The Construction Industry Formbook

A Practical Guide to Reviewing and Drafting Forms
for the Construction Industry

Robert F. Cushman, Esq.
Pepper, Hamilton & Scheetz
Philadelphia, Pennsylvania

Michael S. Simon, Esq.
Vicon Construction Company
Lincoln Park, New Jersey

McNeill Stokes, Esq.
Stokes and Shapiro
Atlanta, Georgia

SHEPARD'S, INC. of Colorado Springs
P.O. Box 1235 Colorado Springs, CO 80901

McGRAW-HILL BOOK COMPANY

New York   St. Louis   San Francisco
Colorado Springs   Auckland   Bogota
Düsseldorf   Johannesburg   London
Madrid   Mexico   Montreal   New Delhi
Panama   Paris   São Paulo   Singapore
Sydney   Tokyo   Toronto

Copyright © 1979 by McGraw-Hill, Inc. All rights reserved. Printed in the United States of America. No part of this publication may be reproduced, stored in a retrieval system, or transmitted, in any form or by any means, electronic, mechanical, photocopying, recording or otherwise, without the prior written permission of Shepard's/McGraw-Hill.

45678910   SHBR   89876

Library of Congress Cataloging in Publication Data

Cushman, Robert Frank, 1931-
   The construction industry formbook.

   Includes index.
   1. Building—Contracts and specifications—United States—Forms. 2. Construction industry—Law and legislation—United States—Forms. I. Simon, Michael S., joint author. II. Stokes, McNeill, joint author. III. Title.
KF902.A3 1978   343'.73'078   78-26427
ISBN 0-07-014976-3

"We are a part of a great industry in a great country. We are builders not destroyers, we are lifters not leaners, and we must be for things, not against them. This is our mission—this is our destiny—let's get on with the job."
Saul Horowitz, Jr. (1925-1975)
President, Associated General Contractors
AGC Convention, March, 1974

Contents

Preface

Disclaimer

How to Use the Forms

PART ONE

The Construction Documents I Advocate Using When Representing the Prime Contractor—Michael S. Simon, Esq.

Chapter One   Agreements with the Owner

	A. Plan and Specification Contract
§1.01	1. Introduction
	2. Standard Form Stipulated Sum Agreement Between Owner and Contractor (AIA Document A101)
§1.02	a. Author's Comments
§1.03	b. Form—AIA Document A101
	3. Standard Form General Conditions (AIA Document A201) with Suggested Modifications
§1.04	a. General Conditions of the Contract for Construction
§1.05	b. Form—AIA Document A201
	B. Construction Management Contracts
§1.06	1. Introduction
	2. Standard Form of Agreement Between Owner and Construction Manager (AGC Document No. 8) with Suggested Modifications
§1.07	a. Author's Comments
§1.08	b. Form—AGC Document No. 8
	3. Amendment to Owner-Construction Manager Agreement (AGC Document No. 8a) Guaranteed Maximum Price
§1.09	a. Author's Comments
§1.10	b. Form—AGC Document No. 8a
	4. General Conditions for the Owner-Construction Manager Agreement (AGC Document No. 8b) with Suggested Modifications

§1.11		a. Author's Comments
§1.12		b. Form—AGC Document No. 8b
	C.	**Turnkey and Design-Build Contracts**
§1.13		1. Introduction
		2. Preliminary Design-Build Agreement Between Owner and Contractor (AGC Document No. 6) with Suggested Modifications
§1.14		a. Author's Comments
§1.15		b. Form—AGC Document No. 6
		3. Standard Form of Design-Build Agreement Between Owner and Contractor (AGC Document No. 6a) with Suggested Modifications
§1.16		a. Author's Comments
§1.17		b. Form—AGC Document No. 6a
		4. General Conditions for Design-Build Agreement (AGC Document No. 6c)
§1.18		a. Author's Comments
§1.19		b. Form—AGC Document No. 6c

Chapter Two   Documents Applicable to Subcontractors and Suppliers

	A.	**Standard Sub-Bid Proposal Form with Suggested Modifications**
§2.01		1. Author's Comments
§2.02		2. Form—Standard Subbid Proposal
	B.	**Subcontract Agreement**
§2.03		1. Author's Comments
§2.04		2. Form—Subcontract Agreement
	C.	**Purchase Order Forms**
§2.05		1. Author's Comments
§2.06		2. Form—Short
§2.07		3. Form—Long
	D.	**Standard Subcontractor's Applications for Payment with Suggested Modifications**
§2.08		1. Author's Comments
§2.09		2. Form—Subcontractor's Application for Payment
	E.	**Waiver, Release and Discharge Forms**
§2.10		1. Author's Comments
§2.11		2. Forms—Waiver, Release and Discharge

Chapter Three   Contractor's Daily Report Form

§3.01	**A.**	**Introduction**
§3.02	**B.**	**Form—Daily Report**

Chapter Four   Joint Venture Documents

§4.01	**A.**	**Introduction**
§4.02	**B.**	**Form—Pre-contract Joint Venture Agreement**

PART TWO

The Construction Documents I Advocate Using When Representing The Subcontractor—McNeill Stokes, Esq.

Chapter Five Documents Applicable to Subcontractors and General Contractors

A. Subcontractor Proposal Forms
- §5.01   1. Introduction
- §5.02   2. Forms—Proposal

B. Standard Subcontract Forms
- §5.03   1. Introduction
- §5.04   2. Payment Terms
- §5.05   3. Scope of Work
- §5.06   4. Scheduling and Liquidated Damages
- §5.07   5. Temporary Site Facilities
- §5.08   6. Conduit Clauses
- §5.09   7. Warranties
- §5.10   8. Hold Harmless and Indemnity Provisions
- §5.11   9. Form—AGC Standard Form of Subcontract Agreement with Suggested Modifications
- §5.12   10. Form—AIA Standard Form of Agreement Between Contractor and Subcontractor (A401—1978 Edition) with Suggested Modifications

C. Authorization for Extra or Changed Work
- §5.13   1. Introduction
- §5.14   2. Form—Work Authorization

Chapter Six Documents Applicable to Suppliers

A. Purchase Orders
- §6.01   1. Introduction
- §6.02   2. Form—Purchase Order

Chapter Seven Joint Venture Agreements

A. Joint Venture Agreements
- §7.01   1. Introduction
- §7.02   2. Parties
- §7.03   3. Introductory Premises
- §7.04   4. Rights and Responsibilities
- §7.05   5. Name and Principal Office
- §7.06   6. Interests of Parties
- §7.07   7. Control of Operations
- §7.08   8. Contributions and Financing
- §7.09   9. Joint Venture Property
- §7.10   10. Labor
- §7.11   11. Employees of Joint Venture

§7.12		12. Accounting
§7.13		13. Insurance
§7.14		14. Conclusion
§7.15	**B.**	**Form—Joint Venture Agreement**

Chapter Eight   Privity Agreements

§8.01	**A.**	**Introduction**
§8.02	**B.**	**Form—Privity Agreement**

PART THREE

Documents to Secure and Obtain Payment—Robert F. Cushman, Esq.

Chapter Nine   Assignments, Joint Checks, Guarantees

A. Assignment of Monies Due or to Become Due

§9.01	1.	Introduction
§9.02	2.	Form—Assignment
§9.03	3.	Form—Notice of Assignment

B. Third Party Joint-Check Arrangement

§9.04	1.	Introduction
§9.05	2.	Form—Agreement by General Contractor to Issue Check to Joint Order of Subcontractor and Supplier of Labor and/or Material to that Subcontractor
§9.06	3.	Form—Agreement by Owner to Issue Check to the Joint Order of General Contractor and Supplier of Labor and/or Material to that General Contractor

C. Guarantees

§9.07	1.	Introduction
§9.08	2.	Form—Guarantee of Payment to Building Material Supplier
	3.	Bank Guarantees
§9.09		a. Generally
§9.10		b. Form—Agreement by Bank to Set Aside, Earmark, and Pay Contractor
§9.11		c. Form—Bank Guarantee to Prime Contractor (Construction Manager-Shell Owner Situation) with Additional Guarantee to Pay Change Orders

Chapter Ten   Mechanics' Liens

A. Mechanics' Lien of Private Projects

§10.01	1.	Introduction
§10.02	2.	Contents of Claim
	B.	**Waivers**
§10.03	1.	Waiver of Lien Clauses in Construction Agreements
	2.	Interim Waiver Affidavits

§10.04		a. Author's Comments
		b. Forms
§10.05		i. Standard Interim Waiver
§10.06		ii. Suggested Form of Interim Waiver
	3.	Final Waiver Affidavit (Release of Liens)
§10.07		a. Author's Comments
§10.08		b. Form—Suggested Final Waiver Affidavit
	4.	Trust Receipt for Waiver
§10.09		a. Author's Comments
§10.10		b. Form—Trust Receipt for Waiver
	C. Mechanics' Lien on Public Projects	
§10.11	1.	Introduction
§10.12	2.	Form—Notice of Municipal Mechanic's Lien
§10.13	3.	Author's Comments

Chapter Eleven   Bonds

§11.01	**A. Payment Bonds**	
§11.02	**B. Obtaining Copies of Bonds and Contracts**	
§11.03	**C. Form—Affidavit to Comptroller General to Obtain a Copy of the Bonded Federal Contract and a Copy of the Payment Bond**	
	D. Notice	
§11.04	1.	Introduction
§11.05	2.	Timeliness of Notice
§11.06	3.	Contents of Notice
§11.07	4.	Form—Notice and Demand for Payment to Contractor and Surety
	E. Time to Institute Suit	
	1.	Miller Act Suit
§11.08		a. Author's Comments
§11.09		b. Form—Miller Act Suit
	2.	Freeze Agreement
§11.10		a. Author's Comments
§11.11		b. Form—Freeze Agreement

Chapter Twelve   Arbitration

§12.01	**A. Advantage of Arbitration**	
	B. Considerations Prior to Commencement of Arbitration Proceedings	
§12.02	1.	Existence of Arbitration Agreement Between Parties
§12.03	2.	Enforcement of Arbitration Agreement by Courts
	C. Initiation of Proceedings Under Contract Arbitration Agreement	
	1.	Demand for Arbitration
		a. Standard American Arbitration Association (AAA) Construction Industry Arbitration Demand Form
§12.04		i. Author's Comments
§12.05		ii. Form—AAA Standard Arbitration Demand
		b. Combining Claim for Unpaid Contract Balance with Claim for Interference and Delay in Undetermined Amount
§12.06		i. Author's Comments
§12.07		ii. Form—Demand for Arbitration

	D. Initiation of Proceedings Under Submission
§12.08	1. Author's Comments
§12.09	2. Form—AAA Submission
	E. Compelling Arbitration
§12.10	1. Author's Comments
§12.11	2. Form—Petition to Compel Arbitration
§12.12	F. Turning Award into Judgment—Form—Motion to Confirm Award of Arbitrators
§12.13	G. Inadvertent Waiver of Arbitration Rights

Preface

Many trade and professional associations have developed form agreements. These documents, however, often reflect a special interest or one-sided approach. Some cause only trouble for the uninitiated who throw caution to the wind and execute them simply because they are printed and therefore "blessed." Some industry-developed agreements, usually finalized after months of give and take among divergent interests, please all for the sake of order and, in doing so, protect none.

Contractors, subcontractors, material suppliers and their attorneys have, for decades, fought the battle of the forms. The battle will continue. The winner in the future will be, as in the past, the knowledgeable drafter with the maximum bargaining power.

Our mission here, and the object of this book, is to depart from the traditional blank form formbook, and to make the drafter knowledgeable by setting forth the specific forms we use (highlighting and analyzing the most important provisions). Where standard industry forms are used, we explain how and why they are modified. For educational purposes we write as advocates—Mr. Simon writes as if he were representing the contractor; Mr. Stokes the subcontractor; and I, as the advocate of the contractor or supplier attempting to secure and obtain payment. By writing in this fashion we hope to make the reader aware of the problem areas in construction documents and of recommended modifications to call for during construction agreement negotiations.

In every case the authors, while writing as advocates, attempt to present a fair and equitable agreement, for an agreement that is too one-sided is an invitation to a breach and a lawsuit.

Robert F. Cushman
Philadelphia, Pennsylvania
December, 1978

Disclaimer

In this book, statements are made and forms are presented with the understanding that the publisher and the co-authors are supplying practical guidelines for educational purposes. The forms are not intended as substitutes for legal advice from experienced attorneys in specific fact situations.

How to Use the Forms

The substantive texts of all standard industry forms presented in this book are reprinted in their entirety. The additions and deletions to the forms, suggested by the authors, are indicated as follows:

1. Recommended additional language is printed in *italics*. For example,

    (original form language) "If the Contractor defaults..."

    (as printed, with the suggested additional language) "If the Contractor *unreasonably and without cause* defaults..."

2. Standard form provisions which the authors suggest be deleted are printed in *italics*, and surrounded by [brackets]. For example,

    (original language) "Contractor warrants to the Owner and the Architect..."

    (as printed, showing the recommended deletion) "Contractor warrants to the Owner *[and the Architect]*..."

PART ONE

The Construction Documents I Advocate Using When Representing The Prime Contractor

Michael S. Simon, Esq.

The prime contractor and its counsel are often faced with the difficult task of selecting appropriate prime contract and subcontract documents. If the prime contractor were obligated to author its own forms productive construction time would be drastically reduced. Part One offers the forms for the prime contractor which I believe to be the best of the standard contract forms. Where an acceptable standard was not found a new form was prepared, drawing from my experience and the experience of other established sources. The forms and suggested modifications presented in Part One are intended to be the foundation for the final, executed document. The forms may be all the prime contractor will need, but more importantly, they offer a basic document, tailored to the needs of the prime contractor.

These "standards" are established so that the prime contractor's position with its subcontractors, suppliers, and owners is on firm ground. Use of standard forms helps eliminate substantial expenditure of time and money in drafting appropriate documents, establishes proper legal protection, and enhances the prospect for a financially successful and amicable completion of work. Reasonable legal protection permits greater attention by subcontractors and suppliers to work performance and order fulfillment, and reduces the risk of litigation.

ONE   Agreements With The Owner

Plan and Specification Contract
§1.01 *Introduction*
§1.02 *Author's Comments—Standard Form Stipulated Sum Agreement Between Owner and Contractor (AIA Document A101)*
§1.03 *Form—AIA Document A101*
§1.04 *General Conditions of the Contract for Construction*
§1.05 *Form—Standard Form General Conditions (AIA Document A201) with Suggested Modifications*

Construction Management Contracts
§1.06 *Introduction*
§1.07 *Author's Comments—Standard Form of Agreement Between Owner and Construction Manager (AGC Document No. 8) with Suggested Modifications*
§1.08 *Form—AGC Document No. 8*
§1.09 *Author's Comments—Amendment to Owner-Construction Manager Agreement (AGC Document No. 8A) Guaranteed Maximum Price*
§1.10 *Form—AGC Document No. 8A*
§1.11 *Author's Comments—General Conditions for the Owner-Construction Manager Agreement (AGC Document No. 8b) with Suggested Modifications*
§1.12 *Form—AGC Document No. 8b*

Turnkey and Design-Build Contracts
§1.13 *Introduction*
§1.14 *Author's Comments—Preliminary Design-Build Agreement Between Owner and Contractor (AGC Document No. 6) with Suggested Modifications*
§1.15 *Form—AGC Document No. 6*
§1.16 *Author's Comments—Standard Form of Design-Build Agreement Between Owner*

and Contractor (AGC Document No. 6a) with Suggested Modifications
§1.17 Form—AGC Document No. 6a
§1.18 Author's Comments—General Conditions for Design-Build Agreement (AGC Document No. 6c)
§1.19 Form—AGC Document No. 6c

A. PLAN AND SPECIFICATION CONTRACTS

§1.01   1. Introduction   The most common standard form of construction agreement between the owner and the contractor is one which calls for a stipulated contract price. The contract plans and specifications, as well as the other technical data, are normally prepared by an independent architect/engineer on behalf of the owner. The owner retains the services of these professionals, and by contract requires the contractor to perform the construction work in strict accordance with these contract documents. The contractor is left little, if any, discretion as to the design, or unilateral deviation from the contract documents. The contractor is essentially precluded from exercising independent "non-construction" judgment.

In this traditional plan and specification type contract, the courts have held that it is the owner who warrants the adequacy of the plans and specifications. The contractor warrants neither the design nor its adequacy, and the contractor who has performed the work in conformity with the contract documents is not denied compensation if the final result is not that which the owner anticipated.

In consideration for the contractor's exact performance of the plans and specifications, the contractor is paid a stipulated contract price. It is the contractor, however, who is expected to accept most risks of price fluctuation.

The most recognized publisher of standard forms for plan and specification contracts is the American Institute of Architects. These contract forms are known quantities in the construction industry. Because they are so well established, prime contractors should accept the use of the AIA documents as the starting point for development of construction agreements. Although other forms either may be similar or more favorable to the prime contractor at the outset, none have the recognition and acceptability of the AIA forms.

The basis for payment and the method of computation can take several forms. The primary contract form is the stipulated lump sum contract. The quantity of the work and the contract sum are set amounts and, excluding subsequent change orders and claims, do not fluctuate. However, the prime contractor must be cognizant of two other basic contract formats. These are the unit price contract and the cost plus some type of mark-up contract.

The unit price contract is usually encountered in heavy and highway projects. However, many lump sum bids include within the bid package various unit prices and line items. In the bid documents, the public or private unit price contract typically is broken down into a list of items or categories of work anticipated, with estimated bid quantities. The prime contractor then is obligated to fill in the unit price for each item. One item might be general conditions; however, general conditions, general and administrative expenses, and profit usually are distributed among the various items. When dealing with a unit price contract, the contractor should make an effort to determine the following:

1. Is the contract award to be based on the unit price times the quantity listed by the owner, or is it to be based on the actual extension of that amount as written by the contractor? Both bases for contract awards are used. This question is important in determining who the low bidder is, and whether or not a mistake in bidding has occurred.
2. Who is to determine the actual quantity, as computed for progress payments and at final completion? If it is the owner or the owner's representative, is the decision final and binding? If so, the prime contractor has drastically limited rights, since many courts have stated that the actual determination of quantities is a factual question and that an engineer's decision, if the contract so states, can be final and binding. The contractor should indicate in the contract the right to appeal any determination as to quantities.
3. If there is a variation in quantities, does the contractor have any right to additional compensation or readjustment of the unit price? Many contracts provide that if the actual quantity of work performed deviates more than 10% above or below the bid quantity (or some other percentage factor), the unit price can be adjusted. However, the contractor must ascertain whether or not that part of the total quantity which is within the permissible percentage differential is to be paid at the readjusted unit price, and whether or not there is a percentage limitation on the extent of the readjustment. The right to negotiate unit prices, without limitation, has been questioned as possibly violating public contract bidding laws. In the contract, the contractor must provide some method of adjusting the unit price if there is a vast difference between actual and bid quantities.
4. Does the unit price take into consideration any overhead factors? As previously indicated, most unit prices include overhead, general and administrative expenses, and profit. However, they normally do not have any provision for extended cost factors to properly compensate the contractor for delays, suspensions or interferences. This is especially true when the actual and bid quantities are within the permissible variation limitations. Therefore, the unit price contractor should insert in its prime contract a specific statement providing that: "If the performance of the work should be altered, delayed, suspended, or interfered with, in whole or in part, due to the fault or negligence of the owner or its representative, or within their control, then the contractor shall be entitled to an equitable adjustment to its unit prices so as to properly compensate it for any increased cost."

The cost plus contract takes various forms. The mark-up factor might be a fixed fee, a percentage of the cost, or some other agreed-upon factor or combination.

A guaranteed maximum upset price also might be combined with this. The prime contractor is urged to review all possible financial factors and contingencies before listing in the contract what cost items should and will be compensated. The contractor is referred to Articles 6 through 11 of AGC Documents Nos. 6 and 8 as included and modified in this book. It is also suggested that AIA Document A111, which is a standard agreement between an owner and contractor "where the basis of payment is the cost of the work plus a fee" as approved and endorsed by the AGC, be reviewed.

2. Standard Form Stipulated Sum Agreement Between Owner and Contractor (AIA Document A101)

§1.02   **a. Author's Comments** The American Institute of Architects Document A101, 1977 edition, is the starting agreement. Although this document indicates that it is to be used with the AIA General Conditions Document A201, 1976 edition, there is no requirement that A201 be so incorporated. The incorporation of A201 as part of the agreement, as hereinafter modified, is recommended in order to set forth the contractor's rights with specificity.

It is imperative that the contractor require the insertion in Article 7 of every document which is intended to be included as part of the contract. When so listing the documents, they should be itemized with specific descriptive facts, such as drawing numbers, revision dates, addenda numbers and dates, etc.

§1.03   b. FORM—   Standard Form of Agreement Between
AIA DOCUMENT A101   Owner and Contractor

WHERE THE BASIS OF PAYMENT IS A STIPULATED SUM

THE AMERICAN INSTITUTE OF ARCHITECTS

1977 EDITION

This document has been reproduced with the permission of The American Institute of Architects under application number 78032. Further reproduction, in part or in whole, is not authorized. Because AIA documents are revised from time to time, users should ascertain from AIA the current edition of the document reproduced below.

AGREEMENT

made as of the _____ day of _____ in the year of Nineteen Hundred and _____

Between the Owner:

and the Contractor:

The Project:

The Architect:

The Owner and the Contractor agree as set forth below.

AIA Document A101 Copyright © 1977 by The American Institute of Architects

ARTICLE 1   The Contract Documents

The Contract Documents consist of this Agreement, the Conditions of the Contract (General, Supplementary and other Conditions), the Drawings, the Specifications, all Addenda issued prior to and all Modifications issued after execution of this Agreement. These form the Contract, and all are as fully a part of the Contract as if attached to this Agreement or repeated herein. An enumeration of the Contract Documents appears in Article 7.

ARTICLE 2   The Work

The Contractor shall perform all the Work required by the Contract Documents for
(Here insert the caption descriptive of the Work as used on other Contract Documents.)

ARTICLE 3   Time of Commencement and Substantial Completion

The Work to be performed under this Contract shall be commenced and, subject to authorized adjustments, Substantial Completion shall be achieved not later than
(Here insert any special provisions for liquidated damages relating to failure to complete on time.)

ARTICLE 4   Contract Sum

The Owner shall pay the Contractor in current funds for the performance of the Work, subject to additions and deductions by Change Order as provided in the Contract Documents, the Contract Sum of

The Contract Sum is determined as follows:
(State here the base bid or other lump sum amount, accepted alternates, and unit prices, as applicable.)

ARTICLE 5   Progress Payments
Based upon Applications for Payment submitted to the Architect by the Contractor and Certificates for Payment issued by the Architect, the Owner shall make progress payments on account of the Contract Sum to the Contractor as provided in the Contract Documents for the period ending the _____ day of the month as follows:
Not later than _____ days following the end of the period covered by the Application for Payment _____ percent (____%) of the portion of the Contract Sum properly allocable to labor, materials and equipment incorporated in the Work and _____ percent (____%) of the portion of the Contract Sum properly allocable to materials and equipment suitably stored at the site or at

---

AIA Document A101 Copyright © 1977 by The American Institute of Architects

some other location agreed upon in writing, for the period covered by the Application for Payment, less the aggregate of previous payments made by the Owner; and upon Substantial Completion of the entire Work, a sum sufficient to increase the total payments to _____ percent (____%) of the Contract Sum, less such amounts as the Architect shall determine for all incomplete Work and unsettled claims as provided in the Contract Documents.

(If not covered elsewhere in the Contract Documents, here insert any provision for limiting or reducing the amount retained after the Work reaches a certain stage of completion.)

Payments due and unpaid under the Contract Documents shall bear interest from the date payment is due at the rate entered below, or in the absence thereof, at the legal rate prevailing at the place of the Project.

(Here insert any rate of interest agreed upon.)

(Usury laws and requirements under the Federal Truth in Lending Act, similar state and local consumer credit laws and other regulations at the Owner's and Contractor's principal places of business, the location of the Project and elsewhere may affect the validity of this provision. Specific legal advice should be obtained with respect to deletion, modification, or other requirements such as written disclosures or waivers.)

ARTICLE 6   Final Payment

Final payment, constituting the entire unpaid balance of the Contract Sum, shall be paid by the Owner to the Contractor when the Work has been completed, the Contract fully performed, and a final Certificate for Payment has been issued by the Architect.

ARTICLE 7   Miscellaneous Provisions

7.1 Terms used in this Agreement which are defined in the Conditions of the Contract shall have the meanings designated in those Conditions.

7.2 The Contract Documents, which constitute the entire agreement between the Owner and the Contractor, are listed in Article 1 and, except for Modifications issued after execution of this Agreement, are enumerated as follows:

(List below the agreement, the Conditions of the Contract (General, Supplementary, and other Conditions), the Drawings, the Specifications, and any Addenda and accepted alternates, showing page or sheet numbers in all cases and dates where applicable.)

This Agreement entered into as of the day and year first written above.

AIA Document A101 Copyright © 1977 by The American Institute of Architects

OWNER   CONTRACTOR

_____   _____

BY   BY

_____   _____

AIA Document A101 Copyright © 1977 by The American Institute of Architects

3. Standard Form General Conditions (AIA Document A201) with Suggested Modifications

§1.04   **a. General Conditions of the Contract for Construction**   The American Institute of Architects Document A201, 1976 edition, is the basic document containing the rights and obligations of the respective parties to be included in the agreement between owner and contractor. It is referenced in the agreement (A101) and, as modified, should be incorporated as a mandatory document. The AIA Document A201 has improved with age and revision. However, the document still places some undue burdens on the prime contractor, limits certain of the owner's responsibilities, and places the architect in a powerful position without any attendant obligations.

The revisions which are proposed are inserted with the intention of equalizing the obligations of owner and contractor, and of placing responsibility on the owner's shoulders, if not on the architect's, for the architect's actions and omissions. It is the author's opinion that many of the adversary positions which are taken on construction projects could be reduced or eliminated by finally placing some of the responsibility on the architect, when, in fact, it is the architect who creates many of the adversary situations. The parties, including the contractor, owner, and architect, should be held accountable for the defaults they create.

The use of AIA Document A201, with as many of the proposed modifications as possible, is strongly advocated. Each revision improves a form which otherwise is the best of the standard forms, as well as being the standard.

§1.05   b. FORM—
AIA DOCUMENT A201

General Conditions of the Contract for Construction

THE AMERICAN INSTITUTE OF ARCHITECTS

1976 EDITION

This document has been reproduced with the permission of The American Institute of Architects under application number 78032. Further reproduction, in part or in whole, is not authorized. Because AIA documents are revised from time to time, users should ascertain from AIA the current edition of the document reproduced below.

TABLE OF ARTICLES

1. CONTRACT DOCUMENTS
2. ARCHITECT
3. OWNER
4. CONTRACTOR
5. SUBCONTRACTORS
6. WORK BY OWNER OR BY SEPARATE CONTRACTORS
7. MISCELLANEOUS PROVISIONS
8. TIME
9. PAYMENTS AND COMPLETION
10. PROTECTION OF PERSONS AND PROPERTY
11. INSURANCE
12. CHANGES IN THE WORK
13. UNCOVERING AND CORRECTION OF WORK
14. TERMINATION OF THE CONTRACT

AIA Document A201 Copyright © 1976 by The American Institute of Architects.

INDEX

Acceptance of Defective or Non-Conforming Work 6.2.2, **13.3**
Acceptance of work 5.4.2, 9.5.5, 9.8.1, 9.9.1, 9.9.3
Access to Work 2.2.5, 6.2.1
Accident Prevention 2.2.4, 10
Acts and Omissions 2.2.4, 4.18.3, 7.4, 7.6.2, 8.3.1, 10.2.5
Additional Costs, Claims for 12.3
Administration of the Contract **2.2,** 4.3.3
All Risk Insurance 11.3.1
Allowances **4.8**
Applications for Payment 2.2.6, 9.2, **9.3,** 9.4, 9.5.3, 9.6.1, 9.8.2, 9.9.1, 9.9.3, 14.2.2
Approvals 2.2.14, 3.4, 4.3.3, 4.5, 4.12.4 through 4.12.6, 4.12.8, 4.18.3, 7.7, 9.3.2
Arbitration 2.2.7 through 2.2.13, 2.2.19, 6.2.5, **7.9,** 8.3.1, 11.3.7, 11.3.8
ARCHITECT **2**
Architect, **Definition** of **2.1**
Architect, Extent of Authority 2.2, 3.4, 4.12.8, 5.2, 6.3, 7.7.2, 8.1.3, 8.3.1, 9.2, 9.3.1, 9.4, 9.5.3, 9.6, 9.8, 9.9.1, 9.9.3, 12.1.1, 12.1.4, 12.3.1, 12.4.1, 13.1, 13.2.1, 13.2.5, 14.2
Architect, Limitations of Authority and Responsibility 2.2.2 through 2.2.4, 2.2.10 through 2.2.14, 2.2.17, 2.2.18, 4.3.3, 4.12.6, 5.2.1, 9.4.2, 9.5.4, 9.5.5, 12.4
Architect's Additional Services 3.4, 7.7.2, 13.2.1, 13.2.5, 14.2.2
Architect's Approvals 2.2.14, 3.4, 4.5, 4.12.6, 4.12.8, 4.18.3
Architect's Authority to Reject Work 2.2.13, 4.5, 13.1.2, 13.2
Architect's Copyright 1.3
Architect's Decisions 2.2.7 through 2.2.13, 6.3, 7.7.2, 7.9.1, 8.3.1, 9.2, 9.4, 9.6.1, 9.8.1, 12.1.4, 12.3.1
Architect's Inspections 2.2.13, 2.2.16, 9.8.1, 9.9.1
Architect's Instructions 2.2.13, 2.2.15, 7.7.2, 12.4, 13.1
Architect's Interpretations 2.2.7 through 2.2.10, 12.3.2
Architect's On-Site Observations 2.2.3, 2.2.5, 2.2.6, 2.2.17, 7.7.1, 7.7.4, 9.4.2, 9.6.1, 9.9.1
Architect's Project Representative 2.2.17, 2.2.18
Architect's Relationship with Contractor 1.1.2, 2.2.4, 2.2.5, 2.2.10, 2.2.13, 4.3.3, 4.5, 4.7.3, 4.12.6, 4.18, 11.3.6

Architect's Relationship with Subcontractors 1.1.2, 2.2.13, 9.5.3, 9.5.4
Architect's Representations 9.4.2, 9.6.1, 9.9.1
Artistic Effect 1.2.3, 2.2.11, 2.2.12, 7.9.1
Attorney's Fees 4.18.1, 6.2.5, 9.9.2
Award of Separate Contracts 6.1.1
Award of Subcontracts and Other Contracts for Portions of the Work **5.2**
Bonds, Lien 9.9.2
Bonds, Performance, Labor and Material Payment 7.5, 9.9.3
Building Permit 4.7
Certificate of Substantial Completion 9.8.1
Certificates of Inspection, Testing or Approval 7.7.3
Certificates of Insurance 9.3.2, 11.1.4
Certificates for Payment 2.2.6, 2.2.16, **9.4,** 9.5.1, 9.5.5, 9.6.1, 9.7.1, 9.8.2, 9.9.1, 9.9.3, 12.1.4, 14.2.2
Change Orders 1.1.1, 2.2.15, 3.4, 4.8.2.3, 5.2.3, 7.7.2, 8.3.1, 9.7, 9.9.3, 11.3.1, 11.3.5, 11.3.7, **12.1,** 13.1.2, 13.2.5, 13.3.1
Change Orders, Definition of 12.1.1
CHANGES IN THE WORK 2.2.15, 4.1.1, **12**
Claims for Additional Cost or Time 8.3.2, 8.3.3, 12.2.1, **12.3**
Claims for Damages 6.1.1, 6.2.5, **7.4,** 8.3, 9.6.1.1
Cleaning Up **4.15,** 6.3
Commencement of the Work, Conditions Relating to 3.2.1, 4.2, 4.7.1, 4.10, 5.2.1, 6.2.2, 7.5, 9.2, 11.1.4, 11.3.4
Commencement of the Work, Definition of 3.1.2
Communications 2.2.2, 3.2.6, 4.9.1, **4.16**
Completion, Conditions Relating to 2.2.16, 4.11, 4.15, 9.4.2, 9.9, 13.2.2
COMPLETION, PAYMENTS AND **9**
Completion, Substantial 2.2.16, 8.1.1, 8.1.3, 8.2.2, 9.8, 13.2.2
Compliance with Laws 1.3, 2.1.1, 4.6, 4.7, 4.13, 7.1, 7.7, 10.2.2, 14
Concealed Conditions **12.2**
Consent, Written 2.2.18, 4.14.2, 7.2, 7.6.2, 9.8.1, 9.9.2, 9.9.3, 11.3.9
Contract, Definition of **1.1.2**
Contract Adminstration 2.2, 4.3.3
Contract Award and Execution, Conditions Relating to 4.7.1, 4.10, 5.2, 7.5, 9.2, 11.1.4, 11.3.4

AIA Document A201 Copyright © 1976 by The American Institute of Architects.

CONTRACT DOCUMENTS   **1**
Contract Documents, Copies Furnished and Use of   1.3, 3.2.5, 5.3
Contract Documents, Definition of   **1.1.1**
Contract Sum, Definition of   **9.1.1**
Contract Termination   **14**
Contract Time, Definition of   8.1.1
CONTRACTOR   **4**
Contractor, **Definition** of   **4.1,** 6.1.2
Contractor's Employees   4.3.2, 4.4.2, 4.8.1, 4.9, 4.18, 10.2.1 through 10.2.4, 10.2.6, 10.3, 11.1.1
Contractor's Liability Insurance   **11.1**
Contractor's Relationship with Separate Contractors and Owner's Forces   3.2.7, 6
Contractor's Relationship with Subcontractors   1.2.4, 5.2, 5.3, 9.5.2, 11.3.3, 11.3.6
Contractor's Relationship with the Architect   1.1.2, 2.2.4, 2.2.5, 2.2.10, 2.2.13, 4.3.3, 4.5, 4.7.3, 4.12.6, 4.18, 11.3.6
Contractor's Representations   1.2.2, 4.5, 4.12.5, 9.3.3
Contractor's Responsibility for Those Performing the Work   4.3.2, 4.18, 10
Contractor's Review of Contract Documents   1.2.2, 4.2, 4.7.3
Contractor's Right to Stop the Work   9.7
Contractor's Right to Terminate the Contract   14.1
Contractor's Submittals   2.2.14, 4.10, 4.12, 5.2.1, 5.2.3, 9.2, 9.3.1, 9.8.1, 9.9.2, 9.9.3
Contractor's Superintendent   4.9, 10.2.6
Contractor's Supervision and Construction Procedures   1.2.4, 2.2.4, 4.3, 4.4, 10
Contractual Liability Insurance   11.1.3
Coordination and Correlation   1.2.2, 1.2.4, 4.3.1, 4.10.1, 4.12.5, 6.1.3, 6.2.1
Copies Furnished of Drawings and Specifications   1.3, 3.2.5, 5.3
Correction of Work   3.3, 3.4, 10.2.5, **13.2**
Cost, Definition of   12.1.4
Costs   3.4, 4.8.2, 4.15.2, 5.2.3, 6.1.1, 6.2.3, 6.2.5, 6.3, 7.7.1, 7.7.2, 9.7, 11.3.1, 11.3.5, 12.1.3, 12.1.4, 12.3, 13.1.2, 13.2, 14
Cutting and Patching of Work   **4.14,** 6.2
Damage to the Work   6.2.4, 6.2.5, 9.6.1.5, 9.8.1, 10.2.1.2, 10.3, 11.3, 13.2.6
Damages, Claims for   6.1.1, 6.2.5, 7.4, 8.3.4, 9.6.1.2
Damages for Delay   6.1.1, 8.3.4, 9.7
Day, Definition of   8.1.4
Decisions of the Architect   2.2.9 through 2.2.12, 6.3, 7.7.2, 7.9.1, 8.3.1, 9.2, 9.4, 9.6.1, 9.8.1, 12.1.4, 12.3.1, 14.2.1
Defective or Non-Conforming Work, Acceptance, Rejection and Correction of   2.2.3, 2.2.13, 3.3, 3.4, 4.5, 6.2.2, 6.2.3, 9.6.1.1, 9.9.4.2, 13
Definitions   1.1, 2.1, 3.1, 4.1, 4.12.1 through 4.12.3, **5.1,** 6.1.2, **8.1,** 9.1.1, 12.1.1, 12.1.4

Delays and Extensions of Time   **8.3**
Disputes   2.2.9, 2.2.12, 2.2.19, 6.2.5, 6.3, 7.9.1
Documents and Samples at the Site   **4.11**
Drawings and Specifications, Use and Ownership of   1.1.1, 1.3, 3.2.5, 5.3
Emergencies   **10.3**
Employees, Contractor's   4.3.2, 4.4.2, 4.8.1, 4.9, 4.18, 10.2.1 through 10.2.4, 10.2.6, 10.3, 11.1.1
Equipment, Labor, Materials and   1.1.3, 4.4, 4.5, 4.12, 4.13, 4.15.1, 6.2.1, 9.3.2, 9.3.3, 11.3, 13.2.2, 13.2.5, 14
Execution and Progress of the Work   1.1.3, 1.2.3, 2.2.3, 2.2.4, 2.2.8, 4.2, 4.4.1, 4.5, 6.2.2, 7.9.3, 8.2, 8.3, 9.6.1, 10.2.3, 10.2.4, 14.2
Execution, Correlation and Intent of the Contract Documents   **1.2,** 4.7.1
Extensions of Time   8.3, 12.1
Failure of Payment by Owner   **9.7,** 14.1
Failure of Payment of Subcontractors   9.5.2, 9.6.1.3, 9.9.2, 14.2.1
Final Completion and Final Payment   2.2.12, 2.2.16, **9.9,** 13.3.1
Financial Arrangements, Owner's   3.2.1
Fire and Extended Coverage Insurance   11.3.1
Governing Law   **7.1**
Guarantees (See Warranty and Warranties)   2.2.16, 4.5, 9.3.3, 9.8.1, 9.9.4, 13.2.2
Indemnification   4.17, **4.18,** 6.2.5, 9.9.2
Identification of Contract Documents   1.2.1
Identification of Subcontractors and Suppliers   5.2.1
Information and Services Required of the Owner   **3.2,** 6, 9, 11.2, 11.3
Inspections   2.2.13, 2.2.16, 4.3.3, 7.7, 9.8.1, 9.9.1
Instructions to Bidders   1.1.1, 7.5
Instructions to the Contractor   2.2.2, 3.2.6, 4.8.1, 7.7.2, 12.1.2, 12.1.4
INSURANCE   9.8.1, **11**
Insurance, Contractor's Liability   11.1
Insurance, Loss of Use   11.4
Insurance, Owner's Liability   11.2
Insurance, Property   11.3
Insurance, Stored Materials   9.3.2, 11.3.1
Insurance Companies, Consent to Partial Occupancy   11.3.9
Insurance Companies, Settlement With   11.3.8
Intent of the Contract Documents   1.2.3, 2.2.10, 2.2.13, 2.2.14, 12.4
Interest   **7.8**
Interpretations, Written   1.1.1, 2.2.7, 2.2.8, 2.2.10, 12.4
Labor and Materials, Equipment   1.1.3, **4.4,** 4.5, 4.12, 4.13, 4.15.1, 6.2.1, 9.3.2, 9.3.3, 11.3, 13.2.2, 13.2.5, 14
Labor and Material Payment Bond   7.5

AIA Document A201 Copyright © 1976 by The American Institute of Architects.

Labor Disputes   8.3.1
Laws and Regulations   1.3, 2.1., 4.6, 4.7, 4.13, 7.1, 7.7, 10.2.2, 14
Liens   9.3.3, 9.9.2, 9.9.4.1
Limitations of Authority   2.2.2, 2.2.17, 2.2.18, 11.3.8, 12.4.1
Limitations of Liability   2.2.10, 2.2.13, 2.2.14, 3.3, 4.2, 4.7.3, 4.12.6, 4.17, 4.18.3, 6.2.2, 7.6.2, 9.4.2, 9.9.4, 9.9.5, 10.2.5, 11.1.2, 11.3.6
Limitations of Time, General   2.2.8, 2.2.14, 3.2.4, 4.2, 4.7.3, 4.12.4, 4.15, 5.2.1, 5.2.3, 7.4, 7.7, 8.2, 9.5.2, 9.6, 9.8, 9.9, 11.3.4, 12.1.4, 12.4, 13.2.1, 13.2.2, 13.2.5
Limitations of Time, Specific   2.2.8, 2.2.12, 3.2.1, 3.4, 4.10, 5.3, 6.2.2, 7.9.2, 8.2, 8.3.2, 8.3.3, 9.2, 9.3.1, 9.4.1, 9.5.1, 9.7, 11.1.4, 11.3.1, 11.3.8, 11.3.9, 12.2, 12.3, 13.2.2, 13.2.5, 13.2.7, 14.1, 14.2.1
Limitations, Statutes of   7.9.2, 13.2.2, 13.2.7
Loss of Use Insurance   **11.4**
Materials, Labor, Equipment and   1.1.3, 4.4, 4.5, 4.12, 4.13, 4.15.1, 6.2.1, 9.3.3, 9.3.3, 11.3.1, 13.2.2, 13.2.5, 14
Materials Suppliers   4.12.1, 5.2.1, 9.3.3
Means, Methods, Techniques, Sequences and Procedures of Construction   2.2.4, 4.3.1, 9.4.2
Minor Changes in the Work   1.1.1, 2.2.15, **12.4**
MISCELLANEOUS PROVISIONS   **7**
Modifications, Definition of   1.1.1
Modifications to the Contract   1.1.1, 1.1.2, 2.2.2, 2.2.18, 4.7.3, 7.9.3, 12
Mutual Responsibility   **6.2**
Non-Conforming Work, Acceptance of Defective or   13.3.1
Notice, Written   2.2.8, 2.2.12, 3.4, 4.2, 4.7.3, 4.7.4, 4.9, 4.12.6, 4.12.7, 4.17, 5.2.1, 7.3, 7.4, 7.7, 7.9.2, 8.1.2, 8.3.2, 8.3.3, 9.4.1, 9.6.1, 9.7, 9.9.1, 9.9.5, 10.2.6, 11.1.4, 11.3.1, 11.3.4, 11.3.5, 11.3.7, 11.3.8, 12.2, 12.3, 13.2.2, 13.2.5, 14
Notices, Permits, Fees and   4.7, 10.2.5
Notice of Testing and Inspections   7.7
Notice to Proceed   8.1.2
Observations, Architect's On-Site   2.2.3, 7.7.1, 7.7.4, 9.4.2
Observations, Contractor's   1.2.2, 4.2.1, 4.7.3
Occupancy   8.1.3, 9.5.5, 11.3.9
On-Site Inspections by the Architect   2.2.3, 2.2.16, 9.4.2, 9.8.1, 9.9.1
On-Site Observations by the Architect   2.2.3, 2.2.6, 2.2.17, 7.7.1, 7.7.4, 9.4.2, 9.6.1, 9.9.1
Orders, Written   3.3, 4.9, 12.1.4, 12.4.1, 13.1
OWNER   **3**
Owner, **Definition** of   **3.1**
Owner, Information and Services Required of the   3.2, 6.1.3, 6.2, 9, 11.2, 11.3

Owner's Authority   2.2.16, 4.8.1, 7.7.2, 9.3.1, 9.3.2, 9.8.1, 11.3.8, 12.1.2, 12.1.4
Owner's Financial Capability   3.2.1
Owner's Liability Insurance   **11.2**
Owner's Relationship with Subcontractors   1.1.2, 9.5.4
Owner's Right to Carry Out the Work   **3.4**, 13.2.4
Owner's Right to Clean Up   4.15.2, **6.3**
Owner's Right to Perform Work and to Award Separate Contracts   **6.1**
Owner's Right to Terminate the Contract   14.2
Owner's Right to Stop the Work   **3.3**
Ownership and Use of Documents   1.1.1, **1.3**, 3.2.5, 5.2.3
Patching of Work, Cutting and   4.14, 6.2.2
Patents, Royalties and   4.17.1
Payment Bond, Labor and Material   7.5
Payment, Applications for   2.2.6, 9.2, 9.3, 9.4, 9.5.3, 9.6.1, 9.8.2, 9.9.1, 9.9.3, 14.2.2
Payment, Certificates for   2.2.6, 2.2.16, 9.4, 9.5.1, 9.5.5, 9.6.1, 9.7.1, 9.8.2, 9.9.1, 9.9.3, 12.1.4, 14.2.2
Payment, Failure of   9.5.2, 9.6.1.3, 9.7, 9.9.2, 14
Payment, Final   2.2.12, 2.2.16, 9.9, 13.3.1
Payments, Progress   7.8, 7.9.3, 9.5.5, 9.8.2, 9.9.3, 12.1.4
PAYMENTS AND COMPLETION   **9**
Payments to Subcontractors   9.5.2, 9.5.3, 9.5.4, 9.6.1.3, 11.3.3, 14.2.1
Payments Withheld   **9.6**
Performance Bond and Labor and Material Payment Bond   **7.5**
Permits, Fees and Notices   3.2.3, **4.7**, 4.13
PERSONS AND PROPERTY, PROTECTION OF   **10**
Product Data, Definition of   4.12.2
Product Data, Shop Drawings, Samples and   2.2.14, 4.2.1, 4.12
Progress and Completion   2.2.3, 7.9.3, **8.2**
Progress Payments   7.8, 7.9.3, 9.5.5, 9.8.2, 9.9.3, 12.1.4
Progress Schedule   **4.10**
Project, Definition of   **1.1.4**
Project Representative   2.2.17
Property Insurance   **11.3**
PROTECTION OF PERSONS AND PROPERTY   **10**
Regulations and Laws   1.3, 2.1.1, 4.6, 4.7, 4.13, 7.1, 10.2.2, 14
Rejection of Work   2.2.13, 4.5.1, 13.2
Releases of Waivers and Liens   9.9.2, 9.9.4
Representations   1.2.2, 4.5, 4.12.5, 9.4.2, 9.6.1, 9.9.1
Representatives   2.1, 2.2.2, 2.2.17, 2.2.18, 3.1, 4.1, 4.9, 5.1, 9.3.3

AIA Document A201 Copyright © 1976 by The American Institute of Architects.

Responsibility for Those Performing the Work 2.2.4, 4.3.2, 6.1.3, 6.2, 9.8.1
Retainage 9.3.1, 9.5.2, 9.8.2, 9.9.2, 9.9.3
Review of Contract Documents by the Contractor 1.2.2, **4.2**, 4.7.3
Reviews of Contractor's Submittals by Owner and Architect 2.2.14, 4.10, 4.12, 5.2.1, 5.2.3, 9.2
Rights and Remedies 1.1.2, 2.2.12, 2.2.13, 3.3, 3.4, 5.3, 6.1, 6.3, 7.6, 7.9, 8.3.1, 9.6.1, 9.7, 10.3, 12.1.2, 12.2, 13.2.2, 14
Royalties and Patents 4.17
Safety of Persons and Property 10.2
Safety Precautions and Programs 2.2.3, 10.1
Samples, Definition of 4.12.3
Samples, Shop Drawings, Product Data and 2.2.14, 4.2, 4.12
Samples at the Site, Documents and 4.11
Schedule of Values 9.2
Schedule, Progress 4.10
Separate Contracts and Contractors 4.14.2, 6, 11.3.6, 13.1.2
Shop Drawings, Definition of 4.12.1
Shop Drawings, Product Data and Samples 2.2.14, 4.2, **4.12**
Site, Use of 4.13, 6.2.1
Site Visits, Architect's 2.2.3, 2.2.5, 2.2.6, 2.2.17, 7.7.1, 7.7.4, 9.4.2, 9.6.1, 9.9.1
Site Inspections 1.2.2, 2.2.3, 2.2.16, 7.7, 9.8.1, 9.9.1
Special Inspection and Testing 2.2.13, 7.7
Specifications 1.1.1, 1.2.4, 1.3
Statutes of Limitations 7.9.2, 13.2.2, 13.2.7
Stopping the Work 3.3, 9.7.1, 10.3, 14.1
Stored Materials 6.2.1, 9.3.2, 10.2.1.2, 11.3.1, 13.2.5
SUBCONTRACTORS 5
Subcontractors, **Definition** of **5.1**
Subcontractors, Work by 1.2.4, 2.2.4, 4.3.1, 4.3.2
Subcontractual Relations 5.3
Submittals 1.3, 4.10, 4.12, 5.2.1, 5.2.3, 9.2, 9.3.1, 9.8.1, 9.9.2, 9.9.3
Subrogation, Waiver of 11.3.6
Substantial Completion 2.2.16, 8.1.1, 8.1.3, 8.2.2, **9.8**, 13.2.2
Substantial Completion, Definition of 8.1.3
Substitution of Subcontractors 5.2.3, 5.2.4
Substitution of the Architect 2.2.19
Substitutions of Materials 4.5, 12.1.4
Sub-subcontractors, Definition of 5.1.2
Subsurface Conditions 12.2.1

Successors and Assigns 7.2
Supervision and Construction Procedures 1.2.4, 2.2.4, **4.3**, 4.4, 10
Superintendent, Contractor's **4.9**, 10.2.6
Surety, Consent of 9.9.2, 9.9.3
Surveys 3.2.2, 4.18.3
Taxes 4.6
Termination by the Contractor 14.1
Termination by the Owner 14.2
Termination of the Architect 2.2.19
TERMINATION OF THE CONTRACT 14
Tests 2.2.13, 4.3.3, **7.7**, 9.4.2
Time 8
Time, **Definition** of **8.1**
Time, Delays and Extensions of 8.3, 12.1, 12.3, 13.2.7
Time Limits, Specific 2.2.8, 2.2.12, 3.2.1, 3.4, 4.10, 5.3, 6.2.2, 7.9.2, 8.2, 8.3.2, 8.3.3, 9.2, 9.3.1, 9.4.1, 9.5.1, 9.7, 11.1.4, 11.3.1, 11.3.8, 11.3.9, 12.2, 12.3, 13.2.2, 13.2.5, 13.2.7, 14.1, 14.2.1
Title to Work 9.3.2, 9.3.3
UNCOVERING AND CORRECTION OF WORK 13
Uncovering of Work 13.1
Unforseen Conditions 8.3, 12.2
Unit Prices 12.1.3, 12.1.5
Use of Documents 1.1.1, 1.3, 3.2.5, 5.3
Use of Site 4.13, 6.2.1
Values, Schedule of 9.2
Waiver of Claims by the Contractor 7.6.2, 8.3.2, 9.9.5, 11.3.6
Waiver of Claims by the Owner 7.6.2, 9.9.4, 11.3.6, 11.4.1
Waiver of Liens 9.9.2
Warranty and Warranties 2.2.16, **4.5**, 9.3.3, 9.8.1, 9.9.4, 13.2.2
Weather Delays 8.3.1
Work, Definition of **1.1.3**
Work by Owner or by Separate Contractors 6
Written Consent 2.2.18, 4.14.2, 7.2, 7.6.2, 9.8.1, 9.9.3, 9.9.4
Written Interpretations 1.1.1, 1.2.4, 2.2.8, 12.3.2
Written Notice 2.2.8, 2.2.12, 3.4, 4.2, 4.7.3, 4.7.4, 4.9, 4.12.6, 4.12.7, 4.17, 5.2.1, 7.3, 7.4, 7.7, 7.9.2, 8.1.2, 8.3.2, 8.3.3, 9.4.1, 9.6.1, 9.7, 9.9.1, 9.9.5, 10.2.6, 11.1.4, 11.3.1, 11.3.4, 11.3.5, 11.3.7, 11.3.8, 12.2, 12.3, 13.2.2, 13.2.5, 14
Written Orders 3.3, 4.9, 12.1.4, 12.4.1, 13.1

AIA Document A201 Copyright © 1976 by The American Institute of Architects.

ARTICLE 1 Contract Documents

1.1 Definitions

1.1.1 The Contract Documents The Contract Documents consist of the Owner-Contractor Agreement, *all written representations by Owner,* the Conditions of the Contract (General, Supplementary and other Conditions), the Drawings, the Specifications, and all *listed* Addenda issued prior to and all Modifications issued after execution of the Contract. A Modification is (1) a written amendment to the Contract signed by both parties, (2) a Change Order, (3) a written interpretation issued by the Architect pursuant to Subparagraph 2.2.8, or (4) a written order for a minor change in the Work issued by the Architect pursuant to Paragraph 12.3. The Contract Documents do not include Bidding Documents such as the Advertisement or Invitation to Bid, the Instructions to Bidders, sample forms, the Contractor's Bid or portions of Addenda relating to any of these, or any other documents, unless specifically enumerated in the Owner-Contractor Agreement.[1]

1.1.2 The Contract The Contract Documents form the Contract for Construction. This Contract represents the entire and integrated agreement between the parties hereto and supersedes all prior negotiations, representations, or agreements, either written or oral. The Contract may be amended or modified only by a Modification as defined in Subparagraph 1.1.1. The Contract Documents shall not be construed to create any contractual relationship of any kind between the Architect and the Contractor, but *both* [*the Architect*] shall be entitled to performance of obligations intended for *its* [*his*] benefit, and to enforcement thereof. Nothing contained in the Contract Documents shall create any contractual relationship between the Owner or the Architect and any Subcontractor or Sub-subcontractor. *The Owner-Architect agreement shall be available for review.*

1.1.3 The Work The Work comprises the completed construction required by the Contract Documents and includes all labor necessary to produce such construction, and all materials and equipment incorporated or to be incorporated in such construction.

1.1.4 The Project The Project is the total construction of which the Work performed under the Contract Documents may be the whole or a part.

1.2 Execution, Correlation and Intent

1.2.1 The Contract Documents shall be signed in not less than triplicate by the Owner and Contractor. If either the Owner or the Contractor or both, do not sign the Conditions of the Contract, Drawings, Specifications, or any of the other Contract Documents, the Architect shall identify such Documents.

1.2.2 By executing the Contract, the Contractor represents that he has visited the site, familiarized himself with the local conditions under which the Work is to be performed, and correlated his observations with the requirements of the Contract Documents.

1.2.3 The intent of the Contract Documents is to include all items *reasonably* necessary for the proper execution and completion of the Work. The Contract Documents are complementary, and what is required by any one shall be as binding as if required by all. Work not covered in the Contract Documents will not be required. [*unless it is consistent therewith and is reasonably inferable therefrom as being necessary to produce the intended results.*] Words and

---

AIA Document A201 Copyright © 1976 by The American Institute of Architects.

abbreviations which have well-known technical or trade meanings are used in the Contract Documents in accordance with such recognized meanings.

1.2.4 The organization of the Specifications into divisions, sections and articles, and the arrangement of Drawings shall not control the Contractor in dividing the Work among Subcontractors or in establishing the extent of Work to be performed by any trade.

1.3 Ownership and Use of Documents

1.3.1 All Drawings, Specifications and copies thereof furnished by the Architect are and shall remain his property. They are to be used only with respect to this Project and are not to be used on any other project. With the exception of one contract set for each party to the Contract, such documents are to be returned or suitably accounted for to the Architect on request at the completion of the Work. Submission or distribution to meet official regulatory requirements or for other purposes in connection with the Project is not to be construed as publication in derogation of the Architect's common law copyright or other reserved rights.

ARTICLE 2   Architect

2.1 Definition

2.1.1 The Architect is the person lawfully licensed to practice architecture, or an entity lawfully practicing architecture identified as such in the Owner-Contractor Agreement, and is referred to throughout the Contract Documents as if singular in number and masculine in gender. The term Architect means the Architect or his authorized representative.

2.2 Administration of the Contract

2.2.1 The Architect will provide administration of the Contract as hereinafter described, *but shall not exceed the authority vested by its contract with the Owner.*

2.2.2 The Architect will be the Owner's representative during construction and until final payment is due. The Architect will advise and consult with the Owner. The Owner's instructions to the Contractor shall be forwarded through the Architect. The Architect will have authority to act on behalf of the Owner only to the extent provided in the Contract Documents, unless otherwise modified by written instrument in accordance with Subparagraph 2.2.18.

2.2.3 The Architect will visit the site at intervals appropriate to the stage of construction to familiarize himself generally with the progress and quality of the Work and to determine in general if the Work is proceeding in accordance with the Contract Documents. However, the Architect will not be required to make exhaustive or continuous on-site inspections to check the quality or quantity of the Work. On the basis of his on-site observations as an architect, he will keep the Owner informed of the progress of the Work, and will endeavor to guard the Owner against defects and deficiencies in the Work of the Contractor. *The Architect will advise the Contractor, in writing, of any defect or deficiency in the work at the time that the Architect observes same, or at such time as the Architect has reason to believe that such exists.*

AIA Document A201 Copyright © 1976 by The American Institute of Architects.

2.2.4 The Architect will not be responsible for and will not have control or charge of construction means, methods, techniques, sequences or procedures, or for safety precautions and programs in connection with the Work, and he will not be responsible for the Contractor's failure to carry out the Work in accordance with the Contract Documents. The Architect will not be responsible for or have control or charge over the acts or omissions of the Contractor, Subcontractors, or any of their agents or employees, or any other persons performing any of the Work.

2.2.5 The Architect shall at all times have access to the Work wherever it is in preparation and progress. The Contractor shall provide facilities for such access so the Architect may perform his functions under the Contract Documents.

2.2.6 Based on the Architect's observations and an evaluation of the Contractor's Applications for Payment, the Architect will determine the amounts owing to the Contractor and will issue Certificates for Payment in such amounts, as provided in Paragraph 9.4.

2.2.7 The Architect will be the interpreter of the requirements of the Contract Documents and the judge of the performance thereunder by both the Owner and Contractor. *Such interpretation is subject to arbitration pursuant to Paragraph 2.2.12.*

2.2.8 The Architect will render interpretations necessary for the proper execution or progress of the Work, with reasonable promptness and in accordance with any time limit agreed upon. Either party to the Contract may make written request to the Architect for such interpretations.

2.2.9 Claims, disputes and other matters in question between the Contractor and the Owner relating to the execution or progress of the Work or the interpretation of the Contract Documents shall be referred initially to the Architect for decision which he will render in writing within a reasonable time, *so as not to delay the Work.*

2.2.10 All interpretations and decisions of the Architect shall be consistent with the intent of and reasonably inferable from the Contract Documents and will be in writing or in the form of drawings. In his capacity as interpreter and judge, he will endeavor to secure faithful performance by both the Owner and the Contractor, will not show partiality to either, and will not be liable for the result of any interpretation or decision rendered in good faith in such capacity.

2.2.11 The Architect's decisions in matters relating to artistic effect will be final if consistent with the intent of the Contract Documents, *which intent is subject to arbitration.*

2.2.12 Any claim, dispute or other matter in question between the Contractor and the Owner referred to the Architect, except those relating to artistic effect as provided in Subparagraph 2.2.11 and except those which have been waived by the making or acceptance of final payment as provided in Subparagraphs 9.9.4 and 9.9.5, shall be subject to arbitration upon the written demand of either party. However, no demand for arbitration of any such claim, dispute or other matter may be made until the earlier of (1) the date on which the Architect has rendered a written decision, or (2) the tenth day after the parties have presented their evidence to the Architect or have been given a reasonable opportunity to do so, if the Architect has not rendered his written decision by that date. When such a written

---

AIA Document A201 Copyright © 1976 by The American Institute of Architects.

decision of the Architect states (1) that the decision is final but subject to appeal, and (2) that any demand for arbitration of a claim, dispute or other matter covered by such decision must be made within thirty days after the date on which the party making the demand receives the written decision, failure to demand arbitration within said thirty days' period will result in the Architect's decision becoming final and binding upon the Owner and the Contractor. If the Architect renders a decision after arbitration proceedings have been initiated, such decision may be entered as evidence but will not supersede any arbitration proceedings unless the decision is acceptable to all parties concerned. *The Contractor may, after receipt of the Architect's decision as specified in paragraph 2.2.12, notify the Owner, in writing, that it is reserving its right to demand arbitration until some future date. Said future date shall not be more than thirty (30) days after the date of substantial completion, as determined by the Architect. In such event, provided the Owner does not object, in writing, to such reservation within five (5) days of the Contractor's notice, the arbitration rights of the respective parties will be reserved and preserved for a period of time up to thirty (30) days after the date of substantial completion.*
2

2.2.13 The Architect will have authority to reject Work which does not conform to the Contract Documents. Whenever, in his opinion, he considers it necessary or advisable for the implementation of the intent of the Contract Documents, he will have authority to require special inspection or testing of the Work in accordance with Subparagraph 7.7.2 whether or not such Work be then fabricated, installed or completed. [*However, neither*] The Architect's authority to act under this Subparagraph 2.2.13, [*nor any decision made by him in good faith either to exercise or not to exercise such authority,*] shall give rise to a [*any*] duty *and* [*or*] responsibility of the Architect to the Contractor, any Subcontractor, any of their agents or employees, or any other person performing any of the Work, *to act reasonably and with good faith.*

2.2.14 The Architect will review and approve or take other appropriate action upon Contractor's submittals such as Shop Drawings, Product Data and Samples, [*but only*] for conformance with the design concept of the Work and with the information given in the Contract Documents. Such action shall be taken with reasonable promptness so as to cause no delay. The Architect's approval of a specific item shall not indicate approval of an assembly of which the item is a component, *unless so noted by Contractor.*

2.2.15 The Architect will prepare Change Orders in accordance with Article 12, and will have authority to order minor changes in the Work as provided in Subparagraph 12.4.1.

2.2.16 The Architect will conduct inspections to determine the dates of Substantial Completion and final completion, will receive and forward to the Owner for the Owner's review written warranties and related documents required by the Contract and assembled by the Contractor, and will issue a final Certificate for Payment upon compliance with the requirements of Paragraph 9.9.

2.2.17 If the Owner and Architect agree, the Architect will provide one or more Project Representatives to assist the Architect in carrying out his responsibilities at the site. The duties, responsibilities and limitations of authority of any such Project Representative shall be as set forth in an exhibit to be incorporated in the Contract Documents.

2.2.18 The duties, responsibilities and limitations of authority of the Architect as the

---

AIA Document A201 Copyright © 1976 by The American Institute of Architects.

Owner's representative during construction as set forth in the Contract Documents will not be modified or extended without written consent of the Owner, the Contractor and the Architect.

2.2.19 In case of the termination of the employment of the Architect, the Owner shall appoint an architect against whom the Contractor makes no reasonable objection whose status under the Contract Documents shall be that of the former architect. Any dispute in connection with such appointment shall be subject to arbitration.

ARTICLE 3   Owner

3.1 Definition

3.1.1 The Owner is the person or entity identified as such in the Owner-Contractor Agreement and is referred to throughout the Contract Documents as if singular in number and masculine in gender. The term Owner means the Owner or his authorized representative.

3.2 Information and Services Required of the Owner

3.2.1 The Owner shall, at the request of the Contractor, at the time of execution of the Owner-Contractor Agreement, furnish to the Contractor reasonable evidence that he has made financial arrangements to fulfill his obligations under the Contract. Unless such reasonable evidence is furnished, the Contractor is not required to execute the Owner-Contractor Agreement or to commence the Work. *The failure of the Contractor to request or receive satisfactory evidence that sufficient funds are available and committed shall not be deemed to be an acquiescence by the Contractor of the existence of the lack of funds, or affect any of the Contractor's rights to payment. The Contractor shall be entitled to an updated financial statement, as to the availability and commitment of funds, as may be reasonably required during the progress of this Contract. If satisfactory evidence that sufficient funds are available is not forthcoming, then the Contractor shall have the right to stop work or any portion thereof. The Owner shall be responsible and liable to the Contractor for any additional costs the Contractor may incur as a result of insufficient funds.*

3.2.2 The Owner shall furnish all surveys describing the physical characteristics, legal limitations and utility locations for the site of the Project, and a legal description of the site. *The Owner warrants that the site and access are free from any encumbrance.*

3.2.3 Except as provided in Subparagraph 4.7.1, the Owner shall secure and pay for necessary approvals, easements, assessments and charges required for the construction, use or occupancy of permanent structures or for permanent changes in existing facilities.

3.2.4 Information or services *required to be furnished by or is* under the Owner's control shall be furnished by the Owner with reasonable promptness to avoid delay in the orderly progress of the Work.

3.2.5 Unless otherwise provided in the Contract Documents, the Contractor will be furnished, free of charge, all copies of Drawings and Specifications reasonably necessary for the execution of the Work.

AIA Document A201 Copyright © 1976 by The American Institute of Architects.

3.2.6 The Owner shall forward all instructions to the Contractor through the Architect.

3.2.7 The foregoing are in addition to other duties and responsibilities of the Owner enumerated herein and especially those in respect to Work by Owner or by Separate Contractors, Payments and Completion, and Insurance in Articles 6, 9 and 11 respectively.

3.3 Owner's Right to Stop the Work

3.3.1 If the Contractor *unreasonably and without cause* fails to correct defective Work as required by Paragraph 13.2 or *unreasonably and without cause* persistently fails to carry out the Work in accordance with the Contract Documents, the Owner, by a written order signed personally or by an agent specifically so empowered by the Owner in writing, may order the Contractor to stop the Work, or any portion thereof, until the cause for such order has been eliminated; however, this right of the Owner to stop the Work shall not give rise to any duty on the part of the Owner to exercise this right for the benefit of the Contractor or any other person or entity, except to the extent required by Subparagraph 6.1.3.

3.4 Owner's Right to Carry Out the Work

3.4.1 If the Contractor *unreasonably and without cause* defaults or neglects to carry out the Work in accordance with the Contract Documents and fails within seven days after receipt of written notice from the Owner to commence and continue correction of such default or neglect with diligence and promptness, the Owner may, after seven days following receipt by the Contractor of an additional written notice and without prejudice to any other remedy he may have, make good such deficiencies. In such case an appropriate Change Order shall be issued deducting from the payments then or thereafter due the Contractor the cost of correcting such deficiencies, including compensation for the Architect's additional services made necessary by such default, neglect or failure. Such action by the Owner and the amount charged to the Contractor are both subject to the prior approval of the Architect. If the payments then or thereafter due the Contractor are not sufficient to cover such amount, the Contractor shall pay the difference to the Owner. *The Owner shall be obligated to mitigate all damages.*

ARTICLE 4   Contractor

4.1 Definition

4.1.1 The Contractor is the person or entity identified as such in the Owner-Contractor Agreement and is referred to throughout the Contract Documents as if singular in number and masculine in gender. The term Contractor means the Contractor or his authorized representative.

4.2 Review of Contract Documents

4.2.1 The Contractor shall carefully study and compare the Contract Documents and shall at once report to the Architect any *patent and material* error, inconsistency or omission he may discover. The Contractor shall not be liable to the Owner or the Architect for any damage resulting from any such errors, inconsistencies or omissions in the Contract Documents. The Contractor shall perform no portion of the Work at any time without Contract

---

AIA Document A201 Copyright © 1976 by The American Institute of Architects.

Documents or, where required, approved Shop Drawings, Product Data or Samples for such portion of the Work.

4.3 Supervision and Construction Procedures

4.3.1 The Contractor shall supervise and direct the Work, using his best skill and attention. He shall be solely responsible for all construction means, methods, techniques, sequences and procedures and for coordinating all portions of the Work under the Contract.

4.3.2 The Contractor shall be responsible to the Owner for the acts and omissions of his employees, Subcontractors and their agents and employees, and other persons performing any of the Work under a contract with the Contractor.

4.3.3 The Contractor shall not be relieved from his obligations to perform the Work in accordance with the Contract Documents either by the activities or duties of the Architect in his administration of the Contract, or by inspections, tests or approvals required or performed under Paragraph 7.7 by persons other than the Contractor.

4.3.4 *Neither the Architect nor the Owner shall unreasonably interfere with the Contractor's performance of any part of the Work unless said performance and Work are not in accord with the contract documents, or are being performed in such a manner as to create imminent damage or injury to person or property.*

4.4 Labor and Materials

4.4.1 Unless otherwise provided in the Contract Documents, the Contractor shall provide and pay for all labor, materials, equipment, tools, construction equipment and machinery, water, heat, utilities, transportation, and other facilities and services necessary for the proper execution and completion of the Work, whether temporary or permanent and whether or not incorporated or to be incorporated in the Work.

4.4.2 The Contractor shall at all times enforce strict discipline and good order among his employees and shall not employ on the Work any unfit person or anyone not skilled in the task assigned to him.

4.5 Warranty

4.5.1 The Contractor warrants to the Owner [*and the Architect*] that all materials and equipment furnished under this Contract will be new unless otherwise specified, and that all Work will be of good quality, free from faults and defects and in conformance with the Contract Documents. All Work not conforming to these requirements, including substitutions not properly approved and authorized, may be considered defective. If required by the Architect, the Contractor shall furnish satisfactory evidence as to the kind and quality of materials and equipment. [*This warranty is not limited by the provisions of Paragraph 13.2.*]

4.6 Taxes

4.6.1 The Contractor shall pay all sales, consumer, use and other similar taxes for the Work or portions thereof provided by the contractor which are legally enacted at the time bids are received, whether or not yet effective.

AIA Document A201 Copyright © 1976 by The American Institute of Architects.

4.7 Permits, Fees and Notices

4.7.1 Unless otherwise provided in the Contract Documents, the Contractor shall secure and pay for the building permit and for all other permits and governmental fees, licenses and inspections necessary for the proper execution and completion of the Work which are customarily secured after execution of the Contract and which are legally required at the time the bids are received.

4.7.2 The Contractor shall give all notices and comply with all laws, ordinances, rules, regulations and lawful orders of any public authority bearing on the performance of the Work. *The Owner warrants that the design is in accord with same.*

4.7.3 It is not the responsibility of the Contractor to make certain that the Contract Documents are in accordance with applicable laws, statutes, building codes and regulations. If the Contractor observes that any of the Contract Documents are at variance therewith in any respect, he shall promptly notify the Architect in writing, and any necessary changes shall be accomplished by appropriate Modification.

4.7.4 If the Contractor performs any Work knowing it to be contrary to such laws, ordinances, rules and regulations, and without such notice to the Architect, he shall assume full responsibility therefor and shall bear all costs attributable thereto.

4.8 Allowances

4.8.1 The Contractor shall include in the Contract Sum all allowances stated in the Contract Documents. Items covered by these allowances shall be supplied for such amounts and by such persons as the Owner may direct, but the Contractor will not be required to employ persons against whom he makes a reasonable objection.

4.8.2 Unless otherwise provided in the Contract Documents:

.1 these allowances shall cover the cost to the Contractor, less any applicable trade discount, of the materials and equipment required by the allowance delivered at the site, and all applicable taxes;

.2 the Contractor's costs for unloading and handling on the site, labor, installation costs, overhead, profit and other expenses contemplated for the original allowance shall be included in the Contract Sum and not in the allowance;

.3 whenever the cost is more than or less than the allowance, the Contract Sum shall be adjusted accordingly by Change Order, the amount of which will recognize changes, if any, in handling costs on the site, labor, installation costs, overhead, profit and other expenses.

4.9 Superintendent

4.9.1 The Contractor shall employ a competent superintendent and necessary assistants who shall be in attendance at the Project site during the progress of the Work. The superintendent shall represent the Contractor and all communications given to the superintendent, *in writing,* shall be as binding as if given to the Contractor. Important communications shall be confirmed in writing. Other communications shall be so confirmed on written request in each case.

AIA Document A201 Copyright © 1976 by The American Institute of Architects.

4.10 Progress Schedule

4.10.1 The Contractor, immediately after being awarded the Contract, shall prepare and submit for the Owner's and Architect's information estimated progress schedule for the Work. The progress schedule shall be related to the entire Project to the extent required by the Contract Documents, and shall provide for expeditious and practicable execution of the Work.

4.11 Documents and Samples at the Site

4.11.1 The Contractor shall maintain at the site for the Owner one record copy of all Drawings, Specifications, Addenda, Change Orders and other Modifications, in good order and marked currently to record all changes made during construction, and approved Shop Drawings, Product Data and Samples. These shall be available to the Architect and shall be delivered to him for the Owner upon completion of the Work.

4.12 Shop Drawings, Product Data and Samples

4.12.1 Shop Drawings are drawings, diagrams, schedules and other data specially prepared for the Work by the Contractor or any Subcontractor, manufacturer, supplier or distributor to illustrate some portion of the Work.

4.12.2 Product Data are illustrations, standard schedules, performance charts, instructions, brochures, diagrams and other information furnished by the Contractor to illustrate a material, product or system for some portion of the Work.

4.12.3 Samples are physical examples which illustrate materials, equipment or workmanship and establish standards by which the Work will be judged.

4.12.4 The Contractor shall review, [*approve*] and submit, with reasonable promptness and in such sequence as to cause no delay in the Work or in the work of the Owner or any separate contractor, all Shop Drawings, Product Data and Samples required by the Contract Documents.

4.12.5 By [*approving and*] submitting Shop Drawings, Product Data and Samples, the Contractor represents that he has determined and verified all materials, field measurements, and field construction criteria related thereto, or will do so, and that he has checked and coordinated the information contained within such submittals with the requirements of the Work and of the Contract Documents.

4.12.6 The Contractor shall not be relieved of responsibility for any deviation from the requirements of the Contract Documents by the Architect's approval of Shop Drawings, Product Data or Samples under Subparagraph 2.2.14 unless the Contractor has specifically informed the Architect in writing of such deviation at the time of submission and the Architect has given written approval to the specific deviation, *or approved the submission*. The Contractor shall not be relieved from responsibility for errors or omissions in the Shop Drawings, Product Data or Samples by the Architect's approval thereof, *unless so noted in the submission.*

4.12.7 The Contractor shall direct specific attention, in writing or on resubmitted Shop

---

AIA Document A201 Copyright © 1976 by The American Institute of Architects.

Drawings, Product Data or Samples, to revisions other than those requested by the Architect on previous submittals.

4.12.8 No portion of the Work requiring submission of a Shop Drawing, Product Data or Sample shall be commenced until the submittal has been approved by the Architect as provided in Subparagraph 2.2.14. All such portions of the Work shall be in accordance with approved submittals.

4.13 Use of Site

4.13.1 The Contractor shall confine operations at the site to areas permitted by law, ordinances, permits and the Contract Documents and shall not unreasonably encumber the site with any materials or equipment.

4.14 Cutting and Patching of Work

4.14.1 The Contractor shall be responsible for all cutting, fitting or patching that may be required to complete the Work or to make its several parts fit together properly, *provided same is reasonably inferred by the Contract.*

4.14.2 The Contractor shall not damage or endanger any portion of the Work or the work of the Owner or any separate contractors by cutting, patching or otherwise altering any work, or by excavation. The Contractor shall not *unreasonably* cut or otherwise alter the work of the Owner or any separate contractor except with the written consent of the Owner and of such separate contractor. The Contractor shall not unreasonably withhold from the Owner or any separate contractor his consent to cutting or otherwise altering the Work. *The Owner shall coordinate the work of others.*

4.15 Cleaning Up

4.15.1 The Contractor at all times shall keep the premises free from accumulation of waste materials or rubbish caused by his operations. At the completion of the Work he shall remove all his waste materials and rubbish from and about the Project as well as all his tools, construction equipment, machinery and surplus materials.

4.15.2 If the Contractor fails to clean up at the completion of the Work, the Owner may do so as provided in Paragraph 3.4 and the cost thereof shall be charged to the Contractor.

4.16 Communications

4.16.1 The Contractor shall forward all communications to the Owner through the Architect.

4.17 Royalties and Patents

4.17.1 The Contractor shall pay all royalties and license fees. He shall defend all suits or claims for infringement of any patent rights and shall save the Owner harmless from loss on account thereof, except that the Owner shall be responsible for all such loss when a

---

AIA Document A201 Copyright © 1976 by The American Institute of Architects.

particular design, process or the product of a particular manufacturer or manufacturers is specified, but if the Contractor knows [*has reason to believe*] that the design, process or product specified is an infringement of a patent, he shall be responsible for such loss unless he promptly gives such information to the Architect.

4.18 Indemnification

4.18.1 To the fullest extent permitted by law, the Contractor shall indemnify and hold harmless the Owner and the Architect and their agents and employees from and against all claims, damages, losses and expenses, including but not limited to attorneys' fees, arising out of or resulting from the performance of the Work, provided that any such claim, damage, loss or expense (1) is attributable to bodily injury, sickness, disease or death, or to injury to or destruction of tangible property (other than the Work itself) including the loss of use resulting therefrom, and (2) is *directly* caused in whole or in part by any negligent act or omission of the Contractor, any Subcontractor, anyone directly [*or indirectly*] employed by any of them or anyone for whose acts any of them may be liable, *provided* [*regardless of whether or not*] it is *not* caused in part by a party indemnified hereunder. Such obligation shall not be construed to negate, abridge, or otherwise reduce any other right or obligation of indemnity which would otherwise exist as to any party or person described in this Paragraph 4.18.

4.18.2 In any and all claims against the Owner or the Architect or any of their agents or employees by any employee of the Contractor, any Subcontractor, anyone directly or indirectly employed by any of them or anyone for whose acts any of them may be liable, the indemnification obligation under this Paragraph 4.18 shall not be limited in any way by any limitation on the amount or type of damages, compensation or benefits payable by or for the Contractor or any Subcontractor under worker's or workmen's compensation acts, disability benefit acts or other employee benefit acts.

4.18.3 The obligations of the Contractor under this Paragraph 4.18 shall not extend to the liability of the Architect, his agents or employees, arising out of (1) the preparation or approval of maps, drawings, opinions, reports, surveys, change orders, designs or specifications, or (2) the giving of or the failure to give directions or instructions by the Architect, his agents or employees providing such giving or failure to give is *a* [*the primary*] cause of the injury or damage.

ARTICLE 5   Subcontractors

5.1 Definition

5.1.1 A Subcontractor is a person or entity who has a direct contract with the Contractor to perform any of the Work at the site. The term Subcontractor is referred to throughout the Contract Documents as if singular in number and masculine in gender and means a Subcontractor or his authorized representative. The term Subcontractor does not include any separate contractor or his subcontractors.

5.1.2 A Sub-subcontractor is a person or entity who has a direct or indirect contract with a Subcontractor to perform any of the Work at the site. The term Sub-subcontractor is

---

AIA Document A201 Copyright © 1976 by The American Institute of Architects.

referred to throughout the Contract Documents as if singular in number and masculine in gender and means a Sub-subcontractor or an authorized representative thereof.

5.2 Award of Subcontracts and Other Contracts for Portions of the Work

5.2.1 Unless otherwise required by the Contract Documents or the Bidding Documents, the Contractor, as soon as practicable after the award of the Contract, shall furnish to the Owner and the Architect in writing the names of the persons or entities (including those who are to furnish materials or equipment fabricated to a special design) proposed for each of the principal portions of the Work. The Architect will promptly reply to the Contractor in writing stating whether or not the Owner [*or the Architect,*] after due investigation, has reasonable objection to any such proposed person or entity. Failure of the Owner or Architect to reply promptly shall constitute notice of no reasonable objection.

5.2.2 The Contractor shall not contract with any such proposed person or entity to whom the Owner [*or the Architect*] has made reasonable objection under the provisions of Subparagraph 5.2.1. The Contractor shall not be required to contract with anyone to whom he has a reasonable objection.

5.2.3 If the Owner [*or the Architect*] has reasonable objection to any such proposed person or entity, the Contractor shall submit a substitute to whom the Owner [*or the Architect*] has no reasonable objection, and the Contract Sum shall be increased or decreased by the difference in cost occasioned by such substitution and an appropriate Change Order shall be issued; however, no increase in the Contract Sum shall be allowed for any such substitution unless the Contractor has acted promptly and responsively in submitting names as required by Subparagraph 5.2.1.

5.2.4 The Contractor shall make no substitution for any *major* Subcontractor, person or entity previously selected *without submitting the new name.* [*if the Owner or Architect makes reasonable objection to such substitution.*]

5.3 Subcontractual Relations

5.3.1 By an appropriate agreement, written where legally required for validity, the Contractor shall require each Subcontractor, to the extent of the Work to be performed by the Subcontractor, to be bound to the Contractor by the terms of the Contract Documents, and to assume toward the Contractor all the obligations and responsibilities which the Contractor, by these Documents, assumes toward the Owner and the Architect. Said agreement shall preserve and protect the rights of the Owner and the Architect under the Contract Documents with respect to the Work to be performed by the Subcontractor so that the subcontracting thereof will not prejudice such rights, and shall allow to the Subcontractor, unless specifically provided otherwise in the Contractor-Subcontractor agreement, the benefit of all rights, remedies and redress against the Contractor that the Contractor, by these Documents, has against the Owner. Where appropriate, the Contractor shall require each Subcontractor to enter into similar agreements with his Sub-subcontractors. The Contractor shall make available to each proposed Subcontractor, prior to the execution of the Subcontract, copies of the Contract Documents to which the Subcontractor will be bound by this Paragraph 5.3. [*and identify to the Subcontractor any terms and conditions of the proposed Subcontract which may be at variance with the Contract Documents.*] Each Subcontractor shall similarly make copies of such Documents available to his Sub-subcontractors.

AIA Document A201 Copyright © 1976 by The American Institute of Architects.

ARTICLE 6 Work By Owner or By Separate Contractors

6.1 Owner's Right to Perform Work and to Award Separate Contracts

6.1.1 The Owner reserves the right to perform work related to the Project with his own forces, and to award separate contracts in connection with other portions of the Project or other work on the site under these or similar Conditions of the Contract. If the Contractor claims that delay or additional cost is involved because of such action by the Owner, he shall make such claim as provided elsewhere in the Contract Documents.

6.1.2 When separate contracts are awarded for different portions of the Project or other work on the site, the term Contractor in the Contract Documents in each case shall mean the Contractor who executes each separate Owner-Contractor Agreement.

6.1.3 The Owner will provide for the coordination of the work of his own forces and of each separate contractor with the Work of the Contractor, who shall cooperate therewith as provided in Paragraph 6.2.

6.1.4 *The Owner represents and warrants that it shall coordinate the work and performance of its own forces and any other contractor on the site or related to this Contractor's work so as not to delay, hinder or interfere with the Contractor's performance thereof, and so as not to create additional costs to this Contractor. If the work or performance of any other contract should be changed, altered, or modified, with or without cause, and should same not be due to the direct fault of this Contractor, then Contractor shall be entitled to reimbursement for any additional costs it may incur resulting therefrom.*

6.2 Mutual Responsibility

6.2.1 The Contractor shall afford the Owner and separate contractors reasonable opportunity for the introduction and storage of their materials and equipment and the execution of their work, and shall connect and coordinate his Work with theirs as required by the Contract Documents.

6.2.2 If any part of the Contractor's Work depends for proper execution or results upon the work of the Owner or any separate contractor, the Contractor shall, prior to proceeding with the Work, promptly report to the Architect any *patent and* apparent discrepancies or defects in such other work that render it unsuitable for such proper execution and results. [*Failure of the Contractor so to report shall constitute an acceptance of the Owner's or separate contractors' work as fit and proper to receive his Work, except as to defects which may subsequently become apparent in such work by others.*]

6.2.3 Any costs caused by defective or ill-timed work shall be borne by the party responsible therefor.

6.2.4 Should the Contractor wrongfully cause damage to the work or property of the Owner, or to other work on the site, the Contractor shall promptly remedy such damage as provided in Subparagraph 10.2.5.

6.2.5 Should the Contractor wrongfully cause damage to the work or property of any separate contractor, the Contractor shall upon due notice promptly attempt to settle with

---

AIA Document A201 Copyright © 1976 by The American Institute of Architects.

such other contractor by agreement, or otherwise to resolve the dispute. If such separate contractor sues or initiates an arbitration proceeding against the Owner on account of any damage alleged to have been caused *solely and directly* by the Contractor, the Owner shall notify the Contractor who shall defend such proceedings at the Owner's expense, and if any judgment or award against the owner arises *solely and directly* therefrom the Contractor shall pay or satisfy it and shall reimburse the Owner for all attorneys' fees and court or arbitration costs which the Owner has incurred.

6.3 Owner's Right to Clean Up

6.3.1 If a dispute arises between the Contractor and separate contractors as to their responsibility for cleaning up as required by Paragraph 4.15, the Owner may clean up and charge the cost thereof to the contractors responsible therefor as the Architect shall determine to be just.

ARTICLE 7 Miscellaneous Provisions

7.1 Governing Law

7.1.1 The Contract shall be governed by the law of the place where the Project is located.

7.2 Successors and Assigns

7.2.1 The Owner and the Contractor each binds himself, his partners, successors, assigns and legal representatives to the other party hereto and to the partners, successors, assigns and legal representatives of such other party in respect to all covenants, agreements and obligations contained in the Contract Documents. Neither party to the Contract shall assign the Contract or sublet it as a whole without the written consent of the other, nor shall the Contractor assign any moneys due or to become due to him hereunder, without the previous written consent of the Owner.

7.3 Written Notice

7.3.1 Written notice shall be deemed to have been duly served if delivered in person to the individual or member of the firm or entity or to an officer of the corporation for whom it was intended, or if delivered at or sent by registered or certified mail to the last business address known to him who gives the notice.

7.4 Claims for Damages

7.4.1 Should either party to the Contract suffer injury or damage to person or property because of any act or omission of the other party or of any of his employees, agents or others for whose acts he is legally liable, claim shall be made in writing to such other party within a reasonable time after the first observance of such injury or damage.

7.5 Performance Bond and Labor and Material Payment Bond

7.5.1 The Owner shall have the right to require the Contractor to furnish bonds covering the faithful performance of the Contract and the payment of all obligations arising thereunder if and as required in the Bidding Documents or in the Contract Documents.

AIA Document A201 Copyright © 1976 by The American Institute of Architects.

7.6 Rights and Remedies

7.6.1 The duties and obligations imposed by the Contract Documents and the rights and remedies available thereunder shall be in addition to and not a limitation of any duties, obligations, rights and remedies otherwise imposed or available by law, *unless so indicated.*

7.6.2 No action or failure to act by the Owner, Architect or Contractor shall constitute a waiver of any right or duty afforded any of them under the Contract, nor shall any such action or failure to act constitute an approval of or acquiescence in any breach thereunder, except as may be specifically agreed in writing; *or specified in the Contract.*

7.7 Tests

7.7.1 If the Contract Documents, laws, ordinances, rules, regulations or orders of any public authority having jurisdiction require any portion of the Work to be inspected, tested or approved, the Contractor shall give the Architect timely notice of its readiness so the Architect may observe such inspection, testing or approval. The Contractor shall bear all costs of such *contractualy specified* inspections, tests or approvals conducted by public authorities. Unless otherwise provided, the Owner shall bear all costs of other inspections, tests or approvals.

7.7.2 If the Architect determines that any Work requires special inspection, testing, or approval which Subparagraph 7.7.1 does not include, he will, upon written authorization from the Owner, instruct the Contractor to order such special inspection, testing or approval, and the Contractor shall give notice as provided in Subparagraph 7.7.1. If such special inspection or testing reveals a failure of the Work to comply with the requirements of the Contract Documents, the Contractor shall bear all costs thereof, including compensation for the Architect's additional services made necessary by such failure; otherwise the Owner shall bear such costs, and an appropriate Change Order shall be issued.

7.7.3 Required certificates of inspection, testing or approval shall be secured by the Contractor and promptly delivered by him to the Architect.

7.7.4 If the Architect is to observe the inspection, tests or approvals required by the Contract Documents, he will do so promptly and, where practicable, at the source of supply.

7.8 Interest

7.8.1 Payments due and unpaid under the Contract Documents shall bear interest from the date payment is due at such rate as the parties may agree upon in writing or, in the absence thereof, at the legal rate prevailing at the place of the Project.

7.9 Arbitration

7.9.1 All claims, disputes and other matters in question between the Contractor and the Owner arising out of, or relating to, the Contract Documents or the breach thereof, [*except as provided in Subparagraph 2.2.11 with respect to the Architect's decisions on matters relating to artistic effect, and*] except for claims which have been waived by the making or acceptance of final payment as provided by Subparagraphs 9.9.4 and 9.9.5, shall be decided by arbitration in accordance with the Construction Industry Arbitration Rules of the American Arbitration Association then obtaining unless the parties mutually agree otherwise. [*No arbitration*

AIA Document A201 Copyright © 1976 by The American Institute of Architects.

arising out of or relating to the Contract Documents shall include, by consolidation, joinder or in any other manner, the Architect, his employees or consultants except by written consent containing a specific reference to the Owner-Contractor Agreement and signed by the Architect, the Owner, the Contractor and any other person sought to be joined.] No arbitration shall include by consolidation, joinder or in any other manner, parties other than the Owner, the Contractor and any other persons substantially involved in a common question of fact or law, whose presence is required if complete relief is to be accorded in the arbitration. No person other than the Owner or Contractor shall be included as an original third party or additional third party to an arbitration whose interest or responsibility is insubstantial. Any consent to arbitration involving an additional person or persons shall not constitute consent to arbitration of any dispute not described therein or with any person not named or described therein. The foregoing agreement to arbitrate and any other agreement to arbitrate with an additional person or persons duly consented to by the parties to the Owner-Contractor Agreement shall be specifically enforceable under the prevailing arbitration law. The award rendered by the arbitrators shall be final, and judgment may be entered upon it in accordance with applicable law in any court having jurisdiction thereof.

7.9.2 Notice of the demand for arbitration shall be filed in writing with the other party to the Owner-Contractor Agreement and with the American Arbitration Association, and a copy shall be filed with the Architect. The demand for arbitration shall be made within the time limits specified in Subparagraph 2.2.12 where applicable, and in all other cases within a reasonable time after the claim, dispute or other matter in question has arisen, and in no event shall it be made after the date when institution of legal or equitable proceedings based on such claim, dispute or other matter in question would be barred by the applicable statute of limitations.

7.9.3 Unless otherwise agreed in writing, the Contractor shall carry on the Work and maintain its progress during any arbitration proceedings, and the Owner shall continue to make payments to the Contractor in accordance with the Contract Documents.

7.9.4 *The Owner acknowledges that it will participate in and be bound by any judicial, administrative, legislative or arbitration proceeding wherein the Owner's participation and presence are demanded or summoned by the Contractor, provided that said proceedings involve a common question of law or fact, or indemnification, and further provided that said proceedings involve a third party and the Contractor, even though said third party might not be specifically bound by or a party to this Contract.*

ARTICLE 8   Time

8.1 Definitions

8.1.1 Unless otherwise provided, the Contract Time is the period of time allotted in the Contract Documents for Substantial Completion of the Work as defined in Subparagraph 8.1.3, including authorized adjustments thereto.

8.1.2 The date of commencement of the Work is the date established in a notice to proceed. If there is no notice to proceed, it shall be the date of the Owner-Contractor Agreement or such other date as may be established therein.

AIA Document A201 Copyright © 1976 by The American Institute of Architects.

8.1.3 The Date of Substantial Completion of the Work or designated portion thereof is the Date certified by the Architect when construction is sufficiently complete, in accordance with the Contract Documents, so the Owner can occupy or utilize the Work or designated portion thereof for the use for which it is intended.

8.1.4 The term day as used in the Contract Documents shall mean calendar day unless otherwise specifically designated.

8.2 Progress and Completion

8.2.1 All time limits stated in the Contract Documents are of the essence of the Contract.

8.2.2 The Contractor shall begin the Work on the date of commencement as defined in Subparagraph 8.1.2. He shall carry the Work forward expeditiously with adequate forces and shall achieve Substantial Completion within the Contract Time.

8.3 Delays and Extensions of Time

8.3.1 If the Contractor is delayed at any time in the progress of the Work by any act or neglect of the Owner or the Architect, or by any employee of either, or by any separate contractor employed by the Owner, or by changes ordered in the Work, or by labor disputes, fire, unusual delay in transportation, adverse weather conditions not reasonably anticipatable, unavoidable casualties, or any causes beyond the Contractor's control, or by delay authorized by the Owner pending arbitration, or by any other cause which the Architect determines may justify the delay, then the Contract Time shall be extended by Change Order for such reasonable time as the Architect may determine.

8.3.2 Any claim for extension of time shall be made in writing to the *Owner or* Architect *within a reasonable time [not more than twenty days]* after the commencement of the delay; otherwise it shall be waived. In the case of a continuing delay only one claim is necessary. The Contractor shall provide an estimate of the probable effect of such delay on the progress of the Work.

8.3.3 If no agreement is made stating the dates upon which interpretations as provided in Subparagraph 2.2.8 shall be furnished, then no claim for delay shall be allowed on account of failure to furnish such interpretations until *three [fifteen]* days after written request is made for them, *unless facts necessitate a shorter time. [and not then unless such claim is reasonable.]*

8.3.4 This Paragraph 8.3 does not exclude the recovery of damages for delay by either party under other provisions of the Contract Documents.

8.3.5 *It is hereby acknowledged that the contract price is based upon the Contractor being able to perform its work in an orderly and sequential manner, as it so determines. That if its performance is delayed, interfered, suspended, or otherwise interrupted, in whole or in part, by the Owner, the Architect, other contractors on the site or project, or by any other party or by any act within the power and/or duty of the Owner to control, then the Owner shall be liable to the Contractor for any and all increased and extended costs, attorneys fees, general and administrative costs, and other damages which are incurred by the Contractor.*

AIA Document A201 Copyright © 1976 by The American Institute of Architects.

ARTICLE 9   Payments and Completion

9.1 Contract Sum

9.1.1 The Contract Sum is stated in the Owner-Contractor Agreement and, including authorized adjustments thereto, is the total amount payable by the Owner to the Contractor for the performance of the Work under the Contract Documents.

9.2 Schedule of Values

9.2.1 Before the first Application for Payment, the Contractor shall submit to the Architect a schedule of values allocated to the various portions of the Work, prepared in such form and supported by such data to substantiate its accuracy as the Architect may require. This schedule, unless objected to by the Architect, shall be used only as a basis for the Contractor's Applications for Payment.

9.3 Applications for Payment

9.3.1 At least ten days before the date for each progress payment established in the Owner-Contractor Agreement, the Contractor shall submit to the Architect an itemized Application for Payment, notarized if required, supported by such data substantiating the Contractor's right to payment as the Owner [*or the Architect*] may require, and reflecting retainage, if any, as provided elsewhere in the Contract Documents.

9.3.2 Unless otherwise provided in the Contract Documents, payments will be made on account of materials or equipment not incorporated in the Work but delivered and suitably stored at the site and, if approved in advance by the Owner, payments may similarly be made for materials or equipment suitably stored at some other location agreed upon in writing. Payments for materials or equipment stored on or off the site shall be conditioned upon submission by the Contractor of bills of sale or such other procedures satisfactory to the Owner to establish the Owner's title to such materials or equipment or otherwise protect the Owner's interest, including applicable insurance and transportation to the site for those materials and equipment stored off the site.

9.3.3 The Contractor warrants that title to all Work, materials and equipment covered by an Application for Payment will pass to the Owner [*either by incorporation in the construction or*] upon the receipt of payment by the Contractor, [*whichever occurs first,*] free and clear of all liens, claims, security interests or encumbrances, hereinafter referred to in this Article 9 as "liens"; and that no Work, materials or equipment covered by an Application for Payment will have been acquired by the Contractor, or by any other person performing Work at the site or furnishing materials and equipment for the Project, subject to an agreement under which an interest therein or an encumbrance thereon is retained by the seller or otherwise imposed by the Contractor or such other person, *which would survive payment to the Contractor.*

9.4 Certificates for Payment

9.4.1 The Architect will, within seven days after the receipt of the Contractor's Application for Payment, either issue a Certificate for Payment to the Owner, with a copy to the Contractor, for such amount as the Architect determines is properly due, or notify the

---

AIA Document A201 Copyright © 1976 by The American Institute of Architects.

Contractor in writing his reasons for withholding a Certificate as provided in Subparagraph 9.6.1.

9.4.2 The issuance of a Certificate for Payment will constitute a representation by the Architect to the Owner, based on his observations at the site as provided in Subparagraph 2.2.3 and the data comprising the Application for Payment, that the Work has progressed to the point indicated; that, to the best of his knowledge, information and belief, the quality of the Work is in accordance with the Contract Documents (subject to [*an evaluation of the Work for conformance with the Contract Documents upon Substantial Completion, to*] the results of any subsequent tests required by or performed under the Contract Documents, to minor deviations from the Contract Documents correctable prior to completion, and to any specific qualifications stated in his Certificate); and that the Contractor is entitled to payment in the amount certified. However, by issuing a Certificate for Payment, the Architect shall not thereby be deemed to represent that he has made exhaustive or continuous on-site inspections to check the quality or quantity of the Work or that he has reviewed the construction means, methods, techniques, sequences or procedures, or that he has made any examination to ascertain how or for what purpose the Contractor has used the moneys previously paid on account of the Contract Sum.

9.5 Progress Payments

9.5.1 After the Architect has issued a Certificate for Payment, the Owner shall make payment in the manner and within the time provided in the Contract Documents.

9.5.2 The Contractor shall promptly pay each Subcontractor, upon receipt of payment from the Owner, out of the amount paid to the Contractor on account of such Subcontractor's Work, the amount to which said Subcontractor is entitled, reflecting the percentage actually retained, if any, from payments to the Contractor on account of such Subcontractor's Work. The Contractor shall, by an appropriate agreement with each Subcontractor, require each Subcontractor to make payments to his Sub-subcontractors in similar manner. *Payments are subject to the Subcontract or Purchase Order terms.*

9.5.3 The Architect may, on request and at his discretion, furnish to any Subcontractor, if practicable, information regarding the percentages of completion or the amounts applied for by the Contractor and the action taken thereon by the Architect on account of Work done by such Subcontractor.

9.5.4 Neither the Owner nor the Architect shall have any obligation to pay or to see to the payment of any moneys to any Subcontractor except as may otherwise be required by law.

9.5.5 No Certificate for a progress payment, nor any progress payment, nor any partial or entire use or occupancy of the Project by the Owner, shall constitute an acceptance of any Work not in accordance with the Contract Documents, *when so listed by the Owner or Architect, or in the event of latent defects.*

9.6 Payments Withheld

9.6.1 The Architect may decline to certify payment and may withhold his Certificate in whole or in part, *only* to the extent necessary reasonably to protect the Owner, if in his

---

AIA Document A201 Copyright © 1976 by The American Institute of Architects.

opinion he is unable to make representations to the Owner as provided in Subparagraph 9.4.2. If the Architect is unable to make representations to the Owner as provided in Subparagraph 9.4.2 and to certify payment in the amount of the Application, he will notify the Contractor as provided in Subparagraph 9.4.1. If the Contractor and the Architect cannot agree on a revised amount, the Architect will promptly issue a Certificate for Payment for the amount for which he is able to make such representations to the Owner. The Architect may also decline to certify payment or, because of subsequently discovered evidence or subsequent observations, he may nullify the whole or any part of any Certificate for Payment previously issued, to such extent as *is* [*may be*] necessary [*in his opinion*] to protect the Owner from loss because of:

.1 defective work not remedied,

.2 third party claims filed [*or reasonable evidence indicating probable filing of such claims*]

.3 failure of the Contractor to make payments properly to Subcontractors or for labor, materials or equipment, *but only if no bond has been furnished,*

.4 reasonable evidence that the Work cannot be completed *by the Contractor* for the unpaid balance of the Contract Sum,

.5 damage to the Owner or another contractor,

.6 reasonable evidence that the Work will not be completed within the *properly adjusted* Contract Time, or

.7 persistent *unreasonable* failure to carry out the Work in accordance with the Contract Documents.

9.6.2 When the above grounds in Subparagraph 9.6.1 are removed, payment shall be made for amounts withheld because of them.

9.7 Failure of Payment

9.7.1 If the Architect does not issue a Certificate for Payment, through no fault of the Contractor, within seven days after receipt of the Contractor's Application for Payment, or if the Owner does not pay the Contractor *by* [*within seven days after*] the date established in the Contract Documents any amount certified by the Architect or awarded by arbitration, then the Contractor may, upon *three* [*seven*] additional days' written notice to the Owner [*and the Architect,*] stop the Work until payment of the amount owing has been received. The Contract Sum shall be increased by the amount of the Contractor's reasonable costs of shut-down, delay and start-up, *legal fees, etc.,* which shall be effected by appropriate Change Order in accordance with Paragraph 12.3.

9.8 Substantial Completion

9.8.1 When the Contractor considers that the Work, or a designated portion thereof which is acceptable to the Owner, is substantially complete as defined in Subparagraph 8.1.3, the Contractor shall prepare for submission to the Architect a list of items to be completed or corrected. The failure to include any items on such list does not alter the responsibility of the Contractor to complete all Work in accordance with the Contract Documents. When the Architect on the basis of an inspection determines that the Work or designated portion thereof is substantially complete, he will then prepare a Certificate of Substantial Completion which shall establish the Date of Substantial Completion, shall state

---

AIA Document A201 Copyright © 1976 by The American Institute of Architects.

the responsibilities of the Owner and the Contractor for security, maintenance, heat, utilities, damage to the Work, and insurance, and shall fix the time within which the Contractor shall complete the items listed therein. Warranties required by the Contract Documents shall commence on the Date of Substantial Completion of the Work or designated portion thereof unless otherwise provided in the Certificate of Substantial Completion. The Certificate of Substantial Completion shall be submitted to the Owner and the Contractor for their written acceptance of the responsibilities assigned to them in such Certificate.

9.8.2 Upon Substantial Completion of the Work or designated portion thereof and upon application by the Contractor and certification by the Architect, the Owner shall make payment, reflecting adjustment in retainage, if any, for such Work or portion thereof, as provided in the Contract Documents.

9.8.3 The Architect shall conduct an inspection of the Work within five days after receipt of notice from the Contractor that the work has been substantially completed. If no itemized list is received from the Contractor, then it shall be assumed that the Contractor claims that no items remain to be completed or corrected. The Owner, by itself or through its Architect, shall furnish a detailed listing of each and every item of work (a) required to be performed prior to acknowledgement of substantial completion; or (b) if substantial completion has taken place, a detailed list of each and every item of work yet to be completed or corrected. These lists shall be forwarded to the Contractor so as not to cause delay to final completion. As work is performed the Owner or Architect shall acknowledge same and those items shall be removed from the list.

9.9 Final Completion and Final Payment

9.9.1 Upon receipt of written notice that the Work is ready for final inspection and acceptance and upon receipt of a final Application for Payment, the Architect will promptly make such inspection and, when he finds the Work acceptable under the Contract Documents and the Contract fully performed, he will promptly issue a final Certificate for Payment stating that to the best of his knowledge, information and belief, and on the basis of his observations and inspections, the Work has been completed in accordance with the terms and conditions of the Contract Documents and that the entire balance found to be due the Contractor, and noted in said final Certificate, is due and payable. The Architect's final Certificate for Payment will constitute a further representation that the conditions precedent to the Contractor's being entitled to final payment as set forth in Subparagraph 9.9.2 have been fulfilled.

9.9.2 Neither the final payment nor the remaining retained percentage shall become due until the Contractor submits to the Architect (1) an affidavit that all payrolls, bills for materials and equipment, and other indebtedness connected with the Work for which the Owner or his property might in any way be responsible, have been paid or otherwise satisfied, (2) consent of surety, if any, to final payment and (3), if required by the Owner, other data establishing payment or satisfaction of all such obligations, such as receipts, releases and waivers of liens arising out of the Contract, to the extent and in such form as may be designated by the Owner. If any Subcontractor refuses to furnish a release or waiver required by the Owner, the Contractor may furnish a bond satisfactory to the Owner to indemnify him against any such lien. If any such lien remains unsatisfied after all payments are made, the Contractor shall refund to the Owner all moneys that the latter may be compelled to pay in discharging such lien, including all costs and reasonable attorneys' fees.

AIA Document A201 Copyright © 1976 by The American Institute of Architects.

9.9.3 If, after Substantial Completion of the Work, final completion thereof is materially delayed through no fault of the Contractor or by the issuance of Change Orders affecting final completion, and the Architect so confirms, the Owner shall, upon application by the Contractor and certification by the Architect, and without terminating the Contract, make payment of the balance due for that portion of the Work fully completed and accepted. If the remaining balance for Work not fully completed or corrected is less than the retainage stipulated in the Contract Documents, and if bonds have been furnished as provided in Paragraph 7.5, the written consent of the surety to the payment of the balance due for that portion of the Work fully completed and accepted shall be submitted by the Contractor to the Architect prior to certification of such payment. Such payment shall be made under the terms and conditions governing final payment, except that it shall not constitute a waiver of claims.

9.9.4 The making of final payment shall constitute a waiver of all claims by the Owner except those arising from:

.1 unsettled liens,

.2 faulty or defective Work appearing after Substantial Completion,

.3 *latent* failures of the Work to comply with the requirements of the Contract Documents, or

.4 terms of any special warranties required by the Contract Documents.

9.9.5 The acceptance of final payment shall constitute a waiver of all claims by the Contractor except those previously made in writing and identified by the Contractor as unsettled at the time of the final Application for Payment.

ARTICLE 10 Protection of Persons and Property

10.1 Safety Precautions and Programs

10.1.1 The Contractor shall be responsible for initiating, maintaining and supervising all safety precautions and programs in connection with the Work.

10.2 Safety of Persons and Property

10.2.1 The Contractor shall take all reasonable precautions for the safety of, and shall provide all reasonable protection to prevent damage, injury or loss to:

.1 all employees on the Work and all other persons who may be affected thereby;

.2 all the Work and all materials and equipment to be incorporated therein, whether in storage on or off the site, under the care, custody or control of the Contractor or any of his Subcontractors or Sub-subcontractors; and

.3 other property at the site or adjacent thereto, including trees, shrubs, lawns, walks, pavements, roadways, structures and utilities not designated for removal, relocation or replacement in the course of construction.

10.2.2 The Contractor shall give all notices and comply with all applicable laws, ordi-

---

AIA Document A201 Copyright © 1976 by The American Institute of Architects.

nances, rules, regulations and lawful orders of any public authority bearing on the safety of persons or property or their protection from damage, injury or loss.

10.2.3 The Contractor shall erect and maintain, as required by existing conditions and progress of the Work, all reasonable safeguards for safety and protection, including posting danger signs and other warnings against hazards, promulgating safety regulations and notifying owners and users of adjacent utilities.

10.2.4 When the use or storage of explosives or other hazardous materials or equipment is necessary for the execution of the Work, the Contractor shall exercise the utmost care and shall carry on such activities under the supervision of properly qualified personnel.

10.2.5 The Contractor shall promptly remedy all damage or loss (other than damage or loss insured under Paragraph 11.3) to any property referred to in Clauses 10.2.1.2 and 10.2.1.3 caused in whole or in part by the Contractor, any Subcontractor, any Sub-subcontractor, or anyone directly or indirectly employed by any of them, or by anyone for whose acts any of them may be liable and for which the Contractor is responsible under Clauses 10.2.1.2 and 10.2.1.3, except damage or loss attributable to the acts or omissions of the Owner or Architect or anyone directly or indirectly employed by either of them, or by anyone for whose acts either of them may be liable, and not attributable to the fault or negligence of the Contractor. The foregoing obligations of the Contractor are in addition to his obligations under Paragraph 4.18.

10.2.6 The Contractor shall designate a responsible member of his organization at the site whose duty shall be the prevention of accidents. This person shall be the Contractor's superintendent unless otherwise designated by the Contractor in writing to the Owner and the Architect.

10.2.7 The Contractor shall not load or permit any part of the Work to be loaded so as to endanger its safety.

10.3 Emergencies

10.3.1 In any emergency affecting the safety of persons or property, the Contractor shall act, at his discretion, to prevent threatened damage, injury or loss. Any additional compensation or extension of time claimed by the Contractor on account of emergency work shall be determined *between the Contractor and Owner.* [*as provided in Article 12 for Changes in the Work.*]

ARTICLE 11   Insurance

11.1 Contractor's Liability Insurance

11.1.1 The Contractor shall purchase and maintain such insurance as will protect him from claims set forth below which may arise out of or result from the Contractor's operations under the Contract, whether such operations be by himself or by any Subcontractor or by anyone directly or indirectly employed by any of them, or by anyone for whose acts any of them may be liable:

AIA Document A201 Copyright © 1976 by The American Institute of Architects.

.1 claims under workers' or workmen's compensation, disability benefit and other similar employee benefit acts;

.2 claims for damages because of bodily injury, occupational sickness or disease, or death of his employees;

.3 claims for damages because of bodily injury, sickness or disease, or death of any person other than his employees;

.4 claims for damages insured by usual personal injury liability coverage which are sustained (1) by any person as a result of an offense directly or indirectly related to the employment of such person by the Contractor, or (2) by any other person;

.5 claims for damages, other than to the Work itself, because of injury to or destruction of tangible property, including loss of use resulting therefrom; and

.6 claims for damages because of bodily injury or death of any person or property damage arising out of the ownership, maintenance or use of any motor vehicle.

11.1.2 The issuance required by Subparagraph 11.1.1 shall be written for not less than any limits of liability specified in the Contract Documents, or required by law, whichever is greater.

11.1.3 The insurance required by Subparagraph 11.1.1 shall include contractual liability insurance applicable to the Contractor's obligations under Paragraph 4.18.

11.1.4 Certificates of Insurance acceptable to the Owner shall be filed with the Owner prior to commencement of the Work. These Certificates shall contain a provision that coverages afforded under the policies will not be cancelled until at least thirty days' prior written notice has been given to the Owner.

11.2 Owner's Liability Insurance

11.2.1 The Owner shall be responsible for purchasing and maintaining his own liability insurance and, at his option, may purchase and maintain such insurance as will protect him against claims which may arise from operations under the Contract.

11.3 Property Insurance

11.3.1 Unless otherwise provided, the Owner shall purchase and maintain property insurance upon the entire Work at the site to the full insurable value thereof. This insurance shall include the interests of the Owner, the Contractor, Subcontractors and Sub-subcontractors in the Work and shall insure against the perils of fire and extended coverage and shall include "all risk" insurance for physical loss or damage including, without duplication of coverage, theft, vandalism and malicious mischief. If the Owner does not intend to purchase such insurance for the full insurable value of the entire Work, he shall inform the Contractor in writing prior to commencement of the Work. The Contractor may then effect insurance which will protect the interests of himself, his Subcontractors and the Sub-subcontractors in the Work, and by appropriate Change Order the cost thereof shall be charged to the Owner. If the Contractor is damaged by failure of the Owner to purchase or maintain such insurance and to so notify the Contractor, then the Owner shall bear all reasonable costs properly attributable thereto. If not covered under the all risk insurance or otherwise provided in the Contract Documents, the Contractor shall effect and maintain similar property

---

AIA Document A201 Copyright © 1976 by The American Institute of Architects.

insurance on portions of the Work stored off the site or in transit when such portions of the Work are to be included in an Application for Payment under Subparagraph 9.3.2.

11.3.2 The Owner shall purchase and maintain such boiler and machinery insurance as may be required by the Contract Documents or by law. This insurance shall include the interests of the Owner, the Contractor, Subcontractors and Sub-subcontractors in the Work.

11.3.3 Any loss insured under Subparagraph 11.3.1 is to be adjusted with the Owner and made payable to the Owner as trustee for the insureds, as their interests may appear, subject to the requirements of any applicable mortgagee clause and of Subparagraph 11.3.8. The Contractor shall pay each Subcontractor a just share of any insurance moneys received by the Contractor, and by appropriate agreement, written where legally required for validity, shall require each Subcontractor to make payments to his Sub-subcontractors in similar manner.

11.3.4 The Owner shall file a copy of all policies with the Contractor before an exposure to loss may occur.

11.3.5 If the Contractor requests in writing that insurance for risks other than those described in Subparagraphs 11.3.1 and 11.3.2 or other special hazards be included in the property insurance policy, the Owner shall, if possible, include such insurance, and the cost thereof shall be charged to the Contractor by appropriate Change Order.

11.3.6 The Owner and Contractor waive all rights against (1) each other and the Subcontractors, Sub-subcontractors, agents and employees each of the other, and (2) the Architect and separate contractors, if any, and their subcontractors, sub-subcontractors, agents and employees, for damages caused by fire or other perils to the extent covered by insurance obtained pursuant to this Paragraph 11.3 or any other property insurance applicable to the Work, except such rights as they may have to the proceeds of such insurance held by the Owner as trustee. The foregoing waiver afforded the Architect, his agents and employees shall not extend to the liability imposed by Subparagraph 4.18.3. The Owner or the Contractor, as appropriate, shall require of the Architect, separate contractors, Subcontractors and Sub-subcontractors by appropriate agreements, written where legally required for validity, similar waivers each in favor of all other parties enumerated in this Subparagraph 11.3.6.

11.3.7 If required in writing by any party in interest, the Owner as trustee shall, upon the occurrence of an insured loss, give bond for the proper performance of his duties. He shall deposit in a separate account any money so received, and he shall distribute it in accordance with such agreement as the parties in interest may reach, or in accordance with an award by arbitration in which case the procedure shall be as provided in Paragraph 7.9. If after such loss no other special agreement is made, replacement of damaged work shall be covered by an appropriate Change Order.

11.3.8 The Owner as trustee shall have power to adjust and settle any loss with the insurers unless one of the parties in interest shall object in writing within five days after the occurrence of loss to the Owner's exercise of this power, and if such objection be made, arbitrators shall be chosen as provided in Paragraph 7.9. The Owner as trustee shall, in that case, make settlement with the insurers in accordance with the directions of such arbitrators. If distribution of the insurance proceeds by arbitration is required, the arbitrators will direct such distribution.

AIA Document A201 Copyright © 1976 by The American Institute of Architects.

11.3.9 If the Owner finds it necessary to occupy or use a portion or portions of the Work prior to Substantial Completion thereof, such occupancy shall not commence prior to a time mutually agreed to by the Owner and Contractor and to which the insurance company or companies providing the property insurance have consented by endorsement to the policy or policies. This insurance shall not be cancelled or lapsed on account of such partial occupancy. Consent of the Contractor and of the insurance company or companies to such occupancy or use shall not be unreasonably withheld.

11.4 Loss of Use Insurance

11.4.1 The Owner, at his option, may purchase and maintain such insurance as will insure him against loss of use of his property due to fire or other hazards, however caused. The Owner waives all rights of action against the Contractor for loss of use of his property, including consequential losses due to fire or other hazards however caused, to the extent covered *or coverable* by insurance under this Paragraph 11.4.

ARTICLE 12 Changes in the Work

12.1 Change Orders

12.1.1 A Change Order is a written order to the Contractor signed by the Owner *or* [*and*] the Architect, issued after execution of the Contract, authorizing a change in the Work or an adjustment in the Contract Sum or the Contract Time. The Contract Sum and the Contract Time may be changed only by Change Order. A Change Order signed by the Contractor indicates his agreement therewith, including the adjustment in the Contract Sum or the Contract Time, *unless so reserved or left open.*

12.1.2 The Owner, without invalidating the Contract, may order changes in the Work within the general scope of the Contract consisting of additions, deletions or other revisions, the Contract Sum and the Contract Time being adjusted accordingly. All such changes in the Work shall be authorized by Change Order, and shall be performed under the applicable conditions of the Contract Documents.

12.1.3 The cost or credit to the Owner resulting from a change in the Work shall be determined in one or more of the following ways:

.1 by mutual acceptance of a lump sum properly itemized; [*and supported by sufficient substantiating data to permit evaluation;*]

.2 by unit prices stated in the Contract Documents or subsequently agreed upon;

.3 by cost to be determined in a manner agreed upon by the parties and a mutually acceptable fixed or percentage fee; or

.4 by the method provided in Subparagraph 12.1.4.

12.1.4 If none of the methods set forth in Clauses 12.1.3.1, 12.1.3.2 or 12.1.3.3 is agreed upon, the Contractor, provided he receives a written order signed by the Owner, shall promptly proceed with the Work involved. The cost of such Work shall then be determined by the Architect on the basis of the reasonable expenditures and savings of those performing the Work attributable to the change, including, in the case of an increase in the Contract Sum, *separate* [*a*] reasonable allowances for *general conditions,* overhead and profit. In such

---

AIA Document A201 Copyright © by The American Institute of Architects.

case, and also under Clauses 12.1.3.3 and 12.1.3.4 above, the Contractor shall keep and present, in such form as the Architect may prescribe, an itemized accounting together with appropriate supporting data for inclusion in a Change Order. Unless otherwise provided in the Contract Documents, cost shall be limited to the following: cost of materials, including sales tax and cost of delivery; cost of labor, including social security, old age and unemployment insurance, and fringe benefits required by agreement or custom; workers' or workmen's compensation insurance; bond premiums; rental value of equipment and machinery; and the additional costs of supervision and field office personnel directly attributable to the change. Pending final determination of cost to the Owner, payments on account shall be made on the Architect's Certificate for Payment. The amount of credit to be allowed by the Contractor to the Owner for any deletion or change which results in a net decrease in the Contract Sum will be the amount of the actual net cost as confirmed by the Architect. When both additions and credits covering related Work or substitutions are involved in any one change, the allowance for overhead and profit shall be figured on the basis of the net increase, if any, with respect to that change.

12.1.5 If unit prices are stated in the Contract Documents or subsequently agreed upon, and if the quantities originally contemplated are so changed in a proposed Change Order that application of the agreed unit prices to the quantities of Work proposed will cause substantial inequity to the Owner or the Contractor, the applicable unit prices shall be equitably adjusted.

12.1.6 *Any change or proposed change submitted to the Architect or Owner for review and signature must be reviewed and finalized within a reasonable period of time so as not to cause any delay or interruption in the Contractor's performance of the Contract or Work, in whole or part.*

12.2 Concealed Conditions

12.2.1 Should *latent or* concealed conditions *be* encountered in the performance of the Work [*below the surface of the ground*] or should concealed or unknown conditions [*in an existing structure*] be at variance with the conditions indicated by the Contract Documents, or should unknown physical conditions [*below the surface of the ground*] or [*should*] concealed or unknown conditions [*in an existing structure*] of an unusual nature, differing materially from those ordinarily encountered and generally recognized as inherent in work of the character provided for in this Contract, be encountered, the Contract Sum *and time* shall be equitably adjusted by Change Order upon claim by either party made within twenty days after the first observance of the conditions.

12.3 CLAIMS FOR ADDITIONAL COST

12.3.1 If the Contractor wishes to make a claim for an increase in the Contract Sum, he shall give the Architect written notice thereof within *a reasonable time,* [*twenty days*] after the occurrence of the event giving rise to such claim. This notice shall be given *where reasonably possible* by the Contractor before proceeding to execute the Work, except in an emergency endangering life or property in which case the Contractor shall proceed in accordance with Paragraph 10.3. [*No such claim shall be valid unless so made.*] If the Owner and the Contractor cannot agree on the amount of the adjustment in the Contract Sum, it shall be determined by the Architect. Any changes in the Contract Sum resulting from such claim shall be authorized by Change Order.

12.3.2 If the Contractor claims that additional cost is involved because of, but not limited

---

AIA Document A201 Copyright © 1976 by The American Institute of Archtects.

to, (1) any written interpretation pursuant to Subparagraph 2.2.8, (2) any order by the Owner to stop the Work pursuant to Paragraph 3.3 where the Contractor was not at fault, (3) any written order for a minor change in the Work issued pursuant to Paragraph 12.4, or (4) failure of payment by the Owner pursuant to Paragraph 9.7, the Contractor shall make such claim as provided in Subparagraph 12.3.1.

12.4 Minor Changes in the Work

12.4.1 The Architect will have authority to order minor changes in the Work not involving an adjustment in the Contract Sum or an extension of the Contract Time and not inconsistent with the intent of the Contract Documents. Such changes shall be effected by written order, and shall be binding on the Owner and the Contractor. The Contractor shall carry out such written orders promptly.

12.5 *If the Contractor is requested in writing, by either the Owner or the Architect, to price proposed changes, and the Contractor so prices the proposed change, and if the Owner or the Architect decide not to effectuate the change, then the Contractor shall be entitled to reimbursement of all costs incurred in the reviewing and pricing of said proposed change, including all home office engineering, estimating, purchasing or other costs, plus a reasonable overhead and profit.*

ARTICLE 13 Uncovering and Correction of Work

13.1 Uncovering of Work

13.1.1 If any portion of the Work should be covered contrary to the request of the Architect or to requirements specifically expressed in the Contract Documents, it must, if required in writing by the Architect, be uncovered for his observation and shall be replaced at the Contractor's expense.

13.1.2 If any portion of the Work has been covered which the Architect has not specifically requested to observe prior to being covered, the Architect may request to see such Work and it shall be uncovered by the Contractor. If such Work be found in accordance with the Contract Documents, *due to the Contractor's default,* the cost of uncovering and replacement shall, by appropriate Change Order, be charged to the Owner. If such Work be found not in accordance with the Contract Documents, the Contractor shall pay such costs unless it be found that this condition was caused by the Owner or a separate contractor as provided in Article 6, in which event the Owner shall be responsible for the payment of such costs.

13.2 Correction of Work

13.2.1 The Contractor shall promptly correct all Work rejected by the Architect as defective or as failing to conform to the Contract Documents whether observed before or after Substantial Completion and whether or not fabricated, installed or completed. The Contractor shall bear all costs of correcting such rejected Work, including compensation for the Architect's additional services made necessary thereby, *where the Contractor was at sole fault.*

13.2.2 If, within one year after the Date of Substantial Completion of the Work or designated portion thereof or within one year after acceptance by the Owner of designated equipment or within such longer period of time as may be prescribed [*by law or*] by the terms

---

AIA Document A201 Copyright © 1976 by The American Institute of Architects.

of any applicable special warranty required by the Contract Documents, any of the Work is found to be defective or not in accordance with the Contract Documents, the Contractor shall correct it promptly after receipt of a written notice from the Owner to do so unless the Owner has previously given the Contractor a written acceptance of such condition. This obligation shall survive termination of the Contract. The Owner shall give such notice promptly after discovery of the condition. *This clause shall limit other remedies.*

13.2.3 The Contractor shall remove from the site all portions of the Work which are defective or nonconforming and which have not been corrected under Subparagraphs 4.5.1, 13.2.1 and 13.2.2, unless removal is waived by the Owner.

13.2.4 If the Contractor fails to correct defective or nonconforming Work as provided in Subparagraphs 4.5.1, 13.2.1 and 13.2.2, the Owner may correct it in accordance with Paragraph 3.4.

13.2.5 If the Contractor does not proceed with the correction of such defective or nonconforming Work within a reasonable time fixed by written notice from the Architect, the Owner may remove it and may store the materials or equipment at the expense of the Contractor. If the Contractor does not pay the cost of such removal and storage within ten days thereafter, the Owner may upon ten additional days written notice sell such Work at auction or at private sale and shall account for the net proceeds thereof, after deducting all the costs that should have been borne by the Contractor, including compensation for the Architect's additional services made necessary thereby. If such proceeds of sale do not cover all costs which the Contractor should have borne, the difference shall be charged to the Contractor and an appropriate Change Order shall be issued. If the payments then or thereafter due the Contractor are not sufficient to cover such amount, the Contractor shall pay the difference to the Owner.

13.2.6 The Contractor shall bear the cost of making good all work of the Owner or separate contractors destroyed or damaged by such correction or removal.

13.2.7 [*Nothing contained in*] This Paragraph 13.2 shall be construed to establish a period of limitation with respect to any [*other*] obligation which the Contractor might have under the Contract Documents, including Paragraph 4.5 hereof. [*The establishment of the time period of one year after the Date of Substantial Completion or such longer period of time as may be prescribed by law or by the terms of any warranty required by the Contract Documents relates only to the specific obligation of the Contractor to correct the Work, and has no relationship to the time within which his obligation to comply with the Contract Documents may be sought to be enforced, nor to the time within which proceedings may be commenced to establish the Contractor's liability with respect to his obligations other than specifically to correct the Work.*]

13.3 Acceptance of Defective of Non-Conforming Work

13.3.1 If the Owner prefers to accept defective or non-conforming Work, he may do so instead of requiring its removal and correction, in which case a Change Order will be issued to reflect a reduction in the Contract Sum where appropriate and equitable. Such adjustment shall be effected whether or not final payment has been made.

AIA Document A201 Copyright © 1976 by The American Institute of Architects.

ARTICLE 14 Termination of the Contract

14.1 Termination by the Contractor

14.1.1 If the Work is stopped for a period of thirty days under an order of any court or other public authority having jurisdiction, or as a result of an act of government, such as a declaration of a national emergency making materials unavailable through no act or fault of the Contractor, *Owner, Architect* or a Subcontractor or their agents or employees or any other persons performing any of the Work under a contract with *any of them, [the Contractor, or if the Work should be stopped for a period of thirty days by the Contractor because the Architect has not issued a Certificate for Payment as provided in Paragraph 9.7 or because the Owner has not made payment thereon as provided in Paragraph 9.7,*] then the Contractor may, upon seven additional days' written notice to the Owner [*and the Architect,*] terminate the Contract and recover from the Owner payment for all Work executed and for any proven loss sustained upon any materials, equipment, tools, construction equipment and machinery, including reasonable profit and damages.

14.1.2 *If the project is stopped or delayed, either in whole or substantial part, for a period of thirty (30) days under an Order of any Court or other public authority having jurisdiction, or as a result of an act of government, due to the fault or negligence of the Owner or Architect, or as a result of any act within either's control; or, if the project should be stopped or delayed, either in whole or substantial part, for a period of thirty (30) days by the Contractor due to the Owner's failure to make proper payment thereon; or, if the Owner or Architect should commit a material breach of any of its responsibilities or obligations under this agreement, then the Contractor may, upon seven (7) days written notice to the Owner, terminate this agreement and recover from the Owner compensation for (1) all work performed; (2) any unpaid costs of and fees for the project; (3) any liability, obligations, damages, commitments and/or claims that the Contractor may have incurred or might incur in good faith in connection with this contract; (4) the contractor's attorney and legal fees; and, (5) all lost anticipated gross profit on the contract work not performed as of the date of termination.*

14.2 Termination by the Owner

14.2.1 If the Contractor is adjudged a bankrupt, or if he makes a general assignment for the benefit of his creditors, or if a receiver is appointed on account of his insolvency, or if he persistently or repeatedly refuses or fails, except in cases for which extension of time is provided, to supply enough properly skilled workmen or proper materials, or if he fails to make prompt payment to Subcontractors or for materials or labor, or persistently disregards laws, ordinances, rules, regulations or orders of any public authority having jurisdiction, or otherwise is guilty of a substantial violation of a provision of the Contract Documents, then the Owner, upon certification by the Architect that sufficient cause exists to justify such action, may, without prejudice to any right or remedy and after giving the Contractor and his surety, if any, seven days' written notice, terminate the employment of the Contractor and take possession of the site and of all materials, equipment, tools, construction equipment and machinery thereon owned by the Contractor and may finish the Work by whatever method he may deem expedient. In such case the Contractor shall not be entitled to receive any further payment until the Work is finished.

14.2.2 If the unpaid balance of the Contract Sum exceeds the costs of finishing the Work, including compensation for the Architect's additional services made necessary thereby,

---

AIA Document A201 Copyright © 1976 by The American Institute of Architects.

such excess shall be paid to the Contractor. If such costs exceed the unpaid balance, the Contractor shall pay the difference to the Owner. The amount to be paid to the Contractor or to the Owner, as the case may be, shall be certified by the Architect, upon application, in the manner provided in Paragraph 9.4, and this obligation for payment shall survive the termination of the Contract.

FOOTNOTES:

1   Note that the contractor's bid is specifically excluded from incorporation into the contract, unless it is specifically included. Thus, if a bid is intended to become part of the contract, and treated as a contract document, it must be incorporated specifically and listed in the actual agreement
2   By this type of clause, the parties can avoid multiple arbitrations during the progress of the job. The parties should be able to perform the work without creating adversary relations. When such a provision is inserted, the disputes usually can be resolved amicably during the progress of the work
3   As referenced in the various general conditions that are reviewed in this book, this article, although for the contractor's benefit, has created concern. It is for this reason that the indicated provision must be inserted as a continuation to paragraph 3.2.1

AIA Document A201 Copyright © 1976 by The American Institute of Architects.

B. CONSTRUCTION MANAGEMENT CONTRACTS

§1.06 1. Introduction The "construction management" concept lacks a simple definition. The terms "construction manager" and "construction management contract" are employed in numerous, differing factual and legal situations. Therefore, it is virtually impossible to standardize a single form for use by a prime contractor who is involved in a construction management situation.

The construction management contract may be best characterized as a conceptual agreement. Unlike the traditional construction contract pattern, in which an owner hires an architect/engineer to prepare the design and bid documents and then obtains competitive bids based upon strict adherence to those plans (which often creates adverse interests), the construction management concept is a multi-disciplined team approach.

It is imperative that the prime contractor educate the owner to the fact that there is no set standard in construction management. The contractor must dispel any preconceived notions of the owner. The construction management contract normally is a negotiated instrument and most frequently involves an executed agreement, even before detailed plans and specifications are finalized. The construction manager becomes the owner's representative, adviser, and consultant, as well as the professional link between the architect/engineer and the owner.

The construction manager's contract must indicate clearly that the manager's professional role is not that of the architect/engineer. A distinct architect/engineer entity should have a separate contract with the owner. The architect/engineer contract should be made available for complete review by the construction manager so that the manager's responsibilities will be consistent with those of the architect/engineer. The construction management contract must differentiate and delineate the roles of the construction manager and the architect/engineer. It must state explicitly that the construction manager neither claims to be the architect/engineer nor accepts that liability. This is a necessary item in a construction management situation in order to avoid conflict with any licensing statute, and to divide clearly the responsibility and liability for the design aspect.

During the design phase, the construction manager should raise the possible and probable construction problems that may occur, and thus avoid adversary situations that may arise during construction under the typical plan and specification contract. The construction manager offers to the owner the expertise that the owner normally lacks when dealing with the architect/engineer. On a properly operating construction management team, the input of all parties is considered before the final design is reached. Often the initial design concept is never realized, as it is subject to changes in objectives, even during construction. For this reason the construction manager must provide sufficient self-protection in order to adjust compensation and completion time.

Since the entire construction management agreement revolves around the owner's needs, the construction manager must establish a fluctuating "time of the essence" clause. Although these may appear to be inconsistent terms, time must remain material to the contract, but it must also be capable of adjustment to meet the changing concept.

There is great confusion in construction management when trying to determine whether the construction manager is also a prime contractor with subcontractors. It is the author's opinion that the pure construction management contract works best when the construction manager remains in a professional consulting capacity, and that the owner should be the party who enters into the various trade prime contracts.

However, in this situation, the construction manager gives up various controls over the trade prime contractors, and therefore should avoid furnishing any absolute, guaranteed maximum price or completion time to the owner. The construction manager should limit the contractual obligation to acting as the professional constructor, rendering advice and directions to the owner. It should be the owner's obligation to effectuate the advice, or at the very least, to accept liability for the results of the owner's actions and omissions.

If the construction manager is the entity which signs with the trade contractor, then the manager must be aware that this action constitutes acceptance of normal prime contractor responsibilities and obligations to both the owner and the subcontractors and suppliers, as well as acceptance of construction manager obligations. If the construction manager is going to guarantee price or completion time to the owner, it is the author's opinion that the construction manager must be the person to select the trade contractors, the subcontract and purchase order forms, and must retain all necessary power and control over the trade contractors. The construction manager must reserve the right to select and discharge the trade contractor. In addition to this right, the construction manager must retain the right to perform the work which otherwise would be performed by a trade contractor. However, the author strongly advises that if the construction manager performs any work as a trade contractor, the manager perform that work with separate and distinct administrative and supervisory personnel. In fact, a separate legal entity is advisable. Too many instances in which the construction manager wears two hats lead to the creation of disputes and claims. This is especially true when someone communicates with the contractor's personnel, but cannot tell, or does not know, whether that person is operating as a trade contractor or as the construction manager. Confusion creates litigation. Retain the right to perform as a trade contractor, but keep a separate identity.

The Associated General Contractors of America have recently published and copyrighted three forms for the construction management contract. These forms incorporate many clauses from the American Institute of Architects form. The modifications seem to make these forms more suitable, although not perfect, for the prime contractor.

AGC Document No. 8 is entitled "Standard Form of Agreement Between Owner And Construction Manager (Guaranteed Maximum Price Option)." This is the best general form that the author has found. From this form the prime contractor can tailor a construction management form. It must be emphasized that since the construction management contract is a conceptual one and differs from contract to contract, *this form must be tailored to the facts.* There are certain recommendations for changes to this standard form, and these are set forth in §§1.08, 1.09.

AGC Document No. 8A is entitled "Amendment To Owner-Construction Manager Contract" and provides for the insertion of the guaranteed maximum price. The form is simple, and, as a standard, general form, needs no correction. Understanding the importance of the form requires understanding the general concept of construction management. Since the construction manager is involved in a team concept, prior to the finalization of plans and specifications, the construction manager should not and cannot guarantee a price at the time of executing the construction management agreement. The construction manager only can make a price commitment after fulfilling numerous obligations under the original agreement. Thus, the furnishing of a guaranteed maximum price must be by amendment or separate agreement with the owner.

AGC Document No. 8b entitled "General Conditions For Owner-Construction Manager Agreement" is well-written, and is the best available "standard" when no standard is possible. It tries to cover too many types of situations in a single document. It would require extensive modification for application to any one of numerous construction management situations. It is the *strong* recommendation of the author that AGC Document No. 8b *not* be used as general conditions or articles of construction or as a document which would be given precedence over conflicting terms, when the construction manager is the party entering into contracts with the trade contractors. If the construction manager is going to play the role of a prime contractor, and if the trade contractor is going to play the role of a subcontractor, it is *strongly* advised that the prime contractor use the standard subcontract form which is included in this book. On the other hand, the general conditions prepared by the Associated General Contractors of America form an excellent basis for preparing specific general conditions between the owner and construction manager, assuming that the owner is the entity which has the contractual relationship with the trade prime contractors, and assuming that the construction manager does not guarantee price or completion date and includes within the construction management contract a basis for additional compensation, should further costs be incurred as a result of problems between the trade contractor and the owner. AGC Document No. 8b with recommended modifications is discussed in §§11.11, 11.12. The document should be used as a starting point for general conditions between the owner and construction manager, or the owner and trade contractor, when the construction manager is only a consultant.

2. Standard Form of Agreement Between Owner and Construction Manager (AGC Document No. 8) with Suggested Modifications

§1.07　　a. Author's Comments Before any modifications are made to a standard form, it is mandatory that the prime contractor carefully read and digest the document. The standard form sets forth in clear and concise language the general phases and concepts of the construction management contract. This AGC document must be read prior to negotiating the construction management agreement with the owner, so that when the parties enter into negotiations, they have a good understanding of the concepts and potential areas for agreement. The form emphasizes the idea that construction management is an integrated team concept running the full spectrum from planning, design, and construction, through completion.

The AGC standard form of construction manager agreement should be slightly modified if the construction manager will or will not be performing work as a trade contractor. It is recommended that the construction manager's management forces and trade work forces be separate entities.

The problem of a construction manager's performing work as a trade contractor becomes complex when change orders are involved, as in paragraph 2.2.4 of the form in §1.08. If the construction manager performs work as a trade contractor, then there might be a conflict of interest. The same is true to a lesser extent when all trade contractors have direct contracts with the construction manager, and when the construction manager's own trade work forces are but one aspect of the overall contract. In this instance the construction manager may have a conflict in fulfilling "neutral" construction manager obligations toward the owner when reviewing the performance of the various trade contractors, and in settling disputes between those trade contractors. There is no solution except that the construction manager not perform any trade contractor work; this is only possible when there is no guaranteed maximum price or time obligation.

Article 4 of the form involves the issue of whether the trade contracts are to be with the owner or with the construction manager. Although this can be determined at a future date, it is recommended that Article 4.3 be changed as indicated to shift the initial burden.

Article 7, entitled "Construction Manager's Fee," and Article 8, entitled "Cost Of The Project," are within the province of the construction manager. They must be carefully reviewed to ensure the inclusion of all actual and reasonably conceivable costs and expenses. It is strongly suggested that the construction manager review these items with an accountant so that all actual and potential cost contingencies are covered.

Article 15, which is left available for miscellaneous provisions, should include an owner-furnished property clause and a provision relating to the insertion of present and future construction contract documents.

§1.08   B. FORM—
AGC DOCUMENT
NO. 8

Standard Form of Agreement Between Owner and Construction Manager (Guaranteed Maximum Price Option)

THE ASSOCIATED GENERAL CONTRACTORS

AGC Document Number 8, Owner-Construction Manager Agreement, Copyright © 1977, reprinted by permission of The Associated General Contractors of America.

Certain Provisions of this document have been derived, with modifications, from documents published by The American Institute of Architects.

Portions of AIA Documents A111, Owner-Contractor Agreement; A201, General Conditions of the Contract for Construction; and B801, Owner-Construction Manager Agreement have been reproduced with the permission of The American Institute of Architects under application number 78036. Further reproduction, in part or in whole, is not authorized. Because AIA documents are revised from time to time, users should ascertain from AIA the current edition of the document of which portions are reproduced below.

TABLE OF ARTICLES

1. The Construction Team and Extent of Agreement
2. Construction Manager's Services
3. The Owner's Responsibilities
4. Trade Contracts
5. Schedule
6. Guaranteed Maximum Price
7. Construction Manager's Fee
8. Cost of the Project
9. Changes in the Project
10. Discounts
11. Payments to the Construction Manager
12. Insurance, Indemnity and Waiver of Subrogation
13. Termination of the Agreement and Owner's Right to Perform Construction Manager's Obligations
14. Assignment and Governing Law
15. Miscellaneous Provisions
16. Arbitration

AGREEMENT

Made this_____day of_____in the year of Nineteen Hundred and_____

BETWEEN_____

_____ the Owner, and

_____ the Construction Manager.

For services in connection with the following described Project: *(Include complete Project location and scope)*

The Architect/Engineer for the Project is

The Owner and the Construction Manager agree as set forth below:

_____

ARTICLE 1   The Construction Team and Extent of Agreement

The CONSTRUCTION MANAGER accepts the relationship of trust and confidence established between him and the Owner by this Agreement. He covenants with the Owner to furnish his best skill and judgment and to cooperate with the Architect/Engineer in furthering the interests of the Owner. He agrees to furnish efficient business administration and superintendence and to use his best efforts to complete the Project in [*a reasonable*] expeditious and economical manner consistent with the interest of the Owner.

1.1 The Construction Team The Construction Manager, the Owner, and the Architect/Engineer called the "Construction Team" shall work from the beginning of design through construction completion. The Construction Manager shall provide leadership to the Construction Team on all matters relating to construction.

1.2 Extent of Agreement This Agreement represents the entire agreement between the Owner and the Construction Manager and supersedes all prior negotiations, representations or agreements. When Drawings and Specifications are complete, they shall be identified by amendment to this Agreement. This Agreement shall not be superseded by any provisions of the documents for construction and may be amended only by written instrument signed by both Owner and Construction Manager.

1.3 Definitions The Project is the total construction to be performed under this Agreement. The Work is that part of the construction that the Construction Manager is to perform with his own forces or that part of the construction that a particular Trade Contractor is to perform. The term day shall mean calendar day unless otherwise specifically designated.

ARTICLE 2   Construction Manager's Services

The Construction Manager will perform the following services under this Agreement in each of the two phases described below.

2.1 Design Phase

   2.1.1 Consultation During Project Development Schedule and attend regular meetings with the Architect/Engineer during the development of conceptual and preliminary design to advise on site use and improvements, selection of materials, building systems and equipment. Provide recommendations on construction feasibility, availability of materials and labor, time requirements for installation and construction, and factors related to cost including costs of alternative designs or materials, preliminary budgets, and possible economies.

2.1.2 Scheduling Develop a Project Time Schedule that coordinates and integrates the Architect/Engineer's design efforts with construction schedules. Update the Project Time Schedule incorporating a detailed schedule for the construction operations of the Project, including realistic activity sequences and durations, allocation of labor and materials, processing of shop drawings and samples, and delivery of products requiring long lead-time procurement. Include the Owner's occupancy requirements showing portions of the Project having occupancy priority.

2.1.3. Project Construction Budget Prepare a Project budget as soon as major Project requirements have been identified, and update periodically for the Owner's approval. Prepare an estimate based on a quantity survey of Drawings and Specifications at the end of the schematic design phase for approval by the Owner as the Project Construction Budget. Update and refine this estimate for Owner's approval as the development of the Drawings and Specifications proceeds, and advise the Owner and the Architect/Engineer if it appears that the Project Construction Budget will not be met and make recommendations for corrective action.

2.1.4. Coordination of Contract Documents Review the Drawings and Specifications as they are being prepared, recommending alternative solutions whenever design details affect construction feasibility or schedules without, however, assuming any of the Architect/Engineer's responsibilities for design.

2.1.5. Construction Planning Recommend for purchase and expedite the procurement of long-lead items to ensure their delivery by the required dates.

2.1.5.1 Make recommendations to the Owner and the Architect/Engineer regarding the division of Work in the Drawings and Specifications to facilitate the bidding and awarding of Trade Contracts, allowing for phased construction taking into consideration such factors as time of performance, availability of labor, overlapping trade jurisdictions, and provisions for temporary facilities.

2.1.5.2 Review the Drawings and Specifications with the Architect/Engineer to eliminate areas of conflict and overlapping in the Work to be performed by the various Trade Contractors and prepare prequalification criteria for bidders.

2.1.5.3 Develop Trade Contractor interest in the Project and as working Drawings and Specifications are completed, take competitive bids on the Work of the various Trade Contractors. After analyzing the bids, either award contracts or recommend to the Owner that such contracts be awarded.

2.1.6. Equal Employment Opportunity Determine applicable requirements for equal employment opportunity programs for inclusion in Project bidding documents.

2.2 Construction Phase

2.2.1 Project Control Monitor the Work of the Trade Contractors and coordinate the Work with the activities and responsibilities of the Owner, Architect/Engineer and Construction Manager to complete the Project in accordance with the Owner's objectives of cost, time and quality.

2.2.1.1 Maintain a competent full-time staff at the Project site to coordinate and provide general direction of the Work and progress of the Trade Contractors on the Project.

2.2.1.2 Establish on-site organization and lines of authority in order to carry out the overall plans of the Construction Team.

2.2.1.3 Establish procedures for coordination among the Owner, Architect/Engineer, Trade Contractors and Construction Manager with respect to all aspects of the Project and implement such procedures.

2.2.1.4 Schedule and conduct progress meetings at which Trade Contractors, Owner, Architect/Engineer and Construction Manager can discuss jointly such matters as procedures, progress, problems and scheduling.

2.2.1.5 Provide regular monitoring of the schedule as construction progresses. Identify potential variances between scheduled and probable completion dates. Review schedule for Work not started or incomplete and recommend to the Owner and Trade Contractors adjustments in the schedule to meet the probable completion date. Provide summary reports of each monitoring and document all changes in schedule.

2.2.1.6. Determine the adequacy of the Trade Contractors' personnel and equipment and the availability of materials and supplies to meet the schedule. Recommend courses of action to the Owner when requirements of a Trade Contract are not being met.

2.2.2 Physical Construction Provide all supervision, labor, materials, construction equipment, tools and subcontract items which are necessary for the completion of the Project which are not provided by either the Trade Contractors or the Owner. To the extent that the Construction Manager performs any Work, with his own forces, he shall, with respect to such Work, be bound to the extent not inconsistent with this Agreement, by the procedures and the obligations with respect to such Work.[1] *[as may govern the Trade Contractors under any General Conditions to the Trade Contract.]*

2.2.3 Cost Control Develop and monitor an effective system of Project cost control. Revise and refine the initially approved Project Construction Budget, incorporate approved changes as they occur, and develop cash flow reports and forecasts as needed. Identify variances between actual and budgeted or estimated costs and advise Owner and Architect/Engineer whenever projected cost exceeds budgets or estimates.

2.2.3.1 Maintain cost accounting records on authorized Work performed under unit costs, actual costs for labor and material, or other bases requiring accounting records. Afford the Owner access to these records and preserve them for a period of three (3) years after final payment.

2.2.4 Change Orders Develop and implement a system for the preparation, review and processing of Change Orders. Recommend necessary or desirable changes to the Owner and the Architect/Engineer, review requests for changes, submit recommendations to the Owner and the Architect/Engineer, and assist in negotiating Change Orders.

2.2.5 Payments to Trade Contractors Develop and implement a procedure for the review, processing and payment of applications by Trade Contractors for progress and final payments.

2.2.6 Permits and Fees Assist the Owner and Architect/Engineer in obtaining all building permits and special permits for permanent improvements, excluding permits for inspection or temporary facilities required to be obtained directly by the various Trade Contractors. Assist in obtaining approvals from all the authorities having jurisdiction.

2.2.7 Owner's Consultants If required, assist the Owner in selecting and retaining professional services of a surveyor, testing laboratories and special consultants, and coordinate these services, *without assuming any responsibility or liability of or for these consultants.*[2]

2.2.8 Inspection Inspect the Work of Trade Contractors for defects and deficiencies in the Work without assuming any of the Architect/Engineer's responsibilities for inspection.

2.2.8.1 Review the safety programs of each of the Trade Contractors and make appropriate recommendations. In making such recommendations and carrying out such reviews, he shall not be required to make exhaustive or continuous inspections to check safety precautions and programs in connection with the Project. The performance of such services by the Construction Manager shall not relieve the Trade Contractors of their responsibilities for the safety of persons and property, and for compliance with all federal, state and local statutes, rules, regulations and orders applicable to the conduct of the Work.

2.2.9 Document Interpretation Refer all questions for interpretation of the documents prepared by the Architect/Engineer *initially* to the Architect/Engineer, *but subject to arbitration as provided in Article 16.*

2.2.10 Shop Drawings and Samples In collaboration with the Architect/Engineer, establish and implement procedures for expediting the processing and approval of shop drawings and samples.

2.2.11 Reports and Project Site Documents Record the progress of the Project. Submit written progress reports to the Owner and the Architect/Engineer including information on the Trade Contractors' Work, and the percentage of completion. Keep a daily log available to the Owner and the Architect/Engineer.

2.2.11.1 Maintain at the Project site, on a current basis: records of all necessary Contracts, Drawings, samples, purchases, materials, equipment, maintenance and operating manuals and instructions, and other construction related documents, including all revisions. Obtain data from Trade Contractors and maintain a current set of record Drawings, Specifications and operating manuals. At the completion of the Project, deliver all such records to the Owner.

2.2.12 Substantial Completion Determine Substantial Completion of the Work or designated portions thereof and prepare for the Architect/Engineer a list of incomplete or unsatisfactory items and a schedule for their completion.

2.2.13 Start-Up With the Owner's maintenance personnel, direct the checkout of utilities, operations systems and equipment for readiness and assist in their initial start-up and testing by the Trade Contractors.

2.2.14 Final Completion Determine final completion and provide written notice to the Owner and Architect/Engineer that the Work is ready for final inspection. Secure and transmit to the Architect/Engineer required guarantees, affidavits, releases, bonds and waivers. Turn over to the Owner all keys, manuals, record drawings and maintenance stocks.

2.2.15 Warranty Where any Work is performed by the Construction Manager's own forces or by Trade Contractors under contract with the Construction Manager, the Construction

Manager shall warrant that all materials and equipment included in such Work will be new, unless otherwise specified, and that such Work will be of good quality, free from improper workmanship and defective materials and in conformance with the Drawings and Specifications. With respect to the same Work, the Construction Manager further agrees to correct all work defective in material and workmanship for a period of one year from the Date of Substantial Completion or for such longer periods of time as may be set forth with respect to specific warranties contained in the trade sections of the Specifications. The Construction Manager shall collect and deliver to the Owner any specific written warranties given by others.

2.3 Additional Services

2.3.1 At the request of the Owner the Construction Manager will provide the following additional services upon written agreement between the Owner and Construction Manager defining the extent of such additional services and the amount and manner in which the Construction Manager will be compensated for such additional services.

2.3.2 Services related to investigation, appraisals or valuations of existing conditions, facilities or equipment, or verifying the accuracy of existing drawings or other Owner-furnished information.

2.3.3 Services related to Owner-furnished equipment, furniture and furnishings which are not a part of this Agreement.

2.3.4 Services for tenant or rental spaces not a part of this Agreement.

2.3.5 Obtaining or training maintenance personnel or negotiating maintenance service contracts.

ARTICLE 3   Owner's Responsibilities

3.1 The Owner shall provide full information regarding his requirements for the project.

3.2 The Owner shall designate a representative who shall be fully acquainted with the project and has authority to *issue and* approve Project Construction Budgets, Changes in the Project, render decisions promptly and furnish information expeditiously.

3.3 The Owner shall retain an Architect/Engineer for design and to prepare construction documents for the Project. The Architect/Engineer's services, duties and responsibilities are described in the Agreement between the Owner and the Architect/Engineer, a copy of which will be furnished to the Construction Manager. The Agreement between the Owner and the Architect/Engineer shall not be modified without written notification to the Construction Manager.

3.4 The Owner shall furnish for the site of the Project all necessary surveys describing the physical characteristics, soil reports and subsurface investigations, legal limitations, utility locations, and a legal description.

3.5 The Owner shall secure and pay for necessary approvals, easements, assessments and charges required for the construction, use or occupancy of permanent structures or for permanent changes in existing facilities.

3.6 The Owner shall furnish such legal services as may be necessary for providing the items set forth in Paragraph 3.5, and such auditing services as he may require.

3.7 The Construction Manager will be furnished without charge all copies of Drawings and Specifications reasonably necessary for the execution of the Work.

3.8 The Owner shall provide the insurance for the Project as provided in Paragraph 12.4, and shall bear the cost of any bonds required.

3.9 The services, information, surveys and reports required by the above paragraphs shall be furnished with reasonable promptness at the Owner's expense, and the Construction Manager shall be entitled to rely upon the accuracy and completeness thereof.

3.10 If the Owner becomes aware of any fault or defect in the Project or non-conformance with the Drawings and Specifications, he shall give prompt written notice thereof to the Construction Manager.

3.11 The Owner shall furnish, *prior to commencing work and at such future times as may be requested,* reasonable evidence satisfactory to the Construction Manager that sufficient funds are available and committed for the entire cost of the Project. Unless such reasonable evidence is furnished, the Construction Manager is not required to commence *or continue* any Work, or may, if such evidence is not presented within a reasonable time, stop the Project upon 15 days notice to the Owner. *The failure of the construction manager to request or receive satisfactory evidence that sufficient funds are available and committed shall not be deemed to be an acquiescence by the construction manager in the lack of funds, or affect any of the construction manager's rights to payment.*[3]

3.12 The Owner shall communicate with the Trade Contractors only through the Construction Manager.

ARTICLE 4   Trade Contracts

4.1 All portions of the Project that the Construction Manager does not perform with his own forces shall be performed under Trade Contracts. The Construction Manager shall request and receive proposals from Trade Contractors and Trade Contracts will be awarded after the proposals are reviewed by the Architect/Engineer, Construction Manager and Owner.

4.2 If the Owner refuses to accept a Trade Contractor recommended by the Construction Manager, the Construction Manager shall recommend an acceptable substitute and the Guaranteed Maximum Price if applicable shall be increased or decreased by the difference in cost occasioned by such substitution and an appropriate Change Order shall be issued.

4.3 Unless otherwise directed by the Owner, Trade Contracts will be between *Owner* [*the Construction Manager and*] the Trade Contractors. Whether the Trade Contracts are with the Construction Manager or the Owner, the form of the Trade Contracts including the General and Supplementary Conditions shall be satisfactory to the Construction Manager.

4.4 The Construction Manager shall be responsible to the Owner for the acts and omissions of his agents and employees, Trade Contractors performing Work under a contract with the Construction Manager, and such Trade Contractors' agents and employees.

ARTICLE 5   Schedule

5.1 The services to be provided under this Contract shall be in general accordance with the following schedule:

5.2 At the time a Guaranteed Maximum Price is established, as provided for in Article 6, a Date of Substantial Completion of the project shall also be established.

5.3 The Date of Substantial Completion of the Project or a designated portion thereof is the date when construction is sufficiently complete in accordance with the Drawings and Specifications so the Owner can *reasonably* occupy or utilize the Project or designated portion thereof for the use for which it is intended. Warranties called for by this Agreement or by the Drawings and Specifications shall commence on the Date of Substantial Completion of the Project or designated portion thereof.

5.4 If the Construction Manager is delayed at any time in the progress of the Project by any act or neglect of the Owner or the Architect/Engineer or by any employee of either, or by any separate contractor employed by the Owner, or by changes ordered in the Project, or by labor disputes, fire, unusual delay in transportation, adverse weather conditions not reasonably anticipatable, unavoidable casualties or any causes beyond the Construction Manager's control, or by delay authorized by the Owner pending arbitration, the Construction Completion Date shall be extended by Change Order for a reasonable length of time.

ARTICLE 6   Guaranteed Maximum Price

6.1 When the design, Drawings and Specifications are sufficiently complete, the Construction Manager will, if desired by the Owner, establish a Guaranteed Maximum Price, guaranteeing the maximum price to the Owner for the Cost of the Project and the Construction Manager's Fee. Such Guaranteed Maximum Price will be subject to modification for Changes in the Project as provided in Article 9, *for the Owner's failure to properly fulfill its obligations* and for additional costs arising from delays caused by the Owner or the Architect/Engineer, *or due to events not within the control or assumed by the Construction Manager.*

6.2 When the Construction Manager provides a Guaranteed Maximum Price, the Trade Contracts will either be with the Construction Manager or will contain the necessary provisions to allow the Construction Manager to control the performance of the Work.

6.3 The Guaranteed Maximum Price will only include those taxes in the Cost of the Project which are legally enacted at the time the Guaranteed Maximum Price is established.

ARTICLE 7   Construction Manager's Fee

7.1 In consideration of the performance of the Contract, the Owner agrees to pay the Construction Manager in current funds as compensation for his services a Construction Manager's Fee as set forth in Subparagraphs 7.1.1. and 7.1.2.

   7.1.1   For the performance of the Design Phase services, a fee of   which shall be paid monthly, in equal proportions, based on the scheduled Design Phase time.

   7.1.2   For work or services performed during the Construction Phase, a fee of
which shall be paid proportionately to the ratio the monthly payment for the Cost of the Project bears to the estimated cost. Any balance of this fee shall be paid at the time of final payment.

7.2 Adjustments in Fee shall be made as follows:

   7.2.1   For Changes in the Project as provided in Article 9, the Construction Manager's Fee shall be adjusted as follows:

7.2.2 For delays in the Project not the responsibility of the Construction Manager, there will be an equitable adjustment in the fee to compensate the Construction Manager for his increased expenses.

7.2.3 The Construction Manager shall be paid an additional fee in the same proportion as set forth in 7.2.1 in the Construction Manager is placed in charge of the reconstruction if any insured or uninsured loss.

7.3 Included in the Construction Manager's Fee are the following:

7.3.1 Salaries or other compensation of the Construction Manager's employees at the principal office and branch offices, except employees listed in Subparagraph 8.2.2.

7.3.2 General operating expenses of the Construction Manager's principal and branch offices other than the field office.

7.3.3 Any part of the Construction Manager's capital expenses, including interest on the Construction Manager's capital employed for the project.

7.3.4 Overhead or general expenses of any kind, except as may be expressly included in Article 8.

7.3.5 Costs in excess of the Guaranteed Maximum Price.

ARTICLE 8   Cost of the Project

8.1 The term Cost of the Project shall mean costs necessarily incurred in the Project during either the Design or Construction Phase, and paid by the Construction Manager, or by the Owner if the Owner is directly paying Trade Contractors upon the Construction Manager's approval and direction. Such costs shall include the items set forth below in this Article.

8.1.1 The Owner agrees to pay the Construction Manager for the Cost of the Project as defined in Article 8. Such payment shall be in addition to the Construction Manager's Fee stipulated in Article 7.

8.2 Cost Items

8.2.1 Wages paid for labor in the direct employ of the Construction Manager in the performance of his Work under applicable collective bargaining agreements, or under a salary or wage schedule agreed upon by the Owner and Construction Manager, and including such welfare or other benefits, if any, as may be payable with respect thereto.

8.2.2 Salaries of the Construction Manager's employees when stationed at the field office, in whatever capacity employed, employees engaged on the road in expediting the production or transportation of materials and equipment, and employees in the main or branch office performing the functions listed below:

8.2.3 Cost of all employee benefits and taxes for such items as unemployment compensation and social security, insofar as such cost is based on wages, salaries, or other remuneration paid to employees of the Construction Manager and included in the Cost of the Project under Subparagraphs 8.2.1 and 8.2.2.

8.2.4 The proportion of reasonable transportation, traveling, moving, and hotel expenses of the Construction Manager or of his officers or employees incurred in discharge of duties connected with the Project.

8.2.5 Cost of all materials, supplies and equipment incorporated in the Project, including costs of transportation and storage thereof.

8.2.6 Payments made by the Construction Manager or Owner to Trade Contractors for their Work performed pursuant to contract under this Agreement.

8.2.7 Cost, including transportation and maintenance, of all materials, supplies, equipment, temporary facilities and hand tools not owned by the workmen, which are employed or consumed in the performance of the Work, and cost less salvage value on such items used but not consumed which remain the property of the Construction Manager.

8.2.8 Rental charges of all necessary machinery and equipment, exclusive of hand tools, used at the site of the Project, whether rented from the Construction Manager or other, including installation, repairs and replacements, dismantling, removal, costs of lubrication, transportation and delivery costs thereof, at rental charges consistent with those prevailing in the area.

8.2.9 Cost of the premiums for all insurance which the Construction Manager is required to procure by this Agreement or is deemed necessary by the Construction Manager.

8.2.10 Sales, use, gross receipts or similar taxes related to the Project imposed by any governmental authority, and for which the Construction Manager is liable.

8.2.11 Permit fees, licenses, tests, royalties, damages for infringement of patents and costs of defending suits therefor, and deposits lost for causes other than the Construction Manager's negligence. If royalties or losses and damages, including costs of defense, are incurred which arise from a particular design, process, or the product of a particular manufacturer or manufacturers specified by the Owner or Architect/Engineer, and the Construction Manager has no reason to believe there will be infringement of patent rights, such royalties, losses and damages shall be paid by the Owner and not considered as within the Guaranteed Maximum Price.

8.2.12 Losses, expenses or damages to the extent not compensated by insurance or otherwise (including settlement made with the written approval of the Owner).

8.2.13 The cost of corrective work subject, however, to the Guaranteed Maximum Price.

8.2.14 Minor expenses such as telegrams, long-distance telephone calls, telephone service at the site, expressage, and similar petty cash items in connection with the Project.

8.2.15 Cost of removal of all debris.

8.2.16 Cost incurred due to an emergency affecting the safety of persons and property.

8.2.17 Cost of data processing services required in the performance of the services outlined in Article 2.

8.2.18 Legal costs reasonably and properly resulting from prosecution of the Project for the Owner.

8.2.19 All costs directly incurred in the performance of the Project and not included in the Construction Manager's Fee as set forth in Paragraph 7.3.

ARTICLE 9   Changes in the Project

9.1 The Owner without invalidating this Agreement, may order Changes in the Project within the general scope of this Agreement consisting of additions, deletions or other revisions, the Guaranteed Maximum Price, if established, the Construction Manager's Fee and the Construction Completion Date being adjusted accordingly. All such Changes in the project shall be authorized by Change Order.

9.1.1. A Change Order is a written order to the Construction Manager signed by the Owner or his authorized agent issued after the execution of this Agreement, authorizing a Change in the Project *or the method or manner of performance* and/or an adjustment in the Guaranteed Maximum Price, the Construction Manager's Fee, or the Construction Completion Date. Each adjustment in the Guaranteed Maximum Price resulting from a Change Order shall clearly separate the amount attributable to the Cost of the Project and the Construction Manager's Fee.

9.1.2 The increase or decrease in the Guaranteed Maximum Price resulting from a Change in the Project shall be determined in one or more of the following ways.

.1 by mutual acceptance of a lump sum properly itemized and supported by sufficient substantiating data to permit evaluation;

.2 by unit prices stated in the Agreement or subsequently agreed upon;

.3 by cost as defined in Article 8 and a mutually acceptable fixed or percentage fee; or

.4 by the method provided in Subparagraph 9.1.3.

9.1.3 If none of the methods set forth in Clauses 9.1.2.1 through 9.1.2.3 is agreed upon, the Construction Manager, provided he receives a written order signed by the Owner, shall promptly proceed with the Work involved. The cost of such Work shall then be determined on the basis of the reasonable expenditures and savings of those performing the Work attributed to the change, including, in the case of an increase in the Guaranteed Maximum Price, a reasonable increase in the Construction Manager's Fee. In such case, and also under Clauses 9.1.2.3 and 9.1.2.4 above, the Construction Manager shall keep and present, in such form as the Owner may prescribe, an itemized accounting together with appropriate supporting data of the increase in the Cost of the Project as outlined in Article 8. The amount of decrease in the Guaranteed Maximum Price to be allowed by the Construction Manager to the Owner for any deletion or change which results in a net decrease in cost will be the amount of the actual net decrease. When both additions and credits are involved in any one change, the increase in Fee shall be figured on the basis of net increase, if any.

9.1.4 If unit prices are stated in the Agreement or subsequently agreed upon, and if the quantities originally contemplated are so changed in a proposed Change Order *or as a result of several Change Orders* that application of the agreed unit prices to the quantities of Work proposed will cause substantial inequity to the Owner or the Construction Manager, the applicable unit prices and Guaranteed Maximum Price shall be equitably adjusted.[4]

9.1.5 Should *unknown or latent* [*concealed*] conditions encountered in the performance of the Work [*below the surface of the ground or should concealed or unknown conditions in an existing structure*] be at variance with the conditions indicated by the Drawings, Specifications, or Owner-furnished information or property or should unknown *or latent* [*physical*] conditions [*below the surface of the ground or should concealed or unknown conditions in an existing structure*] of an unusual nature, differing materially from those ordinarily encountered and generally recognized as inherent in work of the character provided for in this Agreement, be encountered, the Guaranteed Maximum Price and the Construction Completion Date shall be equitably adjusted by Change Order upon claim by either party made within a reasonable time after the first observance of the conditions.

9.2 Claims for Additional Cost or Time

9.2.1 If the Construction Manager wishes to make a claim for an increase in the Guaranteed Maximum Price, an increase in his fee, or an extension in the Construction Completion Date, he shall give the Owner written notice thereof within a reasonable time after the occurrence of the event giving rise to such claim. This notice shall be given by the Construction Manager before proceeding to execute any Work, except in an emergency endangering life or property in which case the Construction Manager shall act, at his discretion, to prevent threatened damage, injury or loss. Claims arising from delay shall be made within a reasonable time after the delay. No such claim shall be valid unless so made. If the Owner and the Construction Manager cannot agree on the amount of the adjustment in the Guaranteed Maximum Price, Construction Manager's Fee or Construction Completion Date, it shall be determined pursuant to the provisions of Article 16. Any change in the Guaranteed Maximum Price, Construction Manager's Fee or Construction Completion Date resulting from such claim shall be authorized by Change Order.

9.3 Minor Changes in the Project

9.3.1 The Architect/Engineer will have authority to order minor Changes in the Project not involving an adjustment in the Guaranteed Maximum Price or an extension of the Construction Completion Date and not inconsistent with the intent of the Drawings and Specifications. Such Changes may be effected by written order and shall be binding on the Owner and the Construction Manager.

9.4 Emergencies

9.4.1 In any emergency affecting the safety of persons or property, the Construction Manager shall act, at his discretion, to prevent threatened damage, injury or loss. Any increase in the Guaranteed Maximum Price or extension of time claimed by the Construction Manager on account of emergency work shall be determined as provided in this Article.

ARTICLE 10   Discounts

All discounts for prompt payment shall accrue to the Owner to the extent the Cost of the project is paid directly by the Owner or from a fund made available by the Owner to the Construction Manager for such payments. To the extent the Cost of the Project is paid with funds of the Construction Manager, all cash discounts shall accrue to the Construction Manager. All trade discounts, rebates and refunds, and all returns from sale of surplus materials and equipment, shall be credited to the Cost of the Project.

ARTICLE 11   Payments to the Construction Manager

11.1 The Construction Manager shall submit monthly to the Owner a statement, sworn to if required, showing in detail all moneys paid out, costs accumulated or costs incurred on account of the Cost of the Project during the previous month and the amount of the

Construction Manager's Fee due as provided in Article 7. Payment by the Owner to the Construction Manager of the statement amount shall be made within ten (10) days after it is submitted.

11.2 Final payment constituting the unpaid balance of the Cost of the Project and the Construction Manager's Fee shall be due and payable when the Project is delivered to the Owner, ready for beneficial occupancy, or when the Owner occupies the Project, whichever event first occurs, provided that the Project be then substantially completed and this Agreement substantially performed. If there should remain minor items to be completed, the Construction Manager and Architect/Engineer shall list such items and the Construction Manager shall deliver, in writing, his unconditional promise to complete said items within a reasonable time thereafter. The Owner may retain a sum equal to 150% of the estimated cost of completing any unfinished items, provided that said unfinished items are listed separately and the estimated cost of completing any unfinished items likewise listed separately. Thereafter, Owner shall pay to Construction Manager, monthly, the amount retained for incomplete items as each of said items is completed.

11.3 The Construction Manager shall promptly pay all the amount due Trade Contractors or other persons with whom he has a contract upon receipt of any payment from the Owner, the application for which includes amounts due such Trade Contractor or other persons. Before issuance of final payment, the Construction Manager shall submit satisfactory evidence that all payrolls, materials bills and other indebtedness connected with the Project have been paid or otherwise satisfied.

11.4 If the Owner should fail to pay the Construction Manager within seven (7) days after the time the payment of any amount becomes due, then the Construction Manager may, upon seven (7) additional days' written notice to the Owner and the Architect/Engineer, stop the Project until payment of the amount owing has been received.

11.5 Payments due but unpaid shall bear interest at the rate the Owner is paying on his construction loan or at the legal rate, whichever is higher.

ARTICLE 12   Insurance, Indemnity and Waiver of Subrogation

12.1 Indemnity

12.1.1   The Construction Manager agrees to indemnify and hold the Owner harmless from all claims for bodily injury and property damage (other than the work itself and other property insured under Paragraph 12.4) that may arise *as a direct result* from the Construction Manager's operations under this Agreement.

12.1.2   The Owner shall cause any other contractor who may have a contract with the Owner to perform construction or installation work in the areas where work will be performed under this Agreement, to agree to indemnify the Owner and the Construction Manager and hold them harmless from all claims for bodily injury and property damage (other than property insured under Paragraph 12.4) that may arise from that contractor's operations. Such provisions shall be in a form satisfactory to the Construction Manager.

12.2 Construction Manager's Liability Insurance

12.2.1   The Construction Manager shall purchase and maintain such insurance as will protect him from the claims set forth below which may arise out of or result from the Construction Manager's operations under this Agreement whether such operations be by himself or by any Trade Contractor or by anyone directly or indirectly employed by any of them, or by anyone for whose acts any of them may be liable:

12.2.1.1 Claims under workers' compensation, disability benefit and other similar employee benefit acts which are applicable to the work to be performed.

12.2.1.2 Claims for damages because of bodily injury, occupational sickness or disease, or death of his employees under any applicable employer's liability law.

12.2.1.3 Claims for damages because of bodily injury, or death of any person other than his employees.

12.2.1.4 Claims for damages insured by usual personal injury liability coverage which are sustained (1) by any person as a result of an offense directly or indirectly related to the employment of such person by the Construction Manager or (2) by any other person.

12.2.1.5 Claims for damages, other than to the work itself, because of injury to or destruction of tangible property, including loss of use therefrom.

12.2.1.6 Claims for damages because of bodily injury or death of any person or property damage arising out of the ownership, maintenance or use of any motor vehicle.

12.2.2 The Construction Manager's Comprehensive General Liability Insurance shall include premises—operations (including explosion, collapse and underground coverage) elevators, independent contractors, completed operations, and blanket contractual liability on all written contracts, all including broad form property damage coverage.

12.2.3 The Construction Manager's Comprehensive General and Automobile Liability Insurance, as required by Subparagraphs 12.2.1 and 12.2.2 shall be written for not less than limits of liability as follows:

a. Comprehensive General Liability
   1. Personal Injury $_____ Each Occurrence
                              $_____ Aggregate
                                          (Completed Operations)
   2. Property Damage $_____ Each Occurrence
                              $_____ Aggregate
b. Comprehensive Automobile Liability
   1. Bodily Injury $_____ Each Person
                              $_____ Each Occurrence
   2. Property Damage $_____ Each Occurrence

12.2.4 Comprehensive General Liability Insurance may be arranged under a single policy for the full limits required or by a combination of underlying policies with the balance provided by an Excess or Umbrella Liability policy.

12.2.5 The foregoing policies shall contain a provision that coverages afforded under the policies will not be cancelled or not renewed until at least sixty (60) days' prior written notice has been given to the Owner. Certificates of Insurance showing such coverages to be in Force shall be filed with the Owner prior to commencement of the Work.

12.3 Owner's Liability Insurance

12.3.1 The Owner shall be responsible for purchasing and maintaining his own liability insurance and, at his option, may purchase and maintain such insurance as will protect him against claims which may arise from operations under this Agreement.

12.4 Insurance to Protect Project

12.4.1 The Owner shall purchase and maintain property insurance in a form acceptable to the Construction Manager upon the entire Project for the full cost of replacement as of the time of any loss. This insurance shall include as named insureds the Owner, the Construction Manager, Trade Contractors and their Trade Subcontractors and shall insure against loss from the perils of Fire, Extended Coverage, and shall include "All Risk" insurance for physical loss or damage including without duplication of coverage at least theft, vandalism, malicious mischief, transit, collapse, flood, earthquake, testing, and damage resulting from defective design, workmanship or material. The Owner will increase limits of coverage, if necessary, to reflect estimated replacement cost. The Owner will be responsible for any co-insurance penalties or deductibles. If the Project covers an addition to or is adjacent to an existing building, the Construction Manager, Trade Contractors and their Trade Subcontractors shall be named as additional insureds under the Owner's Property Insurance covering such building and its contents.

12.4.1.1 If the Owner finds it necessary to occupy or use a portion or portions of the Project prior to Substantial Completion thereof, such occupancy shall not commence prior to a time mutually agreed to by the Owner and Construction Manager and to which the insurance company or companies providing the property insurance have consented by endorsement to the policy or policies. This insurance shall not be cancelled or lapsed on account of such partial occupancy. Consent of the Construction Manager and of the insurance company or companies to such occupancy or use shall not be unreasonably withheld.

12.4.2 The Owner shall purchase and maintain such boiler and machinery insurance as may be required or necessary. This insurance shall include the interests of the Owner, the Construction Manager, Trade Contractors and their Subcontractors in the Work.

12.4.3 The Owner shall purchase and maintain such insurance as will protect the Owner and Construction Manager against loss of use of Owner's property due to those perils insured pursuant to Subparagraph 12.4.1. Such policy will provide coverage for expediting expenses of materials, continuing overhead of the Owner and Construction Manager, necessary labor expense including overtime, loss of income by the Owner and other determined exposures. Exposures of the Owner and the Construction Manager shall be determined by mutual agreement and separate limits of coverage fixed for each item.

12.4.4 The Owner shall file a copy of all policies with the Construction Manager before an exposure to loss may occur. Copies of any subsequent endorsements will be furnished to the Construction Manager. The Construction Manager will be given sixty (60) days notice of cancellation, non-renewal, or any endorsements restricting or reducing coverage. If the Owner does not intend to purchase such insurance, he shall inform the Construction Manager in writing prior to the commencement of the Work. The Construction Manager may then effect insurance which will protect the interest of himself, the Trade Contractors and their Trade Subcontractors in the Project, the cost of which shall be a Cost of the Project pursuant to Article 8, and the Guaranteed Maximum Price shall be increased by Change Order. If the Construction Manager is damaged by failure of the Owner to purchase or maintain such insurance or to so notify the Construction Manager, the Owner shall bear all reasonable costs properly attributable thereto.

12.5 Property Insurance Loss Adjustment

12.5.1 Any insured loss shall be adjusted with the Owner and the Construction Manager and made payable to the Owner and Construction Manager as trustees for the insureds, as their interests may appear, subject to any applicable mortgagee clause.

12.5.2 Upon the occurrence of an insured loss, monies received will be deposited in a separate account and the trustees shall make distribution in accordance with the agreement of the parties in interest, or in the absence of such agreement, in accordance with an arbitration award pursuant to Article 16. If the trustees are unable to agree on the settlement of the loss, such dispute shall also be submitted to arbitration pursuant to Article 16.

12.6 Waiver of Subrogation

12.6.1 The Owner and Construction Manager waive all rights against each other, the Architect/Engineer, Trade Contractors, and their Trade Subcontractors for damages caused by perils covered by insurance provided under Paragraph 12.4, except such rights as they may have to the proceeds of such insurance held by the Owner and Construction Manager as trustees. The Construction Manager shall require similar waivers from all Trade Contractors and their Trade Subcontractors.

12.6.2 The Owner and Construction Manager waive all rights against each other and the Architect/Engineer, Trade Contractors and their Trade Subcontractors for loss or damage to any equipment used in connection with the Project and covered by any property insurance. The Construction Manager shall require similar waivers from all Trade Contractors and their Trade Subcontractors.

12.6.3 The Owner waives subrogation against the Construction Manager, Architect/Engineer, Trade Contractors, and their Trade Subcontractors on all property and consequential loss policies carried by the Owner on adjacent properties and under property and consequential loss policies purchased for the Project after its completion.

12.6.4 If the policies of insurance referred to in this Paragraph require an endorsement to provide for continued coverage where there is a waiver of subrogation, the owners of such policies will cause them to be so endorsed.

ARTICLE 13 Termination of the Agreement and Owner's Right to Perform Construction Manager's Obligations

13.1 Termination by the Construction Manager

13.1.1 If the Project, *in whole or substantial part,* is stopped for a period of thirty days under an order of any court or other public authority having jurisdiction, or as a result of an act of government, such as a declaration of a national emergency making materials unavailable, through no act or fault of the Construction Manager, or if the Project should be stopped for a period of thirty days by the Construction Manager for the Owner's failure to make payment thereon, then the Construction Manager may, upon seven days' written notice to the Owner and the Architect/Engineer, terminate this Agreement and recover from the Owner payment for all work executed, *liabilities incurred or to be incurred,* the Construction Manager's Fee earned to date, and for any proven loss sustained upon any materials, equipment, tools, construction equipment and machinery, including reasonable profit [*and*] damages, *and legal fees.*

13.2 Owner's Right to Perform Construction Manager's Obligations and Termination by the Owner for Cause

13.2.1 If the Construction Manager fails to perform any of his obligations under this

Agreement including any obligation he assumes to perform work with his own forces, the Owner may, after seven days' written notice during which period the Construction Manager fails to perform such obligation, make good such deficiencies. The Guaranteed Maximum Price, if any, shall be reduced by the cost to the Owner of making good such deficiencies.

13.2.2 If the Construction Manager is adjudged a bankrupt, or if he makes a general assignment for the benefit of his creditors, or if a receiver is appointed on account of his insolvency, *and who is unable to maintain reasonable progress,* or if he persistently or repeatedly *unreasonably* refuses or fails, except in cases for which extension of time is provided, to supply enough properly skilled workmen or proper materials, or if he fails to make *proper* [*prompt*] payment to Trade Contractors or for materials or labor, or persistently disregards laws, ordinances, rules, regulations or orders of any public authority having jursciction, or otherwise is guilty of a substantial violation of a provision of the Agreement, then the Owner may, without prejudice to any right or remedy and after giving the Construction Manager and his surety, if any, seven days' written notice, during which period Construction Manager fails to cure the violation, terminate the employment of the Construction Manager and take possession of the site and of all materials, equipment, tools, construction equipment and machinery thereon owned by the Construction Manager and may finish the Project by whatever *reasonable* method he may deem expedient. In such case, the Construction Manager shall not be entitled to receive any further payment until the Project is finished nor shall he be relieved from his obligations assumed under Article 6. *It shall be the Owner's obligation to mitigate any and all damages.*

13.3 Termination by Owner Without Cause

13.3.1 If the Owner *without the Construction Manager being in material default of this Agreement,* terminates this Agreement other than pursuant to Subparagraph 13.2.2 or Subparagraph 13.3.2, he shall reimburse the Construction Manager for any unpaid Cost of the Project due him under Article 8, plus (1) the unpaid balance of the Fee computed upon the *total estimated* Cost of the Project *less Cost of the Project* to the date of termination at the rate of the precentage named in Subparagraph 7.2.1 or if the Construction Manager's Fee be stated as a fixed sum, such an amount as will increase the payment on account of his fee to *that* [*a*] sum. [*which bears the same ratio to the said fixed sum as the Cost of the Project at the time of termination bears to the adjusted Guaranteed Maximum Price, if any, otherwise to a reasonable estimated Cost of the Project when completed.*] The Owner shall also pay to the Construction Manager fair compensation, either by purchase or rental at the election of the Owner, for any equipment *used or* retained. In case of such termination of the Agreement the Owner shall further assume and become liable for obligations, commitments and unsettled claims that the Construction Manager has previously undertaken or incurred in good faith, *including legal fees,* in connection with said Project. The Construction Manager shall, as a condition of receiving the payments referred to in this Article 13, execute and deliver all such papers and take all such steps, including the legal assignment of his contractual rights, as the Owner may require for the purpose of fully vesting in him the rights and benefits of the Construction Manager under such obligations or commitments. *The Owner shall be obligated for all of the Construction Manager's legal fees incurred for this Project, or relating to any breach by the Owner.*

13.3.2 After the completion of the Design Phase, if the final cost estimates make the Project no longer feasible from the standpoint of the Owner, the Owner may terminate this Agreement and pay the Construction Manager his Fee in accordance with Subparagraph 7.1.1 plus any costs incurred pursuant to Article 9.

ARTICLE 14   Assignment and Governing Law

14.1 Neither the Owner nor the Construction Manager shall assign his interest in this Agreement without the written consent of the other except as to the assignment of proceeds.

14.2 This Agreement shall be governed by the law of the place where the Project is located.

ARTICLE 15   Miscellaneous Provisions

15.1 *The Owner agrees to furnish to the Construction Manager, in addition to the Owner's responsibilities specified in Article 3, the property listed in the schedule annexed hereto plus such related data and documentation necessary for use of same. The Owner represents that said property is suitable for the particular use intended, and that it shall be furnished on the date or dates specified, or if none are specified, as reasonably required by the Construction Manager. If the property is unsuitable, or is not furnished as specified, the Construction Manager will be entitled to receive from the Owner all additional costs incurred as a result thereof, plus a reasonable fee.*[5]

15.2 *Those documents set forth in the annexed schedule of contract documents are incorporated into this agreement and made a part hereof. Such additional documents shall be added thereto as may be mutually agreed between the parties.*[6]

15.3 *It is expressly understood that the Owner shall be directly retaining the services of an architect/engineer. The Construction Manager neither undertakes nor assumes any of the responsibility or liability of or for the Architect/Engineer.*[7]

ARTICLE 16   Arbitration

16.1 All claims, disputes and other matters in question arising out of, or relating to, this Agreement or the breach thereof, except with respect to the Architect/Engineer's decision on matters relating to artistic effect, and except for claims which have been waived by the making or acceptance of final payment shall be decided by arbitration in accordance with the Construction Industry Arbitration Rules of the American Arbitration Association then obtaining unless the parties mutually agree otherwise. This agreement to arbitrate shall be specifically enforceable under the prevailing arbitration law.

16.2 Notice of the demand for arbitration shall be filed in writing with the other party to this Agreement and with the American Arbitration Association. The demand for arbitration shall be made within a reasonable time after the claim, dispute or other matter in question has arisen, and in no event shall it be made after the date when institution of legal or equitable proceedings based on such claim, dispute or other matter in question would be barred by the applicable statute of limitations.

16.3 The award rendered by the arbitrators shall be final and judgment may be entered upon it in accordance with applicable law in any court having jurisdiction thereof.

16.4 Unless otherwise agreed in writing, the Construction Manager shall carry on the Work and maintain the Contract Completion Date during any arbitration proceedings, and the Owner shall continue to make payments in accordance with this Agreement.

16.5 All claims which are related to or dependent upon each other, shall be heard by the same arbitrator or arbitrators even though the parties are not the same unless a specific contract prohibits such consolidation.

16.6 *The Owner acknowledges that it will participate in and be bound by any judicial, administra-*

tive, legislative or arbitration proceeding wherein the Owner's participation was demanded or summoned by the Construction Manager and provided that said proceeding involves a third party who is either not a party to or is not bound by the arbitration provisions specified in Article 16.[8]

This Agreement executed the day and year first written above.

OWNER: _____   ATTEST: _____

CONSTRUCTION MANAGER: _____   ATTEST: _____

FOOTNOTES:

1. It is advisable that Article 2.2.2 be slightly modified so that the trade contract given to the construction manager need not be similar to the subcontract form given to other trade contractors. This is especially so since the construction managers already take responsibility for their own acts
2. Limitation of liability clauses are advisable. The construction manager must be careful to avoid assuming or accepting professional liability of others
3. While this clause creates some safeguards for the contractor, it also presents new legal problems. It has been argued that if the construction manager fails to ask for or receive satisfactory evidence of funding, and does not object, that the right is waived or at least damaged should the owner have insufficient funds. Therefore, the scope of this provision must be enlarged to properly protect the construction manager by adding the sentence shown
4. This article fails to define "so changed" as it appears in the second line. The construction manager should consider omitting the word "so" and inserting the words "by a cumulative 15%" after the word "changed". Since the pros and cons of specific limitations could be argued endlessly, as well as what is the appropriate percentage, this article is left to the construction manager's selection and adjustment
5. An owner-furnished property clause could be an enlargement of Article 3, which sets forth the owner's responsibilities, or a new provision
6. The construction contract document clause must, of necessity, be subject to change as the various phases of the construction management agreement are commenced. However, for the purpose of clarity, a specific schedule of contract documents should be annexed to the contract
7. A clear delineation and acknowledgement should be made in this agreement in respect to the architect/engineer agreement
8. The arbitration provision is reasonable as it relates directly to the construction manager and owner. However, there are instances when the construction manager goes into court with the desire to bind the owner to the judicial decision. This might not be possible under the present arbitration clause. Therefore, this provision must be added

3. **Amendment to Owner-Construction Manager Agreement (AGC Document No. 8A) Guaranteed Maximum Price**

§1.09   **a. Author's Comments**   This document is acceptable as written. However, it is emphasized that a separate amendment exhibit must be prepared which specifically lists the construction manager's contract documents. Each document should be listed in detail to avoid subsequent dispute.

§1.10   b. FORM—
AGC DOCUMENT
NO. 8A

Amendment to Owner-Construction Manager Contract

THE ASSOCIATED GENERAL CONTRACTORS OF AMERICA

AGC Document Number 8A, Amendment to Owner-Construction Manager Contract, Copyright © 1977, reprinted by permission of the Associated General Contractors of America.

Pursuant to Article 6 of the original Agreement, AGC Form No. 8, dated _____

between _____ (Owner)

and _____ (the Construction Manager),

for _____ (the Project),

the Owner desires to fix a Guaranteed Maximum Price for the Project and the Construction Manager agrees that the design, plans and specifications are sufficiently complete for such purpose. Therefore, the Owner and Construction Manager agree as set forth below.

ARTICLE I   Guaranteed Maximum Price

The Construction Manager's Guaranteed Maximum Price for the Project, including the Cost of the Work as defined in Article 8 and the Construction Manager's Fee as defined in Article 7 is _____ Dollars ($ _____). This price is for the performance of the Work in accordance with the documents listed and attached to this Amendment and marked Amendment Exhibit A.

(*OPTIONAL SAVINGS CLAUSE*) It is further agreed that if, upon completion of the work, the actual cost of the work plus the Construction Manager's Fee is less than the Guaranteed Maximum Price as set forth herein and as adjusted by approved change orders that the Owner agrees to pay to the Construction Manager an amount equal to _____ % of such savings, as additional compensation.

ARTICLE II   Time Schedule

The Construction Completion date established by this Amendment is:

ATTEST:

_____

OWNER:
By: _____
Date: _____

CONSTRUCTION MANAGER:
_____

ATTEST:

_____

By: _____
Date: _____

4. General Conditions For the Owner-Construction Manager Agreement (AGC Document No. 8b) with Suggested Modifications

§1.11   **a. Author's Comments**   This document is an excellent attempt to fulfill the general condition requirements for all of the numerous types of construction management agreements. As written, it does not answer the construction manager's legal needs if the construction manager enters subcontracts with trade contractors, or if the construction manager is to give a guaranteed maximum price. This agreement should not supersede the standard form subcontract agreement, which is recommended for use when the construction manager and the trade contractor have a direct, contractual relationship. In fact, it is specifically recommended that if the general conditions, as modified, are part of the agreement between the owner and construction manager, and if the construction manager enters into the separate subcontract agreement with a trade contractor, that the subsequent trade subcontract specifically provide that any inconsistencies between the subcontract agreement and the general conditions be interpreted so that the subcontract takes precedence over the general conditions.

The general conditions have been revised so that the form can be used as a general document. The form only should be used as a general document where the construction manager does not guarantee a maximum cost, or where the document will not take precedence over the subcontract agreement between the construction manager and the trade contractor.

§1.12 b. FORM—
AGC DOCUMENT
NO. 8b

General Conditions For Owner-Construction Manager Agreement

THE ASSOCIATED GENERAL CONTRACTORS OF AMERICA

AGC Document Number 8b, Construction Management General Conditions, Copyright © 1977, reprinted by permission of The Associated General Contractors of America.

Certain provisions of this document have been derived, with modifications, from the following document published by The American Institute of Architects:

Portions of AIA Document A201, General Conditions of the Contract For Construction have been reproduced with the permission of The American Institute of Architects under application number 78037. Further reproduction, in part or in whole, is not authorized. Because AIA documents are revised from time to time, users should ascertain from AIA the current edition of the document of which portions are reproduced below.

Instructions For Construction Manager

1. These documents are intended to be used with AGC Document No. 8, Standard Form of Agreement Between Owner and Construction Manager, as the General Conditions. These conditions primarily govern the obligations of the Trade Contractors and in addition establish the general procedures for the administration of construction. They have been drafted to cover Trade Contracts with either the Owner or the Construction Manager.
2. Nothing contained herein is intended to conflict with local, state or federal laws or regulations.
3. It is recommended all insurance matters be reviewed with your insurance consultant and carrier such as implications of errors and omission liability, completed operations, and waiver of subrogation.
4. Each article should be reviewed by the Construction Manager as to the applicability to a given project and contractual conditions.
5. Special conditions and terms for the project or the Trade Contractor Agreements should cover the following:
   —trade contractor retainages
   —payment schedules
   —insurance limits
   —owner's protective insurance if required of trade contractors
   —builder's risk deductible, if any.
6. If the Owner does not provide Builder's Risk Insurance, Paragraph 12.2 will need to be modified.

TABLE OF ARTICLES

1. Contract Documents
2. Owner
3. Architect/Engineer

    4 Construction Manager
    5 Trade Contractors
    6 Trade Subcontractors
    7 Separate Trade Contracts
    8 Miscellaneous Provisions
    9 Time
  10 Payments and Completion
  11 Protection of Persons and Property
  12 Insurance
  13 Changes in the Work
  14 Uncovering and Correction of Work
  15 Termination of the Contract

ARTICLE 1 Contract Documents

1.1 Definitions

1.1.1 The Contract Documents The Contract Documents consist of the Agreement between the Owner or Construction Manager, as the case may be, and the Trade Contractor, the Conditions of the Contract (General, Supplementary and other Conditions), the Drawings (and criteria if the drawings are not complete), the Specifications, all Addenda issued prior to execution of the Contract, and all Modifications issued after the execution of the contract. A Modification is (1) a written amendment to the Contract signed by both parties, (2) a Change Order, (3) a written interpretation issued by the Architect/Engineer pursuant to Subparagraph 3.2.2; or (4) a written order for a minor change in the Work issued on the Owner's behalf pursuant to Paragraph 13.4. The Contract Documents do not include Bidding or Proposal Documents such as the Advertisement or Invitation To Bid, Requests for Proposals, sample forms. Trade Contractors Bid or Proposal, or portions of Addenda relative to any of these, or any other documents other than those set forth in this subparagraph unless specifically set forth in the [*Agreement with the Trade Contractor.*] annexed schedule *of Contract Documents. Any agreement between the Construction Manager and Trade Contractors shall govern that relationship.*

1.1.2 The Contract The Contract Documents form the Contract with the Trade Contractor. This Contract represents the entire and integrated agreement and supersedes all prior negotiations, representations, or agreements, either written or oral. The Contract may be amended or modified only by a Modification as defined in Subparagraph 1.1.1.

1.1.3 The Work The Work comprises the completed construction performed by the Construction Manager with his own forces or required by a Trade Contractor's contract and includes all labor necessary to produce such construction required of the Construction Manager or a Trade Contractor, and all materials and equipment incorporated or to be incorporated in such construction.

1.1.4 The Project The Project is the total construction to be performed under the Agreement between the Owner and Construction Manager of which the Work is a part.

1.2 Execution, Correlation and Intent

1.2.1 By executing his Agreement each Trade Contractor represents that he has visited the site, familiarized himself with the local conditions under which the Work is to be performed and correlated his observations with the requirements of the Contract Documents.

1.2.2 The intent of the Contract Documents is to include all items necessary for the proper execution and completion of the Work. The Contract Documents are complementary, and what is required by any one shall be as binding as if required by all. Work not covered in the Contract Documents will not be required unless it is consistent therewith and is reasonably inferable therefrom as being necessary to produce the intended results. Words and abbreviations in the Contract Documents which have well-known technical or trade meanings are used in accordance with such recognized meanings.

1.2.3 The organization of the Specifications into divisions, sections, and articles, and the arrangements of Drawings shall not control the Construction Manager in dividing the Work among Trade Contractors or in establishing the extent of Work to be performed by any trade.

1.2.4 *It is expressly understood that any trade contractor, who enters into an agreement with the Construction Manager, will be bound to execute the Construction Manager's standard form subcontract agreement or Purchase Order form. The trade contractor further agrees that its agreement with the Construction Manager shall prevail and take precedence over any conflicting or inconsistent terms or provisions set forth in this document, provided that the protection offered to the Construction Manager in said document is equal to or greater than that which is set forth in these General Conditions.*

1.3 Ownership and Use of Documents

1.3.1 Unless otherwise provided in the Contract Documents, the Trade Contractor will be furnished, free of charge, all copies of Drawings and Specifications reasonably necessary for the execution of the Work.

1.3.2 All Drawings, Specifications and copies thereof furnished by the Architect/Engineer are and shall remain his property. They are to be used only with respect to this Project and are not to be used on any other project. With the exception of one contract set for each party, such documents are to be returned or suitably accounted for to the Architect/Engineer on request at the completion of the Work. Submission or distribution to meet official regulatory requirements or for other purposes in connection with the Project is not to be construed as publication in derogation of the Architect/Engineer's common law copyright or other reserved rights.

ARTICLE 2   Owner

2.1 Definition

2.1.1 The Owner is the person or entity identified as such in the Agreement between the Owner and Construction Manager and is referred to throughout the Contract Documents as if singular in number and masculine in gender. The term Owner means the Owner or his authorized representative.

2.2 Information and Services Furnished by the Owner

2.2.1 The Owner will furnish all surveys describing the physical characteristics, legal limitations and utility locations for the site of the Project, and a legal description of the site.

2.2.2 Except as provided in Subparagraph 5.7.1 the Owner will secure and pay for necessary approvals, easements, assessments and charges required for the construction, use, or occupancy of permanent structures or for permanent changes in existing facilities.

2.2.3 Information or services under the Owner's control will be furnished by the Owner with reasonable promptness to avoid delay in the orderly progress of the Work.

2.2.4 The Owner shall forward all instructions to the Trade Contractors through the Construction Manager even when Owner has direct contracts with Trade Contractors.

ARTICLE 3   Architect/Engineer

3.1 Definition

3.1.1 The Architect/Engineer is the person lawfully licensed to practice architecture or engineering or an entity lawfully practicing architecture or engineering and identified as such in the Agreement between the Owner and Construction Manager and is referred to throughout the Contract Documents as if singular in number and masculine in gender. The term Architect/Engineer means the Architect/Engineer or his authorized representative.

3.1.2 Nothing contained in the Contract Documents shall create any contractual relationship between the Architect/Engineer and any Trade Contractor.

3.2 Architect/Engineer's Duties During Construction

3.2.1 The Architect/Engineer shall at all times have access to the Work wherever it is in preparation and progress. When directed by the Construction Manager, the Trade Contractor shall provide facilities for such access so the Architect/Engineer may perform his functions under the Contract Documents.

3.2.2 The Architect/Engineer will be the interpreter of the requirements of the Drawings and Specifications. The Architect/Engineer will, within a reasonable time, render such interpretations as are necessary for the proper execution of the progress of the Work.

3.2.3 All interpretations of the Architect/Engineer shall be consistent with the intent of and reasonably inferable from the Contract Documents and will be in writing or in the form of drawings. All requests for interpretations shall be directed through the Construction Manager. The Architect/Engineer shall not be liable to the Trade Contractor for the result of any interpretation or decision rendered in good faith in such capacity.

3.2.4 The Architect/Engineer's decisions in matters relating to artistic effect will be final if consistent with the intent of the Contract Documents.

3.2.5 The Architect/Engineer will have authority to reject Work which does not conform to the Contract Documents. Whenever, in his opinion, he considers it necessary or advisable for the implementation of the intent of the Contract Documents, he will have authority to require special inspection or testing of the Work in accordance with Subparagraph 8.7.2 whether or not such Work be then fabricated, installed or completed. However, neither the Architect/Engineer's authority to act under this Subparagraph 3.2.5, nor any decision made by him in good faith either to exercise or not to exercise such authority, shall give rise to any duty or responsibility of the Architect/Engineer to the Trade Contractor, any Trade Subcontractor, any of their agents or employees, or any other person performing any of the

Work. *The Architect/Engineer shall not interfere with the Construction Manager's reasonable performance of its Contract.*

3.2.6 The Architect/Engineer will review and approve or take other appropriate action upon Trade Contractor's submittals such as Shop Drawings, Product Data and Samples, but only for conformance with the design concept of the Work and with the information given in the Contract Documents. Such action shall be taken with reasonable promptness so as to cause no delay. The Architect/Engineer's approval of a specific item shall not indicate approval of an assembly of which the item is a component.

3.2.7 The Architect/Engineer along with the Construction Manager will conduct inspections to determine the dates of Substantial Completion and final completion, will receive and review written warranties and related documents required by the Contract and assembled by the Trade Contractor.

3.2.8 The Architect/Engineer will communicate with the Trade Contractors through the Construction Manager.

ARTICLE 4 Construction Manager

4.1 Definition

4.1.1 The Construction Manager is the person or entity who has entered into an agreement with the Owner to serve as Construction Manager and is referred to throughout the Contract Documents as if singular in number and masculine in gender. The term Construction Manager means the Construction Manager acting through his authorized representative.

4.1.2 Whether the Trade Contracts are between the Owner and Trade Contractors, or the Construction Manager and Trade Contractors, it is the intent of these General Conditions to allow the Construction Manager to direct and schedule the performance of all Work and the Trade Contractors are expected to follow all such directions and schedules.

4.2 Administration of the Contract

4.2.1 The Construction Manager will provide, as the Owner's authorized representative, the general administration of the Project as herein described.

4.2.2 The Construction Manager will be the Owner's construction representative during construction until final payment and shall have the responsibility to supervise and coordinate the work of all Trade Contractors.

4.2.3 The Construction Manager shall prepare and update all Construction Schedules and shall direct the Work with respect to such schedules.

4.2.4 The Construction Manager shall have authority to reject Work which does not conform to the Contract Documents and to require any Special Inspection and Testing in accordance with Subparagraph 8.7.2.

4.2.5 The Construction Manager will prepare and issue Change Orders to the Trade Contractors in accordance with Article 13.

4.2.6 The Construction Manager along with the Architect/Engineer will conduct inspections to determine the dates of substantial Completion and final completion, and will receive and review written warranties and related documents required by the Contract and assembled by the Trade Contractor.

4.2.7 *Nothing contained in the Contract Documents between a trade contractor and the Owner shall create any contractual relationship between the Construction Manager and any trade contractor.*[1]

4.3 Owner's and Construction Manager's Right to Stop Work

4.3.1 If the Trade Contractor fails to correct defective Work as required by Paragraph 14.2 or persistently fails to carry out the Work in accordance with the Contract Documents, the Construction Manager or the Owner through the Construction Manager may order the Trade Contractor to stop the Work, or any portion thereof, until the cause for such order has been eliminated.

4.3.2 If the Trade Contractor defaults or neglects to carry out the Work in accordance with the Contract Documents and fails within seven days after receipt of written notice from the Construction Manager to commence and continue correction of such default or neglect with diligence and promptness, the Construction Manager may, by written notice, and without prejudice to any other remedy he or the Owner may have, make good such deficiencies. In such case an appropriate Change Order shall be issued deducting from the payments then or thereafter due the Trade Contractor the cost of correcting such deficiencies, including compensation for the Architect/Engineer's and Construction Manager's additional services made necessary by such default, neglect or failure, *as well as the Construction Manager's legal costs and fees.*

ARTICLE 5 Trade Contractors

5.1 Definition

5.1.1 A Trade Contractor is the person or entity identified as such in the Agreement between the Owner or Construction Manager and a Trade Contractor and is referred to throughout the Contract Document as if singular in number and masculine in gender. The term Trade Contractor means the Trade Contractor or his authorized representative.

5.1.2 The Agreements with the Trade Contractors may either be with the Owner or with the Construction Manager. These conditions in several instances make reference to obligations and rights of the "Owner or Construction Manager" to cover both possibilities. Such references are only to cover either possibility and such use does not create a joint obligation on the Owner and Construction Manager to the Trade Contractor. The contract obligation with the Trade Contractor is solely with the person or entity with whom he has his Agreement.

5.1.3 If the Trade Contracts are with the Construction Manager, the Trade Contractor assumes toward the Construction Manager all the obligations and responsibilities which the Construction Manager assumes toward the Owner under the Agreement between the Owner and the Construction Manager. A copy of the pertinent parts of this Agreement will be made available on request.

5.2 Review of Contract Documents

5.2.1 The Trade Contractor shall carefully study and compare the Contract Documents and shall at once report to the Construction Manager any error, inconsistency or omission he may *or reasonably should* discover. [*The Trade Contractor shall not be liable to the Owner or the Architect/Engineer or Construction Manager for any damage resulting from any such errors, inconsistencies or omissions.*]

5.3 Supervision and Construction Procedures

5.3.1 The Trade Contractor shall supervise and direct the Work, using his best skill and attention. He shall be solely responsible for all construction means, methods, techniques, sequences and procedures and for coordinating all portions of the Work under the Contract subject to the overall coordination of the Construction Manager.

5.3.2 The Trade Contractor shall be responsible to the Owner and the Construction Manager for the acts and omissions of his employees and all his Trade Subcontractors and their agents and employees and other persons performing any of the Work under a contract with the Trade Contractor.

5.3.3 Neither observations nor inspections, tests or approvals by persons other than the Trade Contractor shall relieve the Trade Contractor from his obligations to perform the Work in accordance with the Contract Documents.

5.4 Labor and Materials

5.4.1 Unless otherwise specifically provided in the Contract Documents, the Trade Contractor shall provide and pay for all labor, materials, equipment, tools, construction equipment and machinery, transportation, and other facilities and services necessary for the proper execution and completion of the Work.

5.4.2 The Trade Contractor shall at all times enforce strict discipline and good order among his employees and shall not employ on the Work any unfit person or anyone not skilled in the task assigned to him.

5.5 Warranty

5.5.1 The Trade Contractor warrants to the Owner and the Construction Manager that all materials and equipment furnished under this Contract will be new unless otherwise specified, and that all Work will be of good quality, free from faults and defects and in conformance with the Contract Documents. All Work not so conforming to these requirements, including substitutions not properly approved and authorized, may be considered defective. If required by the Construction Manager, the Trade Contractor shall furnish satisfactory evidence as to the kind and quality of materials and equipment. This warranty is not limited by the provisions of Paragraph 14.2.

5.6 Taxes

5.6.1 The Trade Contractor shall pay all sales, consumer, use and other similar taxes for the Work or portions thereof provided by the Trade Contractor which are legally enacted at the time bids or proposals are received, whether or not yet effective.

5.7 Permits, Fees and Notices

5.7.1 Unless otherwise provided in the Contract Documents, the Trade Contractor shall secure and pay for all permits, governmental fees, licenses and inspections necessary for the proper execution and completion of his Work, which are customarily secured after execution of the contract and which are legally required at the time bids or proposals are received.

5.7.2 The Trade Contractor shall give all notices and comply with all laws, ordinances, rules, regulations and orders of any public authority bearing on the performance of the Work.

5.7.3 Unless otherwise provided in the Contract Documents, it is not the responsibility of the Trade Contractor to make certain that the Contract Documents are in accordance with applicable laws, statutes, building codes and regulations. If the Trade Contractor observes that any of the Contract Documents are at variance therewith in any respect, he shall promptly notify the Construction Manager in writing, and any necessary changes shall be by appropriate Modification.

5.7.4 If the Trade Contractor performs any Work knowing it to be contrary to such laws, ordinances, rules and regulations, and without such notice to the Construction Manager, he shall assume full responsibility therefor and shall bear all costs attributable thereto.

5.8 Allowances

5.8.1 The Trade Contractor shall include in the Contract Sum as defined in 10.1.1 all allowances stated in the Contract Documents. Items covered by these allowances shall be supplied for such amounts and by such persons as the Construction Manager may direct, but the Trade Contractor will not be required to employ persons against whom he makes a reasonable objection.

5.8.2 Unless otherwise provided in the Contract Documents:

.1 These allowances shall cover the cost to the Trade Contractor, less any applicable trade discount, of the materials and equipment required by the allowance delivered at the site, and all applicable taxes;

.2 The Trade Contractor's costs for unloading and handling on the site, labor, installation costs, overhead, profit and other expenses contemplated for the original allowance shall be included in the Contract Sum and not in the allowance;

.3 Whenever the cost is more than or less than the allowance, the Contract Sum shall be adjusted accordingly by Change Order, the amount of which will recognize changes, if any, in handling costs on the site, labor, installation costs, overhead, profit and other expenses.

5.9 Superintendent

5.9.1 The Trade Contractor shall employ a competent superintendent and necessary assistants who shall be in attendance at the Project site during the progress of the Work. The superintendent shall be satisfactory to the Construction Manager, and shall not be changed except with the consent of the Construction Manager, unless the superintendent proves to be unsatisfactory to the Trade Contractor or ceases to be in his employ. The superintendent shall represent the Trade Contractor and all communications given to the superintendent shall be as binding as if given to the Trade Contractor. Important communications shall be confirmed in writing. Other communications shall be so confirmed on written request in each case.

5.10 Progress Schedule

5.10.1 The Trade Contractor, immediately after being awarded the Contract, shall prepare and submit for the Construction Manager's information an estimated progress schedule for the Work. The progress schedule shall be related to the entire Project to the extent required by the Contract Documents and shall provide for expeditious and practicable execution of the Work. This schedule shall indicate the dates for the starting and completion of the various stages of construction, shall be revised as required by the conditions of the Work, and shall be subject to the Construction Manager's approval.

5.11 Drawings and Specifications at the Site

5.11.1 The Trade Contractor shall maintain at the site for the Construction Manager and Architect/Engineer two copies of all Drawings, Specifications, Addenda, Change Orders and other Modifications, in good order and marked currently to record all changes made during construction. These Drawings, marked to record all changes during construction, and approved Shop Drawings, Product Data and Samples shall be delivered to the Construction Manager for the Owner upon completion of the Work.

5.12 Shop Drawings, Product Data and Samples

5.12.1 Shop Drawings are drawings, diagrams, schedules and other data especially prepared for the Work by the Trade Contractor or any Trade Subcontractor, manufacturer, supplier or distributor to illustrate some portion of the Work.

5.12.2 Product Data are illustrations, standard schedules, performance charts, instructions, brochures, diagrams and other information furnished by the Trade Contractor to illustrate a material, product or system for some portion of the Work.

5.12.3 Samples are physical examples which illustrate materials, equipment or workmanship and establish standards by which the Work will be judged.

5.12.4 The Trade Contractor shall review, approve and submit through the Construction Manager with reasonable promptness and in such sequence as to cause no delay in the Work or in the work of any separate contractor, all Shop Drawings, Product Data and Samples required by the Contract Documents.

5.12.5 By approving and submitting Shop Drawings, Product Data and Samples, the Trade Contractor represents that he has determined and verified all materials, field measurements, and field construction criteria related thereto, or will do so, and that he has checked and coordinated the information contained within such submittals with the requirements of the Work and of the Contract Documents.

5.12.6 The Construction Manager, if he finds such submittals to be in order, will forward them to the Architect/Engineer. If the Construction Manager finds them not to be complete or in proper form, he may return them to the Trade Contractor for correction or completion.

5.12.7 The Trade Contractor shall not be relieved of responsibility for any deviation from the requirements of the Contract Documents by the *Construction Manager's forwarding them to the Architect/Engineer, or by the* Architect/Engineer's approval of Shop Drawings, Product Data or Samples under Subparagraph 3.2.6 unless the Trade Contractor has specifically informed the Architect/Engineer and Construction Manager in writing of such deviation at the time of submission and the Architect/Engineer has given written approval to the specific deviation. The Trade Contractor shall not be relieved from responsibility for errors or omissions in the Shop Drawings, Product Data or Samples by the *Construction Manager's or* Architect/Engineer's approval thereof.

5.12.8 The Trade Contractor shall direct specific attention, in writing or on resubmitted

Shop Drawings, Product Data or Samples, to revisions other than those requested by the Architect/Engineer or Construction Manager on previous submittals.

5.12.9 No portion of the Work requiring submission of a Shop Drawing, Product Data or Sample shall be commenced until the submittal has been approved by the Architect/Engineer. All such portions of the Work shall be in accordance with approved submittals.

5.13 Use of Site

5.13.1 The Trade Contractor shall confine operations at the site to areas designated by the Construction Manager, permitted by law, ordinances, permits and the Contract Documents and shall not unreasonably encumber the site with any materials or equipment.

5.14 Cutting and Patching of Work

5.14.1 The Trade Contractor shall be responsible for all cutting, fitting or patching that may be required to complete the Work or to make its several parts fit together properly. He shall provide protection of existing Work as required.

5.14.2 The Trade Contractor shall not damage or endanger any portion of the Work or the work of the Construction Manager or any separate contractors by cutting, patching or otherwise altering any work, or by excavation. The Trade Contractor shall not cut or otherwise alter the work of the Construction Manager or any separate contractor except with the written consent of the Construction Manager and of such separate contractor. The Trade Contractor shall not unreasonably withhold from the Construction Manager or any separate contractor his consent to cutting or otherwise altering the Work.

5.15 Cleaning Up

5.15.1 The Trade Contractor at all times shall keep the premises free from accumulation of waste materials or rubbish caused by his operations. At the completion of the Work he shall remove all his waste materials and rubbish from and about the Project as well as all his tools, construction equipment, machinery and surplus materials.

5.15.2 If the Trade Contractor fails to clean up, the Construction Manager may do so and the cost thereof shall be charged to the Trade Contractor.

5.16 Communications

5.16.1 The Trade Contractor shall forward all communications to the Owner and Architect/Engineer through the Construction Manager.

5.17 Royalties and Patents

5.17.1 The Trade Contractor shall pay all royalties and license fees. He shall defend all suits or claims for infringement of any patent rights and shall save the Owner and Construction Manager harmless from loss on account thereof, except that the Owner shall be responsible for all such loss when a particular design, process or the product of a particular manufacturer or manufacturers is specified, but if the Trade Contractor has reason to believe that the design, process or product specified is an infringement of a patent, he shall be responsible for such loss unless he promptly gives such information to the Construction Manager.

5.18 Indemnification

5.18.1 To the fullest extent permitted by law, the Trade Contractor shall indemnify and hold harmless the Owner, the Construction Manager and the Architect/Engineer and their agents and employees from and against all claims, damages, losses and expenses, including but not limited to attorneys' fees, arising out of or resulting from the performance of the Work, provided that any such claim, damage, loss or expense (1) is attributable to bodily injury, sickness, disease or death, or to injury to or destruction of tangible property (other than the Work itself) including the loss of use resulting therefrom, and (2) is caused in whole or in part by any negligent act or omission of the Trade Contractor, any Trade Subcontractor, anyone directly or indirectly employed by any of them or anyone for whose acts any of them may be liable, regardless of whether or not it is caused in part by a party indemnified hereunder. Such obligation shall not be construed to negate, abridge or otherwise reduce any other right or obligation of indemnity which would otherwise exist as to any party or person described in this Paragraph 5.18.

5.18.2 In any and all claims against the Owner, the Construction Manager or the Architect/Engineer or any of their agents or employees by any employee of the Trade Contractor, any Trade Subcontractor, anyone directly or indirectly employed by any of them or anyone for whose acts any of them may be liable, the indemnification obligation under this Paragraph 5.18 shall not be limited in any way by any limitation on the amount or type of damages, compensation or benefits payable by or for the Trade Contractor or any Trade Subcontractor under workers' or workmen's compensation acts, disability benefit acts or other employee benefit acts.

5.18.3 The obligations of the Trade Contractor under this Paragraph 5.18 shall not extend to the liability of the Architect/Engineer, his agents or employees arising out of (1) the preparation or approval of maps, drawings, opinions, reports, surveys, designs or specifications, or (2) the giving of or the failure to give directions or instruction by the Architect/Engineer, his agents or employees provided such giving or failure to give is the primary cause of the injury or damage.

ARTICLE 6 Trade Subcontractors

6.1 Definition

6.1.1 A Trade Subcontractor is a person or entity who has a direct contract with a Trade Contractor to perform any of the Work at the site. The term Trade Subcontractor is referred to throughout the Contract Documents as if singular in number and masculine in gender and means a Trade Subcontractor or his authorized representative.

6.1.2 A Trade Subsubcontractor is a person or entity who has a direct or indirect contract with a Trade Subcontractor to perform any of the Work at the site. The term Trade Subsubcontractor is referred to throughout the Contract Documents as if singular in number and masculine in gender and means a Trade Subsubcontractor or an authorized representative thereof.

6.2 Award of Trade Subcontracts and Other Contracts for Portions of the Work

6.2.1 Unless otherwise required by the Contract Documents or in the Bidding or Proposal Documents, the Trade Contractor shall furnish to the Construction Manager in writing, for acceptance by the Owner and the Construction Manager in writing, the names of the persons or entities (including those who are to furnish materials or equipment fabricated to a special design) proposed for each of the principal portions of the Work. The Construction Manager will promptly reply to the Trade Contractor in writing if either the Owner or the

Construction Manager, after due investigation, has reasonable objection to any such proposed person or entity. Failure of the Owner or Construction Manager to reply promptly shall constitute notice of no reasonable objection.

6.2.2 The Trade Contractor shall not contract with any such proposed person or entity to whom the Owner or the Construction Manager has made reasonable objection under the provisions of Subparagraph 6.2.1. The Trade Contractor shall not be required to contract with anyone to whom he has a reasonable objection.

6.2.3 If the Owner or Construction Manager refuses to accept any person or entity on a list submitted by the Trade Contractor in response to the requirements of the Contract Documents, the Trade Contractor shall submit an acceptable substitute; however, no increase in the Contract Sum shall be allowed for any such substitution.

6.2.4 The Trade Contractor shall make no substitution for any Trade Subcontractor, person or entity previously selected if the Owner or Construction Manager makes reasonable objection to such substitution.

6.3 Trade Subcontractual Relations

6.3.1 By an appropriate agreement, written where legally required for validity, the Trade Contractor shall require each Trade Subcontractor, to the extent of the work to be performed by the Trade Subcontractor, to be bound to the Trade Contractor by the terms of the Contract Documents, and to assume toward the Trade Contractor all the obligations and responsibilities which the Trade Contractor, by these Documents, assumes toward the Owner, the Construction Manager, or the Architect/Engineer. Said agreement shall preserve and protect the rights of the Owner, the Construction Manager and the Architect/Engineer under the Contract Documents with respect to the Work to be performed by the Trade Subcontractor so that the subcontracting thereof will not prejudice such rights, and shall allow to the Trade Subcontractor, unless specifically provided otherwise in the Trade Contractor-Trade Subcontractor agreement, the benefit of all rights, remedies and redress against the Trade Contractor that the Trade Contractor, by these Documents, has against the Owner or Construction Manager. Where appropriate, the Trade Contractor shall require each Trade Subcontractor to enter into similar agreements with his Trade Subsubcontractors. The Trade Contractor shall make available to each proposed Trade Subcontractor, prior to the execution of the Trade Subcontract, copies of the Contract Documents to which the Trade Subcontractor will be bound by this Paragraph 6.3, and shall identify to the Trade Subcontractor any terms and conditions of the proposed Trade Subcontract which may be at variance with the Contract Documents. Each Trade Subcontractor shall similarly make copies of such Documents available to his Trade Subsubcontractors.

ARTICLE 7   Separate Trade Contracts

7.1 Mutual Responsibility of Trade Contractors

7.1.1 The Trade Contractor shall afford the Construction Manager and other Trade Contractors reasonable opportunity for the introduction and storage of their materials and equipment and the execution of their work, and shall connect and coordinate his work with others under the general direction of the Construction Manager.

7.1.2 If any part of the Trade Contractor's Work depends, for proper execution or results, upon the Work of the Construction Manager or any separate Trade Contractor, the Trade Contractor shall, prior to proceeding with the Work, promptly report to the Construction

Manager any apparent discrepancies or defects in such Work that render it unsuitable for such proper execution and results. Failure of the Trade Contractor so to report shall constitute an acceptance of the other Trade Contractor's or Construction Manager's work as fit and proper to receive his work, except as to defects which may subsequently become apparent in such work by others.

7.1.3 Any costs *including legal fees,* caused by defective or ill-timed work shall be borne by the *Trade Contractor [party]* responsible therefor.

7.1.4 Should the Trade Contractor wrongfully cause damage to the Work or property of the Owner or to other work on the site, the Trade Contractor shall promptly remedy such damage as provided in Subparagraph 11.2.5.

7.1.5 Should the Trade Contractor wrongfully cause damage to the work or property of any separate Trade Contractor or other contractor, the Trade Contractor shall, upon due notice, promptly attempt to settle with the other Contractor by agreement, or otherwise resolve the dispute. If such separate Trade Contractor or other contractor sues the Owner or the Construction Manager or initiates an arbitration proceeding against the Owner or Construction Manager on account of any damage alleged to have been caused by the Trade Contractor, the Owner or Construction Manager shall notify the Trade Contractor who shall defend such proceedings at the Trade Contractor's expense, and if any judgment or award against the Owner or Construction Manager arises therefrom, the Trade Contractor shall pay or satisfy it and shall reimburse the Owner or Construction Manager for all attorney's fees and court or arbitration costs which the Owner or Construction Manager has incurred.

7.2 Construction Manager's Right to Clean Up

7.2.1 If a dispute arises between the separate Trade Contractors as to their responsibility for cleaning up as required by paragraph 5.15, the Construction Manager may clean up and charge the cost thereof to the Trade Contractors responsible therefor as the Construction Manager shall determine to be just.

ARTICLE 8   Miscellaneous Provisions

8.1 Governing Law

8.1.1 The Contract shall be governed by the law of the place where the Project is located.

8.2 Successors and Assigns

8.2.1 The Owner [*or Construction Manager (as the case may be)*] and the Trade Contractor each binds himself, his partners, successors, assigns and legal representatives to the other party hereto and to the partners, successors, assigns and legal representatives of such other party in respect to all covenants, agreements and obligations contained in the Contract Documents. Neither party to the Contract shall assign the Contract or sublet it as a whole without the written consent of the other.

8.3 Written Notice

8.3.1 Written notice shall be deemed to have been duly served if delivered in person to the individual or member of the firm or entity or to an officer of the corporation for whom it was intended, or if delivered at or sent by registered or certified mail to the last business address known to him who gives the notice.

8.4 Claims for Damages

8.4.1 Should either party to the Trade Contract suffer injury or damage to person or property because of any act or omission of the other party or of any of his employees, agents or others for whose acts he is legally liable, claim shall be made in writing to such other party within a reasonable time after the first observance of such injury or damage.

8.5 Performance Bond and Labor and Material Payment Bond

8.5.1 The Owner or Construction Manager shall have the right to require the Trade Contractor to furnish bonds in a form and with a corporate surety acceptable to the Construction Manager covering the faithful performance of the Contract and the payment of all obligations arising thereunder if and as required in the Bidding or Proposal Documents or in the Contract Documents.

8.6 Rights and Remedies

8.6.1 The duties and obligations imposed by the Contract Documents and the rights and remedies available thereunder shall be in addition to and not a limitation of any duties, obligations, rights and remedies otherwise imposed or available by law. *The rights and remedies of any trade contractor who has a contract with the Construction Manager are subject to any and all limitations and conditions provided in said agreement.*

8.6.2 No action or failure to act by the Construction Manager, Architect/Engineer or Trade Contractor shall constitute a waiver of any right or duty afforded any of them under the Contract Documents, nor shall any such action or failure to act constitute an approval of or acquiescence in any breach thereunder, except as may be specifically agreed in writing.

8.7 Tests

8.7.1 If the Contract Documents, laws, ordinances, rules, regulations or orders of any public authority having jurisdiction require any portion of the Work to be inspected, tested or approved, the Trade Contractor shall give the Construction Manager timely notice of its readiness so the Architect/Engineer and Construction Manager may observe such inspection, testing or approval. The Trade Contractor shall bear all costs of such inspections, tests or approvals unless otherwise provided.

8.7.2 If the Architect/Engineer or Construction Manager determines that any Work requires special inspection, testing or approval which Subparagraph 8.7.1 does not include, he will, through the Construction Manager, instruct the Trade Contractor to order such special inspection, testing or approval and the Trade Contractor shall give notice as in Subparagraph 8.7.1. If such special inspection or testing reveals a failure of the Work to comply with the requirements of the Contract Documents, the Trade Contractor shall bear all costs thereof, including compensation for the Architect/Engineer's and Construction Manager's additional services made necessary by such failure. If the work complies, the Owner [*or Construction Manager (as the case may be)*] shall bear such costs and an appropriate Change Order shall be issued.

8.7.3 Required certificates of inspection, testing or approval shall be secured by the Trade Contractor and promptly delivered by him through the Construction Manager to the Architect/Engineer.

8.7.4 If the Architect/Engineer or Construction Manager is to observe the inspections, tests or approvals required by the Contract Documents, he will do so promptly and, where practicable, at the source of supply.

8.8 Interest

8.8.1 Payments due and unpaid under the Contract Documents shall bear interest from the date payment is due at such rate upon which the parties may agree in writing or, in the absence thereof, at the legal rate prevailing at the place of the Project.

8.9 Arbitration

8.9.1 All claims, disputes and other matters in question arising out of, or relating to this Contract or the breach thereof, except as set forth in Subparagraph 3.2.4 with respect to the Architect/Engineer's decisions on matters relating to artistic effect, and except for claims which have been waived by the making or acceptance of final payment provided by Subparagraphs 10.8.4 and 10.8.5, shall be decided by arbitration in accordance with the Construction Industry Arbitration Rules of the American Arbitration Association then obtaining unless the parties mutually agree otherwise. This agreement to arbitrate shall be specifically enforceable under the prevailing arbitration law. The award rendered by the arbitrators shall be final, and judgment may be entered upon it in accordance with applicable law in any court having jurisdiction thereof.

8.9.2 Notice of the demand for arbitration shall be filed in writing with the other party to the Contract and with the American Arbitration Association. The demand for arbitration shall be made within a reasonable time after the claim, dispute or other matter in question has arisen, and in no event shall it be made after the date when institution of legal or equitable proceedings based on such claim, dispute or other matter in question would be barred by the applicable statute of limitations.

8.9.3 The Trade Contractor shall carry on the Work and maintain the progress schedule during any arbitration proceedings, unless otherwise agreed by him and the Construction Manager in writing.

8.9.4 All claims which are related to or dependent upon each other shall be heard by the same arbitrator or arbitrators even though the parties are not the same unless a specific contract prohibits such consolidation.

8.9.5 *The arbitration rights of Article 8.9 do not apply to any trade contract between the trade contractor and Construction Manager, unless expressly and specifically set forth in their subcontract.*[2]

ARTICLE 9   Time

9.1 Definitions

9.1.1 Unless otherwise provided, the Contract Time is the period of time allotted in the Contract Documents for the Substantial Completion of the Work as defined in Subparagraph 9.1.3 including authorized adjustments thereto.

9.1.2 The date of commencement of the Work is the date established in a notice to proceed. If there is no notice to proceed, it shall be the date of the Trade Contractor Agreement or such other date as may be established therein.

9.1.3 The Date of Substantial Completion of the Work or designated portion thereof is the Date certified by the Architect/Engineer when construction is sufficiently complete, in accordance with the Contract Documents, so the Owner can occupy or utilize the Work or designated portion thereof for the use for which it is intended.

9.1.4 The term day as used in the Contract Documents shall mean calendar day unless otherwise specifically designated.

9.2 Progress and Completion

9.2.1 All time limits stated in the Contract Documents are of the essence of the Contract.

9.2.2 The Trade Contractor shall begin the Work on the date of commencement as defined in Subparagraph 9.1.2. He shall carry the Work forward expeditiously with adequate forces and shall achieve Substantial Completion within the Contract Time.

9.3 Delays and Extensions of Time

9.3.1 If the Trade Contractor is delayed at any time in the progress of the Work by any act or neglect of the Owner, Construction Manager, or the Architect/Engineer, or by any employee of either, or by any separate contractor employed by the Owner, or by changes ordered in the Work, or by labor disputes, fire, unusual delay in transportation, adverse weather conditions not reasonably anticipatable, unavoidable casualties or any causes beyond the Trade Contractor's control, or by delay authorized by the Owner or Construction Manager pending arbitration, or by any other cause which the Construction Manager determines may justify the delay, then the Contract Time shall be extended by Change Order for such reasonable time as the Construction Manager may determine. *It is expressly understood that the Trade Contractor shall have no claim for monetary damages or reimbursement from the Construction Manager for any such event.*

9.3.2 Any claim for extension of time shall be made in writing to the Construction Manager not more than twenty (20) days after the commencement of the delay; otherwise, it shall be waived. In the case of a continuing delay only one claim is necessary. The Trade Contractor shall provide an estimate of the probable effect of such delay on the progress of the Work.

9.3.3 If no agreement is made stating the dates upon which interpretations as set forth in Subparagraph 3.2.2 shall be furnished, then no claim for delay shall be allowed on account of failure to furnish such interpretations until fifteen days after written request is made for them, and not then unless such claim is reasonable.

9.3.4 It shall be recognized by the Trade Contractor that he may reasonably anticipate that as the job progresses, the Construction Manager will be making changes in and updating Construction Schedules pursuant to the authority given him in Subparagraph 4.2.3. Therefore, no claim for an increase in the Contract Sum for either acceleration or delay will be allowed for extensions of time pursuant to this Paragraph 9.3 or for other changes in the Construction Schedules which are of the type ordinarily experienced in projects of similar size and complexity.

[**9.3.5** *This Paragraph 9.3 does not exclude the recovery of damages for delay by either party under other provisions of the Contract Documents.*]

ARTICLE 10 Payments and Completion

10.1 Contract Sum

10.1.1 The Contract Sum is stated in the Agreement between the Owner or Construction Manager and the Trade Contractor including adjustments thereto and is the total amount payable to the Trade Contractor for the performance of the Work under the Contract Documents.

10.2 Schedule of Values

10.2.1 Before the first Application for Payment, the Trade Contractor shall submit to the Construction Manager a schedule of values allocated to the various portions of the Work prepared in such form and supported by such data to substantiate its accuracy as the Construction Manager may require. This schedule, unless objected to by the Construction Manager, shall be used only as a basis for the Trade Contractor's Applications for Payment.

10.3 Applications for Payment

10.3.1 At least ten days before the date for each progress payment established in the Trade Contractor's Agreement, the Trade Contractor shall submit to the Construction Manager an itemized Application for Payment, notarized if required, supported by such data substantiating the Trade Contractor's right to payment as the Owner or the Construction Manager may require, and reflecting retainage, if any, as provided elsewhere in the Contract Documents.

10.3.2 Unless otherwise provided in the Contract Documents, payments will be made on account of materials or equipment not incorporated in the Work but delivered and suitably stored at the site and, if approved in advance by the Construction Manager, payments may similarly be made for materials or equipment stored at some other location agreed upon in writing. Payments made for materials or equipment stored on or off the site shall be conditioned upon submission by the Trade Contractor of bills of sale or such other procedures satisfactory to the Construction Manager to establish the Owner's title to such materials or equipment or otherwise protect the Owner's interest, including applicable insurance and transportation to the site for those materials and equipment stored off the site.

10.3.3 The Trade Contractor warrants that title to all Work, materials and equipment covered by an Application for Payment will pass to the Owner either by incorporation in the construction or upon the receipt of payment by the Trade Contractor, whichever occurs first, free and clear of all liens, claims, security interests or encumbrances, hereinafter referred to in this Article 10 as "liens"; and that no Work, materials or equipment covered by an Application for Payment will have been acquired by the Trade Contractor, or by any other person performing his Work at the site or furnishing materials and equipment for his Work, subject to an agreement under which an interest therein or an encumbrance thereon is retained by the seller or otherwise imposed by the Trade Contractor or such other person. All Trade Subcontractors and Trade Sub-subcontractors agree that title will so pass upon their receipt of payment from the Trade Contractor.

10.4 Progress Payments

10.4.1 If the Trade Contractor has made Application for Payment as above, the Construction Manager will, with reasonable promptness but not more than seven days after the receipt of the Application, *review [process]* such Application for payment in accordance with the Contract.

10.4.2 No approval of an application for a progress payment, nor any progress payment, nor any partial or entire use or occupancy of the Project by the Owner, shall constitute an acceptance of any Work not in accordance with the Contract Documents.

10.4.3 The Trade Contractor shall promptly pay each Trade Subcontractor upon receipt of payment out of the amount paid to the Trade Contractor on account of such Trade Subcontractor's Work, the amount to which said Trade Subcontractor is entitled, reflecting the percentage actually retained, if any, from payments to the Trade Contractor on account of such Trade Subcontractor's Work. The Trade Contractor shall, by an appropriate agreement with each Trade Subcontractor, also require each Trade Subcontractor to make payments to his Trade Sub-subcontractors in a similar manner.

10.5 Payments Withheld

10.5.1 The Construction Manager may decline to approve an Application for Payment if in his opinion the Application is not adequately supported. If the Trade Contractor and Construction Manager cannot agree on a revised amount, the Construction Manager shall process the Application for the amount he deems appropriate. The Construction Manager may also decline to approve any Applications for Payment or, because of subsequently discovered evidence or subsequent inspections, he may nullify in whole or in part any approval previously made to such extent as may be necessary in his opinion because of:

.1 defective work not remedied;

.2 third party claims filed or reasonable evidence indicating probable filing of such claims;

.3 failure of the Trade Contractor to make payments properly to Trade Subcontractors or for labor, materials or equipment;

.4 reasonable evidence that the Work cannot be completed for the unpaid balance of the Contract Sum;

.5 damage to the Construction Manager, the Owner, or another contractor working at the Project;

.6 reasonable evidence that the Work will not be completed within the Contract time; or

.7 persistent failure to carry out the Work in accordance with the Contract Documents.

10.5.2 When the above grounds in Subparagraph 10.5.1 are removed, payment shall be made for amounts withheld because of them.

10.6 Failure of Payment

10.6.1 If the Trade Contractor is *to be paid by the Owner, and if it is* not paid within seven days after any amount is approved for payment by the Construction Manager and has become due and payable, then the Trade Contractor may, upon seven additional days' written notice to the Owner and Construction Manager stop the Work until payment of the amount owing has been received. The Contract Sum shall be increased by *the Owner by* the amount of the Trade Contractor's reasonable costs of shutdown, delay and start up, which shall be effected by appropriate Change Order in accordance with Paragraph 13.3

10.7 Substantial Completion

10.7.1 When the Trade Contractor considers that the Work, or a designated portion thereof which is acceptable to the Owner, is substantially complete as defined in Subparagraph 9.1.3, the Trade Contractor shall prepare for submission to the Construction Manager a list of items to be completed or corrected. The failure to include any items on such list does not alter the responsibility of the Trade Contractor to complete all Work in accordance with the Contract Documents. When the Construction Manager and Architect/Engineer on the basis of inspection determine that the Work or designated portion thereof is substantially complete, the Architect/Engineer will then prepare a Certificate of Substantial Completion which shall establish the Date of Substantial Completion, shall state the responsibilities of the Owner, the Construction Manager and the Trade Contractor for security, maintenance, heat, utilities, damage to the Work, and insurance, and shall fix the time within which the Trade Contractor shall complete the items listed therein. Warranties required by the Contract Documents shall commence on the Date of Substantial Completion of the Work or designated portion thereof unless otherwise provided in the Certificate of Substantial Completion. The Certificate of Substantial Completion shall be submitted to the Owner, the Construction Manager and the Trade Contractor for their written acceptance of the responsibilities assigned to them in such Certificate.

10.8 Final Completion and Final Payment

10.8.1 Upon receipt of written notice that the Work is ready for final inspection and acceptance and upon receipt of a final Application for Payment, the Architect/Engineer and Construction Manager will promptly make such inspection and, when they find the Work acceptable under the Contract Documents and the Contract fully performed, the Construction Manager will promptly approve final payment.

10.8.2 Neither the final payment nor the remaining retained percentage shall become due until the Trade Contractor submits to the Construction Manager (1) an affidavit that all payrolls, bills for materials and equipment, and other indebtedness connected with the Work for which the Owner or his property might in any way be responsible, have been paid or otherwise satisfied, (2) consent of surety, if any, to final payment and (3), if required by the Owner, other data establishing payment or satisfaction of all such obligations, such as receipts, releases and waivers of liens arising out of the Contract, to the extent and in such form as may be designated by the Owner. If any Trade Subcontractor refuses to furnish a release or waiver required by the Owner or Construction Manager, the Trade Contractor may furnish a bond satisfactory to the Owner and Construction Manager to indemnify them against any such lien, *including all legal costs and fees.* If any such lien remains unsatisfied after all payments are made, the Trade Contractor shall refund to the Owner or Construction Manager all moneys that the latter may be compelled to pay in discharging such lien, including all costs and reasonable attorneys' fees.

10.8.3 If, after Substantial Completion of the Work, final completion thereof is materially delayed through no fault of the Trade Contractor or by the issuance of Change Orders affecting final completion, and the Construction Manager so confirms, the Owner or Construction Manager shall, upon certification by the Construction Manager, and without terminating the Contract, make payment of the balance due for that portion of the Work fully completed and accepted. If the remaining balance for Work not fully completed or corrected is less than the retainage stipulated in the Contract Documents, and if bonds have been furnished as provided in Paragraph 8.5, the written consent of the surety to the payment of the balance due for that portion of the Work fully completed and accepted shall be submitted by the Trade Contractor to the Construction Manager prior to such payment. Such payment shall be made under the terms and conditions governing final payment, except that it shall not constitute a waiver of claims.

10.8.4 The making of final payment shall constitute a waiver of all claims by the Owner or Construction Manager except those arising from:

.1 unsettled liens;

.2 faulty or defective Work appearing after Substantial Completion;

.3 failure of the Work to comply with the requirements of the Contract Documents; or

.4 terms of any special warranties required by the Contract Documents.

10.8.5 The acceptance of final payment shall constitute a waiver of all claims by the Trade Contractor except those previously made in writing and identified by the Trade Contractor as unsettled at the time of the Final Application for Payment.

ARTICLE 11   Protection of Persons and Property

11.1 Safety Precautions and Programs

11.1.1   The Trade Contractor shall be responsible for initiating, maintaining and supervising all safety precautions and programs in connection with the Work.

11.1.2   If the Trade Contractor fails to maintain the safety precautions required by law or directed by the Construction Manager, the Construction Manager may take such steps as necessary and charge the Trade Contractor therefor.

11.1.3   The failure of the Construction Manager to take any such action shall not relieve the Trade Contractor of his obligations in Subparagraph 11.1.1.

11.2 Safety of Persons and Property

11.2.1   The Trade Contractor shall take all reasonable precautions for the safety of, and shall provide all reasonable protection to prevent damage, injury or loss to:

.1 all employees on the Work and all other persons who may be affected thereby;

.2 all the Work and all materials and equipment to be incorporated therein, whether in storage on or off the site, under the care, custody or control of the Trade Contractor or any of his Trade Subcontractors or Trade Sub-subcontractors; and

.3 other property at the site or adjacent thereto, including trees, shrubs, lawns, walks, pavements, roadways, structures and utilities not designated for removal, relocation or replacement in the course of construction.

11.2.2   The Trade Contractor shall give all notices and comply with all applicable laws, ordinances, rules, regulations and lawful orders of any public authority bearing on the safety of persons or property or their protection from damage, injury or loss.

11.2.3   The Trade Contractor shall erect and maintain, as required by existing conditions and progress of the Work, all reasonable safeguards for safety and protection, including posting danger signs and other warnings against hazards, promulgating safety regulations and notifying owners and users of adjacent utilities. If the Trade Contractor fails to so comply he shall, at the direction of the Construction Manager, remove all forces from the Project without cost or loss to the Owner or Construction Manager, until he is in compliance.

11.2.4   When the use or storage of explosives or other hazardous materials or equipment is necessary for the execution of the Work, the Trade Contractor shall exercise the utmost care and shall carry on such activities under the supervision of properly qualified personnel.

11.2.5   The Trade Contractor shall promptly remedy all damage or loss (other than damage or loss insured under Paragraph 12.2) to any property referred to in Clauses 11.2.1.2 and 11.2.1.3 caused in whole or in part by the Trade Contractor, his Trade Subcontractors, his Trade Sub-subcontractors, or anyone directly or indirectly employed by any of them, or by anyone for whose acts any of them may be liable and for which the Trade Contractor is responsible under Clauses 11.2.1.2 and 11.2.1.3, except damage or loss attributable to the acts or omissions of the Owner or Architect/Engineer or anyone directly or indirectly employed by either of them or by anyone for whose acts either of them may be liable, and not attributable to the fault or negligence of the Trade Contractor. The foregoing obligations of the Trade Contractor are in addition to his obligations under Paragraph 5.18.

11.2.6 The Trade Contractor shall designate a responsible member of his organization at the site whose duty shall be the prevention of accidents. This person shall be the Trade Contractor's superintendent unless otherwise designated by the Trade Contractor in writing to the Construction Manager.

11.2.7 The Trade Contractor shall not load or permit any part of the Work to be loaded so as to endanger its safety.

11.3 Emergencies

11.3.1 In any emergency affecting the safety of persons or property, the Trade Contractor shall act, at his discretion, to prevent threatened damage, injury or loss. Any additional compensation or extension of time claimed by the Trade Contractor on account of emergency work shall be determined as provided in Article 13 for Changes in the Work.

ARTICLE 12 Insurance

12.1 Trade Contractor's Liability Insurance

12.1.1 The Trade Contractor shall purchase and maintain such insurance as will protect him from claims set forth below which may arise out of or result from the Trade Contractor's operations under the Contract, whether such operations be by himself or by any of his Trade Subcontractors or by anyone directly or indirectly employed by any of them, or by anyone for whose acts any of them may be liable:

.1 claims under workers' or workmen's compensation, disability benefit and other similar employee benefit acts which are applicable to the work to be performed including the "Broad Form All States" Endorsement;

.2 claims for damages because of bodily injury, occupational sickness or disease, or death of his employees under any employers liability law including, if applicable, those required under maritime or admiralty law for wages, maintenance, and cure;

.3 claims for damages because of bodily injury, sickness or disease, or death of any person other than his employees;

.4 claims for damages insured by usual personal injury liability coverage which are sustained (1) by any person as a result of an offense directly or indirectly related to the employment of such person by the Trade Contractor, or (2) by any other person;

.5 claims for damages other than to the work itself because of injury to or destruction of tangible property, including loss of use resulting therefrom; and

.6 claims for damages because of bodily injury or death of any person or property damage arising out of the ownership, maintenance or use of any motor vehicle.

12.1.2 The insurance required by Subparagraph 12.1.1 shall be written for not less than any limits of liability specified in the Contract Documents, or required by law, whichever is greater.

12.1.3 The insurance required by Subparagraph 12.1.1 shall include premises-operations (including explosion, collapse and underground coverage), elevators, independent contractors, products and/or completed operations, and contractual liability insurance (on a "blanket basis" designating all written contracts), all including broad form property damage coverage. Liability insurance may be arranged under Comprehensive General Liability policies for the full limits required or by a combination of underlying policies for lesser limits with the remaining limits provided by an Excess or Umbrella Liability Policy.

12.1.4 The foregoing policies shall contain a provision that coverages afforded under the policies will not be cancelled until at least sixty days' prior written notice has been given to the Construction Manager. Certificates of Insurance acceptable to the Construction Manager shall be filed with the Construction Manager prior to commencement of the Work. Upon request, the Trade Contractor shall allow the Construction Manager to examine the actual policies. *The Owner and Construction Manager shall be named insureds.*

12.2 Property Insurance and Waiver of Subrogation

12.2.1 Unless otherwise provided, the Owner will purchase and maintain property insurance upon the entire Work at the site to the full insurable value thereof. This insurance shall include the interests of the Owner, the Construction Manager, the Trade Contractors, and Trade Subcontractors in the Work and shall insure against the perils of fire and extended coverage, and shall include "all risk" insurance for physical loss or damage.

12.2.2 The Owner will effect and maintain such boiler and machinery insurance as may be necessary and/or required by law. This insurance shall include the interest of the Owner, the Construction Manager, the Trade Contractors, and Trade Subcontractors in the Work.

12.2.3 Any loss insured under Paragraph 12.2 and 12.3 is to be adjusted with the Owner and Construction Manager and made payable to the Owner and Construction Manager as trustees for the insureds, as their interests may appear, subject to the requirements of any applicable mortgagee clause.

12.2.4 The Owner, the Construction Manager, the Architect/Engineer, the Trade Contractors, and the Trade Subcontractors waive all rights against each other and any other contractor or subcontractor engaged in the Project for damages caused by fire or other perils to the extent covered by insurance provided under Paragraph 12.2, or any other property or consequential loss insurance applicable to the Project, equipment used in the Project, or adjacent structures, except such rights as they may have to the proceeds of such insurance. If any policy of insurance requires an endorsement to maintain coverage with such waivers, the owner of such policy will cause the policy to be so endorsed. The Owner will require, by appropriate agreement, written where legally required for validity, similar waivers in favor of the Trade Contractors and Trade Subcontractors by any separate contractor and his subcontractors.

12.2.5 The Owner and Construction Manager shall deposit in a separate account any money received as trustees, and shall distribute it in accordance with such agreement as the parties in interest may reach, or in accordance with an award by arbitration in which case the procedure shall be as provided in Paragraph 8.9. If after such loss no other special agreement is made, replacement of damaged work shall be covered by an appropriate Change Order.

12.2.6 The Owner and Construction Manager as trustees shall have power to adjust and settle any loss with the insurers unless one of the parties in interest shall object in writing within five days after the occurrence of loss to the Owner's and Construction Manager's exercise of this power, and if such objection be made, arbitrators shall be chosen as provided in Paragraph 8.9. The Owner and Construction Manager as trustees shall, in that case, make settlement with the insurers in accordance with the directions of such arbitrators. If distribution of the insurance proceeds by arbitration is required, the arbitrators will direct such distribution.

12.2.7 If the Owner finds it necessary to occupy or use a portion or portions of the Work prior to Substantial Completion thereof, such occupancy shall not commence prior to a time mutually agreed to by the Owner and Construction Manager and to which the insurance company or companies providing the property insurance have consented by endorsement to the policy or policies. This insurance shall not be cancelled or lapsed on account of such partial occupancy.

ARTICLE 13 Changes in the Work

13.1 Change Orders

13.1.1 A Change Order is a written order to the Trade Contractor signed by the Owner or Construction Manager, as the case may be, issued after the execution of the Contract, authorizing a Change in the Work or an adjustment in the Contract Sum or the Contract Time. The Contract Sum and the Contract Time may be changed only by Change Order. A Change order signed by the Trade Contractor indicates his agreement therewith, including the adjustment in the Contract Sum or the Contract Time.

13.1.2 The Owner or Construction Manager, without invalidating the Contract, may order Changes in the Work within the general scope of the Contract consisting of additions, deletions or other revisions, the Contract Sum and the Contract Time being adjusted accordingly. All such changes in the Work shall be authorized by Change Order, and shall be performed under the applicable conditions of the Contract Documents.

13.1.3 The cost or credit to the Owner or Construction Manager resulting from a Change in the Work shall be determined in one or more of the following ways:

.1 by mutual acceptance of a lump sum properly itemized and supported by sufficient substantiating data to permit evaluation; or

.2 by unit prices stated in the Contract Documents or subsequently agreed upon; or

.3 by cost to be determined in a manner agreed upon by the parties and a mutually acceptable fixed or percentage fee; or

.4 by the method provided in Subparagraph 13.1.4.

13.1.4 If none of the methods set forth in Clauses 13.1.3.1, 13.1.3.2 or 13.1.3.3 is agreed upon, the Trade Contractor, provided he receives a written order signed by the Owner or the Construction Manager, shall promptly proceed with the Work involved. The cost of such Work shall be determined by the Construction Manager on the basis of the reasonable expenditures and savings of those performing the Work attributable to the change, including, in the case of an increase in the Contract Sum, a reasonable allowance for overhead and profit. In such case, and also under Clauses 13.1.3.3 and 13.1.3.4 above, the Trade Contractor shall keep and present, in such form as the Construction Manager may prescribe, an itemized accounting together with appropriate supporting data for inclusion in a

Change Order. Unless otherwise provided in the Contract Documents, cost shall be limited to the following: cost of materials; including sales tax and cost of delivery; cost of labor, including social security, old age and unemployment insurance, and fringe benefits required by agreement or custom; workers' or workmen's compensation insurance; bond premiums; rental value of equipment and machinery; and the additional costs of supervision and field office personnel directly attributable to the change. Pending final determination of cost, payments on account shall be made as determined by the Construction Manager. The amount of credit to be allowed by the Trade Contractor for any deletion or change which results in a net decrease in the Contract Sum will be the amount of the actual net cost as confirmed by the Construction Manager. When both additions and credits covering related Work or substitutions are involved in any one change, the allowance for overhead and profit shall be figured on the basis of the net increase, if any, with respect to that change.

13.1.5 If unit prices are stated in the Contract Documents or subsequently agreed upon, and if the quantities originally contemplated are so changed in a proposed Change Order that application of the agreed unit prices to the quantities of Work proposed will cause substantial inequity to the Owner, the Construction Manager, or the Trade Contractor, the applicable unit prices shall be equitably adjusted.

13.2 Concealed Conditions

13.2.1 Should concealed conditions encountered in the performance of the Work below the surface of the ground or should concealed or unknown conditions in an existing structure be at variance with the conditions indicated by the Contract Documents, or should unknown physical conditions below the surface of the ground or should concealed or unknown conditions in an existing structure of an unusual nature, differing materially from those ordinarily encountered and generally recognized as inherent in work of the character provided for in this Contract, be encountered, the Contract Sum shall be equitably adjusted by Change Order upon claim by either party made within twenty days after the first observance of the conditions.

13.3 Claims for Additional Cost

13.3.1 If the Trade Contractor wishes to make a claim for an increase in the Contract Sum, he shall give the Construction Manager written notice thereof within twenty days after the occurrence of the event giving rise to such claim. This notice shall be given by the Trade Contractor before proceeding to execute the Work, except in an emergency endangering life or property in which case the Trade Contractor shall proceed in accordance with Paragraph 11.3. No such claim shall be valid unless so made. Any change in the Contract Sum resulting from such claim shall be authorized by Change Order.

13.3.2 If the Trade Contractor claims that additional cost is involved because of, but not limited to, (1) any written interpretation issued pursuant to Subparagraph 3.2.2, (2) any order by the Owner or Construction Manager to stop the Work pursuant to Paragraph 4.3 where the Trade Contractor was not at fault, or (3) any written order for a minor change in the Work issued pursuant to Paragraph 13.4, the Trade Contractor shall make such claim as provided in Subparagraph 13.3.1.

13.4 Minor Changes in the Work

13.4.1 The Architect/Engineer will have authority to order through the Construction Manager minor changes in the Work not involving an adjustment in the Contract Sum or an extension of the Contract Time and not inconsistent with the intent of the Contract Documents. Such changes shall be effected by written order and such changes shall be binding on the Owner, the Construction Manager, and the Trade Contractor. The Trade Contractor shall carry out such written orders promptly.

13.5 *The Trade Contractor's right to any payment in excess of its Contract Price with the Construction Manager is strictly limited to that net additional sum that the Construction Manager actually received for that specific event from the Owner, less all costs and expenses incurred by the Construction Manager in connection therewith.*[3]

ARTICLE 14 Uncovering and Correction of Work

14.1 Uncovering of Work

14.1.1 If any portion of the Work should be covered contrary to the request of the Construction Manager or Architect/Engineer, or to requirements specifically expressed in the Contract Documents, it must, if required in writing by the Construction Manager, be uncovered for their observation and replaced, at the Trade Contractor's expense.

14.1.2 If any other portion of the Work has been covered which neither the Construction Manager nor the Architect/Engineer has specifically requested to observe prior to being covered, the Architect/Engineer or Construction Manager may request to see such Work and it shall be uncovered by the Trade Contractor. If such Work be found in accordance with the Contract Documents, the cost of uncovering and replacement shall, by appropriate Change Order, be charged to the Owner or Construction Manager, as the case may be. If such Work be found not in accordance with the Contract Documents, the Trade Contractor shall pay such costs unless it be found that this condition was caused by a separate trade contractor employed as provided in Article 7, and in that event the separate trade contractor shall be responsible for the payment of such costs.

14.2 Correction of Work

14.2.1 The Trade Contractor shall promptly correct all Work rejected by the Architect/Engineer or the Construction Manager as defective or as failing to conform to the Contract Documents whether observed before or after Substantial Completion and whether or not fabricated, installed or completed. The Trade Contractor shall bear all costs of correcting such rejected Work, including compensation for the Architect/Engineer's and/or Construction Manager's additional services made necessary thereby.

14.2.2 If within one year after the Date of Substantial Completion of Work or designated portion thereof, or within one year after acceptance by the Owner of designated equipment or within such longer period of time as may be prescribed by law or by the terms of any applicable special warranty required by the Contract Documents, any of the Work is found to be defective or not in accordance with the Contract Documents, the Trade Contractor shall correct it promptly after receipt of a written notice from the Owner or Construction Manager to do so unless the Owner [*or Construction Manager*] has previously given the Trade Contractor a written acceptance of such condition. This obligation shall survive the termination of the Contract. The Owner or Construction Manager shall give such notice promptly after discovery of the condition.

14.2.3 The Trade Contractor shall remove from the site all portions of the Work which are defective or non-conforming and which have not been corrected under Subparagraphs 14.2.1, 5.5.1 and 14.2.2, unless removal has been waived by the Owner.

14.2.4 If the Trade Contractor fails to correct defective or non-conforming Work as provided in Subparagraphs 5.5.1, 14.2.1 and 14.2.2, the Owner or Construction Manager may correct it in accordance with Subparagraph 4.3.2.

14.2.5 If the Trade Contractor does not proceed with the correction of such defective or non-conforming Work within *the [a reasonable]* time fixed by written notice from the Construction Manager, the Owner or Construction Manager may remove it and may store the materials or equipment at the expense of the Trade Contractor. If the Trade Contractor does not pay the cost of such removal and storage within ten days thereafter, the Owner or Construction Manager may upon ten additional days' written notice sell such Work at auction or at private sale and shall account for the net proceeds thereof, after deducting all the costs that should have been borne by the Trade Contractor, including compensation for the Construction Manager's additional services made nedessary thereby. If such proceeds of sale do not cover all costs which the Trade Contractor should have borne, the difference shall be charged to the Trade Contractor and an appropriate Change Order shall be issued. If the payments then or thereafter due the Trade Contractor are not sufficient to cover such amount, the Trade Contractor shall pay the difference to the Owner or Construction Manager.

14.2.6 The Trade Contractor shall bear the cost of making good all work of the Construction Manager or other contractors destroyed or damaged by such removal or correction.

14.3 Acceptance of Defective or Nonconforming Work

14.3.1 If the Owner or Construction Manager prefers to accept defective or non-conforming Work, he may do so instead of requiring its removal and correction, in which case a Change Order will be issued to reflect reduction in the Contract Sum where appropriate and equitable. Such adjustment shall be effected whether or not final payment has been made.

ARTICLE 15   Termination of the Contract

15.1 Termination by the Trade Contractor

15.1.1 If the Work is stopped for a period of thirty days under an order of any court or other public authority having jurisdiction, or as a result of an act of government, such as a declaration of a national emergency making materials unavailable, through no act or fault of the Trade Contractor or a Trade Subcontractor or their agents or employees or any other persons performing any of the Work under a contract with the Trade Contractor, or if the Work should be stopped for a period of thirty days by the Trade Contractor because of *a substantial* failure to receive payment in accordance with the Contract, then the Trade Contractor may, upon seven additional days' written notice to the Construction Manager, terminate the Contract and recover from the Owner [*or Construction Manager, as the case may be,*] payment for all Work executed and for any proven loss sustained upon any materials, equipment, tools, construction equipment and machinery, including reasonable profit and damages.

15.2 Termination by the Owner or Construction Manager

15.2.1 If the Trade Contractor is adjudged a bankrupt, or if he makes a general assignment for the benefit of his creditors, or if a receiver is appointed on account of his insolvency, or if he persistently or repeatedly refuses or fails, except in cases for which extension of time is provided, to supply enough properly skilled workmen or proper materials, or if he fails to make prompt payment to Trade Subcontractors or for materials or labor, or persistently disregards laws, ordinances, rules, regulations or orders of any public authority having jurisdiction, or otherwise is guilty of a substantial violation of a provision of the Contract Documents, then the Owner or Construction Manager may, without prejudice to any right or remedy and after giving the Trade Contractor and his surety, if any, seven days' written notice, terminate the employment of the Trade Contractor and take possession of the site and of all materials, equipment, tools, construction equipment and machinery thereon owned by the Trade Contractor and may finish the Work by whatever method he may deem expedient. In such case the Trade Contractor shall not be entitled to receive any further payment until the Work is finished.

15.2.2 If the unpaid balance of the Contract Sum exceeds the costs of finishing the Work, including compensation for the Construction Manager's additional services made necessary thereby, *including legal costs and fees,* such excess shall be paid to the Trade Contractor. If such costs exceed the unpaid balance, the Trade Contractor shall pay the difference to the Owner or Construction Manager.

FOOTNOTES:

1   This new paragraph is added to further amplify and clarify the fact that the standard general conditions form is not binding on the construction manager, assuming the trade contract is with the owner and not the construction manager
2   This new Article 8.9.5 must be added so a trade contractor, who has an agreement with a construction manager, cannot argue that arbitration rights are incorporated by reference
3   The construction manager should insert this paragraph when dealing with changes in the work relating to changes in price

C. Turnkey and Design-Build Contracts

§1.13   1. Introduction   The design-build prime contract agreement is at the far end of the construction contract spectrum. On one end is the plan and specification contract, in which the contractor must comply fully with the construction contract documents prepared for and furnished by the owner. In the middle of the spectrum is the construction manager team concept. In that instance the architect/engineer and the contractor usually are separate entities which work together. The architect/engineer is hired by the owner, and the professional responsibility and liability for the architect/engineer's errors rest with the owner, although sometimes the construction manager accepts responsibility. In the design-build situation, the team concept has been reduced to zero. In the design-build agreement, the contractor customarily is the one who employs the architect/engineer. It is the contractor who furnishes the final plans and specifications to the owner. The contractor is the team.

The legal considerations in a design-build contract are very different from those in a plan and specification contract. In the plan and specification contract, it is the owner who warrants the adequacy of the plans and specifications prepared by the architect/engineer. If the results are not what the owner anticipates, but the contractor has performed the work in accordance with the owner-furnished contract documents, the contractor has a right to rely on the expertise of the owner's architect/engineer. In the design-build contract that expertise shifts from the owner's side to the contractor's side. It is the contractor who employs the architect/engineer. The contractor accepts the liability and responsibility should the architect/engineer's work be defective. It is the owner who relies on the combined expertise and representations of the contractor. The term "turn-key" frequently has been used interchangeably with "design-build" contract. Case law has imposed upon the contractor full responsibility for the design of the project and for any defects in that design "except to the extent that such responsibility is specifically waived or limited by the contract documents." (*Mobile Housing Environments v Barton and Barton* 432 FSupp 1343 [D CO 1977].) The contractor must be prepared to accept this responsibility before entering a design-build contract. In fact, even though the contractor may attempt to preclude design-related liability, the author questions the legal effectiveness of the contractor's attempt to deny responsibility when the contractor actually furnishes the design expertise. Obviously, each situation must rest on its own peculiar facts.

A major problem to be considered prior to entry into a design-build agreement is whether or not the contractor will be violating any state licensing statute regarding the practice of architecture and/or engineering. The contractor must check with counsel to determine whether any governing legislation exists. The contractor can be certain that a violation will occur, resulting in penalties and lawsuits, if that portion of the work requiring a licensed person is not performed by one with a license. Questions might also arise as to the validity of the overall design-build agreement, if the main purpose of the agreement is the performance of licensed work by a non-licensed person. Therefore, the contract should be written so that the main purpose of the agreement is the performance of non-licensed services. The best way to avoid problems is to retain licensed firms for the performance of all licensed services. If this is done, the contractor should consider inclusion, in the contract with the licensed entity, of provisions covering indemnification of the prime contractor if found liable for damages resulting from deficiencies in the licensed services. Careful review of a prime contractor's own insurance policies, as well as of the licensed entity's insurance coverage, is necessary before proceeding with a design-build agreement.

The Associated General Contractors of America Document No.6a, June, 1977, entitled "Standard Form of Design-Build Agreement Between Owner and Contractor," is a superb, standard prime contractor form. There are several recommended modifications and additions to the form, but as a single design-build agreement, there is none better.

2. Preliminary Design-Build Agreement Between Owner and Contractor (AGC Document No. 6) with Suggested Modifications

§1.14   a. Author's Comments Since the design-build agreement often starts with a concept, and does not necessarily result in going forward with actual construction, the contractor must have some form of agreement for protection in the initial stages. In this instance, it is recommended that the architect/engineer be a separate entity, or that the contractor be licensed to render this type of service, according to the law of the jurisdiction involved. The Associated General Contractors of America Document No. 6, June, 1977, represents a fair agreement between the parties. However, since there is no obligation on the owner's part to proceed with final design and construction, the contractor should be careful to include sufficient compensation in Article 3 to cover this contingency. Therefore, it is recommended that, even if a total credit eventually is allowed the owner for this phase of the work when the guaranteed maximum price is determined, the agreement include sufficient compensation to the design-build contractor to properly compensate for the constructor's time plus profit. When dealing with a preliminary design-build agreement, a cost plus basis should be used for determining compensation. The advantage of this approach can be seen readily when the owner has not made a commitment to go ahead with final design and construction. The contractor will be consulting continually with the owner and, by fulfilling obligations to the client, the contractor may talk the owner out of the project. Thus, the numerous hours that may be spent on this type of work only may be compensable on a cost plus basis.

§1.15 b. FORM—AGC DOCUMENT NO. 6

Preliminary Design-Build Agreement

THE ASSOCIATED GENERAL CONTRACTORS

AGC Document Number 6, Preliminary Design-Build Agreement, Copyright © 1977, reprinted by permission of the Associated General Contractors of America.

Certain provisions of this document have been derived, with modifications, from the following document published by The American Institute of Architects:

Portions of AIA Document B141, Owner-Architect Agreement have been reproduced with the permission of The American Institute of Architects under application number 78038. Further reproduction, in part or in whole, is not authorized. Because AIA documents are revised from time to time, users should ascertain from AIA the current edition of the document of which portions are reproduced below.

This AGREEMENT made this_____day of_____19____between _____hereinafter called the OWNER, and _____, hereinafter called the CONTRACTOR.

The Owner and Contractor agree as set forth below:

---

1. The Owner engages the Contractor to cause certain preliminary design work and construction estimates to be made to determine the cost of designing and constructing

hereinafter called the "Project," for the Owner.

2. The Contractor shall be responsible for furnishing the Design of the Project. The Owner and Contractor shall develop a design phase schedule. Based upon the Owner's Project requirements, Schematic Design Studies will be prepared by the Architect/Engineer. Upon approval of Schematic Designs, the Architect/Engineer shall prepare Design Development Documents to fix the size and character of the Project as to structural, mechanical and electrical systems, materials and other appropriate essential items in the Project. From approved Design Development Documents, the Architect/Engineer will prepare working Drawings and Specifications setting forth in detail the requirements for the

construction of the Project, and based upon codes, laws or regulations which have been enacted at the time of their preparation. Construction of the Project shall be in accordance with these Drawings and Specifications as approved by the Owner. The drawings and Specifications shall remain the property of the Contractor and are not to be used by the Owner on other projects without the written consent of the Contractor.

3. For performing or causing the performance of these services, the Owner agrees to pay the Contractor as follows:

This compensation is to be paid

4. The Architect and/or Engineer will be

5. After the design is sufficiently complete, the Contractor shall submit to the Owner a Guaranteed Maximum Price for the design and construction of the Project. If the Owner and Contractor agree on such a price for the Project and the Owner desires to proceed with the final design and construction of the Project, the Owner and Contractor will enter into a further agreement in the form attached hereto and marked Exhibit A. If the Owner elects not to proceed with final design and construction, he shall have no further obligation to the Contractor other than the payment of his compensation as set out in paragraph 3.

6. If the Owner provides full information regarding his requirements for the Project and makes the necessary decisions for the design and construction estimates to proceed in an orderly manner, it is anticipated that the design will be sufficiently complete for the development of a Guaranteed Maximum Price by

7. *In case of any default by the Owner, the Contractor shall be entitled to all of its costs, damages and fees, including Accounting, Architectural, Building, Engineering and Legal incurred to date or arising therefrom, plus its profit.*[1]

CONTRACTOR

_____

ATTEST:

_____   By _____

Date _____

OWNER

_____

ATTEST:
_____ By _____

Date _____

FOOTNOTE

1   This paragraph is inserted in order to protect the contractor against the legal principle of law which precludes a party from the right to collect attorney fees unless so provided in the contract

3. Standard Form of Design-Build Agreement Between Owner and Contractor (AGC Document No. 6a) with Suggested Modifications

§1.16   **a. Author's Comments** This form requires certain modifications and revisions. The present form places on the contractor responsibilities which should be minimized. The changes in the standard agreement are recommended in order to lessen undue burdens and responsibilities which otherwise would be placed upon the design-build contractor.

The standard form tries to please too many parties. The agreement seems to stress the use of an outside architect/engineer. While this might be desirable in some situations, in others it might not be what the design-build contractor is selling. Therefore, this agreement must be reviewed by the contractor for modification to fit the facts if the contractor is not using an outside, independent architect/engineer.

Article 2 lists certain liabilities and responsibilities of the contractor, but it should also provide limitations on the contractor's legal obligations. It must be remembered that an architect/engineer, acting under an independent agreement with the owner, normally is liable for negligence only if it fails to exercise that degree of reasonable care and skill which is to be exercised by persons of similar license who have similar expertise. Therefore, the liability of the architect/engineer is not absolute when dealing with the owner. However, the law is unsettled with respect to design-build contracts, and case law seems to place upon the design-build contractor a greater liability for design errors than that placed upon the architect/engineer, who deals directly with the owner. There is a difference because the design-build contractor guarantees a performance contract, rather than merely selling a licensed service. For this reason, paragraph 2.1.4 should be added to Article 2.

According to many contractors, the use of a guaranteed maximum price, as provided in Article 6, will place an undue restriction on the contractor. However, from an equitable and realistic point of view, the placing of a guaranteed maximum price on design-build contracts is reasonable. Entering into an open-ended contract would be highly unrealistic. It is the contractor's responsibility to make sure that the price which is inserted will cover fully all anticipated and reasonably conceivable costs. The contractor also must insist upon the insertion of clauses in the contract which will permit recovery of increased costs if the truly unanticipated occurs. It is for this reason that Article 9.1.5 is modified and 9.5 inserted.

Article 13, involving terminations, is the only basic article about which the author is concerned. It does not provide any clear basis for the contractor's holding the owner in default, for terminating the contract, or for collecting damages. For that reason, Article 13 has been changed so that this standard agreement, which is to take precedence, specifies the contractor's rights.

Although the standard form has been revised, it is emphasized that the form is well conceived and well executed. With the proposed modifications, subject to particular factual situations, a good, basic format is presented. Since design-build contracts vary in concept and intent, each form must be specifically analyzed and modified. The starting foundation is laid by the standard form.

§1.17 b. FORM—AGC DOCUMENT NO. 6a

Standard Form of Design-Build Agreement Between Owner and Contractor

THE ASSOCIATED GENERAL CONTRACTORS

AGC Document Number 6a, Design-Build Agreement, Copyright © 1977, reprinted by permission of The Associated General Contractors of America.

Certain provisions of this document have been derived, with modifications, from the following documents published by The American Institute of Architects:

Portions of AIA Documents A111, Owner-Contractor Agreement; and A201, General Conditions of the Contract for Construction have been reproduced with the permission of The American Institute of Architects under application number 78039. Further reproduction in part or in whole, is not authorized. Because AIA documents are revised from time to time, users should ascertain from AIA the current edition of the document of which portions are reproduced below.

TABLE OF ARTICLES

1. The Construction Team and Extent of Agreement
2. Contractor's Responsibilities
3. Owner's Responsibilities
4. Subcontracts
5. Contract Time Schedule
6. Guaranteed Maximum Price
7. Contractor's Fee
8. Cost of the Project
9. Changes in the Project
10. Discounts
11. Payments to the Contractor
12. Insurance, Indemnity and Waiver of Subrogation
13. Termination of the Agreement and Owner's Right to Perform Contractor's Obligations
14. Assignment and Governing Law
15. Miscellaneous Provisions
16. Arbitration

AGREEMENT

Made this_____day of_____in the year of Nineteen Hundred and _____

BETWEEN

_____ the Owner, and
_____ the Contractor.

For services in connection with the following described Project: (Include complete Project location and scope)

The Owner and The Contractor agree as set forth below:

ARTICLE 1   The Construction Team and Extent of Agreement

THE CONTRACTOR accepts the relationship of trust and confidence established between him and the Owner by this Agreement. He agrees to furnish the architectural, engineering and construction services set forth herein and agrees to furnish efficient business administration and superintendence, and to use his best efforts to complete the Project in the best and soundest way and in [*a reasonable,*] expeditious and economical manner consistent with the interests of the Owner.

1.1 The Construction Team: The Contractor, the Owner and the Architect/Engineer called the "Construction Team" shall work from the beginning of design through construction completion. The services of_____, as the Architect/Engineer, will be furnished by the Contractor pursuant to an agreement between the Contractor and the Architect/Engineer.

1.2 Extent of Agreement: This Agreement represents the entire agreement between the Owner and the Contractor and supersedes all prior negotiations, representations or agreements. When the Drawings and Specifications are complete, they shall be identified by amendment to this agreement. This Agreement shall not be superseded by any provisions of the documents for construction and may be amended only by written instrument signed by both Owner and Contractor. *This Agreement shall govern in case of any inconsistency with any other document.*[1]

1.3 Definitions: The Project is the total construction to be designed and constructed of which the Work is a part. The Work comprises the completed construction required by the Drawings and Specifications. The term day shall mean calendar day unless otherwise specifically designated.

ARTICLE 2   Contractor's Responsibilities

2.1 Contractor's Services

   2.1.1 The Contractor shall be responsible for furnishing the Design and for the construction of the Project. The Owner and Contractor shall develop a design and construction phase schedule and the Owner shall be responsible for prompt decisions and approvals so as to maintain the approved schedule.

   2.1.2 If the working Drawings and Specifications have not been completed and a Guaranteed Maximum Price has been established, the Contractor, the Architect/Engineer and Owner will work closely together to monitor the design in accordance with prior approvals so as to ensure that the Project can be constructed within the Guaranteed Maximum Price. As these working Drawings and Specifications are being completed, the Contractor will keep the Owner advised of the effects of any Owner requested changes on the Contract Time Schedule and/or the Guaranteed Maximum Price.

2.1.3 The Contractor will assist the Owner in securing permits necessary for the construction of the Project.

2.1.4 Any design, engineering, architectural, or other professional service incorporated as part of this Contract, which is to be furnished by the Contractor, and which requires the employment of licensed personnel, will be performed by licensed personnel. The Contractor will be held to the same degree, but only to the same degree, that a licensed person would be liable, obligated or responsible for rendering such licensed services. The Contractor will not be liable for any greater degree of care, skill or obligation for such licensed services than would be imposed upon licensed personnel had they dealt directly with the Owner.

2.2 Responsibilities With Respect to Construction

2.2.1 The Contractor will provide all construction supervision, inspection, labor, materials, tools, construction equipment and subcontracted items necessary for the execution and completion of the Project.

2.2.2 The Contractor will pay all sales, use, gross receipts and similar taxes related to the Work provided by the Contractor which have been legally enacted at the time of execution of this Agreement, *as provided in Article 8.*

2.2.3 The Contractor will prepare and submit for the Owner's approval an estimated progress schedule for the Project. This schedule shall indicate the dates for the starting and completion of the various stages of the design and construction. It shall be revised as required by the conditions of the Work and those conditions and events which are beyond the Contractor's control.

2.2.4 The Contractor shall at all times keep the premises *reasonably* free from the accumulation of waste materials or rubbish caused by his operations. At the completion of the Work, he shall remove all of his waste material and rubbish from and around the Project as well as all his tools, construction equipment, machinery and surplus materials.

2.2.5 The Contractor will give all notices and comply with all laws and ordinances legally enacted at the date of the execution of the Agreement, which govern the proper execution of the Work.

2.2.6 The Contractor shall take necessary precautions for the safety of his employees on the Work, and shall comply with all applicable provisions of federal, state and municipal safety laws to prevent accidents or injury to persons on, about or adjacent to the Project site. He shall erect and properly maintain, at all times, as required by the conditions and progress of Work, necessary safeguards for the protection of workmen and the public. It is understood and agreed, however, that the Contractor shall have no responsibility for the elimination or abatement of safety hazards created or otherwise resulting from Work at the job site carried on by other persons or firms directly employed by the Owner as separate contractors or by the Owner's tenants, and the Owner agrees to cause any such separate contractors and tenants to abide and adhere fully to all applicable provisions of federal, state and municipal safety laws and regulations and to comply with all reasonable requests and directions of the Contractor for the elimination or abatement of any such safety hazards at the job site.

2.2.7 The Contractor shall keep such full and detailed accounts as may be necessary for proper financial management under this Agreement. The [*system shall be satisfactory to the*] Owner, [*who*] shall be afforded *reasonable* access to all the Contractor's records, books, correspondence, instructions, drawings, receipts, vouchers, memoranda and similar data relating to this Agreement. The Contractor shall preserve all such records for a period of three years after the final payment or longer where required by law.

2.3 Royalties and Patents

2.3.1 The Contractor shall pay all royalties and license fees. He shall defend all suits or claims for infringement of any patent rights and shall save the Owner harmless from loss on account thereof except when a particular design, process or product is specified by the Owner. In such case the Contractor shall be responsible for such loss only if he has *actual knowledge* [*reason to believe*] that the design, process or product so specified is an infringement of a patent, and fails to give such information promptly to the Owner.

2.4 Warranties and Completion

2.4.1 The Contractor warrants to the Owner that all materials and equipment furnished under this Agreement will be new, unless otherwise specified, and that all Work will be of good quality, free from improper workmanship and defective materials and in conformance with the Drawings and Specifications. The Contractor agrees to correct all Work performed by him under this Agreement which proves to be defective in material and workmanship within a period of one year from the Date of Substantial Completion as defined in Paragraph 5.2, or for such longer periods of time as may be set forth with respect to specific warranties contained in the Specifications. *This warranty period is the exclusive period, and the warranty is in lieu of all other rights and remedies at law or equity.*[2]

2.4.2 The Contractor will secure required certificates of inspection, testing or approval and deliver them to the Owner.

2.4.3 The Contractor will collect all written warranties and equipment manuals and deliver them to the Owner.

2.4.4 The Contractor with the assistance of the Owner's maintenance personnel, will direct the checkout of utilities and operation of systems and equipment for readiness, and will assist in their initial start-up and testing.

2.5 Additional Services

2.5.1 The Contractor will provide the following additional services upon the request of the Owner. A written agreement between the Owner and Contractor shall define the extent of such additional services and the amount and manner in which the Contractor will be compensated for such additional services.

2.5.2 Services related to investigation, appraisals or evaluations of existing conditions, facilities or equipment, or verification of the accuracy of existing drawings or other Owner-furnished information.

2.5.3 Services related to Owner-furnished equipment, furniture and furnishings which are not a part of this Agreement.

2.5.4 Services for tenant or rental spaces not a part of this Agreement.

2.5.5 Obtaining and training maintenance personnel or negotiating maintenance service contracts.

ARTICLE 3   Owner's Responsibilities

3.1 The Owner shall provide full information regarding his requirements for the Project.

3.2 The Owner shall designate a representative who shall be fully acquainted with the Project, and has authority to *issue and* approve changes in the scope of the Project, render decisions promptly, and furnish information expeditiously and in time to meet the dates set forth in Subparagraph 2.2.3.

3.3 The Owner shall furnish for the site of the Project all necessary surveys describing the physical characteristics, soils reports and subsurface investigations, legal limitations, utility locations, and a legal description.

3.4 The Owner shall secure and pay for necessary approvals, easements, assessments and charges required for the construction, use, or occupancy of permanent structures or for permanent changes in existing facilities.

3.5 The Owner shall furnish such legal services as may be necessary for providing the items set forth in Paragraph 3.4, and such auditing services as he may require.

3.6 If the Owner becomes aware of any fault or defect in the Project or non-conformance with the Drawings or Specifications, he shall give prompt written notice thereof to the Contractor.

3.7 The Owner shall provide the insurance for the Project as provided in Paragraph 12.4, and shall bear the cost of any bonds that may be required.

3.8 The services and information required by the above paragraphs shall be furnished with reasonable promptness at Owner's expense and the Contractor shall be entitled to rely upon the accuracy and the completeness thereof.

3.9 The Owner shall furnish reasonable evidence satisfactory to the Contractor, prior to signing the Agreement, that sufficient funds are available and committed for the entire Cost of the Project. If the Contractor elects to execute this Agreement without having received such evidence, the Owner shall provide it within a reasonable time. The Contractor may stop work upon fifteen days notice if such evidence has not been furnished within a reasonable time. *The Owner agrees to furnish to the Contractor, in addition to all other responsibilities in this Agreement, the property listed in the schedule annexed hereto, plus such related data and documentation necessary for proper use of same. The Owner represents that said property is suitable for the particular use intended, and that it shall be furnished on the date or dates specified, or if none are specified, as may be reasonably required by the Contractor. If the property is unsuitable, or is not furnished as specified, the Contractor shall be entitled to receive from the Owner all additional costs incurred as a result thereof, plus a reasonable fee.*[3]

3.10 The Owner shall have no contractual obligation to the Contractor's subcontractors and shall communicate with such subcontractors only through the Contractor.

3.11 *The failure of the Contractor to request or receive satisfactory evidence that sufficient funds are available and committed, shall not be deemed to be an acquiescence by the Contractor in the existence of lack of funds, or affect any of the Contractor's rights to payment. The Contractor shall be entitled to an updated financial statement as to the availability and commitment of funds as it may reasonably require during the progress of this Contract.*[4]

ARTICLE 4 Subcontracts

4.1 All portions of the Work that the Contractor does not perform with his own forces shall be performed under subcontracts.

4.2 A Subcontractor is a person or entity who has a direct contract with the Contractor to perform any Work in connection with the Project. The term Subcontractor does not include any separate contractor employed by the Owner or the separate contractors' subcontractors.

4.3 No contractual relationship shall exist between the Owner and any Subcontractor and the Contractor shall be responsible for the management of the Subcontractors in the performance of their Work.

ARTICLE 5 Contract Time Schedule

5.1 The Work to be performed under this Agreement shall be commenced on or about _____ and shall be substantially completed on or about _____

5.2 The Date of Substantial Completion of the Project or a designated portion thereof is the date when construction is sufficiently complete in accordance with the Drawings and Specifications so the Owner can occupy or utilize the Project or designated portion thereof for the use for which it is intended. Warranties called for by this Agreement or by the Drawings and Specifications shall commence on the Date of Substantial Completion of the Project or designated portion thereof. This date shall be established by a Certificate of Substantial Completion signed by the Owner and Contractor and shall state their respective responsibilities for security, maintenance, heat, utilities, damage to the Work and insurance. This Certificate shall also list the items to be completed or corrected and fix the time for their completion and correction.

5.3 If the Contractor is delayed at any time in the progress of the Project by any act or neglect of the Owner or by any separate contractor employed by the Owner, or by changes ordered in the Project, or by labor disputes, fire, unusual delay in transportation, adverse weather conditions not reasonably anticipatable, unavoidable casualties, or any causes beyond the Contractor's control, or a delay authorized by the Owner pending arbitration, then the Date for Substantial Completion shall be extended by Change Order for the period of such delay.

ARTICLE 6 Guaranteed Maximum Price

6.1 The Contractor guarantees that the maximum price to the Owner for the Cost of the Project as set forth in Article 8, and the Contractor's Fee as set forth in Article 7, will not exceed_____ Dollars ($_____), which sum shall be called the Guaranteed Maximum Price.

6.2 The Guaranteed Maximum Price is based upon laws, codes, and regulations in existence at the date of its establishment and upon criteria, Drawings, and Specifications as set forth below:

6.3 The Guaranteed Maximum Price will be modified for delays *not* caused by the *Contractor and due to its fault,* [*Owner*] and for Changes in the Project, all pursuant to Article 9.

6.4 Allowances included in the Guaranteed Maximum Price are as set forth below:

6.5 Whenever the cost is more than or less than the Allowance, the Guaranteed Maximum Price shall be adjusted by Change Order.

ARTICLE 7   Contractor's Fee

7.1 In consideration of the performance of the Agreement, the Owner agrees to pay to the Contractor in current funds as compensation for his services a Fee as follows:

7.2 Adjustments in Fee shall be made as follows:

7.2.1 For Changes in the Project as provided in Article 9, the Contractor's Fee shall be adjusted as follows:

7.2.2 For delays in the Project not the responsibility of the Contractor, there will be an equitable adjustment in the fee to compensate the Contractor for his increased expenses, *plus compensation for all extended overhead and general administrative and operating expenses.*

7.2.3 In the event the Cost of the Project plus the Contractor's Fee shall be less than the Guaranteed Maximum Price as adjusted by Change Orders, the resulting savings will be shared by the Owner and the Contractor as follows:

7.2.4 The Contractor shall be paid an additional fee in the same proportion as set forth in 7.2.1 if the Contractor is placed in charge of managing the replacement of insured or uninsured loss.

7.3 The Contractor shall be paid monthly that part of his Fee proportionate to the percentage of Work completed, the balance, if any, to be paid at the time of final payment.

7.4 Included in the Contractor's Fee are the following:

7.4.1 Salaries or other compensation of the Contractor's employees at the principal office and branch offices, except employees listed in Subparagraph 8.2.3.

7.4.2 General operating expenses of the Contractor's principal and branch offices other than the field office.

7.4.3 Any part of the Contractor's capital expenses, including interest on the Contractor's capital employed for the Project.

7.4.4 Overhead or general expenses of any kind, except as may be expressly included in Article 8, *or 7.2.2*.

7.4.5 Costs in excess of the Guaranteed Maximum Price.

ARTICLE 8   Cost of the Project

8.1 The term Cost of the Project shall mean costs necessarily incurred in the design and construction of the Project and shall include the items set forth below in this Article. The Owner agrees to pay the Contractor for the Cost of the Project as defined in this Article. Such payment shall be in addition to the Contractor's Fee stipulated in Article 7.

8.2 Cost Items

8.2.1 All architectural, engineering and consulting fees and expenses incurred in designing and constructing the Project.

8.2.2 Wages paid for labor in the direct employ of the Contractor in the performance of the Work under applicable collective bargaining agreements, or under a salary or wage schedule agreed upon by the Owner and the Contractor, and including such welfare or other benefits, if any, as may be payable with respect thereto.

8.2.3 Salaries of Contractor's employees when stationed at the field office, in whatever capacity employed, employees engaged on the road expediting the production or transportation of material and equipment and employees from the main or branch office performing the functions listed below:

8.2.4 Cost of all employee benefits and taxes for such items as unemployment compensation and social security, insofar as such cost is based on wages, salaries, or other remuneration paid to employees of the Contractor and included in the Cost of the Project under Subparagraphs 8.2.1, 8.2.2 and 8.2.3.

8.2.5 The [*proportion of reasonable*] transportation, traveling and hotel and moving expenses of the Contractor or of his officers or employees incurred in discharge of duties connected with the Project.

8.2.6 Cost of all materials, supplies and equipment *used or* incorporated in the Project, including costs of transportation and storage thereof.

8.2.7 Payments made by the Contractor to Subcontractors *and suppliers* for Work performed pursuant to contract under this Agreement.

8.2.8 Cost, including transportation and maintenance, of all materials, supplies, equipment, temporary facilities and hand tools not owned by the workmen, which are employed or consumed in the performance of the Work, and cost less salvage value on such items used, but not consumed, which remain the property of the Contractor.

8.2.9 Rental charges of all [*necessary*] machinery and equipment, exclusive of hand tools, used *for the Project or* at the site of the Work, whether rented from the Contractor or others, including installations, repairs and replacements, dismantling, removal, costs of lubrication, transportation and delivery costs thereof, at rental charges consistent with those prevailing in the area.

8.2.10 Cost of the premiums for all insurance which the Contractor is required to procure by this Agreement or is deemed necessary by the Contractor.

8.2.11 Sales, use, gross receipts or similar *and other* taxes related to the Project, imposed by any governmental authority, and for which the Contractor is liable.

8.2.12 Permit fees, licenses, tests, royalties, damages for infringement of patents and costs of defending suits therefor for which the Contractor is responsible under Subparagraph 2.3.1 and deposits lost for causes other than the Contractor's *direct* negligence.

8.2.13 Losses, expenses or damages to the extent not compensated by insurance or otherwise (including settlement made with the written approval of the Owner), and the cost of corrective work.

8.2.14 Minor expenses such as telegrams, long-distance telephone calls, telephone service at the site, expressage, and similar petty cash items in connection with the Project.

8.2.15 Cost of removal of all debris.

8.2.16 Costs incurred due to an emergency affecting the safety of persons and property.

8.2.17 Cost of data processing services required in the performance of the services outlined in Article 2.

8.2.18 Legal *Accounting and Architectural/Engineering* costs reasonably and properly resulting from prosecution of the Project for the Owner.

8.2.19 All costs directly incurred in the performance of the Project and not included in the Contractor's Fee as set forth in Paragraph 7.3.

ARTICLE 9 Changes in the Project

9.1 The Owner, without invalidating this Agreement, may order Changes in the Project within the general scope of this Agreement consisting of additions, deletions or other revisions, the Guaranteed Maximum Price, if established, the Contractor's Fee, and the Contract Time Schedule being adjusted accordingly. All such Changes in the Project shall be authorized by Change Order.

9.1.1 A Change Order is a written order to the Contractor signed by the Owner or his authorized agent and issued after the execution of this Agreement, authorizing a Change in the Project and/or an adjustment in the Guaranteed Maximum Price, the Contractor's Fee or the Contract Time Schedule. Each adjustment in the Guaranteed Maximum Price resulting from a Change Order shall clearly separate the amount attributable to the Cost of the Project and the Contractor's Fee.

9.1.2 The increase or decrease in the Guaranteed Maximum Price resulting from a Change in the Project shall be determined in one or more of the following ways:

9.1.2.1 by mutual acceptance of a lump sum [*properly itemized and supported by sufficient substantiating data to permit evaluation;*] or

9.1.2.2 by unit prices stated in this Agreement or subsequently agreed upon; or

9.1.2.3 by cost to be determined as defined in Article 8 and a mutually acceptable fixed or percentage fee; or

9.1.2.4 by the method provided in Subparagraph 9.1.3.

9.1.3 If none of the methods set forth in Clauses 9.1.2.1 through 9.1.2.3 is agreed upon, the Contractor, provided he receives a written order signed by the owner, shall promptly proceed with the work involved. The cost of such work shall then be determined on the basis of the reasonable expenditures and savings of those performing the work attributed to the change, including, in the case of an increase in the Guaranteed Maximum Price, a reasonable increase in the Contractor's Fee. In such case, and also under Clauses 9.1.2.3 and 9.1.2.4 above, the Contractor shall keep and present, [*in such form as the Owner may prescribe,*] an itemized accounting together with appropriate supporting data of the increase in the Cost of the Project as outlined in Article 8. The amount of decrease in the Guaranteed Maximum Price to be allowed by the Contractor to the Owner for any deletion or change which results in a net decrease in cost will be the amount of the actual net decrease. When both additions and credits are involved in any one change, the increase in Fee shall be figured on the basis of net increase, if any. *Contractor shall be entitled to an increase in the Guaranteed Maximum Price and fee if the performance of changed work affects unchanged work.*

9.1.4 If unit prices are stated in this Agreement or Subsequently agreed upon, and if the quantities originally contemplated are so changed in a proposed Change Order that application of the agreed unit prices to the quantities of Work proposed will cause substantial inequity to the Owner or the Contractor, the applicable unit prices shall be equitably adjusted.

9.1.5 Should concealed *or unknown* conditions encountered in the performance of the Work [*below the surface of the ground or should concealed or unknown conditions in an existing structure*] be at variance with the conditions indicated by the Drawings, Specifications, or Owner-furnished information [*or should unknown physical conditions below the surface of the ground*] or should concealed or unknown conditions [*in an existing structure*] of an unusual nature, differing materially from those ordinarily encountered and generally recognized as inherent in work of the character provided for in this Agreement, be encountered, the Guaranteed Maximum Price and the Contract Time Schedule shall be equitably adjusted by Change Order upon claim by either party made within a reasonable time after the first observance of the conditions.[5]

9.2 Claims for Additional Cost or Time

9.2.1 If the Contractor wishes to make a claim for an increase in the Guaranteed Maximum Price, or increase in his Fee or an extension in the Contract Time Schedule, he shall give the Owner written notice thereof within a reasonable time after the occurrence of the event giving rise to such claim. This notice shall be given by the Contractor *if reasonably possible* before proceeding to execute the Work, except in an emergency endangering life or property in which case the Contractor shall act, at his discretion, to prevent threatened damage, injury or loss. Claims arising from delay shall be made within a reasonable time after the delay. Increases based upon design and estimating costs with respect to possible changes requested by the Owner, shall be made within a reasonable time after the decision is made not to proceed with the change. No such claim shall be valid unless so made. If the Owner and the Contractor cannot agree on the amount of the adjustment in the Guaranteed Maximum Price, the Contractor's Fee or Contract Time Schedule, it shall be determined pursuant to the provisions of Article 16. Any change in the Guaranteed Maximum Price, the Contractor's Fee or Contract Time Schedule resulting from such claim shall be authorized by Change Order.

9.3 Minor Changes in the Project

9.3.1 The Owner will have authority to order minor Changes in the Work not involving an adjustment in the Guaranteed Maximum Price or an extension of the Contract Time Schedule and not inconsistent with the intent of the Drawings and Specifications. Such Changes may be effected by written order and shall be binding on the Owner and the Contractor.

9.4 Emergencies

9.4.1 In any emergency affecting the safety of persons or property, the Contractor shall act, at his discretion, to prevent threatened damage, injury or loss. Any increase in the Guaranteed Maximum Price or extension of time claimed by the Contractor on account of emergency work shall be determined as provided in this Article.

9.5 *In the event of any delay, suspension or interference with any part of the Work, not due to the fault or within the direct control of the Contractor, there shall be an equitable adjustment in the Contract Price, time, and fee, to properly compensate Contractor for its increased costs and time.*

ARTICLE 10   Discounts

All discounts for prompt payment shall accrue to the Owner to the extent the Cost of the Project is paid directly by the Owner or from a fund made available by the Owner to the Contractor for such payments. To the extent the Cost of the Project is paid with funds of the Contractor, all cash discounts shall accrue to the Contractor. All trade discounts, rebates and refunds, and all returns from sale of surplus materials and equipment, shall be credited to the Cost of the Project.

ARTICLE 11   Payments to the Contractor

11.1 Payments shall be made by Owner to Contractor according to the following procedure:

11.1.1 On or before the_____day of each month after work has commenced, the Contractor shall submit to the Owner an Application for Payment in such detail as may be required by the Owner based on the Work completed and materials stored on the site and/or at locations approved by the Owner along with a proportionate amount of the Contractor's Fee for the period ending on the_____day of the month.

11.1.2 Within ten (10) days after his receipt of each monthly Application for Payment, the Owner shall pay directly to the Contractor the appropriate amounts for which Application for Payment is made therein. This payment request shall deduct the aggregate of amounts previously paid by the Owner.

11.1.3 If the Owner should fail to pay the Contractor at the time the payment of any amount becomes due, then the Contractor may, at any time thereafter, upon serving written notice that he will stop work within five (5) days after receipt of the notice by the Owner, and after such five (5) day period, stop the Project until payment of the amount owing has been received. Written notice shall be deemed to have been duly served if sent by certified mail to the last business address known to him who gives the notice.

11.1.4 Payments due but unpaid shall bear interest at the rate the Owner is paying on his construction loan or at the legal rate, which ever is higher.

11.2 The Contractor warrants and guarantees that title to all Work, materials and equipment covered by an Application for Payment whether incorporated in the Project or not, will pass to the Owner upon receipt of such payment by Contractor free and clear of all liens, claims, security interests or encumbrances hereinafter referred to as Liens.

11.3 No Progress Payment nor any partial or entire use or occupancy of the Project by the Owner shall constitute an acceptance of any *latently defective* Work not in accordance with the Drawings and Specifications.

11.4 Final payment constituting the unpaid balance of the Cost of the Project and the Contractor's Fee shall be due and payable when the Project is delivered to the Owner, ready for beneficial occupancy, or when the Owner occupies the Project, whichever event first occurs, provided that the Project be then substantially completed and this Agreement substantially performed. If there should remain minor items to be completed, the Contractor and the Owner shall list such items and the Contractor shall deliver, in writing, his guarantee to complete said items within a reasonable time thereafter. The Owner may retain a sum equal to 150% of the estimated cost of completing any unfinished items, provided that said unfinished items are listed separately and the estimated cost of completing any unfinished items is likewise listed separately. Thereafter, the Owner shall pay to Contractor, monthly, the amount retained for incomplete items as each of said items is completed.

11.5 Before issuance of Final Payment, the Contractor shall submit *reasonable* [*satisfactory*] evidence that all payrolls, materials bills and other indebtedness connected with the Project have been paid or otherwise satisfied.

11.6 The making of Final Payment shall constitute a waiver of all claims by the Owner except those rising from:

11.6.1 Unsettled Liens.

11.6.2 Improper workmanship or defective materials appearing within one year after the Date of Substantial Completion.

11.6.3 *Latent* failures of the Work to comply with the Drawings and Specifications, *subject to Article 2.4.1.*

11.6.4 Terms of any special guarantees required by the Drawings and Specifications.

11.7 The acceptance of Final Payment shall constitute a waiver of all claims by the Contractor except those previously made in writing and unsettled.

ARTICLE 12 Insurance, Indemnity and Waiver of Subrogation

12.1 Indemnity

12.1.1 The Contractor agrees to indemnify and hold the Owner harmless *provided the Owner is free from fault* from all claims for bodily injury and property damage (other than the

Work itself and other property insured under Paragraph 12.4) that may arise *as a direct result* from the Contractor's operations under this Agreement.

12.1.2 The Owner shall cause any other contractor who may have a contract with the Owner to perform work in the areas where work will be performed under this Agreement, to agree to indemnify the Owner and the Contractor and hold them harmless from all claims for bodily injury and property damage (other than property insured under Paragraph 12.4) that may arise from that contractor's operations. Such provisions shall be in a form satisfactory to the Contractor.

12.2 Contractor's Liability Insurance

12.2.1 The Contractor shall purchase and maintain such insurance as will protect him from the claims set forth below which may arise out of or result from the Contractor's operations under this Agreement whether such operations be by himself or by any Subcontractor or by anyone directly or indirectly employed by any of them, or by anyone for whose acts any of them may be liable:

12.2.1.1 Claims under workers' compensation, disability benefit and other similar employee benefit acts which are applicable to the work to be performed.

12.2.1.2 Claims for damages because of bodily injury, occupational sickness or disease, or death of his employees under any applicable employer's liability law.

12.2.1.3 Claims for damages because of bodily injury, or death of any person other than his employees.

12.2.1.4 Claims for damages insured by usual personal injury liability coverage which are sustained (1) by any person as a result of an offense directly or indirectly related to the employment of such person by the Contractor or (2) by any other person.

12.2.1.5 Claims for damages, other than to the Work itself, because of injury to or destruction of tangible property, including loss of use therefrom.

12.2.1.6 Claims for damages because of bodily injury or death of any person or property damage arising out of the ownership, maintenance or use of any motor vehicle.

12.2.2 The Comprehensive General Liability Insurance shall include premises-operations (including explosion, collapse and underground coverage) elevators, independent contractors, completed operations, and blanket contractual liability on all written contracts, all including broad form property damage coverage.

12.2.3 The Contractor's Comprehensive General and Automobile Liability Insurance, as required by Subparagraphs 12.2.1 and 12.2.2 shall be written for not less than limits of liability as follows:

    a. Comprehensive General Liability
        1. Personal Injury $_____ Each Occurrence
                                                   (Completed Operations)
                                       $_____Aggregate

        2. Property Damage $_____ Each Occurrence

                                       $_____Aggregate

b. Comprehensive Automobile Liability
   1. Bodily Injury $_____ Each Person

                             $_____ Each Occurrence

   2. Property Damage $_____ Each Occurrence

12.2.4 Comprehensive General Liability Insurance may be arranged under a single policy for the full limits required or by a combination of underlying policies with the balance provided by an Excess or Umbrella Liability policy.

12.2.5 The foregoing policies shall contain a provision that coverages afforded under the policies will not be cancelled or not renewed until at least sixty (60) days' prior written notice has been given to the Owner. Certificates of Insurance showing such coverages to be in force shall be filed with the Owner prior to commencement of the Work.

12.3 Owner's Liability Insurance

12.3.1 The Owner shall be responsible for purchasing and maintaining his own liability insurance and, at his option, may purchase and maintain such insurance as will protect him against claims which may arise from operations under this Agreement.

12.4 Insurance to Protect Project

12.4.1 The Owner shall purchase and maintain property insurance in a form acceptable to the Contractor upon the entire Project for the full cost of replacement as of the time of any loss. This insurance shall include as named insureds the Owner, the Contractor, Subcontractors and Subsubcontractors and shall insure against loss from the perils of Fire, Extended Coverage, and shall include "All Risk" insurance for physical loss or damage including without duplication of coverage at least theft, vandalism, malicious mischief, transit, collapse, flood, earthquake, testing, and damage resulting from defective design, workmanship or material. The owner will increase limits of coverage, if necessary, to reflect estimated replacement cost. The Owner will be responsible for any co-insurance penalties or deductibles. If the Project covers an addition to or is adjacent to an existing building, the Contractor, Subcontractors and Subsubcontractors shall be named as additional insureds under the Owner's Property Insurance covering such building and its contents.

12.4.1.1 If the Owner finds it necessary to occupy or use a portion or portions of the Project prior to Substantial Completion thereof, such occupancy shall not commence prior to a time mutually agreed to by the Owner and Contractor and to which the insurance company or companies providing the property insurance have consented by endorsement to the policy or policies. This insurance shall not be cancelled or lapsed on account of such partial occupancy. Consent of the Contractor and of the insurance company or companies to such occupancy or use shall not be unreasonably withheld.

12.4.2 The Owner shall purchase and maintain such boiler and machinery insurance as may be required or necessary. This insurance shall include the interests of the Owner, the Contractor, Subcontractors and Subsubcontractors in the Work.

12.4.3 The Owner shall purchase and maintain such insurance as will protect the Owner and Contractor against loss of use of Owner's property due to those perils insured pursuant to Subparagraph 12.4.1. Such policy will provide coverage for expediting expenses of materials, continuing overhead of the Owner and Contractor, necessary labor expense including overtime, loss of income by the Owner and other determined exposures. Exposures of the Owner and the Contractor shall be determined by mutual agreement and separate limits of coverage fixed for each item.

12.4.4 The Owner shall file a copy of all policies with the Contractor before an exposure to loss may occur. Copies of any subsequent endorsements will be furnished to the Contractor. The Contractor will be given sixty (60) days notice of cancellation, non-renewal, or any endorsements restricting or reducing coverage. If the Owner does not intend to purchase such insurance, he shall inform the Contractor in writing prior to the commencement of the Work. The Contractor may then effect insurance which will protect the interest of himself, the Subcontractors and their Subsubcontractors in the Project, the cost of which shall be a Cost of the Project pursuant to Article 8, and the Guaranteed Maximum Price shall be increased by Change Order. If the Contractor is damaged by failure of the Owner to purchase or maintain such insurance or to so notify the Contractor, the Owner shall bear all reasonable costs properly attributable thereto.

12.5 Property Insurance Loss Adjustment

12.5.1 Any insured loss shall be adjusted with the Owner and the Contractor and made payable to the Owner and Contractor as trustees for the insureds, as their interests may appear, subject to any applicable mortgagee clause.

12.5.2 Upon the occurrence of an insured loss, monies received will be deposited in a separate account and the trustees shall make distribution in accordance with the agreement of the parties in interest, or in the absence of such agreement, in accordance with an arbitration award pursuant to Article 16. If the trustees are unable to agree between themselves on the settlement of the loss, such dispute shall also be submitted to arbitration pursuant to Article 16.

12.6 Waiver of Subrogation

12.6.1 The Owner and Contractor waive all rights against each other, the Architect/Engineer, Subcontractors, and Subsubcontractors for damages caused by perils covered by insurance provided under Paragraph 12.4, except such rights as they may have to the proceeds of such insurance held by the Owner and Contractor as trustees. The Contractor shall require similar waivers from all Subcontractors and Subsubcontractors.

12.6.2 The Owner and Contractor waive all rights against each other and the Architect/Engineer, Subcontractors and Subsubcontractors for loss or damage to any equipment used in connection with the Project which loss is covered by any property insurance. The Contractor shall require similar waivers from all Subcontractors and Subsubcontractors.

12.6.3 The Owner waives subrogation against the Contractor, Architect/Engineer, Subcontractors, and Subsubcontractors on all property and consequential loss policies carried by the Owner on adjacent properties and under property and consequential loss policies purchased for the Project after its completion.

12.6.4 If the policies of insurance referred to in this Paragraph require an endorsement to provide for continued coverage where there is a waiver of subrogation, the **owners** of such policies will cause them to be so endorsed.

ARTICLE 13   Termination of the Agreement And Owner's Right to Perform Contractor's Obligations

13.1 Termination by the Contractor

13.1.1   If the Project is stopped *or delayed, in whole or substantial part,* for a period of thirty (30) days under an order of any court or other public authority having jurisdiction, or as a result of an act of government, such as a declaration of a national emergency making materials unavailable, through no [*act or*] fault of the Contractor or *the Owner* [*if the Project should be stopped for a period of thirty (30) days by the Contractor for the Owner's failure to make payment thereon*], then the Contractor may, upon seven days' written notice to the Owner, terminate this Agreement and recover from the Owner payment for all work executed, *liabilities incurred,* the Contractor's Fee earned to date, and for any proven loss sustained upon any materials, equipment, tools, construction equipment and machinery, including reasonable profit and damages.

13.1.2   *If the Project is stopped or delayed, either in whole or substantial part, for a period of thirty (30) days under an Order of any Court or other public authority having jurisdiction, or as a result of an act of government, and due to the fault or negligence of the Owner or as a result of an act within its control; or, if the Project should be stopped or delayed, either in whole or substantial part, for a period of thirty (30) days by the Contractor due to the Owner's failure to make proper payment thereon; or, if the Owner should commit a material breach of any of its responsibilities or obligations under this Agreement, then the Contractor may, upon seven days' written notice to the Owner, terminate this Agreement and recover from the Owner payment for all work performed; for any unpaid costs of and fees for the Project; for any liability, obligations, damages, commitments and/or claims that the Contractor may have incurred or might incur in good faith in connection with this Agreement; as well as receiving payment for the Contractor's attorney and legal fees, and all lost anticipated gross profits on the Contract work not performed as of the date of termination.*[6]

13.2 Owner's Right to Perform Contractor's Obligations and Termination by the Owner for Cause

13.2.1   If the Contractor fails to perform any of his *material* obligations under this Agreement, including any obligation he assumes to perform work with his own forces, the Owner may, after seven days' written notice, during which period the Contractor fails to *attempt, in good faith, to* perform such obligation, make good such deficiencies. The Guaranteed Maximum Price, if any, shall be reduced by the cost to the Owner of making good such deficiencies.

13.2.2   If the Contractor is adjudged a bankrupt, or if he makes a general assignment for the benefit of his creditors, or if a receiver is appointed on account of his insolvency, or if he *unreasonably and without cause* persistently or repeatedly refuses or fails, except in cases for which extension of time is provided, to supply enough properly skilled workmen or proper materials, or if he, *without cause,* fails to make prompt payment to Subcontractors or for materials or labor, or *unreasonably and without cause* persistently disregards laws, ordinances, rules, regulations or orders of any public authority having jurisdiction, or otherwise is guilty of a substantial violation of a provision of this Agreement, then the Owner may, without prejudice to any right or remedy and after giving the Contractor and his surety, if any, seven (7) days' written notice, during which period Contractor fails to *attempt, in good faith, to* cure the violation, terminate the employment of the Contractor and take possession of the site and of all materials, equipment, tools, construction equipment and machinery thereon owned by the Contractor and may finish the Work by whatever method he may deem expedient. In such case, the Contractor shall not be entitled to receive any further payment until the Work is finished nor shall he be relieved from his obligations assumed under Article 6. *The Owner shall take all reasonable steps to mitigate damages.*

13.3 Termination by Owner Without Cause

13.3.1 If *the Owner is not in default or subject to termination pursuant to Article 13.1.2, and if* the Owner terminates the Agreement other than pursuant to Article 13.2.2, he shall reimburse the Contractor for any unpaid Cost of the Project due him under Article 8, plus (1) the unpaid balance of the Fee computed upon the Cost of the Work to the date of termination at the rate of the percentage named in Article 7.2.1 or if the Contractor's Fee be stated as a fixed sum, such an amount as will increase the payment on account of his Fee to a sum which bears the same ratio to the said fixed sum as the Cost of the Project at the time of termination bears to the adjusted Guaranteed Maximum Cost, if any, otherwise to a reasonable estimated Cost of the Project when completed. The Owner shall also pay to the Contractor fair compensation, either by purchase or rental at the election of the *Contractor* [*Owner*], for any equipment *the Owner* retained. In case of such termination of this Agreement the Owner shall further assume and become liable for obligations, commitments and unsettled claims that the Contractor has previously undertaken or incurred *or might incur* in good faith in connection with said Work, *plus legal and accounting fees.* The Contractor shall *upon receipt of* [*as a condition of receiving*] the payments referred to in this Article 13, execute and deliver all such papers and take all such steps, including the legal assignment of his contractual rights, as the Owner may require for the purpose of fully vesting in the Owner the rights and benefits of the Contractor under such obligations or commitments. *The Owner shall compensate Contractor for all costs incurred in discontinuing the Work.*

ARTICLE 14 Assignment and Governing Law

14.1 Neither the Owner nor the Contractor shall assign his interest in this Agreement without the written consent of the other except as to the assignment of proceeds.

14.2 This Agreement shall be governed by the law in effect at the location of this Project.

ARTICLE 15 Miscellaneous Provisions

ARTICLE 16 Arbitration

16.1 All claims, disputes and other matters in question arising out of, or relating to, this Agreement or the breach thereof, except with respect to the Architect/Engineer's decision on matters relating to artistic effect, and except for claims which have been waived by the making or acceptance of Final Payment shall be decided by arbitration in accordance with the Construction Industry Arbitration Rules of the American Arbitration Association then obtaining unless the parties mutually agree otherwise. This agreement to arbitrate shall be specifically enforceable under the prevailing arbitration law.

16.2 Notice of the demand for arbitration shall be filed in writing with the other party to this Agreement and with the American Arbitration Association. The demand for arbitration shall be made within a reasonable time after the claim, dispute or other matter in question has arisen, and in no event shall it be made after the date when institution of legal or equitable proceedings based on such claim, dispute or other matter in question would be barred by the applicable *contractual or* statute of limitations.

16.3 The award rendered by the arbitrators shall be final and judgment may be entered upon it in accordance with applicable law in any court having jurisdiction thereof.

16.4 Unless otherwise agreed in writing, the Contractor shall carry on the Work and maintain the Contract Time Schedule during any arbitration proceedings and the Owner shall continue to make payments in accordance with this Agreement.

[**16.5** *All claims which are related to or dependent upon each other shall be heard by the same arbitrator or arbitrators, even though the parties are not the same, unless a specific contract prohibits such consolidation.*]

16.5 *The Owner acknowledges that it will participate in and be bound by any judicial, administrative, legislative or arbitration proceeding wherein the Owner's participation and presence are demanded or summoned by the Contractor, provided that said proceedings involve a third party and the Contractor, even though said third party might not be specifically bound by the terms of this Contract.*

This Agreement entered into as of the day and year first written above.

ATTEST: OWNER:

ATTEST: CONTRACTOR:

FOOTNOTES

1. It is of utmost importance that the contractor specifically set forth, in this form, all those terms and conditions which are intended to prevail. However, it must be remembered that if there are conflicting terms, then although this sentence states that the agreement will prevail, the entire document, including any conflicting document, will be interpreted together against the party who prepared it—the prime contractor. The contract will be read in favor of the party to whom it was given—the owner. The applicable principle of law is that a document will be interpreted against the party who drafted it, provided that the other party's interpretation is reasonable. Since the design-build contractor is in a position of superior knowledge and expertise, and is the primary party preparing the documents, in order to avoid liability the contractor must make absolutely sure not to create an ambiguity

2. Case law has established the proposition that a warranty period, even for one year, does not preclude an owner's right of action for breach of contract during the longer Statute of Limitation period. Therefore, in order to shorten the Statute of Limitation time period to the same period as the warranty, this clause is inserted. This is basically what is bargained for and agreed upon between the parties, and it should be stated expressly

3. Although Article 3.9 was inserted for the contractor's benefit, it has become the subject of much discussion among construction attorneys. Questions have been raised as to what would happen if the owner did, in fact, have insufficient funds and the contractor failed to seek evidence as to these funds. Would the contractor then have waived the right to receive payment? In order to avoid this type of situation, a provision should be added to 3.9

4. The owner often finds it advantageous, for varying reasons, to furnish to the contractor different items of property. These items of property must be listed in a separate schedule and made a part of the contract. If the property is not as represented, the contractor should be entitled to additional compensation. This is the reason for inserting paragraph 3.11

5. In order to eliminate many of the contingency costs which might be inserted into the guaranteed maximum price, and in order to reach a more equitable agreement, a general floating price factor should be added to the contract. It is a modification of the "changed conditions" clause which will best fulfills this need, as well as the insertion of a "pay for delay" paragraph
6. As presently written, the contractor is subject to termination for default, but has limited rights relating to the owner's default. In case of the owner's default, the contractor should be entitled to collect damages, as in other contractual situations. To eliminate the present inequities of Article 13, paragraph 13.1.2 is required

4. General Conditions for Design-Build Agreement (AGC Document No. 6c)

§1.18 **a. Author's Comments** The Associated General Contractors of America Document No.6c, June, 1977, is neither a true prime contract document nor apparently meant to serve as general conditions between the owner and contractor. Rather, it is written as if it were part of the subcontract.

Since the conditions of the contract are set forth in the agreement between the owner and contractor, it easily can be indicated that no general conditions are required. Since the design-build agreement will normally be negotiated, special conditions can be written to meet the specific facts at hand.

In reviewing the AGC Document No. 6c, many modifications are recommended before giving the document to the subcontractor. There are too many open ends and too many statements and relationships which are less than favorable to the prime contractor. This document has many clauses which would not be recommended, and probably should not be included, in a document which is being proposed by a prime contractor advocate. For the establishment of a subcontractor relationship, the design-build prime contractor should use the standard form subcontract agreement that is set forth in §1.19.

Since the AGC Document No. 6c is a well-written document, it is included for reference and review. In this document the contractor may find specific areas which should be included within the special conditions.

§1.19 B. FORM—
AGC DOCUMENT
NO. 6c

General Conditions for Design-Build Agreement Between Owner and Contractor

THE ASSOCIATED GENERAL CONTRACTORS OF AMERICA

AGC Document Number 6c, Design-Build General Conditions, Copyright © 1977, reprinted by permission of The Associated General Contractors of America.

Certain provisions of this document have been derived, with modifications, from the following document published by The American Institute of Architects:

Portions of AIA Document A201, General Conditions of the Contract for Construction have been reproduced with the permission of The American Institute of Architects under application number 78040. Further reproduction, in part or whole, is not authorized. Because AIA documents are revised from time to time, users should ascertain from AIA the current edition of the document of which portions are reproduced below.

INSTRUCTIONS FOR CONTRACTOR
1. These documents are intended to be used with AGC Document No. 6a, Standard Form of Design-Build Agreement Between Owner and Contractor, Revised 1977, as the General Conditions. These conditions primarily govern the obligations of the Subcontractors and in addition establish the general procedures for the administration of construction.
2. In all cases your attorney should be consulted to advise you on their use and any modifications.
3. Nothing contained herein is intended to conflict with local, state or federal laws or regulations.
4. It is recommended all insurance matters be reviewed with your insurance consultant and carrier such as implications of errors and omission liability, completed operations, and waiver of subrogation.
5. Each article should be reviewed by the Contractor as to the applicability to a given project and contractual conditions.
6. Special conditions and terms for the project or the subcontracts should cover the following:
   —subcontractor retainages
   —payment schedules
   —insurance limits
   —builder's risk deductible, if any.
7. If the Owner does not provide Builder's Risk Insurance, Paragraph 12.2 will need to be modified.

TABLE OF ARTICLES

1. Contract Documents
2. Owner
3. Architect/Engineer
4. Contractor
5. Subcontractors
6. Sub-Subcontractors
7. Separate Subcontracts

     8 Miscellaneous Provisions
     9 Time
    10 Payments and Completion
    11 Protection of Persons and Property
    12 Insurance
    13 Changes in the Work
    14 Uncovering and Correction of Work
    15 Termination of the Contract

ARTICLE 1 Contract Documents

1.1 Definitions

1.1.1 The Contract Documents The Contract Documents consist of the Contract between the Contractor and the Subcontractor, the Conditions of the Contract (General, Supplementary and other Conditions), the Drawings (and Criteria if the drawings are not complete), the Specifications, all Addenda issued prior to execution of the Contract, and all Modifications issued after the execution of the contract. A Modification is (1) a written amendment to the Contract signed by both parties, (2) a Change Order, (3) a written interpretation issued by the Architect/Engineer pursuant to Subparagraph 3.2.2; or (4) a written order for a minor change in the Work issued on the Owner's behalf pursuant to Paragraph 13.4. In addition, the Subcontractor assumes toward the Contractor all the obligations and responsibilities which the Contractor assumes toward the Owner under the Agreement between the Owner and the Contractor. A copy of the pertinent parts of the Agreement will be made available on request. The Contract Documents do not include Bidding or Proposal Documents such as the Advertisement or Invitation To Bid, Requests for Proposals, sample forms, Subcontractors Bid or Proposal, or portions of Addenda relative to any of these, or any other documents other than those set forth in this subparagraph unless specifically set forth in the Agreement with the Subcontractor.

1.1.2 The Contract The Contract Documents form the Contract with the Subcontractor. This Contract represents the entire and integrated agreement and supersedes all prior negotiations, representations, or agreements, either written or oral. The Contract may be amended or modified only by a Modification as defined in Subparagraph 1.1.1.

1.1.3 The Work The Work comprises the completed construction performed by the Contractor with his own forces or, as to the Subcontractor, the completed construction required by a Subcontractor's Contract and includes all labor necessary to reproduce such construction required of the Contractor or a particular Subcontractor, and all materials and equipment incorporated or to be incorporated in such construction.

1.1.4 The Project The Project is the total construction to be performed under the Agreement between the Owner and Contractor of which the Work is a part.

1.2 Execution, Correlation and Intent

1.2.1 By executing his Agreement, each Subcontractor represents that he has visited the site, familiarized himself with the local conditions under which the Work is to be performed and correlated his observations with the requirements of the Contract Documents.

1.2.2 The intent of the Contract Documents is to include all items necessary for the proper execution and completion of the Work. The Contract Documents are complementary, and what is required by any one shall be as binding as if required by all. Work not covered in the Contract Documents will not be required unless it is consistent therewith and is reasonably inferable therefrom as being necessary to produce the intended results. Words and abbreviations in the Contract Documents which have well-known technical or trade meanings are used in accordance with such recognized meanings.

1.2.3 The organization of the Specifications into divisions, sections and articles, and the arrangements of Drawings shall not control the Contractor in dividing the Work among Subcontractors or in establishing the extent of Work to be performed by any trade.

1.3 Ownership and Use of Documents

1.3.1 Unless otherwise provided in the Contract Documents, the Subcontractor will be furnished, free of charge, all copies of Drawings and Specifications reasonably necessary for the execution of the Work.

1.3.2 All Drawings, Specifications and copies thereof furnished by the Contractor are and shall remain his property. They are to be used only with respect to this Project and are not to be used on any other project. With the exception of one contract set for each party, such documents are to be returned or suitably accounted for to the Contractor on request at the completion of the Work. Submission or distribution to meet official regulatory requirements or for other purposes in connection with the Project is not to be construed as publication in derogation of the Contractor's common law copyright or other reserved rights.

ARTICLE 2   Owner

2.1 Definition

2.1.1 The Owner is the person or entity identified as such in the Agreement between the Owner and Contractor and is referred to throughout the Contract Documents as if singular in number and masculine in gender. The term Owner means the Owner or his authorized representative.

2.2 Information and Services Required of the Owner

2.2.1 The Owner will furnish all surveys describing the physical characteristics, legal limitations and utility locations for the site of the Project, and a legal description of the site.

2.2.2 Except as provided in Subparagraph 5.7.1 the Owner will secure and pay for necessary approvals, easements, assessments and charges required for the construction, use, or occupancy of permanent structures or permanent changes in existing facilities.

2.2.3 Information or services under the Owner's control will be furnished by the Owner with reasonable promptness to avoid delay in the orderly progress of the Work.

2.2.4 The Owner shall forward all instructions to the Subcontractors through the Contractor.

ARTICLE 3   Architect/Engineer

3.1 Definition

3.1.1 The Architect/Engineer is the person lawfully licensed to practice architecture or engineering or an entity lawfully practicing architecture or engineering and identified as such in the Agreement between the Owner and Contractor and is referred to throughout the Contract Documents as if singular in number and masculine in gender. The term Architect/Engineer means the Architect/Engineer or his authorized representative.

3.1.2 Nothing contained in the Contract Documents shall create any contractual relationship between the Architect/Engineer and any Subcontractor.

3.2 Architect/Engineer's Duties During Construction

3.2.1 The Architect/Engineer shall at all times have access to the Work wherever it is in preparation and progress. When directed by the Contractor, the Subcontractor shall provide facilities for such access so the Architect/Engineer may perform his functions under the Contract Documents.

3.2.2 The Architect/Engineer will be the interpreter of the requirements of the Drawings and Specifications. The Architect/Engineer will, within a reasonable time, render such interpretations as are necessary for the proper execution of the progress of the Work.

3.2.3 All interpretations of the Architect/Engineer shall be consistent with the intent of and reasonably inferable from the Contract Documents and will be in writing or in the form of drawings. All requests for interpretations shall be directed through the Contractor. Neither the Architect/Engineer nor the Contractor will be liable to the Subcontractor for the result of any interpretation or decision rendered in good faith in such capacity.

3.2.4 The Architect/Engineer's decisions in matters relating to artistic effect will be final if consistent with the intent of the Contract Documents.

3.2.5 The Architect/Engineer will have authority to reject Work which does not conform to the Contract Documents. Whenever, in his opinion, he considers it necessary or advisable for the implementation of the intent of the Contract Documents, he will have authority to require special inspection or testing of the Work in accordance with Subparagraph 8.7.2 whether or not such Work be then fabricated, installed or completed. However, neither the Architect/Engineer's authority to act under this Subparagraph 3.2.5, nor any decision made by him in good faith either to exercise or not to exercise such authority, shall give rise to any duty or responsibility of the Architect/Engineer to the Subcontractor, any Sub-Subcontractor, any of their agents or employees, or any other person performing any of the Work.

3.2.6 The Architect/Engineer will review and approve or take other appropriate action upon Subcontractor's submittals such as Shop Drawings, Product Data and Samples, but only for conformance with the design concept of the Work and with the information given in the Contract Documents. Such action shall be taken with reasonable promptness so as to cause no delay. The Architect/Engineer's approval of a specific item shall not indicate approval of an assembly of which the item is a component.

3.2.7 The Architect/Engineer along with the Contractor will conduct inspections to determine the dates of Substantial Completion and final completion.

3.2.8 The Architect/Engineer will communicate with the Subcontractors through the Contractor.

ARTICLE 4 Contractor

4.1 Definition

4.1.1 The Contractor is the person or entity which has entered into an agreement with the Owner to design and construct the Project and is referred to throughout the Contract Documents as if singular in number and masculine in gender. The Contractor is authorized to enter into agreements with Subcontractors to perform the Work necessary to complete the Project and to perform some of the construction with his own forces. The term Contractor means the Contractor acting through his authorized representative.

4.2 Administration of the Contract

4.2.1 The Contractor will provide the general administration of the Project as herein described.

4.2.2 The Contractor shall have the responsibility to supervise and coordinate the work of all Subcontractors.

4.2.3 The Contractor shall prepare and update all Construction Schedules and shall direct the Work with respect to such schedules.

4.2.4 The Contractor shall have authority to reject Work which does not conform to the Contract Documents and to require any Special Inspection and Testing in accordance with Subparagraph 8.7.2.

4.2.5 The Contractor will prepare and issue Change Orders to the Subcontractors in accordance with Article 13.

4.2.6 The Contractor along with the Architect/Engineer will conduct inspections to determine the dates of Substantial Completion and final completion, and will receive and review written warranties and related documents required by the Contract and assembled by the Subcontractor.

4.3 Contractor's Right to Stop the Work

4.3.1 If the Subcontractor fails to correct defective Work as required by Paragraph 14.2 or persistently fails to carry out the Work in accordance with the Contract Documents, the Contractor may order the Subcontractor to stop the Work, or any portion thereof, until the cause for such order has been eliminated.

4.3.2 If the Subcontractor defaults or neglects to carry out the Work in accordance with the Contract Documents and fails within seven days after receipt of written notice from the Contractor to commence and continue correction of such default or neglect with diligence and promptness, the Contractor may, by written notice, and without prejudice to any other remedy he or the Owner may have, make good such deficiencies. In such case an appropriate Change Order shall be issued deducting from the payments then or thereafter due the Subcontractor the cost of correcting such deficiencies, including compensation for the Architect/Engineer's and Contractor's additional services made necessary by such default, neglect or failure.

ARTICLE 5 Subcontractors

5.1 Definition

5.1.1 A Subcontractor is the person or entity identified as such in the Agreement between the Contractor and a Subcontractor and is referred to throughout the Contract Documents as if singular in number and masculine in gender. The term Subcontractor means the Subcontractor or his authorized representative.

5.2 Review of Contract Documents

5.2.1 The Subcontractor shall carefully study and compare the Contract Documents and shall at once report to the Contractor any error, inconsistency or omission he may discover. The Subcontractor shall not be liable to the Owner, the Contractor or the Architect/Engineer for any damage resulting from any such errors, inconsistencies or omissions.

5.3 Supervision and Construction Procedures

5.3.1 The Subcontractor shall supervise and direct the Work, using his best skill and attention. He shall be solely responsible for all construction means, methods, techniques, sequences and procedures and for coordinating all portions of the Work under the Contract subject to the overall coordination of the Contractor.

5.3.2 The Subcontractor shall be responsible to the Contractor for the acts and omissions of his employees and all his Sub-subcontractors and their agents and employees and other persons performing any of the Work under a contract with the Subcontractor.

5.3.3 Neither observations nor inspections, tests or approvals by persons other than the Subcontractor shall relieve the Subcontractor from his obligations to perform the Work in accordance with the Contract Documents.

5.4 Labor and Materials

5.4.1 Unless otherwise specifically provided in the Contract Documents, the Subcontractor shall provide and pay for all labor, materials, equipment, tools, construction equipment and machinery, transportation, and other facilities and services necessary for the proper execution and completion of the Work.

5.4.2 The Subcontractor shall at all times enforce strict discipline and good order among his employees and shall not employ on the Work any unfit person or anyone not skilled in the task assigned to him.

5.5 Warranty

5.5.1 The Subcontractor warrants to the Owner and the Contractor that all materials and equipment furnished under this Contract will be new unless otherwise specified, and that all Work will be of good quality, free from faults and defects and in conformance with the Contract Documents. All Work not so conforming to these requirements, including substitutions not properly approved and authorized, may be considered defective. If required by the Contractor, the Subcontractor shall furnish satisfactory evidence as to the kind and quality of materials and equipment. This warranty is not limited by the provisions of Paragraph 14.2.

5.6 Taxes

5.6.1 The Subcontractor shall pay all sales, consumer, use and other similar taxes for the Work or portions thereof provided by the Subcontractor which are legally enacted at the time bids or proposals are received, whether or not yet effective.

5.7 Permits, Fees and Notices

5.7.1 Unless otherwise provided in the Contract Documents, the Subcontractor shall secure and pay for all permits, governmental fees, licenses and inspections necessary for the proper execution and completion of the Work, which are customarily secured after execution of the contract and which are legally required at the time bids or proposals are received.

5.7.2 The Subcontractor shall give all notices and comply with all laws, ordinances, rules, regulations and orders of any public authority bearing on the performance of the Work.

5.7.3 Unless otherwise provided in the Contract Documents, it is not the responsibility of the Subcontractor to make certain that the Contract Documents are in accordance with applicable laws, statutes, building codes and regulations. If the Subcontractor observes that any of the Contract Documents are at variance therewith in any respect, he shall promptly notify the Contractor in writing, and any necessary changes shall be by appropriate Modification.

5.7.4 If the Subcontractor performs any Work knowing it to be contrary to such laws, ordinances, rules and regulations, and without such notice to the Contractor, he shall assume full responsibility therefor and shall bear all costs attributable thereto.

5.8 Allowances

5.8.1 The Subcontractor shall include in the Contract Sum as defined in 10.1.1 all allowances stated in the Contract Documents. Items covered by these allowances shall be supplied for such amounts and by such persons as the Contractor may direct.

5.8.2 Unless otherwise provided in the Contract Documents:

.1 These allowances shall cover the cost to the Subcontractor, less any applicable trade discount, of the materials and equipment required by the allowance delivered at the site, and all applicable taxes;

.2 The Subcontractor's costs for unloading and handling on the site, labor, installation costs, overhead, profit and other expenses contemplated for the original allowance shall be included in the Contract Sum and not in the allowance;

.3 Whenever the cost is more than or less than the allowance, the Contract Sum shall be adjusted accordingly by Change Order, the amount of which will recognize changes, if any, in handling costs on the site, labor, installation costs, overhead, profit and other expenses.

5.9 Superintendent

5.9.1 The Subcontractor shall employ a competent superintendent and necessary assistants who shall be in attendance at the Project site during the progress of the Work. The superintendent shall be satisfactory to the Contractor, and shall not be changed except with the consent of the Contractor, unless the superintendent proves to be unsatisfactory to the Subcontractor or ceases to be in his employ. The superintendent shall represent the Subcontractor and all communications given to the superintendent shall be as binding as if given to the Subcontractor. Important communications shall be confirmed in writing. Other communications shall be so confirmed on written request in each case.

5.10 Progress Schedule

5.10.1 The Subcontractor, immediately after being awarded the Contract, shall prepare and submit for the Contractor's information an estimated progress schedule for the Work. The progress schedule shall be related to the entire Project to the extent required by the Contract Documents and shall provide for expeditious and practicable execution of the Work. This schedule shall indicate the dates for the starting and completion of the various stages of construction, shall be revised as required by the conditions of the Work, and shall be subject to the Contractor's approval.

5.11 Drawings and Specifications at the Site

5.11.1 The Subcontractor shall maintain at the site for the Contractor one copy of all Drawings, Specifications, Addenda, Change Orders and other Modifications, in good order and marked currently to record all changes made during construction. These Drawings, marked to record all changes during construction, and approved Shop Drawings, Product Data and Samples shall be delivered to the Contractor for the Owner upon completion of the Work.

5.12 Shop Drawings, Product Data and Samples

5.12.1 Shop Drawings are drawings, diagrams, schedules and other data especially prepared for the Work by the Subcontractor or any Sub-subcontractor, manufacturer, supplier or distributor to illustrate some portion of the Work.

5.12.2 Product Data are illustrations, standard schedules, performance charts, instructions, brochures, diagrams and other information furnished by the Subcontractor to illustrate a material, product or system for some portion of the Work.

5.12.3 Samples are physical examples which illustrate materials, equipment or workmanship and establish standards by which the Work will be judged.

5.12.4 The Subcontractor shall review, approve and submit through the Contractor with reasonable promptness and in such sequence as to cause no delay in the Work or in the work of any separate contractor, all Shop Drawings, Product Data and Samples required by the Contract Documents.

5.12.5 By approving and submitting Shop Drawings, Product Data and Samples, the Subcontractor represents that he has determined and verified all materials, field measurements, and field construction criteria related thereto, or will do so, and that he has checked and coordinated the information contained within such submittals with the requirements of the Work and of the Contract Documents.

5.12.6 The Contractor, if he finds such submittals to be in order, will forward them to the Architect/Engineer. If the Contractor finds them not to be complete or in proper form, he may return them to the Subcontractor for correction or completion.

5.12.7 The Subcontractor shall not be relieved of responsibility for any deviation from the requirements of the Contract Documents by the Architect/Engineer's approval of Shop Drawings, Product Data or Samples under Subparagraph 3.2.6 unless the Subcontractor has specifically informed the Architect/Engineer and Contractor in writing of such deviation at the time of submission and the Architect/Engineer has given written approval to the specific deviation. Subcontractor shall not be relieved from responsibility for errors or omissions in the Shop Drawings, Product Data or Samples by the Architect/Engineer's approval thereof.

5.12.8 The Subcontractor shall direct specific attention, in writing or on resubmitted Shop Drawings, Product Data or Samples, to revisions other than those requested by the Architect/Engineer or Contractor on previous submittals.

5.12.9 No portion of the Work requiring submission of a Shop Drawing, Product Data or Sample shall be commenced until the submittal has been approved by the Architect/Engineer. All such portions of the Work shall be in accordance with approved submittals.

5.13 Use of Site

5.13.1 The Subcontractor shall confine operations at the site to areas designated by the Contractor, permitted by law, ordinances, permits and the Contract Documents and shall not unreasonably encumber the site with any materials or equipment.

5.14 Cutting and Patching of Work

5.14.1 The Subcontractor shall be responsible for all cutting, fitting or patching that may be required to complete the Work or to make its several parts fit together properly. He shall provide protection of existing Work as required.

5.14.2 The Subcontractor shall not damage or endanger any portion of the Work or the work of the Contractor or any separate contractors or subcontractors by cutting, patching or otherwise altering any work, or by excavation. The Subcontractor shall not cut or otherwise alter the work of the Contractor or any separate contractor except with the written consent of the Contractor and of such separate contractor. The Subcontractor shall not unreasonably withhold from the Contractor or any separate contractor his consent to cutting or otherwise altering the Work.

5.15 Cleaning Up

5.15.1 The Subcontractor at all times shall keep the premises free from accumulation of waste materials or rubbish caused by his operations. At the completion of the Work he shall remove all his waste materials and rubbish from and about the Project as well as all his tools, construction equipment, machinery and surplus materials.

5.15.2 If the Subcontractor fails to clean up, the Contractor may do so and the cost thereof shall be charged to the Subcontractor.

5.16 Communications

5.16.1 The Subcontractor shall forward all communications to the Owner and Architect/Engineer through the Contractor.

5.17 Royalties and Patents

5.17.1 The Subcontractor shall pay all royalties and license fees. He shall defend all suits or claims for infringement of any patent rights and shall save the Owner and Contractor harmless from loss on account thereof, except that the Owner shall be responsible for all such loss when a particular design, process or the product of a particular manufacturer or manufacturers is specified, but if the Subcontractor has reason to believe that the design, process or product specified is an infringement of a patent, he shall be responsible for such loss unless he promptly gives such information to the Contractor.

5.18 Indemnification

5.18.1 To the fullest extent permitted by law, the Subcontractor shall indemnify and hold harmless the Owner, the Contractor and the Architect/Engineer and their agents and employees from and against all claims, damages, losses, and expenses including but not limited to, attorneys' fees, arising out of or resulting from the performance of the Work, provided that any such claim, damage, loss or expense (1) is attributable to bodily injury, sickness, disease or death, or to injury to or destruction of tangible property (other than the Work itself) including the loss of use resulting therefrom, and (2) is caused in whole or in part by any negligent act or omission of the Subcontractor, any Sub-subcontractor, anyone directly or indirectly employed by any of them or anyone for whose acts any of them may be liable, regardless of whether or not it is caused in part by a party indemnified hereunder. Such obligation shall not be construed to negate, abridge or otherwise reduce any other right or obligation of indemnity which would otherwise exist as to any party or person described in this Paragraph 5.18.

5.18.2 In any and all claims against the Owner, the Contractor or the Architect/Engineer or any of their agents or employees by any employee of the Subcontractor, any Sub-subcontractor, anyone directly or indirectly employed by any of them or anyone for whose acts any of them may be liable, the indemnification obligation under this Paragraph 5.18 shall not be limited in any way by any limitation on the amount or type of damages, compensation or benefits payable by or for the Subcontractor or any Sub-subcontractor under workers' or workmen's compensation acts, disability benefit acts or other employee benefit acts.

5.18.3 The obligations of the Subcontractor under this Paragraph 5.18 shall not extend to the liability of the Architect/Engineer, his agents or employees arising out of (1) the preparation or approval of maps, drawings, opinions, reports, surveys, designs or specifications, or (2) the giving of or the failure to give directions or instruction by the Architect/Engineer, his agents or employees provided such giving or failure to give is the primary cause of the injury or damage.

ARTICLE 6   Sub-Subcontractors

6.1 Definition

6.1.1 A Sub-subcontractor is a person or entity who has a direct contract with a Subcontractor to perform any of the Work at the site. The term Sub-subcontractor is referred to throughout the Contract Documents as if singular in number and masculine in gender and means a Sub-subcontractor or his authorized representative.

6.2 Award of Sub-Subcontracts and Other Contracts for Portions of the Work

6.2.1 Unless otherwise required by the Contract Documents or in the Bidding or Proposal Documents, the Subcontractor shall furnish to the Contractor in writing, for acceptance by the Contractor in writing, the names of the persons or entities (including those who are to furnish materials or equipment fabricated to a special design) proposed for each of the principal portions of the Work. The Contractor will promptly reply to the Subcontractor in writing if the Contractor, after due investigation, has reasonable objection to any such proposed person or entity. Failure of the Contractor to reply promptly shall constitute notice of no reasonable objection.

6.2.2 The Subcontractor shall not contract with any such proposed person or entity to whom the Contractor has made reasonable objection under the provisions of Subparagraph 6.2.1. The Subcontractor shall not be required to contract with anyone to whom he has a reasonable objection.

6.2.3 If the Contractor refuses to accept any person or entity on a list submitted by the Subcontractor in response to the requirements of the Contract Documents, the Subcontractor shall submit an acceptable substitute; however, no increase in the Contract Sum shall be allowed for any such substitution.

6.2.4 The Subcontractor shall make no substitution for any Sub-subcontractor, person or entity previously selected if the Contractor makes reasonable objection to such substitution.

6.3 Sub-Subcontractual Relations

6.3.1 By an appropriate agreement, written where legally required for validity, the Subcontractor shall require each Sub-subcontractor, to the extent of the work to be performed by the Sub-subcontractor, to be bound to the Subcontractor by the terms of the Contract Documents and to assume toward the Subcontractor all the obligations and responsibilities which the Subcontractor, by these Documents, assumes toward the Owner, the Contractor, or the Architect/Engineer. Said agreement shall preserve and protect the rights of the Owner, the Contractor and the Architect/Engineer under the Contract Documents with respect to the Work to be performed by the Sub-subcontractor so that the subcontracting thereof will not prejudice such rights, and shall allow to the Sub-subcontractor, unless specifically provided otherwise in the Subcontractor—Sub-subcontractor agreement, the benefit of all rights, remedies and redress against the Subcontractor that the Subcontractor, by these Documents has against the Contractor. Where appropriate, the Subcontractor shall require each Sub-subcontractor to enter into similar agreements with his Sub-subcontractors. The Subcontractor shall make available to each proposed Sub-subcontractor, prior to the execution of the Sub-subcontract, copies of the Contract Documents to which the Sub-subcontractor will be bound by this Paragraph 6.3, and shall identify to the Sub-subcontractor any terms and conditions of the proposed Sub-subcontract which may be at variance with the Contract Documents. Each Sub-subcontractor shall similarly make copies of such Documents available to his Sub-subcontractors.

ARTICLE 7   Separate Subcontracts

7.1 Mutual Responsibility of Subcontractors

7.1.1 The Subcontractor shall afford the Contractor and other Subcontractors reasonable opportunity for the introduction and storage of their materials and equipment and the execution of their work, and shall connect and coordinate his Work with others under the general direction of the Contractor.

7.1.2 If any part of the Subcontractor's Work depends, for proper execution or results, upon the Work of the Contractor or any separate Subcontractor, the Subcontractor shall, prior to proceeding with the Work, promptly report to the Contractor any apparent discrepancies or defects in such Work that render it unsuitable for such proper execution and results. Failure of the Subcontractor so to report shall constitute an acceptance of the other Subcontractor's or Contractor's Work as fit and proper to receive his Work, except as to defects which may subsequently become apparent in such work by others.

7.1.3 Any costs caused by defective or ill-timed work shall be borne by the party responsible therefor.

7.1.4 Should the Subcontractor wrongfully cause damage to the Work or property of the Owner or to other work on the site, the Subcontractor shall promptly remedy such damage as provided in Subparagraph 11.2.5.

7.1.5 Should the Subcontractor wrongfully cause damage to the work or property of any separate Subcontractor or other contractor, the Subcontractor shall, upon due notice, promptly attempt to settle with the other contractor by agreement, or otherwise resolve the dispute. If such separate contractor sues the Owner or the Contractor or initiates an arbitration proceeding against the Owner or Contractor on account of any damage alleged to have been caused by the Subcontractor, the Owner or Contractor shall notify the Subcontractor who shall defend such proceedings at the Subcontractor's expense, and if any judgment or award against the Owner or Contractor arises therefrom, the Subcontractor shall pay or satisfy it and shall reimburse the Owner or Contractor for all attorneys' fees and court or arbitration costs which the Owner or Contractor has incurred.

7.2 Contractor's Right to Clean Up

7.2.1 If a dispute arises between the separate Subcontractors as to their responsibility for cleaning up as required by Paragraph 5.15, the Contractor may clean up and charge the cost thereof to the Subcontractors responsible therefor as the Contractor shall determine to be just.

ARTICLE 8 Miscellaneous Provisions

8.1 Governing Law

8.1.1 The Contract shall be governed by the law of the place where the Project is located.

8.2 Successors and Assigns

8.2.1 The Contractor and the Subcontractor each binds himself, his partners, successors, assigns and legal representatives of such other party in respect to all covenants, agreements and obligations contained in the Contract Documents. Neither party to the Contract shall assign the Contract or sublet it as a whole without the written consent of the other.

8.3 Written Notice

8.3.1 Written notice shall be deemed to have been duly served if delivered in person to the individual or member of the firm or entity or to an officer of the corporation for whom it was intended, or if delivered at or sent by registered or certified mail to the last business address known to him who gives the notice.

8.4 Claims for Damages

8.4.1 Should either party to the subcontract agreements suffer injury or damage to person or property because of any act or omission of the other party or of any of his employees, agents or others for whose acts he is legally liable, claim shall be made in writing to such other party within a reasonable time after the first observance of such injury or damage.

8.5 Performance Bond and Labor and Material Payment Bond

8.5.1 The Contractor shall have the right to require the Subcontractor to furnish bonds in a form and with a corporate surety acceptable to the Contractor covering the faithful performance of the Contract and the payment of all obligations arising thereunder if and as required in the Bidding or Proposal Documents or in the Contract Documents.

8.6 Rights and Remedies

8.6.1 The duties and obligations imposed by the Contract Documents and the rights and remedies available thereunder shall be in addition to and not a limitation of any duties, obligations, rights and remedies otherwise imposed or available by law.

8.6.2 No action or failure to act by the Contractor, Architect/Engineer or Subcontractor shall constitute a waiver of any right or duty afforded any of them under the Contract documents, nor shall any such action or failure to act constitute an approval of or acquiescence in any breach thereunder, except as may be specifically agreed in writing.

8.7 Tests

8.7.1 If the Contract Documents, laws, ordinances, rules, regulations or orders of any public authority having jurisdiction require any portion of the Work to be inspected, tested or approved, the Subcontractor shall give the Architect/Engineer timely notice of its readiness so the Architect/Engineer and Contractor may observe such inspection, testing, or approval. The Subcontractor shall bear all costs of such inspections, tests or approvals unless otherwise provided.

8.7.2 If the Architect/Engineer or Contractor determines that any Work requires special inspection, testing or approval which Subparagraph 8.7.1 does not include, he will, through the Contractor, instruct the Subcontractor to order such special inspection, testing or approval and the Subcontractor shall give notice as in Subparagraph 8.7.1. If such special inspection or testing reveals a failure of the Work to comply with the requirements of the Contract Documents, the Subcontractor shall bear all costs thereof, including compensation for the Architect/Engineer's and Contractor's additional services made necessary by such failure. If the work complies, the Contractor shall bear such costs and an appropriate Change Order shall be issued.

8.7.3 Required certificates of inspection, testing or approval shall be secured by the Subcontractor and promptly delivered by him through the Contractor to the Architect/Engineer.

8.7.4 If the Architect/Engineer or Contractor is to observe the inspections, tests or approvals required by the Contract Documents, he will do so promptly and, where practicable, at the source of supply.

8.8 Arbitration

8.8.1 All claims, disputes and other matters in question arising out of, or relating to this Contract or the breach thereof, except as set forth in Subparagraph 3.2.4. with respect to the Architect/Engineer's decisions on matters relating to artistic effect, and except for claims which have been waived by the making or acceptance of final payment provided by Subparagraphs 10.8.4. and 10.8.5, shall be decided by arbitration in accordance with the Construction Industry Arbitration Rules of the American Arbitration Association then obtaining unless the parties mutually agree otherwise. This agreement to arbitrate shall be specifically enforceable under the prevailing arbitration law. The award rendered by the arbitrators shall be final, and judgment may be entered upon it in accordance with applicable law in any court having jurisdiction thereof.

8.8.2 Notice of the demand for arbitration shall be filed in writing with the other party to the Contract and with the American Arbitration Association. The demand for arbitration shall be made within a reasonable time after the claim, dispute or other matter in question has arisen, and in no event shall it be made after the date when institution of legal or equitable proceedings based on such claim, dispute or other matter in question would be barred by the applicable statute of limitations.

8.8.3 The Subcontractor shall carry on the Work and maintain the progress schedule during any arbitration proceedings, unless otherwise agreed by him and the Contractor in writing.

8.8.4 All claims which are related to or dependent upon each other shall be heard by the same arbitrator or arbitrators even though the parties are not the same unless a specific contract prohibits such consolidation.

ARTICLE 9 Time

9.1 Definitions

9.1.1 Unless otherwise provided, the Contract Time is the period of time allotted in the Contract Documents for the Substantial Completion of the Work as defined in Subparagraph 9.1.3 including authorized adjustments thereto.

9.1.2 The date of commencement of the Work is the date established in a notice to proceed. If there is no notice to proceed, it shall be the date of the Subcontractor Agreement or such other date as may be established therein.

9.1.3 The Date of Substantial Completion of the Work or designated portion therof is the Date certified by the Architect/Engineer when construction is sufficiently complete, in accordance with the Contract Documents, so the Owner can occupy or utilize the Work or designated portion thereof for the use for which it is intended.

9.1.4 The term day as used in the Contract Documents shall mean calendar day unless otherwise specifically designated.

9.2 Progress and Completion

9.2.1 All time limits stated in the Contract Documents are of the essence of the Contract.

9.2.2 The Subcontractor shall begin the Work on the date of commencement as defined in Subparagraph 9.1.2. He shall carry the Work forward expeditiously with adequate forces and shall achieve Substantial Completion within the Contract Time.

9.3 Delays and Extensions of Time

9.3.1 If the Subcontractor is delayed at any time in the progress of the Work by any act or neglect of the Owner, Contractor, or the Architect/Engineer, or by any employee of either, or by any separate contractor employed by the Owner, or by changes ordered in the Work, or by labor disputes, fire, unusual delay in transportation, adverse weather conditions not reasonably anticipatable, unavoidable casualties or any causes beyond the Subcontractor's control, or by delay authorized by the Owner or the Contractor pending arbitration, or by any other cause which the Contractor determines may justify the delay, then the Contract Time shall be extended by Change Order for such reasonable time as the Contractor may determine.

9.3.2 Any claim for extension of time shall be made in writing to the Contractor no more than twenty days after the commencement of the delay; otherwise it shall be waived. In the case of a continuing cause of delay only one claim is necessary. The Subcontractor shall provide an estimate of the probable effect of such delay on the progress of the Work.

9.3.3 If no agreement is made stating the dates upon which interpretations as set forth in Subparagraph 3.2.2 shall be furnished, then no claim for delay shall be allowed on account of failure to furnish such interpretations until fifteen days after written request is made for them, and not then unless such claim is reasonable.

9.3.4 It shall be recognized by the Subcontractor that he may reasonably anticipate that as the job progresses, the Contractor will be making changes in and updating Construction Schedules pursuant to the authority given him in Subparagraph 4.2.3. Therefore, no claim for an increase in the Contract Sum for either acceleration or delay will be allowed for extensions of time pursuant to this paragraph 9.3 or for other changes in Construction Schedules which are of the type ordinarily experienced in projects of similar size and complexity.

9.3.5 This Paragraph 9.3 does not exclude the recovery of damages for delay by either party under other provisions of the Contract Documents.

ARTICLE 10   Payments and Completion

10.1 Contract Sum

10.1.1 The Contract Sum is stated in the agreement between the Contractor and the Subcontractor including adjustments thereto and is the total amount payable to the Subcontractor for the performance of the Work under the Contract Documents.

10.2 Schedule of Values

10.2.1 Before the first Application for Payment, the Subcontractor shall submit to the Contractor a schedule of values allocated to the various portions of the Work prepared in such form and supported by such data to substantiate its accuracy as the Contractor may require. This schedule, unless objected to by the Contractor, shall be used only as a basis for the Subcontractor's Applications for Payment.

10.3 Applications for Payment

10.3.1 At least ten days before the date for each progress payment established in the Subcontractor's Agreement, the Subcontractor shall submit to the Contractor an itemized Application for Payment, notarized if required, supported by such data substantiating the Subcontractor's right to payment as the Owner or the Contractor may require, and reflecting such retainage as provided in the Contractor's Subcontract.

10.3.2 Unless otherwise provided in the Contract Documents, payments will be made on account of materials or equipment not incorporated in the Work but delivered and suitably stored at the site and, if approved in advance by the Contractor, payments may similarly be made for materials or equipment stored at some other location agreed upon in writing. Payments made for materials or equipment stored on or off the site shall be conditioned upon submission by the Subcontractor of bills of sale or such other procedures satisfactory to the Contractor to establish the Owner's title to such materials or equipment or otherwise protect the Owner's interest, including applicable insurance and transportation to the site for those materials and equipment stored off the site.

10.3.3 The Subcontractor warrants that title to all Work, materials and equipment covered by an Application for Payment will pass to the Owner either by incorporation in the construction or upon the receipt of payment by the Subcontractor, whichever occurs first, free and clear of all liens, claims, security interests or encumbrances, hereinafter referred to in this Article 10 as "liens"; and that no Work, materials or equipment covered by an Application for Payment will have been acquired by the Subcontractor, or by any other person performing the Work at the site or furnishing materials and equipment for the Project, subject to an agreement under which an interest therein or an encumbrance thereon is retained by the seller or otherwise imposed by the Subcontractor or such other person. All Subcontractors and Sub-subcontractors agree that title will so pass upon their receipt of payment from the Subcontractor.

10.4 Progress Payments

10.4.1 If the Subcontractor has made Application for Payment as above, the Contractor will, with reasonable promptness but not more than seven days after the receipt of payment from the Owner make payment in accordance with the subcontract.

10.4.2 No approval of an application for a progress payment, nor any progress payment, nor any partial or entire use or occupancy of the Project by the Owner, shall constitute an acceptance of any Work not in accordance with the Contract Documents.

10.4.3 The Subcontractor shall promptly pay each Sub-subcontractor upon receipt of payment out of the amount paid to the Subcontractor on account of such Sub-subcontractor's Work, the amount to which said Sub-subcontractor is entitled, reflecting the percentage actually retained, if any, from payments to the Subcontractor on account of such Sub-subcontractor's Work. The Subcontractor shall, by an appropriate agreement with each Sub-subcontractor, also require each Sub-subcontractor to make payments to his subcontractors in a similar manner.

10.5 Payments Withheld

10.5.1 The Contractor may decline to approve an Application for Payment if in his opinion the Application is not adequately supported. If the Subcontractor and Contractor cannot agree on a revised amount, the Contractor shall process the Application for the amount he deems appropriate. The Contractor may also decline to approve any Applications for Payment or, because of subsequently discovered evidence or subsequent inspections, he may nullify in whole or in part any approval previously made to such extent as may be necessary in his opinion because of:

.1 defective work not remedied:

.2 third party claims filed or reasonable evidence indicating probable filing of such claims;

.3 failure of the Subcontractor to make payments properly to Sub-subcontractors or for labor, materials or equipment;

.4 reasonable evidence that the Work cannot be completed for the unpaid balance of the Contract Sum;

.5 damage to the Contractor, the Owner or another contractor working at the Project;

.6 reasonable evidence that the Work will not be completed within the Contract time; or

.7 persistent failure to carry out the Work in accordance with the Contract Documents.

10.5.2 When the above grounds in Subparagraph 10.5.1 are removed, payment shall be made for amounts withheld because of them.

10.6 Failure of Payment

10.6.1 If the Subcontractor is not paid within seven days after payment to the Contractor by the Owner, then the Subcontractor may, upon seven days additional written notice to the Contractor, stop the work until payment of the amount owing has been received. The Contract Sum shall be increased by the amount of the Subcontractor's reasonable costs of shut-down, delay and start-up, which shall be effected by appropriate Change Order in accordance with Paragraph 13.3.

10.7 Substantial Completion

10.7.1 Warranties required by the Contract Documents shall commence on the Date of Substantial Completion of the Project as established by the Certificate of Substantial Completion between the Contractor and Owner.

10.8 Final Completion and Final Payment

10.8.1 Upon receipt of written notice that the Work is ready for final inspection and acceptance and upon receipt of a final Application for Payment, the Architect/Engineer and Contractor will promptly make such inspection and, when they find the Work acceptable under the Contract Documents and the Contract fully performed, the Contractor will promptly approve final payment.

10.8.2 Neither the final payment nor the remaining retained percentage shall become due until the Subcontractor submits to the Contractor (1) an affidavit that all payrolls, bills for materials and equipment, and other indebtedness connected with the Work for which the Owner or his property might in any way be responsible, have been paid or otherwise satisfied, (2) consent of surety, if any, to final payment and (3), if required by the Owner, other data establishing payment or satisfaction of all such obligations, such as receipts, releases and waivers of liens arising out of the Contract, to the extent and in such form as may be designated by the Owner. If any Sub-subcontractor refuses to furnish a release or waiver required by the Owner or Contractor, the Subcontractor may furnish a bond satisfactory to the Owner and Contractor to indemnify them against any such lien. If any such lien remains unsatisfied after all payments are made, the Subcontractor shall refund to the Owner or Contractor all moneys that the latter may be compelled to pay in discharging such lien, including all costs and reasonable attorneys' fees.

10.8.3 If, after Substantial Completion of the Work, final completion thereof is materially delayed through no fault of the Subcontractor or by the issuance of Change Orders affecting final completion, and the Contractor so confirms, the Owner or Contractor shall, upon certification by the Contractor, and without terminating the Contract, make payment of the balance due for that portion of the Work fully completed and accepted. If the remaining balance for Work not fully completed or corrected is less than the retainage stipulated in the Contract Documents, and if bonds have been furnished as provided in Paragraph 8.5, the written consent of the surety to the payment of the balance due for that portion of the Work fully completed and accepted shall be submitted by the Subcontractor to the Contractor prior to such payment. Such payment shall be made under the terms and conditions governing final payment, except that it shall not constitute a waiver of claims.

10.8.4 The making of final payment shall constitute a waiver of all claims by the Contractor except those arising from:

.1 unsettled liens;

.2 faulty or defective Work appearing after Substantial Completion;

.3 failure of the Work to comply with the requirements of the Contract Documents; or

.4 terms of any special warranties required by the Contract Documents.

10.8.5 The acceptance of final payment shall constitute a waiver of all claims by the Subcontractor except those previously made in writing and identified by the Subcontractor as unsettled at the time of the Final Application for Payment.

ARTICLE 11   Protection of Persons and Property

11.1 Safety Precautions and Programs

11.1.1 The Subcontractor shall be responsible for initiating, maintaining and supervising all safety precautions and programs in connection with the Work.

11.1.2 If the Subcontractor fails to maintain the safety precautions required by law or directed by the Contractor, the Contractor may take such steps as necessary and charge the Subcontractor therefor.

11.1.3 The failure of the Contractor to take any such action shall not relieve the Subcontractor of his obligations in Subparagraph 11.1.1.

11.2 Safety of Persons and Property

11.2.1 The Subcontractor shall take all reasonable precautions for the safety of, and shall provide all reasonable protection to prevent damage, injury or loss to:

.1 all employees on the Work and all other persons who may be affected thereby;

.2 all the Work and all materials and equipment to be incorporated therein, whether in storage on or off the site, under the care, custody or control of the Subcontractor or any of his Sub-subcontractors or Sub-subsubcontractors; and

.3 other property at the site or adjacent thereto, including trees, shrubs, lawns, walks, pavements, roadways, structures and utilities not designated for removal, relocation or replacement in the course of construction.

11.2.2 The Subcontractor shall give all notices and comply with all applicable laws, ordinances, rules, regulations and lawful orders of any public authority bearing on the safety of persons or property or their protection from damage, injury or loss.

11.2.3 The Subcontractor shall erect and maintain, as required by existing conditions and progress of the Work, all reasonable safeguards for safety and protection, including posting danger signs and other warnings against hazards, promulgating safety regulations and notifying owners and users of adjacent utilities. If the Subcontractor fails to so comply he shall, at the direction of the Contractor, remove all forces from the Project without cost or loss to the Owner or Contractor, until he is in compliance.

11.2.4 When the use or storage of explosives or other hazardous materials or equipment is necessary for the execution of the Work the Subcontractor shall exercise the utmost care and shall carry on such activities under the supervision of properly qualified personnel.

11.2.5 The Subcontractor shall promptly remedy all damage or loss (other than damage or loss insured under Paragraphs 12.2 and 12.3) to any property referred to in Clauses 11.2.1.2 and 11.2.1.3 caused in whole or in part by the Subcontractor, his Sub-contractors; his Sub-subcontractor, or anyone directly or indirectly employed by any of them or by anyone for whose acts any of them may be liable and for which the Subcontractor is responsible under Clauses 11.2.1.2 and 11.2.1.3, except damage or loss attributable to the acts or omissions of the Owner or Architect/Engineer or anyone directly or indirectly employed by either of them or by anyone for whose acts either of them may be liable, and not attributable to the fault of negligence of the Subcontractor. The foregoing obligations of the Subcontractor are in addition to his obligation under Paragraph 5.17.

11.2.6 The Subcontractor shall designate a responsible member of his organization at the site whose duty shall be the prevention of accidents. This person shall be the Subcontractor's superintendent unless otherwise designated by the Subcontractor in writing to the Contractor.

11.2.7 The Subcontractor shall not load or permit any part of the Work to be loaded so as to endanger its safety.

11.3 Emergencies

11.3.1 In any emergency affecting the safety of persons or property, the Subcontractor shall act, at his discretion, to prevent threatened damage, injury or loss. Any additional compensation or extension of time claimed by the Subcontractor on account of emergency work shall be determined as provided in Article 13 for Changes in the Work.

ARTICLE 12   Insurance

12.1 Subcontractor's Liability Insurance

12.1.1 The Subcontractor shall purchase and maintain such insurance as will protect him from claims set forth below which may arise out of or result from the Subcontractor's operations under the Contract, whether such operations be by himself or by any of his Sub-subcontractors or by anyone directly or indirectly employed by any of them, or by anyone for whose acts any of them may be liable:

.1 claims under workers' compensation, disability benefit and other similar employee benefit acts which are applicable to the work to be performed;

.2 claims for damages because of bodily injury, occupational sickness or disease, or death of his employees under any employer's liability law including, if applicable, those required under maritime or admiralty law for wages, maintenance, and cure;

.3 claims for damages because of bodily injury, sickness or disease, or death of any person other than his employees;

.4 claims for damages insured by usual personal injury liability coverage which are sustained (1) by any person as a result of an offense directly or indirectly related to the employment of such person by the Subcontractor, or (2) by any other person;

.5 claims for damages other than to the work itself because of injury to or destruction of tangible property, including loss of use resulting therefrom; and

.6 claims for damages because of bodily injury or death of any person or property damage arising out of the ownership, maintenance or use of any motor vehicle.

12.1.2 The insurance required by Subparagraph 12.1.1 shall be written for not less than any limits of liability specified in the Contract Documents, or required by law, whichever is greater.

12.1.3 The insurance required by Subparagraph 12.1.1 shall include premises-operations (including explosion, collapse and underground coverage), elevators, independent contractors, products and completed operations, and contractual liability insurance (on a "blanket basis" designating all written contracts), all including broad form property damage coverage. Liability insurance may be arranged under Comprehensive General Liability policies for the full limits required or by a combination of underlying policies for lesser limits with the remaining limits provided by an Excess or Umbrella Liability Policy.

12.1.4 The foregoing policies shall contain a provision that coverages afforded under the policies will not be cancelled or not renewed until at least sixty days' prior written notice has been given to the Contractor. Certificates of Insurance acceptable to the Contractor shall be filed with the Contractor prior to commencement of the Work. Upon request, the Subcontractor shall allow the Contractor to examine the actual policies.

12.2 Property Insurance

12.2.1 Unless otherwise provided, the Owner will purchase and maintain property insurance upon the entire Work at the site to the full insurable value thereof. This insurance shall include the interests of the Owners, the Contractor, the Subcontractors, and Sub-subcontractors in the Work and shall insure against the perils of fire and extended coverage; and shall include "all risk" insurance for physical loss or damage.

12.2.2 The Owner will effect and maintain such boiler and machinery insurance as may be necessary and/or required by law. This insurance shall include the interest of the Owner, the Contractor, the Subcontractors, and Sub-subcontractors in the Work.

12.2.3 Any loss insured under Paragraph 12.2 and 12.3 is to be adjusted with the Owner and Construction Manager and made payable to the Owner and Construction Manager as trustees for the insureds, as their interests may appear, subject to the requirements of any applicable mortgagee clause.

12.2.4 The Owner, the Contractor, the Architect/Engineer, the Subcontractors, and the Sub-subcontractors waive all rights against each other and any other contractor or subcontractor engaged in the project for damages caused by fire or other perils to the extent covered by insurance provided under Paragraphs 12.2 and 12.3, or any other property or consequential loss insurance applicable to the Project, equipment used in the Project, or adjacent structures, except such rights as they may have to the proceeds of such insurance. If any policy of insurance requires an endorsement to maintain coverage with such waivers, the owner of such policy will cause the policy to be so endorsed. The Owner will require, by appropriate agreement, written where legally required for validity, similar waivers in favor of the Subcontractors and Sub-subcontractors by any separate contractor and his subcontractors.

12.2.5 The Owner and Contractor shall deposit in a separate account any money received as trustees, and shall distribute it in accordance with such agreement as the parties in interest may reach, or in accordance with an award by arbitration in which case the procedure shall be as provided in Paragraph 8.8. If after such loss no special agreement is made, replacement of damaged work shall be covered by an appropriate Change Order.

12.2.6 The Owner and Contractor as trustees shall have power to adjust and settle any loss with the insurers unless one of the parties in interest shall object in writing within five days after the occurrence of loss to the Owner's and Contractor's exercise of this power, and if such objection be made, arbitrators shall be chosen as provided in Paragraph 8.8. The Owner and Contractor as trustees shall, in that case, make settlement with the insurers in accordance with the directions of such arbitrators. If distribution of the insurance proceeds by arbitration is required, the arbitrators will direct such distribution.

12.2.7 If the Owner finds it necessary to occupy or use a portion or portions of the Work prior to Substantial Completion thereof, such occupancy shall not commence prior to a time mutually agreed to by the Owner and Contractor and to which the insurance company or companies providing the property insurance have consented by endorsement to the policy or policies. This insurance shall not be cancelled or lapsed on account of such partial occupancy. Consent of the Contractor and of the insurance company or companies to such occupancy or use shall not be unreasonably withheld.

ARTICLE 13   Changes in the Work

13.1 Change Orders

13.1.1 A Change Order is a written order to the Subcontractor signed by the Contractor, issued after the execution of the Contract, authorizing a Change in the Work or an adjustment in the Contract Sum or the Contract Time. The Contract Sum and the Contract Time may be changed only by Change Order. A Change Order signed by the Subcontractor indicates his agreement therewith, including the adjustment in the Contract Sum or the Contract Time.

13.1.2 The Contractor, without invalidating the Contract, may order Changes in the Work within the General scope of the Contract consisting of additions, deletions or other revisions, the Contract Sum and the Contract Time being adjusted accordingly. All such changes in the Work shall be authorized by Change Order, and shall be performed under the applicable conditions of the Contract Documents.

13.1.3 The cost or credit to the Contractor resulting from a Change in the Work shall be determined in one or more of the following ways:

.1 by mutual acceptance of a lump sum properly itemized and supported by sufficient substantiating data to permit evaluation; or

.2 by unit prices stated in the Contract Documents or subsequently agreed upon; or

.3 by cost to be determined in a manner agreed upon by the parties and a mutually acceptable fixed or percentage fee; or

.4 by the method provided in Subparagraph 13.1.4.

13.1.4 If none of the methods set forth in Clauses 13.1.3.1, 13.1.3.2 or 13.1.3.3 is agreed upon, the Subcontractor, provided he receives a written order signed by the Contractor, shall promptly proceed with the Work involved. The cost of such Work shall be determined by the Contractor on the basis of the reasonable expenditures and savings of those performing the Work attributable to the change, including, in the case of an increase in the Contract Sum, a reasonable allowance for overhead and profit. In such case, and also under

Clauses 13.1.3.3 and 13.1.3.4 above, the Subcontractor shall keep and present, in such form as the Contractor may prescribe, an itemized accounting together with appropriate supporting data for inclusion in a Change Order. Unless otherwise provided in the Contract Documents, cost shall be limited to the following: cost of materials, including sales tax and cost of delivery; cost of labor, including social security, old age and unemployment insurance, and fringe benefits required by agreement or custom; workers' or workmen's compensation insurance; bond premiums; rental value of equipment and machinery; and the additional costs of supervision and field office personnel directly attributable to the change. Pending final determination of cost, payments on account shall be made as determined by the Contractor. The amount of credit to be allowed by the Subcontractor for any deletion or change which results in a net decrease in the Contract Sum will be the amount of the actual net cost as confirmed by the Contractor. When both additions and credits covering related Work or substitutions are involved in any one change, the allowance for overhead and profit shall be figured on the basis of the net increase, if any, with respect to that change.

13.1.5 If unit prices are stated in the Contract Documents or subsequently agreed upon, and if the quantities originally contemplated are so changed in a proposed Change Order that application of the agreed unit prices to the quantities of Work proposed will cause substantial inequity to the Owner, the Contractor, or the Subcontractor, the applicable unit prices shall be equitably adjusted.

13.2 Concealed Conditions

13.2.1 Should concealed conditions encountered in the performance of the Work below the surface of the ground or should concealed or unknown conditions in an existing structure be at variance with the conditions indicated by the Contract Documents or should unknown physical conditions below the surface of the ground or should concealed or unknown conditions in an existing structure of an unusual nature, differing materially from those ordinarily encountered and generally recognized as inherent in work of the character provided for in this Contract, be encountered, the Contract Sum shall be equitably adjusted by Change Order upon claim by either party made within twenty days after the first observance of the conditions.

13.3 Claims for Additional Cost

13.3.1 If the Subcontractor wishes to make a claim for an increase in the Contract Sum, he shall give the Contractor written notice thereof within twenty days after the occurrence of the event giving rise to such claim. This notice shall be given by the Subcontractor before proceeding to execute the Work, except in an emergency endangering life or property in which case the Subcontractor shall proceed in accordance with Paragraph 11.3. No such claim shall be valid unless so made. Any change in the Contract Sum resulting from such claim shall be authorized by Change Order.

13.3.2 If the Subcontractor claims that additional cost is involved because of, but not limited to, (1) any written interpretation issued pursuant to Subparagraph 3.2.2, (2) any order by the Contractor to stop the Work pursuant to Paragraph 4.3 where the Subcontractor was not at fault, or (3) any written order for a minor change in the Work issued pursuant to Paragraph 13.4, the Subcontractor shall make such claim as provided in Subparagraph 13.3.1.

13.4 Minor Changes in the Work

13.4.1 The Architect/Engineer will have authority to order through the Contractor minor changes in the Work not involving an adjustment in the Contract Sum or an extension of the Contract Time and not inconsistent with the intent of the Contract Documents. Such changes shall be effected by written order and such changes shall be binding on the Owner, the Contractor and the Subcontractor. The Subcontractor shall carry out such written orders promptly.

ARTICLE 14   Uncovering and Correction of Work

14.1 Uncovering of Work

14.1.1 If any portion of the Work should be covered contrary to the request of the Contractor or Architect/Engineer, or to requirements specifically expressed in the Contract Documents, it must, if required in writing by the Contractor, be uncovered for their observation and replaced, at the Subcontractor's expense.

14.1.2 If any other portion of the Work has been covered which the Contractor or the Architect/Engineer has not specifically requested to observe prior to being covered, the Architect/Engineer or Contractor may request to see such Work and it shall be uncovered by the Subcontractor. If such Work be found in accordance with the Contract Documents, the cost of uncovering and replacement shall, by appropriate Change Order, be charged to the Contractor. If such Work be found not in accordance with the Contract Documents, the Subcontractor shall pay such costs unless it be found that this condition was caused by a separate subcontractor employed as provided in Article 7, and in that event the separate subcontractor shall be responsible for the payment of such costs.

14.2 Correction of Work

14.2.1 The Subcontractor shall promptly correct all Work rejected by the Architect/Engineer or the Contractor as defective or a failing to conform to the Contract Documents whether observed before or after Substantial Completion and whether or not fabricated, installed or completed. The Subcontractor shall bear all costs of correcting such rejected Work, including compensation for the Architect/Engineer's and/or Contractor's additional services made necessary thereby.

14.2.2 If, within one year after the Date of Substantial Completion of Work or designated portion thereof, or within one year after acceptance by the Owner of designated equipment or within such longer period of time as may be prescribed by law or by the terms of any applicable special warranty required by the Contract Documents, any of the Work is found to be defective or not in accordance with the Contract Documents, the Subcontractor shall correct it promptly after receipt of a written notice from the Owner or Contractor to do so unless the Owner or Contractor has previously given the Subcontractor a written acceptance of such condition. This obligation shall survive the termination of the Contract. The Owner or Contractor shall give such notice promptly after discovery of the condition.

14.2.3 The Subcontractor shall remove from the site all portions of the Work which are defective or non-conforming and which have not been corrected under Subparagraphs 14.2.1, 5.5.1 and 14.2.2 unless removal has been waived by the Owner.

14.2.4 If the Subcontractor fails to correct defective or non-conforming Work as provided in Subparagraphs 5.5.1, 14.2.1 and 14.2.2, the Owner or Contractor may correct it in accordance with Subparagraph 4.3.2.

14.2.5 If the Subcontractor does not proceed with the correction of such defective or non-conforming Work within a reasonable time fixed by written notice from the Contractor, the Owner or Contractor may remove it and may store the materials or equipment at the expense of the Subcontractor. If the Subcontractor does not pay the cost of such removal and storage within ten days thereafter, the Owner or Contractor may upon ten additional days' written notice sell such Work at auction or at private sale and shall account for the net proceeds thereof, after deducting all the costs that should have been borne by the Subcontractor, including compensation for the Contractor's additional services made necessary thereby. If such proceeds of sale do not cover all costs which the Subcontractor and an appropriate Change Order shall be issued. If the payments then or thereafter due the Subcontractor are not sufficient to cover such amount, the Subcontractor shall pay the difference to the Owner or Contractor.

14.2.6 The Subcontractor shall bear the cost of making good all work of the Contractor, other Subcontractors other contractors destroyed or damaged by such removal or correction.

14.3 Acceptance of Defective or Nonconforming Work

14.3.1 If the Owner or Contractor prefers to accept defective or non-conforming Work, he may do so instead of requiring its removal and correction, in which case a Change Order will be issued to reflect reduction in the Contract Sum where appropriate and equitable. Such adjustment shall be effected whether or not final payment has been made.

ARTICLE 15   Termination of the Contract

15.1 Termination by the Subcontractor

15.1.1 If the Work should be stopped for a period of thirty days by the Subcontractor because of failure to receive payment in accordance with the Contract, then the Subcontractor may, upon seven additional days' written notice to the Contractor, terminate the Contract and recover from the Contractor payment for all Work executed and for any proven loss sustained upon any materials, equipment, tools, construction equipment and machinery, including reasonable profit and damages.

15.2 Termination by the Contractor

15.2.1 If the Subcontractor is adjudged a bankrupt, or if he makes a general assignment for the benefit of his creditors, or if a receiver is appointed on account of his insolvency, or if he persistently or repeatedly refuses or fails, except in cases for which extension of time is provided, to supply enough properly skilled workmen or proper materials, or if he fails to make prompt payment to Sub-subcontractors or for materials or labor, or persistently disregards laws, ordinances, rules, regulations or orders of any public authority having jurisdiction, or otherwise is guilty of a substantial violation of a provision of the Contract Documents, then the Contractor may, without prejudice to any right or remedy and after giving the Subcontractor and his surety, if any, seven days' written notice, terminate the employment of the Subcontractor and take possession of the site and of all materials, equipment, tools, construction equipment and machinery thereon owned by the Subcontractor and may finish the Work by whatever method he may deem expedient. In such case the Subcontractor shall not be entitled to receive any further payment until the Work is finished.

15.2.2 If the unpaid balance of the Contract Sum exceeds the cost of finishing the Work, including compensation for the Contractor's additional services made necessary thereby, such excess shall be paid to the Subcontractor. If such costs exceed the unpaid balance, the Subcontractor shall pay the difference to the Contractor.

15.2.3 The Contractor has the option to terminate his Agreement with the Owner if the Work is stopped for a period of thirty days under an order of any court or other public authority having jurisdiction, or as a result of an act of government, such as a declaration of a national emergency making materials unavailable, or from the failure of the Owner to make payment. If the Contractor exercises such option he may then terminate the contracts with the Subcontractors and the Subcontractors shall be entitled to recover such amounts for his proven losses as the Contractor may be able to recover from the Owner.

TWO   Documents Applicable to Subcontractors and Suppliers

Standard Subbid Proposal Form with Suggested Modifications
§2.01 *Author's Comments*
§2.02 *Form—Standard Subbid Proposal*

Subcontract Agreement
§2.03 *Author's Comments*
§2.04 *Form—Subcontract Agreement*

Purchase Order Forms
§2.05 *Author's Comments*
§2.06 *Form—Short*
§2.07 *Form—Long*

Standard Subcontractor's Applications for Payment with Suggested Modifications
§2.08 *Author's Comments*
§2.09 *Form—Subcontractor's Application for Payment*

Waiver, Release and Discharge Forms
§2.10 *Author's Comments*
§2.11 *Forms—Waiver, Release and Discharge*

A. STANDARD SUBBID PROPOSAL FORM WITH SUGGESTED MODIFICATIONS

§2.01   **1. Author's Comments**   This form has received general recognition by various construction associations. It is a clear document. Its regular use could and would avoid numerous areas of litigation. There are, however, certain major changes which should be made.

A provision should be inserted into the subbid proposal which would form the written basis for precluding the subcontractor from withdrawing the bid, and which would be evidence for the enforcement of that promise on the basis of promissory estoppel. The subbid proposal should be the basis for the future subcontract, if it is relied upon by the prime contractor.

The second major change is that the subcontractor, with the submission of the bid, should agree to execute the prime contractor's standard form subcontract agreement.

This would avoid subsequent disputes and delays. If this is stated in the bid document, then the parties know where they stand at the time of bidding.

§2.02 1. FORM Standard Subbid Proposal

SUBCONTRACTOR _____ Project _____

Address _____ Location _____
_____ Location _____

PRIME [GENERAL] CONTRACTOR __ A&E _____

_____ Bid Time & Date _____
Address _____ Subbid Time & Date _____

Type of work (including specification sections) _____

(List the category(ies) this proposal will cover, such as plumbing, heating, air conditioning and ventilation, electrical and elevators.)
This proposal includes furnishing all materials and performing all work in the category(ies) listed above, as required by the plans, specifications, general and special conditions and addenda _____, *and the prime contract.*
       (Here list addenda by numbers)
Identify work to be excluded by specification paragraph otherwise the subcontractor will be responsible for all work in the above category(ies) required by the specifications and plans, *and other prime contract documents.*

If this proposal, including prices, is accepted, the subcontractor agrees to enter into *the prime contractor's standard form [a]* subcontract and, if required, furnish performance and payment bonds from _____
                    (Name of surety company or agency)
guaranteeing full performance of the work and payment of all costs incident thereto, and the cost of the bond is not included in this proposal. *The subcontractor submits this subbid with the intent and knowledge that the prime contractor may rely on it.*
This proposal will remain in effect and will not be withdrawn by the subcontractor for a period of 30 days or for the same period of time required by the *prime* contract documents for the *prime [general]* contractor in regard to the prime bid, plus 15 days, whichever period is longer.

_____
Subcontractor

_____
By   (Title)

BASE BID _____

_____

Alternates

	Add	Deduct
1.	$	$
2.	$	$
3.	$	$
4.	$	$
5.	$	$
6.	$	$
7.	$	$
8.	$	$

UNIT PRICES

(Insert Unit Prices if Requested)

	Unit	Add	Deduct
1.		$	$
2.		$	$
3.		$	$
4.		$	$
5.		$	$
6.		$	$
7.		$	$
8.		$	$

(Any Additional Information)

FOOTNOTE:

1 General Services Administration procurement regulations and the CMSCI and the AGC urge that this proposal be submitted to the general contractor at least 48 hours before the opening of the prime bids. As contained in Title 41—Public Contracts & Property Management, Chapter 5B—Public Buildings Service, General Services Administration—Subpart 5B–2.2, paragraph (j), these regulations specifically state: "In order to effectively implement the objectives of the foregoing provisions and to assure the timely receipt of accurate bids, the bidder is requested to urge all subcontractors intending to submit a proposal for work involved in the project to submit to all bidders to whom they intend to bid, a written proposal (or written abstract) with or without price, outlining in detail the specific sections of the specifications to be included in their work as well as any exceptions or exclusions therefrom. It is suggested that such written proposal be submitted to the bidder at least 48 hours in advance of the bid opening."

Standard Subbid Proposal, reprinted by permission of The Associated General Contractors of America, The National Electrical Contractors Association, The Mechanical Contractors Association of America, The Sheet Metal and Air Conditioning Contractors National Association, and The National Association of Plumbing-Heating-Cooling Contractors.

B. SUBCONTRACT AGREEMENT

§2.03   1. Author's Comments   The subcontract can make the difference between success and failure. It is the agreement under which a substantial part of the work will be done. Although the author advocates a very strict subcontract which limits the prime contractor's liability, the subcontract is not meant to be unconscionable. It must always be remembered that as a prime contractor, not only is there an obligation to the owner to perform in accordance with the prime contract documents, but also there is an obligation with respect to the various subcontractors and suppliers. Seldom is the subcontractor's or supplier's potential liability equal to that of the prime contractor. The death rate for the prime contractor due to a single bad job is believed to be substantially higher than the mortality rate for the subcontractor due to a single bad contract. With the risk of loss and dual fronts present, the prime contractor must take great care in the preparation of a firm subcontract agreement. It must be remembered that standard forms can always be negotiated and modified for particular circumstances to fit specific needs; however, the original standard should be drafted to offer as much legal protection as possible.

Even with the use of a standard form, it must be remembered that courts often will interpret similar provisions differently in different jurisdictions. Each case stands on its own facts, existing law, and future concepts. Therefore, there is no absolute position. The prime contractor cannot hide behind clauses which are patently obscene. Courts will not enforce provisions of prime contracts or subcontracts which are so reprehensible and unconscionable that they are contrary to public policy. On the other hand, the courts will enforce strict provisions which are unfavorable to the subcontractor, provided that the clauses are not against public policy.

A rule of law which must be remembered is that a contract will be interpreted against the party who drafted it, provided that the party to whom it is furnished interprets that document in a reasonable manner. Since it is the prime contractor who is presenting the document to the subcontractor, it probably will be construed in favor of the subcontractor. Before the work even is commenced, this rule of law is a strike against the prime contractor. Therefore, it is imperative that the document, which is and should be prepared by the prime contractor, be strict, reasonable, and unambiguous.

The first concern of the prime contractor should be the incorporation into the subcontract of the prime contract documents. The subcontractor should be bound by the same obligations as the prime contractor. See the following articles in §2.04:

II DOCUMENTS AND DEFINITIONS
III SCOPE OF WORK
IV MUTUALITY OF DOCUMENTS.

Although many subcontractors try to deny these obligations, the reasons for subjecting the subcontractor to the obligations of the prime contract far outweigh the disadvantages. To subcontract in any other fashion can only create litigation. There is a single project being constructed, and those documents (the prime contract) must be made part of the subcontract.

The prime contractor must try to fill the gaps that may result from the division of work between the various subcontractors and suppliers, as well as the contractor's employees. This legal and practical concern is covered by the articles of construction which are incorporated in the standard form subcontract. See the following articles in §2.04:

III SCOPE OF WORK
IV MUTUALITY OF DOCUMENTS
V RELATED WORK
VI LAWS, REGULATIONS, ETC.

The changes clause, Article VII, must offer protection to the prime contractor, as well as tie the subcontractor into the prime contract. The prime contractor must also retain the right to order changes, in writing, even when terms have not been agreed upon. However, the prime contractor should have a mechanism to establish a dollar ceiling and other limits on future changes. Unless the prime contractor is clearly at fault, the subcontractor's rights should be linked to the prime contract. This and the assumption of risks that the prime contractor undertakes are found in Article VIII, covering claims. The claims clause is a form of liquidating agreement, and it often deters or eliminates litigation. In other instances it reduces the prime contractor's potential liability. It is an important contractual safeguard.

The subcontractor cannot be divorced from the prime contract. The mutuality of obligation of the subcontractor is evidenced by all the provisions of the subcontract, and is specifically noted in the following articles in §2.04:

IX MATERIAL, INSPECTION, STORAGE AND APPROVALS
XI PROGRESS AND PERFORMANCE
XII INSURANCE AND INDEMNIFICATION
XVII BONDS
XVIII TERMINATION
XIX LABOR RELATIONS
XX PAYMENTS
XXV CONDITIONAL CONTRACT
XXVI APPROVAL OF SUBMITTALS
XXVII GUARANTY AND WARRANTY
XXVIII CANCELLATION
XXX SUB-SUBCONTRACTS.

It should not be forgotten that the project is not being built for the prime contractor's benefit; rather, the prime contractor is performing work for another party and is substantially in the same position as the subcontractor. The prime contractor has greater risks and has obligations to more parties. This is evidenced in the progress and performance provision, as well as in Article XX, concerning payments. The prime contractor must be able to control the work in order to perform the prime contract. The subcontractor's obligation to the prime contractor must be such that the prime contractor can take the various parts and put them together as required. Neither the prime contractor nor the subcontractor should finance the project for the owner. This means that both should wait for payment until the owner pays. The subcontractor should not be able to force payment prior to the prime contractor's receipt of funds. To assure that the prime contract is being performed properly requires the subcontractor to accept full, technical responsibility and to warranty and guarantee obligations. This is covered in the following articles on §2.04:

VI LAWS, REGULATIONS, ETC.
IX MATERIAL, INSPECTION, STORAGE AND APPROVALS
XI PROGRESS AND PERFORMANCE
XVI SUBLET AND ASSIGNMENT

XVIII TERMINATION
XX PAYMENTS
XXVI APPROVAL OF SUBMITTALS
XXVII GUARANTY AND WARRANTY

The majority of the mandatory clauses relate to the prime contractor's securing its relationship with the owner. If the relationship with the owner should terminate, the prime contractor must also be able to cancel the subcontract. This is provided in Article XXVIII CANCELLATION. However, the prime contractor must also consider the position it maintains with the various other subcontractors and suppliers. This risk is partially protected by all provisions, but more specifically by the following articles in §2.04:

XI PROGRESS AND PERFORMANCE
XII INSURANCE AND INDEMNIFICATION
XVIII TERMINATION
XIX LABOR RELATIONS
XX PAYMENTS
XXVIII CANCELLATION.

Many of the articles are necessary simply for the prime contractor to perform the overall obligation under the prime contract, to maintain control of the orderly progression of the work, and to protect the prime contractor. These clauses include the following articles in §2.04:

XI PROGRESS AND PERFORMANCE
XIII PRINCIPAL RELATIONSHIP
XV SUBCONTRACTOR'S REPRESENTATIVE
XVI SUBLET AND ASSIGNMENT
XVII BONDS
XVIII TERMINATION
XIX LABOR RELATIONS
XXIV DAMAGES
XXVIII CANCELLATION
XXX SUB-SUBCONTRACTS.

In case of breach, and more importantly to try to avoid problems, remembering that the prime contractor is on the hook for a greater liability with the owner than is a single subcontractor, and remembering the fact that the prime contractor has a complex coordination obligation, the prime contractor must assure itself of certain legal rights in order to protect itself against liability. It must also establish a means for pursuing its rights against the subcontractor. Although all clauses offer some protection, specific clauses are incorporated with this being their primary objective. These articles in §2.04 include those relating to:

VI LAWS, REGULATIONS, ETC.
VIII CLAIMS
XI PROGRESS AND PERFORMANCE
XII INSURANCE AND INDEMNIFICATION
XIV TAXES, CHARGES, ETC.
XVII BONDS
XVIII TERMINATION

XX PAYMENTS
XXI LIENS AND ENCUMBRANCES
XXII GOVERNING LAW
XXIII ORAL MODIFICATIONS
XXIV DAMAGES
XXVIII CANCELLATION
XXIX LEGAL FORUM.

The subcontract form, set out in §2.04, offers the prime contractor reasonable protection. The articles overlap, but each has a purpose. As stated, the form can be altered through negotiations, but each modification will dilute the rights of the prime contractor. The subcontract form is not as massive as some construction documents which exist, but be assured that it is written by an attorney who is an advocate of the prime contractor.

§2.04 2. FORM Subcontract Agreement

Agreement made this _____ day of _____, 19____ by and between
_____,
_____ ,
with its principal place of business located at _____ ,
(hereinafter designated as "Contractor") and _____ ,
with its principal place of business located at _____ ,
(hereinafter designated as "Subcontractor"):

WHEREAS, the Contractor has heretofore entered a contract (hereinafter designated as the "Prime Contract") with _____ ,
(hereinafter designated as the "Principal"), to furnish certain work, labor and services necessary for the construction of a _____
(hereinafter designated as the "Project"), in accordance with Prime Contract documents including certain Plans and Specifications prepared by _____
(hereinafter designated as the "A/E"):

WITNESS: The Contractor and the Subcontractor, in consideration of mutual covenants do hereby enter this Agreement, incorporating the Articles of Construction, Prime Contract, Plans, Specifications, and other incorporated documents (hereinafter collectively designated as "Contract") and agree as follows:

The Subcontractor shall provide and furnish all labor, materials, tools, supplies, equipment, services, facilities, supervision, administration, etc. necessary for the proper and complete performance and acceptance of the following work:

In consideration of the Subcontractor's performance of this Contract, the Articles of Construction and the Prime Contract, the Contractor shall pay to the Subcontractor the total sum of _____ Dollars ($_____).

Articles Of Construction

I. **Articles of Construction:** These Articles are made part of and are incorporated into the

Contract between the Contractor and the Subcontractor. The terms and conditions contained herein shall be binding on the Subcontractor.

II. Documents and Definitions: The Prime Contract is incorporated herein by reference and made an integral part of this Contract. The Prime Contract includes, but is not limited to, the agreement between the Contractor and Principal, all addendum, modifications, revisions, drawings, specifications, details, all general, technical, supplementary and special terms and conditions, as well as any and all other documents listed in or referred to by the Prime Contract. The Prime Contract can be reviewed by the Subcontractor at the Contractor's principal place of business during normal business hours. The Subcontractor is bound, responsible, obligated and liable to the Contractor as the Contractor is bound, responsible, obligated and liable under the Prime Contract. The term "Contract" as used herein shall include all documents incorporated into and made a part of the Agreement between the Contractor and Subcontractor, and any revisions thereto. The term "Architect/Engineer" (hereinafter referred to as "A/E") shall be deemed to be that representative directing the work for the Principal, or any other person authorized by the Prime Contract to direct, judge, approve or reject any matter or thing connected with the performance of the Prime Contract. The Prime Contract and this Contract shall be interpreted together and in harmony with one another. However, in case of conflict between the Prime Contract and this Contract, this Contract shall govern the relationship between the Contractor and the Subcontractor. The Subcontractor must call any such conflict or discrepancy to the Contractor's attention, in writing, prior to executing this Contract.

III. Scope of Work: All work included in the Contract shall be done under the direction of the Contractor, and to the satisfaction of the Contractor, Principal and A/E. Said work shall be performed in strict accord with the Prime Contract. The work to be performed by the Subcontractor includes that work specifically set forth in this Contract, as well as any and all other work incident or related thereto, including but not limited to that work reasonably necessary for a complete and proper Project, or which is necessary to have a properly working and totally acceptable system and Project. All work covered by this Contract shall be performed in a skillful and workmanlike manner with material, equipment, etc. being both new and of the best kind and grade for the purpose intended. It being the express intent that all work usually performed by the trades covered by this Contract and required by the Prime Contract shall be performed by the Subcontractor, in addition to that work specifically set forth herein. Said work shall be deemed to include any and all work required to be performed by the Contractor, Principal, A/E and by any judicial or administrative tribunal. The Subcontractor agrees, without additional compensation, to perform, conform and abide by all decisions issued by the Contractor, when the Contractor has been directed to perform, conform and abide by similar decisions, without additional compensation, issued by the Principal or A/E. The Subcontractor shall provide, at its own expense, all temporary and permanent tools, scaffolding, hoisting facilities, elevator service, implements, water, heat, light, power, electric, ventilation, storage space, shop and working drawings, test, samples, models, guarantees, permits, licenses, unloading facilities and services, temporary utilities, etc., and all other items necessary for the proper performance of this Contract and acceptance of the Project. The Subcontractor shall pay for all inspection fees, royalties, and license fees. The Subcontractor shall make all necessary arrangements and agreements so as not to infringe any patents, trademarks, or copyrights.

IV. Mutality of Documents: The Subcontractor hereby acknowledges that it has carefully reviewed and examined this Contract with all of its contract documents, and all other documents directly or indirectly relating to this Contract; and that any and all prior ambiguities and discrepancies have previously been clarified and/or corrected. The Subcontractor agrees that it will not make any claim or demand upon the Contractor based upon or arising out of any misunderstanding or misconception on its part of the provisions and requirements of the Prime Contract or this Contract. Any information given or statements made to the Subcontractor by the Contractor or others as to nature or characteristics of the work included herein, or as to the particular details relating to the Subcontractor's work, shall not reduce the work to be performed by the Subcontractor under this Contract. The Subcontractor acknowledges that it has fully examined and analyzed all conditions that could affect its performance and that no conditions exist which would affect the progress, performance or price of this Contract. The Subcontractor will perform and furnish any and all work, labor, services and/or materials, mentioned, shown, depected or required in any Contract document. In case of any ambiguity or discrepancy in this Contract, the Subcontractor shall promptly submit the matter to the Contractor, in writing, otherwise the Subcontractor will be held solely liable to make any change necessary to correct same. Any decision or adjustment by the Subcontractor without a written determination by the Contractor shall be at the Subcontractor's sole risk and expense. Any and all decisions by the Principal or the A/E relative to any ambiguity or discrepancy shall be binding on the Subcontractor when furnished to the Subcontractor by the Contractor. The Subcontractor shall be required to do all things and be bound by all rulings of the Principal or A/E to the same extent and degree as the Contractor is bound thereto.

V. Related Work: The Subcontractor, before proceeding with any work under this Contract will accurately check and verify all previous and surrounding work done by others and determine the correctness of same. The Subcontractor shall field measure all work relating to its work. The failure of the Subcontractor to detect and disclose any existing discrepancies or nonconformities and report same to the Contractor, in writing, before commencing its work shall relieve the Contractor of any and all responsibility for same, and the Subcontractor shall be responsible and liable for all resulting damages, costs and expenses arising as a result of discrepancies and nonconformities which should have been discovered by the Subcontractor.

VI. Laws, Regulations, Etc.: All work, labor, services and materials to be furnished, supplied or performed by the Subcontractor must strictly comply with all Federal, State, Local, Municipal, as well as any and all other governing jurisdictions' and authorities' Laws, Rules, Regulations, Statutes, Ordinances, and Directives (hereinafter designated as "Laws"). All work, labor, services or materials, in addition to that specifically required by this Contract, but necessary to fully comply with said Laws, will be furnished by the Subcontractor as part of this Contract and without any additional compensation. If the Subcontractor discovers or should have discovered any variance between its Contract and any of the governing Laws or legislation, the Subcontractor shall be responsible to promptly notify the Contractor, in writing, and to make the necessary changes before proceeding with its work. The Subcontractor agrees to indemnify and save the Contractor, Principal and A/E harmless from and against any and all claims, loss or expense caused or occasioned directly or indirectly by its failure to fully comply herewith. Subcontractor shall comply with all safety and health laws.

VII. Changes: The Contractor may order Changes in the work. The Subcontractor shall not be entitled to nor shall it receive any increase or upward adjustment in its Contract price unless said amount and liability are acknowledged, in writing, by Contractor's authorized representative, which representative must have written authority for such acts, otherwise the Subcontractor shall proceed at its own risk and expense. No alteration, addition, omission or change shall be made in the work, or the method or manner of performance of same, except upon the written Change Order of the Contractor. Any change or adjustment in the Contract price by virtue of such Change Order shall be specifically stated in said Change Order. Change Orders are subject to the terms of these Articles and all other Contract documents. Prior to the issuance of any Change Order, the Contractor may require the Subcontractor to furnish to the Contractor a detailed breakdown showing the difference in value of the work, labor, services, and materials altered, added, omitted or changed by the proposed Change Order. If an agreement as to monetary allowance or other term in the Change Order cannot be reached, the Contractor, by an authorized representative, may direct, in writing, the Subcontractor to perform the work with the final adjustment reserved until final completion of both this Contract, and the Prime Contract. The monetary amount for the performance of any Change Order shall not exceed the allowance set forth in the Subcontractor's prior price breakdown. The failure of the Subcontractor to immediately commence performance of any Change Order, when so directed, in executed written form by the Contractor, whether or not all terms have been agreed upon, may be deemed a material breach and the Subcontractor held in default of this Contract. Any extension of time needed as a result of a proposed Change Order shall be requested by the Subcontractor, in writing, prior to the issuance of the Change Order, and shall be incorporated therein. There shall be no other monetary or time allowance, direct or indirect, to the Subcontractor other than what is specifically written in the Change Order, including, but not limited to, delays, suspensions, escalations, impact or other cost factors. Ordinary field modifications which do not substantially increase Subcontractor's cost of this Contract will be performed without any price adjustment. Where unit prices are stipulated in the Contract, all adjustments, whether increases or decreases, shall be made in accordance with said units. Said units shall be deemed to include all general and administrative expenses, overhead, profit, supervision, extended performance cost factors, and all other direct and indirect expenses. If the Contractor elects the option to direct the Change Order work to be done by the Subcontractor on a time and material basis, the Subcontractor shall prepare daily time and material invoices which shall be submitted to the Contractor on a daily basis. Said daily time and material invoices shall include only direct out-of-pocket material and labor costs with a maximum total markup of 10 percent. The 10 percent mark-up on time and material invoices is deemed to be full and complete compensation to the Subcontractor for all general and administrative expenses, overhead, supervision, and profit. No payment shall be made for holiday or other nonworking time. The Subcontractor shall in no event be entitled to, nor shall it receive any compensation or allowance for any Change Order in an amount greater than that which the Contractor actually receives from the Principal, less a reasonable deduction for work performed by the Contractor, as well as for the Contractor's overhead and profit. The issuance of any Change Order and payment thereof, prior to completion and acceptance of the Project, shall not preclude the Contractor from questioning the validity thereof and recouping payment therefor, where, on final settlement, it appears that the Change Order work was neither extra nor additional work under a proper interpretation of this Contract or the Prime Contract. No Change Order shall vary, abrogate, avoid, or otherwise affect the terms, conditions and provisions of this Contract except as specifically set forth in the Change Order.

VIII. Claims: The Contractor may, upon the written request of the Subcontractor, appeal on behalf of the Subcontractor from any ruling or decision of the Principal or A/E, or institute any action or proceeding to recover damages by reason of any affirmative claim by the Subcontractor, or by reason of any deduction or refusal to pay by the Principal, for any reason, involving the work or performance of the Subcontractor. In that event, the Subcontractor shall pay all costs attributable thereto and shall render all assistance requested by Contractor. The Subcontractor shall be bound by the determination of the Principal, the A/E, or in the event of an appeal or further action or proceeding, by the determination of same, and shall be entitled only to its proportionate share of any actual net recovery, less overhead and profit to the Contractor and less the Contractor's expenses and attorney's fees in handling said matter. The Subcontractor hereby waives and releases any and all claims, causes of actions, and rights to further payment beyond the Contract amount, except as the Contractor may receive funds or extensions of time from the Principal or A/E. The Subcontractor shall post whatever security may be required by the Contractor to cover the

Contractor's cost and expenses, including attorney's fees, prior to and as a condition to the Contractor's proceeding on the Subcontractor's behalf.

IX. Material, Inspection, Storage and Approvals: The Subcontractor shall provide at its own place of business, at the places of business of its subcontractors and suppliers, and at the Project, sufficient safe and proper facilities for the inspection of the Subcontractor's work by the Contractor, Principal, A/E, or any other authorized representative. The Subcontractor must be prepared, at all times, to prove the exact quantities and qualities of the materials and equipment being used. If the Subcontractor is assigned a storage area for its equipment, material and tools, it shall not store any item outside of the designated area. The Subcontractor shall be responsible for the receipt, delivery, unloading, storage, warehousing, protection, insurance and all other risk of loss relating to any materials or equipment it is to furnish, install, provide, or have provided to it under this Contract. If the Contractor furnishes material to the Subcontractor, then the Subcontractor shall be obligated to inspect all material and equipment at time of receipt or delivery to it. The Subcontractor shall be responsible to immediately notify the Contractor, in writing, of any defects or non-conformity in the material or equipment so received or delivered. Failure to notify the Contractor shall be deemed an acknowledgment and acceptance of the material as being in accord with this Contract. The Subcontractor shall be liable for any damages incurred by the Contractor as a result of its failure to so notify the Contractor. It is the Subcontractor's obligation, upon direction by the Contractor, to take all necessary steps, including but not limited to delivery of samples, tests and reports, guarantees, drawings, manuals, certificates, details, warranties, inspections, etc., to obtain any and all required approvals necessary or required under this Contract or the Prime Contract. The Subcontractor shall, within 24 hours after receiving specific written notice from the Contractor, commence to take down and remove any designated portion of its work which is condemned, disapproved, or is questioned as not being in strict compliance and conformity with the requirements of this Contract or the Prime Contract. The Subcontractor shall promptly, at its own expense, correct and rectify same. If the Contractor determines that it will accept non-conforming work, the Contractor shall be entitled to a credit for the non-conformity, plus all other costs incurred. The Subcontractor shall, at its own expense, fully protect, insure and secure its work from injury or damage. Any damage prior to final acceptance and payment for the Project shall be immediately corrected and rectified by the Subcontractor at its sole expense. Inspection or supervision by the Contractor shall not relieve the Subcontractor of its obligations herein. The Subcontractor shall promptly perform any and all punch list work submitted to it by the Contractor.

X. Cleanup: The Subcontractor shall continuously maintain the Project free from all dirt, rubbish, debris, and any other waste materials. The Subcontractor shall be responsible for the removal and disposal of all receptacles and containers into which same is deposited. On the completion of the various portions of the work, the Subcontractor shall broom clean its work areas. The Subcontractor shall perform whatever additional cleanup work is so directed, at no additional cost, by the Contractor's field superintendent.

XI. Progress and Performance: The Subcontractor shall proceed with each and every part of this Contract in a prompt and diligent manner. The Subcontractor, without additional compensation, shall perform this Contract at such times, in such order, and in such manner as the Contractor may direct. The Subcontractor shall commence, continue and complete its performance of the Project so as not to delay the Contractor, the Principal, other contractors or subcontractors, completion of this Contract, the Prime Contract, or any portions thereof, and so as to insure completion as directed by the Contractor. Any time specified for the completion of this Contract, or portion thereof, is a material provision of this Contract, and time is of the essence. The Subcontractor shall furnish sufficient forces to assure proper performance of its Contract in strict compliance with all performance schedules. Subcontractor shall, from time to time, on demand of the Contractor, give adequate evidence to the Contractor to substantiate the planned performance and progress of the Contract and the various parts thereof. The Subcontractor shall promptly increase its work force, accelerate its performance, work overtime, work Saturdays, Sundays and holidays, all without additional compensation, if, in the opinion of the Contractor, such work is necessary to maintain proper progress. The Subcontractor shall conform to the Contractor's hours of work. No premium time will be acknowledged or paid unless pursuant to a written authorization by the Contractor. The Subcontractor shall neither delay nor adversely effect the performance of the Contractor or any other contractor or subcontractor working on or related to the Project. If the Subcontractor should so delay or threaten to delay the progress or performance of its Contract, or cause any actual or potential damage or liability to the Contractor, then Subcontractor may be deemed in breach of this Contract, and shall indemnify and hold the Contractor harmless. The Subcontractor will fully cooperate and coordinate its work with the Contractor and any other contractor or subcontractor at the Project. The Subcontractor shall bear the costs of all damages done to other contractors and shall be directly responsible to such other contractors or subcontractors for any damages caused by or resulting from acts or omissions of the Subcontractor. The liability of the Subcontractor shall not be deemed waived by any assent or acquiescence by the Contractor to the Subcontractor's late performance. The Contractor shall be entitled to terminate the Contract due to late or threatened late performance. In the event any other contractor or subcontractor should damage the Subcontractor, the Subcontractor shall neither seek nor be entitled to any compensation from the Contractor, but will seek its damages directly from such other party. Subcontractor will not interfere with Contractor's contract with any other party. The Subcontractor acknowledges that the Contract price is based on the fact that the Contractor is not liable to the Subcontractor, absent any actual fraud or intentional and active tortious act, for any damages or costs due to delays, accelerations, non-performance, interferences with performance, suspensions, or changes in the performance or sequence of the Subcontractor's work. Should the Subcontractor's performance, in whole or part, be interfered with or delayed, or be suspended in the commencement, prosecution or completion, for reasons beyond the Subcontractor's control and without its fault or negligence, the Subcontractor shall be entitled to an extension of time in which to complete its Contract; but only if it shall have notified, in writing, the Contractor of the cause of delay within two days of the occurrence of the event, and provided a similar extension of time, if needed, is allotted to the Contractor by the Principal. The Contractor owes no damage, duty, obligation, or liability to the Subcontractor as a result of any delay, interference, suspension, or other event, except for seeking an extension of time from the Principal.

XII. Insurance and Idemnification: The Contractor shall not be liable for any loss or casualty incurred or caused by the Subcontractor. The Subcontractor shall maintain full and complete insurance on its work until final acceptance of the Prime Contract. The Subcontractor assumes all risk of loss for all of its work regardless of whether the Subcontractor had previously been paid for same. The Contractor is not responsible to provide any protective service for the Subcontractor's benefit, and is not liable for any loss or damage to the Subcontractor's work. The Subcontractor shall hold the Contractor harmless from any and all liability, costs, damages, attorney's fees, and expenses from any claims or causes of action of whatsoever nature arising while on or near the Project, or while performing Contract related work, including those claims relating to its subcontractors, suppliers or employees, or by reason of any claim or dispute of any person or entity for damages from any cause directly or indirectly relating to any action or failure to act by the Subcontractor, its representatives, employees, subcontractors, or suppliers and whether or not it is alleged that the Contractor, Principal or A/E, in any way contributed to the alleged wrongdoing or is liable due to a non-delegable duty. Subcontractor acknowledges that specific consideration has been received by it for this indemnification. The Subcontractor will maintain whatever security or insurance the Contractor deems necessary to fully protect the Contractor against any loss or liability. The Contractor may retain any and all monies due or to become due to the Subcontractor, under this or any other contract, sufficient to save itself harmless and indemnity itself against any liability or damage, including attorney fees. As part of the Subcontractor's overall obligation to protect others and hold the Contractor harmless from all liability, the Subcontractor shall obtain, before commencement, and maintain until final acceptance of the Prime Contract, full insurance coverage as may be specified in the Prime Contract or elsewhere in this Contract, and in amounts not less than those so specified. All insurance shall be procured at the Subcontractor's expense and shall have the Contractor listed as a named insured. All insurance shall be maintained in the form and with a company satisfactory to the Contractor. All certificates of insurance must be filed with the Contractor five days prior to scheduled commencement of Contract work. In no case, however, shall the Subcontractor procure and maintain less than the following insurance coverages:

(1) Workmen's Compensation including Occupational Disease, and Employer's Liability Insurance covering all Subcontractor's employees directly or indirectly engaged in the performance of this Contract. The latter insurance shall provide $500,000 coverage.

(2) Comprehensive General Liability Insurance including Contractor's Protective Liability and Contractual Liability Insurance with minimum limits of $500,000/$1,000,000 for property and personal damage. The latter insurance shall insure the hold harmless and indemnification agreements of the Subcontractor running to the Contractor.

(3) Other insurance, including Comprehensive Automobile Liability Insurance as may be required by law or the Contractor.

The Subcontractor shall not sublet or subcontract any part of this Contract without assuming absolute responsibility for requiring similar insurance from its subcontractors and suppliers. No policy will permit cancellation without 15 days prior written notice of cancellation to the Contractor. Failure of the Subcontractor to maintain complete insurance may be deemed a material breach allowing the Contractor to terminate this Contract, or to provide insurance at the Subcontractor's sole expense; in neither case, however, shall the Subcontractor's liability be lessened.

XIII. Principal Relationship: The Subcontractor shall not interfere with the Contractor's relationship with the Principal. The Subcontractor will not enter any other contract relating to the Project without the Contractor's written consent.

XIV. Taxes, Charges, Etc.: The Subcontractor shall be responsible for and shall pay any and all taxes, contributions, fees, etc., imposed directly or indirectly on account of its work, labor, material and services required under or relating to this Contract. At no time shall there be any increase or escalation in the Contract price on account of any such charge. The Subcontractor shall, on demand, substantiate that all taxes and other charges are being properly paid.

XV. Subcontractor's Representative: The Subcontractor shall have a competent representative at the Project at all times who shall have absolute authority to act, in all respects, on behalf and for the Subcontractor. The Subcontractor shall replace said representative, without additional charge, if so demanded by the Contractor. The Subcontractor shall be deemed to be on notice when its representative is so notified, either orally or in writing, or three days after written notice is forwarded to the Subcontractor's designated principal place of business, whichever is sooner.

XVI. Sublet and Assignment: The Subcontractor shall not assign or sublet this Contract or any part or interest therein, or any money due or to become due without the Contractor's prior written consent. If the Contractor so consents, such assignment is subject and subordinated to all labor preferences and other liabilities, actual or potential, as may be imposed on the Contractor due to any obligation or liability of the Subcontractor.

XVII. Bonds: The Subcontractor shall, as part of this Contract, furnish to the Contractor full and duly executed Performance and Payment Bonds issued by a surety company and in such format as is satisfactory to the Contractor. If such are not furnished with this Contract, the Contractor may, at any time prior to or during performance of this Contract, demand that the Subcontractor furnish same. The cost of said bonds shall be separately itemized and be paid for by the Contractor. The Subcontractor's failure to deliver satisfactory bonds within ten days after demand may be deemed a material breach of this Contract. The Subcontractor's officers and the signatory of this Contract accept full personal liability should bonds, for whatsoever reason, not be furnished.

XVIII. Termination: Should the Subcontractor fail to perform in strict accordance with the Prime Contract, this Contract, where or as the Contractor may so direct, or should the Subcontractor become insolvent, unable to or fail to pay its obligations as they mature, or, in any other respect, fail, in the opinion of the Contractor, to properly prosecute and perform any part of its work, fail to exert its best performance efforts, be involved in labor disputes, or be terminated under any other contract with the Contractor, then the Subcontractor may be deemed by the Contractor to have materially breached this Contract. In case of a breach, as indicated herein or as might otherwise be determined by law, then the Contractor may, at its discretion, terminate this Contract, or any part thereof, by giving written notice thereof to the Subcontractor. In case of such termination, the Contractor may use any and all materials, equipment, tools, or chattels furnished by or belonging to the Subcontractor either at or for the Project. The Subcontractor, on termination, will be deemed to have offered to the Contractor an assignment of all of its subcontracts and purchase orders relating to this Project. The Contractor may, at its discretion, do whatever is necessary to assure performance of any terminated work, and to take such action, if necessary, in the Subcontractor's name. The Contractor may withhold from Subcontractor any monies due or to become due under this or any other contract to offset the damages incurred or possibly incurred as a result of the breach. In case of a breach, the Subcontractor and its surety company shall be liable to the Contractor for any and all additional costs, expenses, attorney's fees, and other damages, both liquidated and unliquidated, which directly or indirectly result from the Subcontractor's breach or threatened breach.

XIX. Labor Relations: The Subcontractor shall do whatever is necessary in the prosecution of its work to assure harmonious labor relations at the Project and to prevent strikes or other labor disputes. The Subcontractor shall fully abide by all labor agreements and jurisdictional decisions presently in force or subsequently executed with or by the Contractor. The Subcontractor's failure to so act may be deemed a material breach of this Contract.

XX. Payments: The Subcontractor shall become entitled to receive progress payments, if included in the Prime Contract, for its work performed during the payment periods established in the Prime Contract. Progress payments become payable ten days after such payment has been received by the Contractor. Unless the Subcontractor submits its requisition in a form satisfactory to the Contractor and at least five days prior to the requisition date set forth in the Prime Contract, then no progress payment can be requisitioned for that payment period. All progress payment requisitions are subject to audit, and if any doubt as to the truth exists, the right to progress payments may be denied. The estimate by the Principal or A/E of the value of work performed during a payment period or any deduction, offset or counterclaim against the requisitioned amount shall be binding on the Subcontractor. Progress payments to the Subcontractor for any payment period shall not exceed 90 percent of the amount requisitioned by the Subcontractor, and then acknowledged and paid by the Principal. Final payment shall become payable thirty days after final completion and acceptance of the Prime Contract and receipt of final payment by the Contractor. In no event shall Subcontractor be entitled to receive any form of payment prior to the Contractor's actual receipt of that payment. Subcontractor waives all right of action until said monies are received by the Contractor. Payment is subject to the Contractor's withholding an amount reasonably necessary to fully protect and insure itself against any actual or potential liability or damage directly or indirectly relating to this Contract, or the Subcontractor's breach or threatened breach of any other contract. Payment may be withheld until the Subcontractor furnishes an affidavit detailing each and every unpaid obligation directly or indirectly relating to that Payment and this Contract, including but not limited to the name of each party, the amount due or to become due, the due dates thereof, the nature of any offset relating thereto, along with a consent of its surety that payment be made. If the Contractor deems it necessary, payment may be withheld to assure payment of the Subcontractor's unpaid obligations, or the Contractor may demand that each unpaid obligation be paid, and that an affidavit be furnished from each party to whom the Subcontractor owed money indicating that no other monies are due and owing to them except for the designated amount covered by the particular payment in question. Prior to final payment the Subcontractor shall submit from each and every subcontractor and supplier releases of the Contractor and its surety, and indicating full payment of all monies due or to become due relating to this Contract. Before any payment is made to the Subcontractor, it shall prove that the Project is free and clear from all liens and claims. The Contractor's withholding of monies from the Subcontractor shall be interest free. The acceptance of any progress payments by the Subcontractor shall constitute a release of the Contractor from any other liability, except retainage, due to any reason, arising or incurred during the payment period. Acceptance of final payment by the Subcontractor constitutes a general release of the Contractor and its Surety. If the Subcontractor takes exception to so releasing the Contractor by acceptance of payments, the Subcontractor must return said payment with an affidavit by an Officer listing each and every exception to the release, and stating that no other claim exists. No payment, including final payment, shall be evidence of the performance of this Contract by the Subcontractor, either in whole or in part, and no payment shall be construed as an acceptance of defective or incomplete work, and the Subcontractor shall remain responsible and liable for its performance being in strict compliance with this Contract and the Prime Contract.

XXI. Liens and Encumbrances: The Subcontractor for itself, its subcontractors, suppliers, materialmen and employees, waives, releases and relinquishes all rights to file any Stop Work Notice, Notice of Intent, Notice of Lien, Mechanic's Lien or other encumbrance against the Contractor, Surety, Principal, Project, or any monies earned by the Contractor. The filing or effectuating of such encumbrance shall constitute a material breach. The Subcontractor shall be responsible and liable for all damages and expenses, including bond premiums, attorney's fees, etc. to discharge and/or defend against same. The existence of any encumbrance shall preclude the Subcontractor's right to receive payment until such encumbrance has been satisfied and removed.

XXII. Governing Law: The validity, interpretation and performance of this Contract shall be governed by the Laws of the State where the designated principal place of business of the Contractor is located. The Subcontractor hereby accepts said State's jurisdiction and agrees to accept service of process as if it were personally served within said jurisdiction. Titles, captions or headings to any provision, Article, etc., shall not limit the full contents of same. These Articles have the full force and effect as if no titles existed. If any term or provision of this Contract is found invalid, it shall not affect the validity and enforcement of all remaining terms and provisions of the Contract.

XXIII. Oral Modifications: The Contract cannot be changed, modified, altered, or terminated orally. This Contract supersedes all prior representations made by Contractor.

XXIV. Damages: The Subcontractor shall be responsible and liable for all costs, disbursements, and expenses, including attorney's fees, incurred by the Contractor (a) as a result of the Contractor's pursuing any extra, change, addition, claim or dispute against any other party on behalf of the Subcontractor; or (b) as a result of the Subcontractor's breach or threatened breach of any Article, term or condition of this Contract; or (c) as a result of the Contractor's having to defend or take part in any action or proceeding which directly or indirectly relates to acts or omissions of the Subcontractor or its subcontractors or suppliers.

XXV. Conditional Contract: This Contract is made conditional upon the approval of the Subcontractor by the Principal or A/E, where such approval is required. However, the Subcontractor is responsible to maintain and abide by all statements and quotes given to Contractor, and upon which the Contractor is relying.

XXVI. Approval of Submittals: The approval by the Contractor, Principal, or A/E of any submittals of the Subcontractor shall not relieve it of liability for any deviations from the Prime Contract or this Contract, unless specifically called to the Contractor's attention, in writing, and it is then so acknowledged by the Contractor in writing.

XXVII. Guaranty and Warranty: The Subcontractor, in addition to all other guarantees and warranties contained in this Contract and the Prime Contract and not in limitation of the Contractor's other legal rights, warrants and guarantees that its work is in strict and absolute accord with the Contract, and that it shall, for a minimum of one year after the date of final acceptance of the Prime Contract, perform any maintenance or corrective work, without cost, as directed by the Contractor. The Contractor may demand assurance, by bond or otherwise, from the Subcontractor that it will abide by its guarantee and warranty as specified herein and as might otherwise be specified to a greater extent in the Contract or Prime Contract.

XXVIII. Cancellation: The Contractor, by written notice executed by an Officer, shall have the right to terminate and cancel this Contract, without the Subcontractor being at fault, for any cause or for its own convenience, and require the Subcontractor to immediately stop work. In such event, the Contractor shall pay the Subcontractor for that work actually performed in an amount proportionate to this Contract price. The Contractor shall not be liable to the Subcontractor for any other costs, including prospective profits on work not performed. However, if the reason for the termination and cancellation of this Contract is due to any default or action by the Principal, A/E or as a result of Court Order or public authority, then the Contractor shall not be liable to the Subcontractor for any sum greater than that which the Contractor receives from the Principal on behalf of the Subcontractor's performance, less any costs incurred by the Contractor.

XXIX. Legal Forum: Any dispute or claim arising out of this Contract, or from a breach of this Contract, and which is not resolved by the terms and provisions of this Contract, shall be submitted to the Judicial Court within the County and State of the Contractor's designated principal place of business for decision. The Subcontractor agrees to participate in, join in, and be bound by any proceeding, be it Judicial, Administrative, Arbitration or other, which directly or indirectly relates to this Contract or Project and for which the Contractor demands, by written notice, that the Subcontractor participate. Any claim or action by the Subcontractor must be commenced within two years of the date the cause of action accrued, but in no event later than one year after substantial performance of this Contract, and in no event after final payment to the Subcontractor. If any claim or dispute arises relating to this Contract, the Subcontractor shall immediately make all of its books and records available to the Contractor for review and audit.

XXX. Sub-Subcontracts: The Subcontractor hereby agrees to incorporate into any subcontracts or purchase orders it has with any other party, all those provisions required by law to be incorporated therein, and all those provisions of this Contract which affect the rights of the Contractor. This Contract shall neither create a contractual relationship between Contractor and the Subcontractor's subcontractors or suppliers; nor between the Subcontractor and the A/E or Principal.

This Contract is hereby acknowledged and executed:

Dated: _____

Witnessed: _____

Subcontractor
by: _____
    Officer

Seal:

_____
Contractor

Please Return:
1. Both copies of this Contract duly executed for execution and return by Contractor.
2. Executed Certification of Non-Segregated Facilities.
3. Executed Certification of Equal Employment Opportunity.
4. Executed Certificate of Insurance Compliance.
5. Executed Performance and Payment Bonds.

C. PURCHASE ORDER FORMS

§2.05   1. Author's Comments   The purchase order is often neglected by the prime contractor and thus becomes the source of much litigation. The purchase order is as important to the prime contractor as the subcontract form. The prime contractor must tie the supplier into the obligations of the prime contract and also must have the supplier accept responsibility for the portion of work relating to the prime contractor's functions and obligations to other suppliers, subcontractors, and third parties. In fact, three different purchase orders can be used.

The first purchase order form, which is not included in this book, is nothing more than a plain piece of paper. This form can be used where the prime contractor purchases pure, off-the-shelf, stock items, where the supplier has made no representations as to the adequacy or capability of the product and has not indicated an ability to fulfill the requirements of the prime contract, and where the supplier has no interest in the prime contract. However, once the materials to be furnished are removed from this supermarket classification, then the rights of the prime contractor must be protected.

The argument made by many suppliers is that they are not performing any field labor and therefore must be treated differently from subcontractors. This argument has lost much of its legal and factual force in today's environment. While it may be true that no labor is being performed on the site, more and more suppliers are performing field work in their own shops to meet the prime contract requirements, and then are delivering that work to the field. The requirements of the prime contract are as much a part of that supplier's commitment as they would be if the actual fabrication were done in the field. There is a need to recognize the supplier's obligations, and for the supplier to accept those obligations in order to meet time schedules, codes, insurance requirements, plans and specifications, as well as nearly every other provision of the contract documents. Often the core of the construction project is furnished by the supplier. The supplier cannot be separated from the prime contract obligations. Once the supplier delivers to the site, stores materials on the site, sets equipment, and gets involved with adjustments, erection, or any other field work, the supplier is no different from any other subcontractor.

The two purchase order forms that follow are long and short forms. As with all standard forms, they are subject to negotiation. The short form does not offer the legal protection that the long form does. However, the short form binds the purchaser to the prime contract, sets time limitations in delivery requirements, and places upon the supplier the responsibility and liability for any breach of the agreement by the supplier.

The long form amplifies these items, as well as offering the prime contractor greater legal protection. It must be remembered that a clearly written understanding between the parties will lessen the chances of litigation. The purchase order is not intended to force upon the supplier any liability which would be unconscionable; the form merely sets forth the necessary responsibilities.

In both purchase orders, the scope of work must be itemized clearly by the prime contractor. This cannot be left to chance, and often a rider must be added to the form so that all the specific requirements and quantities are understood by both parties.

The typed purchase order form used by many suppliers, which eliminates the supplier from the prime contract, must be avoided at all costs. Many owners side with prime contractors and, in the prime contract, require bonds or other security from suppliers. The prime contractor must use the form to protect the contractor's rights.

§2.06   2. FORM   **Purchase Order—Short**

PURCHASE ORDER NO. _____ SHIP TO:

TO:

Purchase Order Agreement made this _____ day of _____, 19____,

between _____

_____ located

at _____ ("Contractor")

and _____

located at _____ ("Vendor")

Contractor has entered a contract ("Prime Contract") with _____

_____ ("Principal")

to furnish certain work, labor, services and equipment necessary for the construction of a

_____

_____ ("Project")

in accordance with Prime Contract documents including certain Plans and Specifications

prepared by _____

_____ ("A/E")

Contractor and Vendor enter this Agreement ("Contract"), incorporating the Prime Contract, and agree as follows:

The Vendor shall provide and furnish all materials, supplies, equipment, services, facilities, administration, etc. for the complete performance and acceptance, in exact accord with and subject to the Prime Contract, the following work:
        Total Contract Price $_____

(continued on Rider A)

§2.06 FORM—SHORT   173

Proper Approval Drawings and Data must be to Contractor no later than _____, 19_____. Failure to comply with this schedule may be deemed a breach. Vendor is allowed _____ weeks for completion of work. A firm delivery requirement will be issued by Contractor. Vendor shall insure its work against all risks of loss and damage. No shipment is to be made without release and consent by Contractor. Delivery will be F.O.B. Project at a time and place directed by Contractor. Units must be shipped complete and in the proper sequence. All material delivered to the Project shall have attached identification. Vendor will furnish notarized certificates of compliance stating that all work is in full compliance with the Prime Contract, as relates to this Contract. Delivery, installation or erection of equipment shall not be considered complete until all spare parts and approved copies of the instruction, operation and maintenance manuals are furnished. These manuals shall include drawings of all equipment. Any and all samples, test reports, certificates of compliance, warranties, guarantees, or the like, required by the Prime Contract, shall be furnished at no additional cost. Vendor shall be liable to Contractor as Contractor is liable to the Principal under Prime Contract. Contractor shall not be liable for any delays, suspensions or cost escalations. This Contract may be terminated by Contractor without cause and Vendor shall be entitled to payment only for work performed pro-rata to this Contract price, and in no case to profit on unperformed work.

Materials, supplies, or services covered by this Contract (are) (are not) exempt from Sales Tax.

The Vendor, and any other manufacturer of the work supplied under this Contract, shall indemnify and save harmless the Contractor and Principal, and all persons acting for or on behalf of these parties, from all claims and liability of any nature or kind, including costs, attorney fees, and expenses arising from or occasioned by any breach of this Contract, or by infringement or alleged infringement of patent rights on any invention, process, article, or apparatus, furnished to Contractor or arising from or occasioned by the use thereof. Vendor shall be liable for all damages, costs, and expenses, including Contractor's attorney fees, resulting from any breach of this Contract. Contractor shall pay the total sum of $_____ (including) (excluding) taxes. Vendor shall be entitled to payment, upon payment to Contractor, equal to _____% of the approved amount on the last day of month following delivery and acceptance of the complete unit. Balance on completion of testing, acceptance, compliance with all guarantee and warranty obligations, and payment.

_____   _____
Contractor   Vendor

§2.07 3. FORM Purchase Order—Long

PURCHASE ORDER NO. _____ SHIP TO:
TO:

Agreement made this _____ day of _____, 19___, by and between _____ with its principal place of business located at _____ (hereinafter designated as "Contractor") and _____ _____ with its principal place of business located at _____ (hereinafter designated as "Vendor"):

WHEREAS, the Contractor has heretofore entered a contract (hereinafter designated as the "Prime Contract") with _____ _____ , (hereinafter designated as the "Principal") to furnish certain work, labor, services and equipment necessary for the construction of a _____ _____ (hereinafter designated as the "Project") in accordance with Prime Contract documents including certain Plans and Specifications prepared by _____ _____ (hereinafter designated as the "A/E");

WITNESS: The Contractor and Vendor, in consideration of mutual covenants do hereby enter this Agreement, including the Purchase Order Articles of Construction, (hereinafter collectively referred to as "Contract") and agree as follows:

The Vendor shall provide and furnish all materials, supplies, equipment, services, facilities, administration, etc. for the complete performance and acceptance, in exact accord with, and subject to the Prime Contract, the following work:

Total Contract Price $_____

(continued on Rider A)

PURCHASE ORDER ARTICLES OF CONSTRUCTION ON REVERSE SIDE

This Project is being scheduled on the basis of a progress schedule. Proper Approval Drawings and other Data must be to the Contractor no later than _____, 19__. Failure to comply with this schedule may be deemed a breach. Vendor shall immediately make all required corrections. Specification Section *MUST* appear on all drawings and correspondence. Vendor is allowed _____ weeks for fabrication and completion of equipment and work after return of approved drawings. A firm delivery requirement will be issued by Contractor. Vendor shall insure its work against all risks of loss and damage. All shippers must notify the jobsite 48 hours before attempting delivery. No shipment is to be made without release and consent by Contractor. Delivery will be F.O.B. Project at a time and place directed by Contractor. Units must be shipped complete and in the proper sequence for installation. No partial shipments will be accepted unless requested and approved in writing. All material delivered to the Project shall have attached identification. Each accessory or component which is shipped "loose" shall be marked or tagged the same as the basic item. Vendor will furnish notarized certificates of compliance stating that all work is in full compliance with the Prime Contract before any material is processed, fabricated or delivered.

Bound instruction manuals, if specified, including parts lists and certifications, to be forwarded within _____ days after receipt of approved drawings. Delivery, installation or erection of equipment shall not be considered to be _____ percent complete until approved copies of the operation and maintenance manuals are in the hands of the Contractor. These manuals shall include drawings of all equipment, including minor parts and sub-assemblies, in such detail as will permit disassembly of each piece of equipment for maintenance. Parts drawings shall show such fabrication and assembly details as are required to permit disassembly and assembly of the equipment. Vendor shall furnish start-up and instructional service, if specified.

Vendor shall furnish, with each piece of equipment, the complete set of tools recommended by the manufacturer for the servicing of the equipment. Each piece of equipment shall be furnished with the spare parts listed or referenced in the Prime Contract for the equipment, in addition to the standard set of spare parts recommended by the manufacturer of the equipment. The recommended list of spare parts shall be submitted to the A/E prior to the delivery of the equipment. All spare parts shall be plainly tagged and marked for identification and ordering. They shall be treated with suitable preservatives, wrapped and packaged to provide adequate protection during storage.

Any and all samples, test reports, certificates of compliance, warranties, guarantees, or the like, required by the Prime Contract, shall be furnished at no additional cost. Vendor shall be liable to Contractor as Contractor is liable to the Principal under Prime Contract.

Materials, supplies, or services covered by this Contract (are) (are not) exempt from Sales Tax. Tax Exempt Purchase Certificates (are) (are not) attached.

The Vendor and manufacturer of the work supplied under this Contract shall indemnify and save harmless the Contractor, A/E and Principal, and all persons acting for or on behalf of these parties, from all claims and liability of any nature or kind, including costs, attorney fees, expenses arising from or occasioned by any breach of this Contract, or infringement or alleged infringement of patent rights on any invention, process, article, or apparatus, or any part thereof, or arising from or occasioned by the use thereof, including their use by the Principal. Vendor shall be liable for all damages, costs, and expenses, direct and indirect, including Contractor's attorney fees, resulting from any breach of this Contract.

In consideration of the Vendor's performance of this Contract, which incorporates the

Purchase Order Articles of Construction and the Prime Contract as a part hereof, the Contractor shall pay the total sum of $ _____ (including) (excluding) Taxes. Vendor shall be entitled to payment, upon payment to Contractor, equal to _____% of the approved amount on the last day of month following delivery and acceptance of the complete unit; and, _____% upon acceptance of and payment for the installation. Balance on completion of testing, acceptance, compliance with all guarantee and warranty obligations, and payment to Contractor by Principal.

_____
Vendor

Witnessed: _____ By: _____
Officer

Witnessed: _____ _____
Contractor

PURCHASE ORDER ARTICLES OF CONSTRUCTION ON REVERSE SIDE

PURCHASE ORDER
ARTICLES OF CONSTRUCTION

I These Articles are made part of and are incorporated into the Contract between the Contractor and Vendor. The terms and conditions contained herein shall be binding on Vendor.

II The Prime Contract, including all of its contract documents, is incorporated herein by reference and made an integral part of this Contract. The Prime Contract can be reviewed by the Vendor at the Contractor's principal place of business. The Vendor is bound, responsible, obligated and liable to the Contractor as the Contractor is bound, responsible, obligated, and liable under the Prime Contract. The term "Contract" as used herein shall include all documents incorporated into and made a part of the Agreement, between the Contractor and Vendor; and any revisions thereto. The term "Architect/Engineer" (hereinafter referred to as "A/E") shall be deemed to be that representative directing the work for the Principal, or any other person authorized by the Prime Contract to direct, judge, approve or reject any matter or thing connected with the performance of the Prime Contract. The Prime Contract and this Contract shall be interpreted together and, in harmony with one another. However, in case of conflict between the Prime Contract and this Contract, this Contract shall govern. The Vendor must call any such conflict or discrepancy to the Contractor's attention, in writing, prior to executing this Contract, for written decision, otherwise the Vendor agrees to be bound by the more onerous provision.

III All work included in the Contract shall be done under the direction of the Contractor, and to the satisfaction of the Contractor, Principal and A/E. Said work shall be performed in exact accord with the Prime Contract. The work to be performed by the Vendor includes that work specifically set forth in this Contract, as well as any and all other work reasonably necessary to have a properly working and totally acceptable system and Project. All work covered by this Contract shall be performed in a skillful and workmanlike manner with material, equipment, etc. being both new and of the best kind and grade for the exact purpose intended. Said work shall be deemed to include any and all work required to be performed by the Contractor, Principal, A/E or by any judicial or administrative tribunal. The Vendor agrees, without additional compensation, to perform, conform and abide by all decisions issued by the Contractor, when the Contractor has been directed to perform, conform and abide by similar decisions, without additional compensation, issued by the Principal or A/E. The Vendor shall provide, at its own expense, all working drawings, tests, samples, models, guarantees, insurance and delivery services, and all other items necessary for the proper performance of this Contract and acceptance of the Project. The Vendor shall pay for all inspection fees, royalties, and license fees. The Vendor shall make all necessary arrangements and agreements so as not to infringe any patents, trademarks, or copyrights, and shall hold the Contractor, Principal and A/E harmless from any infringement, claim or suit.

IV The Vendor acknowledges that it has carefully reviewed and examined this Contract with all of its contract documents, and all other documents directly or indirectly relating to the Contract; and the Vendor will not make any claim of the Contractor based upon or arising out of any misunderstanding or misconception on its part of the provisions and requirements of the Prime Contract or this Contract. Any information given or statements made to the Vendor shall not reduce the work to be performed by the Vendor under this Contract. The Vendor acknowledges that it has fully examined and analyzed all conditions that could affect its performance and that no conditions exist which would affect the progress, performance or price of this Contract. The Vendor will perform and furnish any and all work, labor, services, and/or materials, mentioned, shown, depicted or required in one Contract document and not mentioned, shown, depicted, or required in another document, as if it were clearly mentioned, shown, depicted or required in all Contract documents. The Vendor shall be required to do all things and be bound by all rulings of the Principal or A/E to the same extent and degree as the Contractor is bound thereto. The Vendor shall be responsible for all its own field measurements where applicable.

v All work, labor, services and materials to be furnished, supplied or performed by Vendor must strictly comply with all Federal, State, Local, Municipal, as well as any and all other governing Jurisdictions and Authorities. Laws, Rules, Regulations, Statutes, Ordinances, and Directives (hereinafter designated as "Laws"). All work, labor services or materials, in addition to that specifically required by this Contract, but necessary to fully comply with said Laws, will be furnished by Vendor as part of this Contract, without additional compensation.

vi The Vendor shall not be entitled to nor shall it receive any increase or upward adjustment in its Contract price unless said amount and liability are acknowledged, in writing, by an Officer of the Contractor. No alteration, addition, omission or change shall be made in the work, except upon the written Change Order of the Contractor. Any change or adjustment in the Contract price by virtue of such Change Order shall be specifically stated in said Change Order. Change Orders are subject to the terms of these Articles and all other Contract documents. Prior to the issuance of any Change Order, the Contractor may require the Vendor to furnish to the Contractor a detailed breakdown showing the difference in value of the work, labor, services, and materials altered, added omitted or changed by the proposed Change Order. If an agreement as to monetary allowance or other term in the Change Order cannot be reached, the Contractor, by an authorized representative, may direct, in writing, the Vendor to perform the work with the final determination reserved until final completion of this Contract and the Prime Contract. The monetary amount for the performance of any Change Order shall not exceed the allowance set forth in the Vendor's prior price breakdown. Any extension of time needed as a result of a proposed Change Order shall be requested by the Vendor, in writing, prior to the issuance of the Change Order, and shall be incorporated therein. There shall be no other monetary or time allowance, direct or indirect, to the Vendor other than that which is specifically written in the Change Order. Ordinary field modifications which do not substantially increase Vendor's cost of this Contract will be performed without any price adjustment. Where unit prices are stipulated in the Contract, all adjustments, whether increases or decreases shall be made in accordance with said units. Said units shall be deemed to include all general and administrative expenses, overhead, profit, supervision, extended performance time cost factors, and all other direct and indirect expenses. If the Contractor elects the option to direct the Change Order work to be done on a time and material basis, the Vendor shall prepare daily time and material invoices. Said daily time and material invoices shall include only direct out-of-pocket material and labor costs with a maximum total additional mark-up of 10 percent. The 10 percent mark-up is deemed to be full compensation for all administrative expenses, overhead, and profit. The Vendor shall in no event receive any compensation or allowance for any Change Order in an amount greater than that which the Contractor actually receives from the Principal, less a reasonable deduction for the Contractor's overhead and profit. No Change Order shall vary, abrogate, avoid, or otherwise affect the terms, conditions and provisions of this Contract except as specifically set forth in the Change Order.

vii The Contractor may upon the written request of the Vendor, appeal on behalf of the Vendor from any ruling or decision of the Principal or A/E, or institute any action or proceeding to recover damages by reason of any affirmative claim by the Vendor, or by reason of any deduction or refusal to pay by the Principal for any reason, involving the work or performance of the Vendor. In that event, the Vendor shall pay all costs attributable thereto and shall render all assistance requested by Contractor. The Vendor shall be bound by the determination of the Principal, the A/E, or in the event of an appeal or further action or proceeding, by the determination of same, and shall be entitled only to its proportionate share of any actual net recovery, less overhead and profit to the Contractor, and less the Contractor's expenses and attorney's fees. The Vendor hereby waives and releases any and all claims, causes of actions, and rights to further payment, beyond the Contract amount, except as the Contractor may receive funds or extensions of time from the Principal or A/E.

VIII The Vendor shall provide at its own place of business, at the places of business of its subcontractors and suppliers, and at the Project, sufficient safe and proper facilities for the inspection of the Vendor's work by the Contractor, Principal, A/E, or any other authorized representative. The Vendor must be prepared, at all times, to prove the exact quantities and qualities of the materials and equipment being used. If the Vendor is assigned a storage area for its equipment, material and tools, it shall not store any item outside of the designated area. The Vendor shall be responsible for the receipt, delivery, unloading, storage, warehousing, protection, insurance and all other risk of loss relating to any materials or equipment it is to furnish, provide, or have provided to it under this Contract. The Vendor shall be obligated to inspect all material and equipment furnished to it at time of receipt. The Vendor shall be responsible to immediately notify the Contractor, in writing, of any defects or non-conformity in the material or equipment so received. Failure to notify the Contractor shall be deemed an acknowledgment and acceptance of the material as being in accord with this Contract. The Vendor shall be liable for any damages incurred by the Contractor as a result of its failure to so notify the Contractor. It is the Vendor's obligation, upon direction by the Contractor, to take all necessary steps, including but not limited to delivery of samples, tests and reports, guarantees, drawings, manuals, certificates, details, warranties, inspections etc., to obtain any and all required approvals necessary or requested under this Contractor or the Prime Contract. The Vendor shall, within 24 hours after receiving specific written notice from the Contractor, commence to take down and remove any designated portion of its work which is condemned, disapproved, improper, or is questioned as not being in strict compliance and conformity with the requirements of this Contract. The Vendor shall promptly, at its own expense, correct and rectify same. If the Contractor determines that it will accept non-conforming work, the Contractor shall be entitled to a credit for the non-conformity. Any damage prior to final acceptance and payment shall be corrected by the Vendor at its sole expense. Inspection or supervision by the Contractor shall not relieve the Vendor of its obligations.

IX The Vendor shall proceed with each and every part of this Contract in a prompt and diligent manner. The Vendor shall commence, continue and complete its performance of the Project so as not to delay the Contractor, the Principal, other contractors or subcontractors, completion of this Contract, the Prime Contract, or any portions thereof, and so as to insure completion as directed by the Contractor. Any time specified for the completion of this Contract, or a portion thereof, is a material provision of this Contract, and time is of the essence. The Vendor shall, from time to time, on demand of the Contractor, give adequate evidence to the Contractor to substantiate the planned performance and progress of the Contract and the various parts thereof. If the Vendor should delay or threaten to delay the progress or performance of its contract, or cause any actual or potential damage or liability to the Contractor, the Vendor may be deemed in breach of this Contract, and shall indemnify and hold the Contractor harmless from all liability and costs. The Vendor shall bear the costs of all damages done to others and shall be directly responsible to same for any damages caused by or resulting from acts or omissions of the Vendor. In the event any other vendor, contractor or subcontractor should damage the Vendor, the Vendor shall neither seek nor be entitled to any compensation from the Contractor, but will seek its damages directly from such other party. The Vendor acknowledges that the Contract price is based on the fact that the Contractor is not liable, absent any actual fraud or intentional and active tortious conduct, for any damages or costs due to delays, accelerations, non-performance, interferences with performance, suspensions, or changes in the performance or sequence of the Vendor's work. Should this Contract, in whole or part, be interfered with or delayed, or be suspended in the commencement, prosecution or completion, for reasons beyond the Vendor's control and without its fault or negligence, the Vendor shall be entitled to an extension of time in which to complete its Contract; but, only if it shall have notified, in writing, the Contractor of the cause of delay within two days of the occurance of the event, and provided a similar extension of time, if needed, is alloted to the Contractor by the Principal.

X The Contractor shall not be liable for any loss or casualty incurred or caused by the Vendor. The Vendor shall hold the Contractor, Principal, and A/E harmless from any and all liability, costs, damages, attorney's fees, and expenses from any claims or causes of action of whatsoever nature arising while on or near the Project, or while performing Contract related work, including those claims relating to its subcontractors, suppliers or employees, or by reason of any claim or dispute of any person or entity for damages from any cause directly or indirectly relating to any action or failure to act by the Vendor, its representatives, employees, subcontractors, or suppliers and whether or not it is alleged that the Contractor, Principal or A/E, in any way contributed to the alleged wrongdoing or is liable due to a non-delegable duty. The Vendor will maintain whatever security or insurance the Contractor deems necessary to fully protect the Contractor against any loss or liability.

XI The Vendor shall be responsible for and shall pay any and all taxes, contributions, increased wages and material costs, fees, etc., imposed directly or indirectly on account of its work, labor, material and services required under or relating to this Contract. At no time shall there by any increase or escalation in the Contract price.

XII The Vendor shall, as part of this Contract, furnish to the Contractor a full and duly executed Performance and Payment Bond issued by a surety company and in such format as is satisfactory to the Contractor. If such is not furnished with this Contract, the Contractor may, at any time prior to or during performance of this Contract, demand that the Vendor furnish same. The cost of said bonds shall be separately itemized and be paid for by the Contractor. The Vendor's failure to deliver satisfactory bonds within ten days after demand may be deemed a material breach of this Contract.

XIII Should the Vendor fail to perform in strict accordance with the Prime Contract or this Contract, become insolvent, unable to or fail to pay its obligations as they mature, or, in any other respect, fail, in the opinion of the Contractor, to properly prosecute and perform any part of its work, or be terminated under any other contract with the Contractor, then the Vendor may be deemed by the Contractor to have breached this Contract. In case of a breach, the Contractor may, at its discretion, terminate this Contract, or any part thereof, by written notice to the Vendor. In case of termination, the Contractor may use any and all materials, equipment, tools, or chattles furnished by or belonging to the Vendor either at or for the Project. The Vendor, on termination, will be deemed to have offered to the Contractor an assignment of all its subcontracts or purchase orders relating to this Project.

XIV The Vendor shall do whatever is necessary in the prosecution of its work to assure harmonious labor relations at the Project.

XV The Vendor shall become entitled to receive progress payments, if included in the Prime Contract, for work performed during the payment periods established in the Prime Contract, based upon a payment breakdown furnished to the Contractor upon return of this executed Contract. Progress payments become payable ten days after such payment has been received by the Contractor. All progress payment requisitions are subject to audit. The estimate by the Principal or A/E of the value of work performed during a payment period or any deduction, offset or counterclaim against the requisitioned amount shall be binding on the Vendor. Progress payments shall not exceed 90 percent of the amount requisitioned, and then paid by the Principal. Final payment shall become payable thirty days after final completion and acceptance of the Prime Contract and receipt of final payment by the Contractor. In no event shall Vendor be entitled to receive any form of payment prior to the Contractor's actual receipt of that payment. Payment is subject to the Contractor's withholding an amount reasonably necessary to protect itself against any liability directly or indirectly relating to this or any other Contract. Payment may be withheld until the Vendor furnishes an affidavit detailing each and every unpaid obligation directly or indirectly relating to that payment and this Contract. Prior to final payment the Vendor shall submit from each and every subcontractor and supplier releases of the Contractor and its Surety, and indicating full payment of all monies due or to become due relating to this Contract. Before any payment is made to the Vendor, it shall prove that the Project is free and clear from all liens and claims. The Contractor's withholding of monies from the Vendor shall be interest free. The acceptance of any payment shall constitute a release of the Contractor from any liability, except retainage, due to any reason, to date. No payment, including final payment, shall be evidence of the performance of this Contract by the Vendor, and payment shall not be construed as an acceptance of defective or incomplete work.

XVI The Vendor waives, releases and relinquishes all rights to file any Stop Work Notice, Notice of Intent, Notice of Lien, Mechanic's Lien or other encumbrance against the Contractor, Surety, Principal, Project, or any monies earned by the Contractor.

XVII The validity, interpretation and performance of this Contract shall be governed by the Laws of the State where the designated principal place of business of the Contractor is located. Titles, captions or headings to any provision, Article, etc., shall not limit the full contents of same. If any term or provision of this Contract is found invalid, it shall not affect the validity and enforcement of all remaining terms and provisions of the Contract.

XVIII This Contract cannot be changed, modified, altered, or terminated orally.

XIX The Vendor shall be responsible and liable for all costs, disbursements, and expenses, including attorney's fees, incurred by the Contractor as a result of the Vendor's breach or threatened breach of any Article, term or condition of this Contract.

XX Vendor shall not deal directly with the Principal or A/E without Contractor's written consent.

XXI This Contract is made conditional upon the approval of the Vendor by the Principal or A/E, where such approval is required. However, the Vendor is responsible to maintain and abide by all statements and quotes given to Contractor.

XXII The approval by the Contractor, Principal, or A/E of any submittals of the Vendor shall not relieve it of liability for any deviations from the Prime Contract or this Contract, unless specifically called to the Contractor's attention, in writing, and is then so acknowledged by the Contractor, in writing.

XXIII The Vendor, in addition to all other guarantees and warranties contained in this Contract and the Prime Contract, and not in limitation of the Contractor's other legal rights, warrants and guarantees that its work is in strict and absolute accord with the Contract, and that it shall, for a minimum of one year after the date of final acceptance of the Prime Contract, perform any maintenance or corrective work, without cost, as directed by the Contractor. The Contractor may demand assurance, by bond or otherwise, from the Vendor that it will abide by its guarantee and warranty.

XXIV The Contractor, by written notice, shall have the right to terminate and cancel this

Contract, for any cause or for its own convenience. In such event, the Contractor shall pay the Vendor for that work actually performed in an amount proportionate to this Contract price. The Contractor shall not be liable for any other costs, including prospective profits on work not performed. However, if the reason for the termination is due to any default or action by the Principal, A/E or as a result of Court Order or public authority, then the Contractor shall not be liable to the Vendor for any sum greater than that which the Contractor has actually received from the Principal on behalf of the Vendor's performance, less any costs incurred by the Contractor.

xxv The Vendor agrees to incorporate into any subcontracts or purchase orders it has with any other party, all those provisions required by law to be incorporated therein, and all those provisions of this Contract which affect the rights of the Contractor.

D. STANDARD SUBCONTRACTOR'S APPLICATIONS FOR PAYMENT WITH SUGGESTED MODIFICATIONS

§2.08   1. Author's Comments This form has received approval from numerous national construction associations, as evidenced by the credits at the top of the form. Looking only at the computation, the form sets forth the basic and essential cost factors. If unit prices form a basis for payment, then an itemized statement of quantities with substantiating backup data must be attached to the application for payment. If any part of the work is being performed on a cost plus or time and material basis, an itemized statement with all substantiating, backup data must be annexed to the application. However, more than a factual computation should be included in the application for payment.

The right to and time for submission of the application for payment, as well as all other payment procedures, should be governed by the subcontract agreement between the parties. The prime contractor must be assured that the monies paid to the subcontractor are disbursed properly. If the prime contractor posts a payment bond, even if payment is made to the subcontractor, the contractor may be liable again for payment if the subcontractor fails to pay other subcontractors, suppliers, or employees. Therefore, it is advisable that the prime contractor have the subcontractor's application for payment backed by affidavits from the other parties who may be beneficiaries of the payment bond.

Before payment the prime contractor should clarify the relationship with the subcontractor. Thus, the prime contractor should seek written reassurance from the subcontractor of compliance with the contract and of proper disbursement of payments.

§2.09 2. FORM Subcontractor's Application for Payment

Developed as a guide by The Associated General Contractors of America, The National Electrical Contractors Association, The Mechanical Contractors Association of America. The Sheet Metal and Air Conditioning Contractors National Association and The National Association of Plumbing-Heating-Cooling Contractors

TO: _____
    (Prime Contractor)

FROM: _____

_____

PROJECT:
PAYMENT IS SUBJECT TO THE TERMS OF THE CONTRACT DATED[1]
PAYMENT REQUEST NO. _____

PERIOD_____, 19____, to _____, 19____.

STATEMENT OF CONTRACT ACCOUNT:

1. Original Contract Amount $_____

2. Approved Change Order Nos. _____ (As per attached breakdown)
(Net) $_____

3. Adjusted Contract Amount $_____

4. Value of Work Completed to Date: (As per attached breakdown) $_____

5. Value of Approved Change Orders Completed: (As per attached breakdown) $_____

6. Materials Stored on Site: (As per attached breakdown) $_____

7. Total to Date $_____

8. Less Amount Retained (_____%)   ($_____)

9. Total Less Retainage $_____

10. Total Previously Certified (Deduct) $_____

11. AMOUNT DUE THIS REQUEST $_____

CERTIFICATE OF THE SUBCONTRACTOR: *FALSE STATEMENTS MAY FORM THE BASIS FOR PERJURY.*[2]

I hereby certify that the work performed and the materials supplied to date, as shown on the above represent the actual value of accomplishment under the terms of the Contract (and all authorized changes thereto) between the undersigned and _____ relating to the above referenced project. *No other monies are claimed to be or are due from the Prime Contractor, except as listed on the reverse side.*[3]

I also certify that payments, less applicable retention, have been made through the period covered by previous payments received from the contractor, to (1) all my subcontractors (sub-subcontractors) and (2) for all materials and labor used in or in connection with the performance of this Contract. I further certify I have complied with Federal, State and local tax laws, including Social Security laws and Unemployment Compensation laws and Workmen's Compensation laws insofar as applicable to the performance of this Contract; *and have paid all applicable union obligations.*[4] *Subcontractor shall indemnify and hold Prime Contractor harmless from any claims, liens or damages alleged by its sub-subcontractors, suppliers, work forces or others.*[5]

Date _____   _____
Subscribed and sworn before me this   SUBCONTRACTOR
_____ day of

_____, 19____   BY: _____
Notary Public: _____   *(authorized signature)*
My Commission Expires: _____ TITLE: _____

(The following should appear on the reverse of this form.)

Subcontractor hereby waives and releases Prime Contractor from any and all claims, disputes or controversies, and acknowledges that no other monies are due and owing, or are claimed to be due and owing, relating to this contract, or breach thereof, except for those monies specifically listed in this application for payment.

DESCRIPTION   AMOUNT

FOOTNOTES:

1. The mere submission of the application for payment should not be construed as the subcontractor's immediate right to payment. The application for payment should reference the contract between the parties, and specifically make payment subject to its terms

2. Although false statements under oath may form the basis for perjury without stating this fact, it seems that the physical presence of these words foster the stating of the full truth

3. The prime contractor should know at this point whether or not there are any other claims being asserted against it. With the exception of any listed claims, the subcontractor should be obligated to waive all other potential claims

4. Union funds seem to be one of the first items overlooked by subcontractors when financial problems are present. By stating that the subcontractor has complied with all union obligations, the subcontractor will be more hesitant to execute the application for payment, assuming it has not so

complied, when it knows it is being subject to perjury. From a practical point of view, if the prime contractor questions the stability of the subcontractor, it should consider mandating the furnishing of a bond by the subcontractor for the union's benefit

5 The subcontractor's continued indemnification, prior to payment, is the seeking of nothing more than that which the prime contractor is entitled to. If there are claims being made by any party against the prime contractor as a result of the subcontractor's acts or omissions, the prime contractor should ascertain that fact at this junction

E. WAIVER, RELEASE AND DISCHARGE FORMS

§2.10   1. Author's Comments Before making final payment, the relative positions of the prime contractor and the subcontractor or supplier must be ascertained. Many prime contractors have found themselves making final payments to the subcontractors or suppliers, only to be confronted later with various claims by the subcontractors. At this point the prime contractor is in a weak position for negotiating, and the contractor's rights to assert back charges and counterclaims already have been prejudiced.

At the time of final payment the prime contractor should have in hand an affidavit from the subcontractor/supplier requesting and specifying the amount of final payment. The affidavit must acknowledge specifically that the stated amount is the total amount due or alleged to be due to the subcontractor/supplier from the prime contractor and the sureties or other guarantors. In exchange for this payment, the subcontractor/supplier must release the parties from further liability. However, the document should not stop here. It should acknowledge and extend the subcontractor's indemnification of the prime contractor from claims asserted by third parties. The subcontractor must certify that all necessary payments have been made.

All of this information should be set forth in an affidavit. The affidavit, as opposed to a simple statement or letter, adds credibility to the document and assures its usefulness as evidence. It must be understood, however, that further release of lien documents probably will be needed, as most states have separate statutory forms or requirements for that type of document.

The information contained in the waiver, release and discharge document is often hard to obtain after payment. The problem should be avoided by making full execution and submission of the document conditions precedent to final payment.

§2.11 2. FORM   Waiver, Release and Discharge

Certificate and Affidavit made this _____ day of _____ 19____,
by _____ ("Releasor"), a subcontractor/supplier to _____ ("Contractor") relating to a relationship and/or Contract for the performing and/or furnishing of work, labor, services, materials and/or equipment in connection with a Prime Contract and Project known as _____

For and in consideration of _____ Dollars ($_____), and other good and valuable consideration, which sum is acknowledged as being the final and total amount due or alleged due or owing from the Contractor, its sureties _____ and all other guarantors on any performance, payment, labor and/or material bond or other undertaking, (hereinafter collectively referred to as "Releasee") the receipt of which, by Releasor from Releasee, and payment thereof, is hereby acknowledged; the Releasor for and on behalf of itself and all parties claiming any interest in or through it, and for its successors and assigns, does waive, release and discharge the Releasee from all causes of action, suits, debts, accounts, bonds, contracts, promises, damages, liens, encumbrances, judgments, claims and demands whatsoever, in law or equity, which against the Releasee, jointly or separately, the Architect/Engineer and the Owner of the Project, Releasor ever had, now has, or might hereinafter have, relating directly or indirectly to the aforesaid relationship, Contract, Prime Contract and/or Project. The Releasor hereby agrees to indemnify and hold the Releasee harmless from any and all damages, costs, expenses, demands, suits, liens and legal fees, directly or indirectly relating to any claim for compensation by any other party for work, labor, services, materials and/or equipment which directly or indirectly relates to that which was performed or should have been performed by the Releasor, and from and against any claim relating to any work, labor, services, materials and/or equipment allegedly performed by the Releasor.

The Releasor hereby certifies and warrants that it has fully paid for all work, labor, services, materials and/or equipment provided to it in connection with the Contract, Prime Contract and/or Project. The Releasor hereby grants to the Contractor the right to review and audit any and all books and records of the Releasor at any time for verficiation.

In witness whereof, this Waiver, Release and Discharge has been executed this _____ day of _____ 19_____.

_____
Releasor

By: _____

State of _____, County of _____: ss:
I _____ being duly sworn, depose and say that I make this Waiver, Release and Discharge Certificate and Affidavit under penalty or perjury and according to law, and state that I am the _____ of the Releasor identified herein, that I am fully authorized to execute this document on its behalf, and that the statements contained herein are true and correct.

By: _____

Sworn to before me this _____ day of _____ 19_____.

_____
Notary Public (Signature and seal)

THREE Contractor's Daily Report Form

§3.01 Introduction
§3.02 Form—Daily Report

§3.01 A. INTRODUCTION

If it can't be proved, forget it. This statement should be heeded by every contractor. No matter what contract form is used or what problems or claims may exist, if the **facts** cannot be proved by reliable, admissible evidence, forget the claim. A proper daily report is the most important document concerning a construction project. If the daily report is kept in a complete, detailed and trustworthy fashion, for the purpose of running a business and not for the purpose of litigation, it will become evidence. The daily report, if it complies with the business record statutes of the state or other jurisdiction involved, can become evidence even without testimony of the person who wrote it.

Since business record statutes differ among jurisdictions (and since, even when similar statutes are involved, the courts' interpretations may differ), it is advisable for the prime contractor to try to adhere to the most stringent.

For the document, under the strictest guidelines, to be admissible evidence:

1. The daily report must be prepared and kept in the regular course of the contractor's business.

2. The person who keeps the daily report must do so as part of that person's business function.

3. The daily report should be handwritten, and the original should be kept as the official record.

4. The record must be made from the personal knowledge of the person writing it.

5. The record must be written at the time events occur, which should be daily.

6. It must not omit items which normally would be included.

The daily report form in §3.02 is not intended to be the sole report kept in the field. Many of the items in the daily report suggest further business records and documents which should be kept. These include a separate visitor's log, material/equipment log, accident reports, memoranda and minutes of meetings, test reports, quality control reports, detailed force reports, etc.

The intent of this daily report is to put as many facts on a single sheet as possible. In addition to serving as a record of the facts, the report should stimulate communication between field and office.

The time necessary to complete a form properly is a minor investment compared to the potential product. A properly completed form never should have to be used as evidence. It will stimulate the author of the document to think about the day's activities and to be prepared for the subsequent days. Use of the document will establish a direct line of communication between the field and office, and will aid in the performance of the project so as to avoid litigation.

§3.02   B. FORM   Daily Report

PROJECT NO. _____   REPORT NO. _____

PROJECT _____ DATE: _____ DAY: _____

WEATHER CONDITIONS: _____ At _____ .M
  (Temp.-Precipitation-Etc.)
WEATHER CHANGES: _____ At _____ .M
SITE CONDITIONS: _____ At _____ .M

FORCE REPORT (Own) TRADES/PERSONNEL	CAT.	HOURS S.1 | 0.1	ACTIVITY DESCRIPTION LOCATION CONTRACT CHANGE EXTRAWORK — ETC.

TIME SHEETS (ARE) (ARE NOT) ATTACHED

COMMENTS:

CRAFT (Trade)	EMPLOYER: *(Sub.)(Owner)* *(Prime Contr.) (Other)*	Admn.	Supt.	Fore.	Jry.	App.	Etc.	Total	ACTIVITY DESCRIPTION

TIME SHEETS (ARE) (ARE NOT) ATTACHED

COMMENTS:

EQUIPMENT REPORT DESCRIPTION	Own	Rent	Hours	Transfer Date	ACTIVITY DESCRIPTION: LOCATION CONTRACT — CHANGE — EXTRA WORK — IDLE%

COMMENTS:

CONTRACT WORK COMMENTS:

WORK STARTED: _____ WORK COMPLETED: _____

TESTS CONDUCTED: _____

NON-CONTRACT WORK COMMENTS *(CHANGES, EXTRAS, CLAIMS)*:

_____ EFFECT: _____

MATERIAL, & EQUIPMENT RECEIVED: Annex Written Slips

DESCRIPTION	QUANTITY	CARRIER	CONDITION	TIMELINESS	COMMENTS

ORDERS & DIRECTIVES: Written and Oral: Annex Copies of Written

FROM	TO	RELATING TO	RESPONSE	COMMENT & ACTION

NOTICES & PROTESTS: Written and Oral: Annex Copies of Written

FROM	TO	RELATING TO:	RESPONSE	COMMENT & ACTION

VISITORS:

NAME	REPRESENTING	PURPOSE	COMMENT & ACTION

DOCUMENTS RECEIVED: Annex Copies

FROM	TO	RELATING TO	RESPONSE	COMMENT & ACTION

194 CONTRACTOR'S DAILY REPORT FORM

SCHEDULE & PERFORMANCE STATUS: *(Change in Sequence and Operations, Delays, Accelerations, On Schedule, Suspensions)*

DESCRIPTION	CAUSE	WORK AFFECTED	COMMENT & ACTION

ADDITIONAL — EXTRA — UNANTICIPATED COST FACTORS: *(New & Previous Problems & Claims)*

_____

ASSISTANCE NEEDED: *(HELP)*

_____

MEETINGS:

BETWEEN	PURPOSE	RESULT	COMMENT & ACTION

ACCIDENT REPORT:

_____

REMARKS

_____

SIGNATURE

FOUR   Joint Venture Documents

§4.01 Introduction
§4.02 Form—Pre-Contract Joint Venture Agreement

§4.01   A. INTRODUCTION

The joint venture agreement is a legal mechanism needed to accomplish practical results. The joint venture agreement is a means by which two or more independent entities can be brought together to act as a single entity for particular purposes. The reasons for forming a joint venture are as varied as the number of practical problems which face a contractor who cannot tackle them without the aid of another.

The contractor might desire to submit a bid which calls for bondability beyond the contractor's financial capability. To overcome this problem, a joint venture may be formed in order to create financial responsibility. This is only one example of the numerous financial concerns which can give rise to the need for a joint venture.

Another reason for the establishment of a joint venture is the desire to pool talents, skills, and expertise. Many of the design-build prime contracts involve joint ventures where mental as well as financial resources are pooled. The same situation occurs in many construction projects where several major areas of expertise must be pooled. For example, this happens in the bidding and construction of many large sewerage and solid waste treatment facilities.

A major political or moral reason for the formation of joint ventures has come to the fore in recent years. This involves the governmental desire for creating and expanding minority involvement in construction. Governmental encouragement of minority participation is shown by public laws which call for a ten percent requirement of minority business enterprise involvement. Meeting the ten percent requirement often necessitates some form of joint venture participation.

At the time of creation of any joint venture, the entities involved must check all local, state, national and international rules and regulations. If an architectural or engineering firm is involved, licensing statutes, as well as canons of ethics, must be investigated.

The joint venture agreement can be used to create a form of partnership or corporate entity. The partnership joint venture appears to be more flexible. However, the joint venture, when it operates as a partnership, seems to have greater potential for individual problems. The corporate joint venture typically will give greater security and limitation of potential liability. This issue must be discussed with counsel at the time of formation of the joint venture. The tax consequences also must be considered in deciding which type of joint venture to form, especially when a foreign entity or factor is involved.

If the joint venture is entered into for the purpose of negotiations with a third party or for bidding, then it is recommended that two agreements be formed. The first agreement should be the pre-contract joint venture agreement. A more detailed and comprehensive joint venture agreement should be formalized when the negotiations or bidding is successful.

The post-contract joint venture agreement cannot be set forth as a single, standard form. There are too many reasons for the formation of the joint venture, and too many variables which preclude any standard form. A joint venture agreement checklist should include the following items:

1. name of the joint venture;
2. type of joint venture;
3. purpose of the joint venture;
4. capital and resource contribution of the respective entities;
5. restrictions on the use of joint venture assets;
6. banking and finance limitations on the joint venture and each of the entities;
7. control of the joint venture;
8. board of directors;
9. percentage of ownership;
10. percentage of participation;
11. basis for compensation to the entities and the joint venture;
12. liability and obligations, and limits on them, between the respective entities;
13. duration of the joint venture;
14. geographical limitations on the joint venture;
15. distribution of assets, profits, capital, etc.;
16. restrictive covenants against competition between the joint venture entities and the joint venture;
17. bonding provisions;
18. expense allocations and computations;
19. contracting methods;
20. accounting procedures;
21. legal counsel and representation;
22. default and penalties;
23. arbitration;
24. termination and dissolution.

§4.02 B. FORM Pre-Contract Joint Venture Agreement

This Agreement entered into this _____ day of _____ 19____ by and between _____, (hereinafter referred to as "_____") and _____ (hereinafter referred to as "_____"), the said joint venture parties (hereinafter collectively referred to as "Parties"): Witness:

Whereas, the Parties desire to submit a joint venture proposal and if successful to perform, as a joint venture, the construction of a contract and project known and described as _____, the Parties agree as follows:

A proposal for said contract and project shall be submitted in the name of the Parties as a Joint Venture.

The Joint Venture proposal responsibilities and expenses shall be delegated to the respective parties hereto in the following manner:

The terms and amounts for the Joint Venture proposal are to be agreed upon by the Parties, and if said agreement cannot be reached, then no proposal shall be submitted under the Joint Venture name.

Appropriate bid bond or other bid security shall be divided between the respective parties as follows:

In the event the Joint Venture proposal is rejected, this precontract agreement, the Joint Venture, and the rights and liabilities of the Parties shall be terminated with the exception of fulfilling those obligations specified in this agreement.

The Joint Venture is being sponsored by _____.

The name of said Joint Venture shall be _____. In the event such Joint Venture proposal is accepted, and the contract is to be awarded to the Joint Venture, a more detailed Joint Venture agreement will be promptly entered into providing for the performance of the work, furnishing of the necessary capital, monies, equipment, machinery, labor, supervision and engineering, and providing for the imposing of penalties upon any defaulting party and providing for the surviving party to complete the contract in the event any participant should become bankrupt or otherwise unable to perform its full share of the contract. The Parties acknowledge that, as of this date, the obligations of the respective parties under the desired post-contract Joint Venture Agreement are as follows:

As working capital is needed, each party will promptly contribute its share according to the percentage as listed below. The Joint Venture management, rights, and obligations, and their respective interests and participation in the Joint Venture shall be as follows:
_____%
_____%
This Joint Venture shall be for this contract and project only, and shall be conducted separate and apart from all other business of either of the respective parties.

The Parties hereto shall not sell, assign, or in any manner encumber or transfer its interest or any part thereof, by operation of law or otherwise, in this Joint Venture agreement or the proposal without obtaining prior written consent of the other party hereto. Each party shall bear, in accordance with the above percentages, the costs, obligations and liabilities for the operation of the Joint Venture if the proposal is successful.

This Pre-Contract Joint Venture Agreement is executed and acknowledged on this date.

(seal)   _____
                                    A Joint Venture Party

(seal)   _____
                                    A Joint Venture Party

PART TWO

The Construction Documents I Advocate Using When Representing The Subcontractor

McNeill Stokes, Esq.

The forms set out in this Part evolved during many years of representing subcontractors all across the country. In the course of that practice, one of the biggest problems I have encountered is that subcontractors are often presented with inequitable forms by other parties. Subcontractors, along with all the other members of the construction team, have a right to expect construction documents that are fair and equitable. If such forms are not offered, the subcontractor must be prepared to provide its own.

That problem has resulted in the forms offered here. Standard subcontract forms that balance the sometimes conflicting interests of subcontractors and general contractors are needed. Subcontractor bidding is a legally treacherous process demanding a written proposal form. Dealing with suppliers requires simple purchase order forms that contain the legal language necessary to protect the purchaser. General contractor's oral change orders create a need for a work authorization form to reduce the oral order to writing. A privity agreement has been included since disputes with the owner do occur. The instrument most often used by contractors for the purpose of a specific construction project is the joint venture agreement, to which a chapter is devoted.

The forms in Part Two are not meant to be exhaustive of all the forms necessary in representing subcontractors. They are, however, representative of the forms more frequently requested of the counsel for subcontractors.

FIVE Documents Applicable to Subcontractors and General Contractors

Subcontractor Proposal Forms
§5.01 *Introduction*
§5.02 *Forms—Proposal*

Standard Subcontract Forms
§5.03 *Introduction*
§5.04 *Payment Terms*
§5.05 *Scope of Work*
§5.06 *Scheduling and Liquidated Damages*
§5.07 *Temporary Site Facilities*
§5.08 *Conduit Clauses*
§5.09 *Warranties*
§5.10 *Hold Harmless and Indemnity Provisions*
§5.11 *Form—AGC Standard Form of Subcontract Agreement with Suggested Modifications*
§5.12 *Form—AIA Standard Form of Agreement Between Contractor and Subcontractor (A401—1978 Edition) with Suggested Modifications*

Authorization for Extra or Changed Work
§5.13 *Introduction*
§5.14 *Form*

A. SUBCONTRACTOR PROPOSAL FORMS

§5.01   1. Introduction   The proposal form normally is the blueprint for the offer to enter into a contract. Taking time to complete the proposal form fully and accurately is a must for a subcontractor. The description of the scope of the work in the proposal should be precise. The description should state the plans and specifications by sheet numbers, date, date of last revisions and addenda. If the work is not described in detail, the subcontractor may bid on a version of the plans which includes a later revision that materially changes the work. An example of a precise description of the work is:

> The subcontractor will furnish labor, material and supervision necessary to construct the mechanical work shown on drawings M1–M8, dated March 1, 1977 and last revisions October 1, 1977 and drawings M9–M12, dated March 1, 1977 as revised August 10, 1977 in

accordance with the specifications 15A and 15B, (mechanical only) dated October 14, 1977, and addenda 1–3, and excluding the following. . . .

This proposal form is recommended for use by the subcontractor when bidding because it stipulates that areas will be in a condition acceptable for work; that there will be sufficient areas completed to insure continued work; that all work will be done during regular working hours; that overtime will be an extra; that the subcontractor will not be responsible for breakage or protection of the work; and that the buyer will furnish all temporary site facilities, including storage and hoisting.

This proposal form contains the very important financial stipulations that monthly progress payments will be made on or before the 10th day of each month; that final payment is to be made within thirty days after substantial completion; that no backcharges will be valid without the subcontractor's agreement; and that all subcontracts which are not paid when due will accrue 1 1/2% interest, plus reasonable attorney's fees. It provides that the subcontractor has the right to stop work and file a lien for nonpayment. No demand for liquidated damages will be valid unless it is stated expressly in the proposal. The work will be insured by the party with whom the subcontractor is dealing. The form also provides that the year's warranty covers only workmanship. Furthermore, consequential damages are excluded. There is also an excusable delay clause covering delays for reasons beyond the subcontractor's control. Some payment terms have been left to be stipulated on the front, such as no retention or escalation clauses, which provide for an increase in the contract price if a delay occurs through no fault of the subcontractor.

If the contractor signs the subcontractor's proposal, then a binding contract comes into existence. The goal is to make sure that the terms and conditions of the subcontractor's proposal are incorporated by reference into any contract so that the terms and conditions of the proposal take precedence. The terms and conditions of the proposal should be incorporated into any contract that is subsequently signed, by adding the words: "The scope of the work and terms and conditions which are as stated in subcontractor's proposal dated _____, are incorporated by reference which shall take precedence." The subcontractor may not always accomplish this goal, but a proposal form that protects the subcontractor's interests is a good starting point.

§5.02   2. FORMS   **Proposal**

FOR: _____   PROJECT: _____

_____   LOCATION: _____

_____   DESIGN PROFESSIONAL _____

DATE: _____   DRAWINGS NO: __ DATED: _____

SPECIFICATION DATED: _____

Subject to prompt acceptance within _____ days and to all conditions stipulated on the reverse side, we propose to furnish materials and labor at the prices as stipulated below:

PRICE:

The undersigned accepts this proposal and all its terms and conditions as a binding contract subject only to the approval of the credit of the Buyer by the Seller which shall not be unreasonably withheld.

SELLER: _____

BY: _____

TITLE: _____

COMPANY: _____

BY: _____

TITLE: _____

DATE: _____

CONDITIONS OF PROPOSAL

1. Acceptance of this proposal by Buyer shall be acceptance of all terms and conditions recited herein or incorporated by reference. Allowing the Seller to commence work or preparation for work will constitute acceptance by Buyer of this Proposal and all its terms and conditions. Quotations herein, unless otherwise stated, are for immediate acceptance and subject to change.

2. The Seller shall be paid monthly progress payments on or before the 10th of each month for the value of work completed plus the amount of materials and equipment suitably stored applied to the contract sum less the aggregate of previous payments to the Seller. Final payment shall be due 30 days after the work described in this Proposal is substantially completed. Sales of materials are payable in cash on delivery of the goods.

3. No back charges or claim of the Buyer for services shall be valid except by the agreement in writing by the Seller before work is executed.

4. All sums not paid when due shall bear interest at the rate of 1 1/2% per month from due date until paid or the maximum legal rate permitted by law whichever is less; and all costs of collection, including a reasonable attorney's fee, shall be paid by Buyer.

5. If the Buyer fails to make payment to the Seller as herein provided, then the Seller may stop work without prejudice to any other remedy it may have.

6. Buyer is to prepare all work areas so as to be acceptable for Seller's work under the contract. Seller will not be called upon to start work until sufficient areas are ready to insure continued work until job completion.

7. After acceptance of this Proposal as provided, Seller shall be given a reasonable time in which to make delivery of materials and/or labor to commence and complete the performance of the contract. Seller shall not be responsible for delays or defaults where occasioned by any causes of any kind and extent beyond its control, including but not limited to: delays caused by the owner, general contractor, architect and/or engineers; armed conflict or economic dislocation resulting therefrom; embargos, shortages of labor, equipment or materials production facilities or transportation; labor difficulties, civil disorders of any kind; action of a civil or military authorities; vendor priorities and allocations, fires, floods, accidents and acts of God.

8. All workmanship is guaranteed against defects in workmanship for a period of one year from the date of installation. THIS WARRANTY IS IN LIEU OF ALL OTHER WARRANTIES EXPRESS OR IMPLIED INCLUDING ANY WARRANTIES OF MERCHANTABILITY OR FITNESS FOR A PARTICULAR PURPOSE. Seller will not be responsible for special, incidental, or consequential damages. Seller shall not be responsible for damage to its work by other parties. Any repair work necessitated by caused damage will be considered as an order for extra work. Our responsibility for damage or loss in transit ceases upon delivery in good condition to a public carrier.

9. Work called for herein is to be performed during Seller's regular working hours. Overtime rates will be charged for all work performed outside such hours at extra costs.

10. All materials shall be furnished in accordance with the respective industry tolerance of color variation, thickness, size, finish, texture and performance standards.

11. Notwithstanding any provision contained in this Proposal or the contract documents between Owner and Contractor, Seller may file a lien or claim on its behalf in the event that any payment to Seller is not made as and when provided for by the agreement.

12. The subcontract form used between the Seller and the Buyer will be the current AIA

Standard Form Subcontract Document A401. Where there is a conflict between provisions of either the AIA Subcontract Form, or the contract documents between Owner and Contractor, and this Proposal, then this Proposal shall govern.

13 The Buyer shall furnish all temporary site facilities including suitable covered storage space and hoisting at no cost to Seller.

14 The Buyer shall make no demand for liquidated damages for delays or actual damages for delays in any sum in excess of such amount as may be specifically named in this Proposal and no liquidated damages may be assessed against the Seller for delays or causes attributed to other contractors or arising outside the scope of this Proposal.

15 Buyer shall purchase and maintain property insurance upon the full value of the entire work and/or materials to be supplied which shall include the interest of the Seller.

B. STANDARD SUBCONTRACT FORMS

§5.03   1. Introduction   Too often subcontractors sign subcontract forms, which are furnished to them by general contractors, without having knowledge of the very serious legal implications of many of the subcontract clauses that give the general contractors unnecessary legal and practical advantages. Many subcontractors only check to see that their names are spelled properly and that the amounts of money are stated correctly before they sign subcontract forms which create unsuspected liabilities for them.

Not only are subcontractors met by strict provisions imposed on them by the terms of the general contract, which frequently are incorporated by reference into the subcontractor's scope of the work, but also subcontractors often are faced with additional harsh provisions in the subcontract forms, which give the general contractors unnecessary advantages. These subcontract forms usually have been drafted intentionally by the general contractors' attorneys to obtain maximum advantages over the subcontractors. The subcontractors may fail to appreciate fully the legal implications and consequences of the language. These loaded subcontract forms have become increasingly longer and more complicated. They are devised deliberately by the attorneys to protect the interests of the general contractors at the expense of the subcontractors.

It is a sound approach for the subcontractors, in lieu of any subcontract forms devised by individual general contractors, to substitute more neutral standard subcontract forms—either the American Institute of Architects standard subcontract form (AIA Document A-401, 1978 edition) or the AGC-ASC form (1966 edition) sponsored by the Associated General Contractors and other national specialty and subcontractor associations. If a subcontractor is presented with a subcontract form that obviously has been devised to protect the interest of the general contractor, then the subcontractor should retype the special contract terms on either an AIA or an AGC standard subcontract form and present it to the general contractor for execution as a neutral subcontract form. General contractors readily accept these two neutral forms, which have come into wide national use. Copies of the AIA subcontract form can be obtained either from AIA national headquarters, or from virtually any blueprint company, for a small charge. Copies of the AGC subcontract form may be obtained from the national or local chapters of Associated General Contractors, from the national or many of the local chapters of the American Subcontractors Association, or from many other specialty contractor associations who sponsor the AGC form.

The wise subcontractor takes a practical approach by filling out the terms and conditions of an AIA standard subcontract form A-401 and sending filled out copies to the general contractor with a polite letter proposing to substitute the form in lieu of the obviously loaded subcontract form initially forwarded by the general contractor. The subcontractor may sign the filled-out, neutral form or await the general contractor's signature before signing, and may request that the general contractor sign all copies and return one copy to the subcontractor. More often than not, the subcontract form, signed by the general contractor, is returned in the mail. The difference between presenting a properly filled-out, neutral standard subcontract form and orally proposing the substitution of a neutral subcontract form is that the general contractor can see readily that the filled-out, AIA standard subcontract form A-401 is more or less neutral and protects the general contractor as well as the subcontractor. In order to form a legally binding subcontract and to continue with the work, all the general contractor needs to do is to sign the subcontract form.

Where the general contractor responds to the subcontractor that the AIA standard subcontract form A-401 is unacceptable, the subcontractor is in an excellent position to propose the AGC standard subcontract form as a compromise. The subcontractor may state that, since neither party was pleased with the subcontract forms initially proposed, the use of the AGC standard subcontract form would be an adequate compromise. More often than not, this will be acceptable to both the general contractor and the subcontractor. The AGC subcontract form is more readily accepted by general contractors than the AIA subcontract form, since the AGC's form is sponsored and approved by the general contractor's own national association. Either the AIA or the AGC standard subcontract form contains terms that protect both the general contractor and the subcontractor. Certainly both forms are more neutral to the subcontractors than the loaded subcontract forms devised by the general contractors.

Many subcontractors also put in their bids the stipulation that the subcontractor's bid is premised on the condition that an AIA or AGC standard subcontract form be used between the parties if the bid is accepted. If the subcontractor's bid is accepted, the subcontractor is in a better legal position to insist on the use of the stipulated standard form subcontract. Many subcontractors also draft either the AIA or AGC subcontract form and send the form to the general contractor after the contractor indicates that the subcontractor's bid has been accepted.

§5.04 2. Payment Terms The subcontractor runs the risk of not getting paid if payment to the subcontractor is contingent upon payment by the owner to the general contractor, or upon the architect's approving the subcontractor's work. A typical example of the contingent payment clause is:

> Contractor agrees to pay the subcontractor thirty days after completion of the work, certification by the architect and payment by the owner or general contractor.

In a substantial number of recent decisions by the courts of Massachusetts, Maryland, North Carolina, California, New York and Florida, contingent payment clauses have been interpreted to allow recovery by subcontractors even though the general contractor is not paid by the owner.[1] These recent cases have construed contingent payment clauses as not barring a subcontractor's right to recovery. The payment by the owner is not a condition precedent to the subcontractor's right to payment after a reasonable length of time. In other words, courts in recent cases have construed the contingent payment language as a procedural timing device to defer the subcontractor's payment for a reasonable length of time, but typical contingent payment clauses ultimately do not bar the subcontractor's right to recover from the general contractor.

The law relating to contingent payment clauses is moving toward upholding the subcontractor's right to recovery of payment after a reasonable time, in spite of the owner's failure to pay the general contractor. The courts are likely to allow the subcontractor to recover when the owner's failure to pay the general contractor is the general

---

1   *A J Wolfe & Co v Baltimore Contractors Inc* 355 MA 636, 244 NE2d 717 (1969); *Atlantic States Constr Co v Drummond & Co* 251 MD 77, 246 A2d 251 (1968); *Howard-Green Elec Co v Chaney & James Constr Inc* 12 NCAp 63, 182 SE2d 601 (1971). Similar results were reached in the case of *Thomas J Dyer Co v Bishop Intl Engineering Co* 303 F2d 655 (6th Cir 1962); *Midland Engineering Co v John A Hall Constr Co* 398 FSupp 981 (ND IN 1975); *Schuler-Hass Elec Corp v Aetna Casualty & Surety* 649 AD2d 260 (NY 1975).

contractor's own fault.[2] The law does not allow parties to benefit from their own wrongs, and general contractors should not be allowed to raise contingent payment clauses to bar payment of subcontractors when the owners' refusal to pay the general contractors is caused by the general contractors.

However, the last thing that a subcontractor wants is to resort to litigation to override a contingent payment clause that the subcontractor has signed. Even if the subcontractor successfully proves the right to payment when the owner does not pay the general contractor, the general contractor will read the language literally and will stand on that language to deny payment to the subcontractor. Of course, a subcontractor can strike out the words that make payment contingent upon payment from the owner to the general contractor or contingent upon the architect's certifying the work. A better solution for the subcontractor is to add a savings clause which clearly establishes that the subcontractor will be paid if the general contractor is not paid by the owner, or if the architect does not certify the work for any reason not the fault of the subcontractor. Ordinarily general contractors accept such savings clauses, and subcontractors should not sign contingent payment clauses unless language similar to the following savings clause is included:

> If the architect fails to issue a certificate for payment or the contractor does not receive payment for any cause which is not the fault of the subcontractor, the contractor shall pay the subcontractor, on demand, progress payments and the final payment.

The above clause essentially uses the language of Article 12.4.3 of the AIA standard subcontract form A-401. If a subcontractor substitutes the AIA standard subcontract form, the subcontractor automatically includes the savings clause which insures the right to payment.

The AGC standard form subcontract contains a savings provision similar to the AIA payment clause, which gives the subcontractor the right to demand progress payments if payment certificates are not issued for any cause not the fault of the subcontractor, with the added requirement that the failure of the architect to certify the work must also be caused by the fault of the contractor. It is questionable whether the AGC form permits a subcontractor to obtain final payment if the owner or architect does not issue a certificate for payment. The AGC clause states in Article XX(22):

> The Contractor shall pay the Subcontractor on demand for his work and/or materials as far as executed and fixed in place, less the retained percentage, at the time the payment should be made to the Subcontractor if the Architect or Owner's authorized agent fails to issue the certificate for any fault of the Contractor and not the fault of the Subcontractor or as otherwise provided herein.

It is recommended that the words "and final payment" be inserted in this clause in AGC forms to ensure the subcontractor's right to final payment, and that the words "for any fault of the contractor and" be deleted to avoid having to establish the fault of the general contractor to ensure payment to the subcontractor.

Ostensibly, retention is withheld to ensure that performance of the work will be completed by the subcontractor. After a subcontractor completes the work, the reason for withholding retention ceases. In practice, almost all of the subcontract forms which

---

2 *Standard Asbestos Mfg Co v Kaiser* 316 ILAp 441, 45 NE2d 75 (1942)

are drafted by general contractors allow the general contractors to withhold retention until the entire construction project has been completed. Those subcontractors, such as the clearing, grading, foundation, roofing, concrete and steel erection subcontractors, who complete their work at an early stage of construction on the project, may have to wait many months or even years for their retention under such retention clauses. Of course, for those subcontractors in the finishing trades, who work on the project up to its completion, delays in receiving final payment of retention are not as severe.

For a subcontractor to avoid having to wait until completion of the entire project to receive the subcontract retention, the payment clauses should be modified to state that:

> Final payment shall be due thirty (30) days after completion of the work by the subcontractor.

Under this language the subcontractor does not have to wait until after final acceptance of the project to receive full payment for the work. The subcontractor's warranty is adequate to protect the general contractor against problems that might arise after completion of the subcontractor's work.

One of the traps that the subcontractor must avoid is the general contractor's withholding a greater amount of retention from the subcontractor than is withheld from the general contractor by the owner. If the general contractor has the retention reduced at the 50% completion stage to 5%, yet continues to hold 10% retention on the subcontractors until completion of the job, a tremendous pool of working capital is created for the general contractor's use at the expense of the subcontractors. When the general contractor withholds more retention funds from the subcontractor than the owner withholds from the general contractor, the general contractor is not greatly motivated to finish the work, because finishing the work will actually cost the general contractor money when the general contractor must pay more retention to the subcontractor than the owner pays the contractor.

To keep the general contractor from withholding more retention from the subcontractor than is withheld from the general contractor by the owner, the subcontractor should always insert a clause that states:

> The general contractor will withhold no more retention from the subcontractor than is withheld by the owner from the general contractor for the subcontractor's work.

§5.05   3. Scope of Work

A subcontractor should be extremely careful not to sign a subcontract which expands the scope of the work beyond that which was anticipated in the subcontractor's bid. The subcontract should contain a very definite and concise statement of the work, which is limited to the exact work contemplated by the subcontractor.

The clause in a subcontract document describing the work to be performed is one of the most important clauses in the subcontract. The description of the subcontractor's work must be precise. Otherwise, the subcontractor may be required to perform work not contemplated when the subcontractor bid the job or negotiated the subcontract.

Subcontractors should take pains to make sure that there are no ambiguous or dragnet clauses that would require the performance of any work other than that specifically included in the subcontractor's bid. Furthermore, if certain work is excluded from the subcontractor's bid, it also should be excluded from the subcontract. If it is not excluded from the subcontract, the subcontractor may have to perform the work even though it was excluded from the bid.

In the subcontracts relating to the scope of the work, there are troublesome provisions which make the subcontractor liable for providing not only the work and materials described in the trade section of the plans and specifications, but also any work and materials relating to the subcontractor's trade which may be found elsewhere in the plans and specifications. The subcontractor who, in pricing a job, pays attention only to the plans and specifications which relate to the subcontractor's particular trade, may not recognize the additional requirements under this broad scope of work, and consequently may drastically underprice the subcontract. The subcontractor must delete broad statements relating to the scope of the work and must describe the work exactly as bid by specifying sections, divisions or paragraph numbers and related plans.

The description of the work should begin with the classification of the type of work that the subcontractor is going to perform, e.g., mechanical, electrical, roofing, plumbing, grading, structural, concrete rebar, scaffolding, tile or terrazzo, etc. The description should be precise and should use words that exactly define the type of work the subcontractor is going to do. In the next part of the description of the work, the subcontract scope of work should denominate the plans by sheet numbers, date and date of last revision. If the subcontractor does not describe the work in detail, the subcontractor may bid on a version of the plans and specifications which is later revised and may sign a contract which specifies a later revision date that materially changes the work. The next part of the description should state that the work shown on the plans will be in accordance with designated sections of the specifications. If the subcontractor is bidding only part of a trade, e.g., the plumbing work as part of the mechanical, then only those specifications that relate to plumbing work should be listed.

A good example of a precise description of the work in a subcontract document is as follows:

> The Subcontractor shall furnish the labor, materials, equipment and supervision necessary to construct the mechanical work shown on drawing numbers M-1 through M-8, dated March 1, 1977, and last revised August 10, 1977, in accordance with specification sections 15A and 15B (mechanical only) dated October 14, 1977, and Addenda 1–3, and excluding the following. . . .

Dragnet clauses should be avoided by the subcontractors. These clauses provide that the subcontractors will perform the work of their trades, regardless of the sections in which the specifications may appear, and regardless of the drawings on which the work may appear. Frequently, architects will place work out of their normal specifications section in a different category of drawings than that in which the work is normally encountered. The following type of dragnet clause should *not* be agreed to by the subcontractor to define the scope of the work: "All mechanical work shown on the plans and specifications."

It is unthinkable that a subcontractor would fail to check to see that the subcontract contains a precise statement of the amount of money that the subcontractor is to receive under the subcontract, yet subcontractors tend to ignore or be sloppy in defining the scope of the work, which is the corollary of the payment clause. The scope of work is the other side of the payment coin. It is just as important that the subcontractor be precise in defining the scope of the work as it is that the subcontractor be precise in stating the amount of money to be received under the subcontract.

§5.06   4. Scheduling and Liquidated Damages   Without being aware of any liquidated damages provision in the subcontract, a subcontractor may be subjected to the liquidated damages imposed on the general contractor. Such imposition is caused by providing that the subcontractor is bound to the general contractor in the same manner that the general contractor is bound to the owner. Implicit in such a statement is the fact that if the general contractor is bound to the owner for liquidated damages, the subcontractor may be bound to the general contractor for liquidated damages. Often the general contractor loses time in the early phases of the work, attempts to impose unrealistic time schedules upon subcontractors, and then tries to impose liquidated damages if the subcontractors do not finish within the unrealistic time schedules. Many subcontracts provide that the subcontractor will meet the performance schedules established from time to time by the general contractor. This leaves too much discretion in the general contractor.

Subcontractors would be well advised to include in their subcontract provisions allowing them reasonable time within which to perform their work, plus extensions for any delays which are beyond their control. The subcontract also should specify that the work will be scheduled in proper sequence for continuous work. This will guard against staggered scheduling on a job, which would cost more because of problems of mobilization and demobilization of the job and the loss of job momentum.

The subcontract should stipulate that the contractor will consult with the subcontractor in developing the progress schedule. This will afford the subcontractor an opportunity to establish the activities and working time necessary to perform and complete the subcontractor's work. The following suggested clause requires that the contractor develop a progress schedule with necessary input from the subcontractor and stipulates that the subcontractor will have a reasonable time and proper sequence for the performance of the work:

> Subcontractor shall be responsible for maintaining job progress in accordance with the owner-approved schedule of performance; provided, however, that the Subcontractor shall be afforded an opportunity to establish the activities and working time necessary to perform and complete the work under this Subcontract. In the event a schedule of progress is approved without Subcontractor's input, Contractor agrees that Subcontractor at all times shall have reasonable and sufficient time within which to complete the phases of work as they may occur. Contractor shall be responsible for providing within said schedule reasonable time in proper sequence of the performance of the Subcontractor's work.

The AIA subcontract form requires the general contractor to cooperate with the subcontractor in scheduling the work to avoid conflicts or interferences with the subcontractor's work. The AIA scheduling clause appears in Article 12.2.1 and provides:

> 12.2.1 The Contractor shall cooperate with the Subcontractor in scheduling and performing his Work to avoid conflicts or interference in the Subcontractor's Work, and shall expedite written responses to submittals made by the Subcontractor in accordance with Paragraphs 11.2, 11.9, and 11.10. As soon as practicable after execution of this Agreement, the Contractor shall provide the Subcontractor a copy of the estimated progress schedule of the Contrac-

tor's entire Work which the Contractor has prepared and submitted for the Owner's and the Architect's information, together with such additional scheduling details as will enable the Subcontractor to plan and perform his Work properly. The Subcontractor shall be notified promptly of any subsequent changes in the progress schedule and the additional scheduling details.*

Both the AIA and AGC standard form subcontracts contain provisions which do not allow the general contractor to assess liquidated damages against subcontractors unless specifically stipulated in the subcontract. The following is the language of the AIA standard form subcontract Article 12.5.1 relating to liquidated damages:

> 12.5.1 The Contractor shall make no demand for liquidated damages for delay in any sum in excess of such amount as may be specifically named in this Subcontract, and liquidated damages shall be assessed against this Subcontractor only for his negligent acts and his failure to act in accordance with the terms of this Agreement, and in no case for delays or causes arising outside the scope of this Subcontract, or for which other Subcontractors are responsible.*

The AGC subcontract form contains similar language. The scheduling, coordination and progress of the job is the responsibility of the general contractor. The subcontractors do not have any control over the time of construction other than over the number of days required for the subcontractor to complete the work unobstructed or without interference by other trades. The subcontractor should not accept any liquidated damage provision inserted into the subcontract, unless it is specifically tied to the delays caused by the subcontractor in addition to the number of days stipulated to be required for the work.

§5.07   5. Temporary Site Facilities The question of responsibility for temporary site facilities which are common to all contractors on a job site has been very troublesome. It leads to myriads of disputed backcharges because of general contractors' charging subcontractors for the temporary facilities. The responsibility for furnishing and paying for temporary site facilities should be designated in the subcontract. The best way to avoid backcharges by the general contractor for temporary site facilities is to settle the questions at the bidding and the subcontract stages, rather than waiting until the end of the work, when unsuspecting subcontractors may be surprised with backcharges by the general contractor.

The AIA and the AGC standard form subcontracts have blank spaces to be filled in to designate the responsibility for furnishing and paying for temporary site facilities which the general contractor is to provide at no cost to the subcontractor. These normally will be temporary site facilities and services which the general contractor furnishes that are common to all subcontractors on the job site. To foreclose the general contractor from attempting to backcharge the subcontractors for the cost of these temporary facilities or services, the subcontractor should stipulate that all temporary site facilities and services should be supplied by the general contractor at no cost to the subcontractor, using language such as the following:

> Contractor shall, at no cost to Subcontractor, furnish utilities, services and facilities, as listed

---

* AIA Document A401 Copyright © 1978 by The American Institute of Architects.

below, conveniently located at the construction site for use by Subcontractor to install its work, and of sufficient capacity to service Subcontractor's equipment and employees as well as the equipment and employees of all other subcontractors or contractors including Contractor on the job: (a) Electricity at each floor rated for small tools, hoists, derricks, scaffolds, and welder's equipment, (b) Toilets, (c) Personnel elevators so positioned that Subcontractor personnel are not required to walk up or down more than two floors to get to or from their place of work at the construction site, (d) Drinking water, (e) Rubbish removal from an area designated by the Contractor at each floor, (f) Accessible and adequate storage area within the building for Subcontractor's materials and equipment, (g) Adequate clear area to enable Subcontractor to perform its work without interference, (h) Should Subcontractor elect to use the Contractor's hoist, such use shall be available during regular working hours at no cost to Subcontractor and at such other times which do not cause any interference with Subcontractor's personnel working below prior trades, Contractor will be responsible for furnishing and erecting such protection and moving it as required by Subcontractor, (k) Temporary heat, (l) Perimeter protection and barricades shall be installed in compliance with OSHA regulations at no cost to Subcontractor. Such protection shall not interfere with the normal installation of the work covered under this Subcontract. Where protection or barricades must be removed to allow installation of the work under this Subcontract, it shall be removed and reinstalled by Contractor at no expense to Subcontractor.

The responsibility for furnishing and paying for temporary site facilities is standardized in many cities by recommended bidding conditions established between local chapters of the American Subcontractors Association and local chapters of Associated General Contractors of America, Inc. The typical recommended bidding conditions of these local areas designate responsibility for hoist facilities, temporary electrical service, construction water, trash removal, temporary heat, drinking water, toilet facilities and other necessary temporary site facilities. The bidding conditions normally provide that the general contractor will be responsible for furnishing or contracting to furnish, at no cost to the subcontractor, all temporary facilities. All subcontractors who follow these local recommended bidding conditions have no responsibility for providing or paying for the stipulated temporary site facilities, which are the designated responsibility of the general contractors.

These recommended bidding conditions also may settle the question of whether a subcontractor's price should include a payment or performance bond. The recommended bidding conditions may designate the responsibility for compliance with safety requirements which are common to all contractors on the job site, such as the general contractor's responsibility for furnishing perimeter protection and barricades, and for complying with first aid requirements.

The American Institute of Architects Standard Subcontract Form A-401 expressly limits the authority of the general contractor to backcharge a subcontractor for services unless the contractor gives the subcontractor advance notice and confirms the notice in writing within the first ten days of the following calendar month. Article 12.5.2 of the AIA Standard Subcontract form provides as follows:

12.5.2 Except as may be indicated in this Agreement, the Contractor agrees that no claim for payment for services rendered or materials and equipment furnished by the contractor to the Subcontractor shall be valid without prior notice to the Subcontractor and unless written notice thereof is given by the Contractor to the Subcontractor not later than the tenth day of the calendar month following that in which the claim originated.*

---

* AIA Document A401 Copyright © 1978 by The American Institute of Architects.

The AGC Standard Subcontract Form in Article X(26) requires written confirmation within the first ten days of the following month. Subcontractors should be very wary of clauses which permit the general contractor to backcharge the subcontractor for services rendered.

§5.08   6. Conduit Clauses The general contractor naturally will be motivated to bind the subcontractors to the general contractor as the general contractor is bound to the owner. Conversely, the general contractor should be willing to provide the subcontractors with the same rights, redress and remedies which the general contractor has against the owner. Conduit clauses, also called flow down clauses, provide that the subcontract incorporates the general contract provisions which are applicable to the subcontractor's work. If conduit clauses are used, the same rights and duties should flow equally from the owner down through the general contractor to the subcontractor, as well as flowing from the subcontractor up through the general contractor to the owner. Both the AIA standard subcontract form A-401 and AGC standard subcontract form contain conduit clauses which provide that the subcontractor is bound to the same responsibilities and duties, which are applicable to the subcontracted work, as the general contractor has to the owner. In turn the subcontractor has the same rights, redress and remedies against the general contractor that the general contractor has against the owner. The AIA subcontract form contains the following conduit clause in Article 11.1.1 and the reciprocal rights and responsibilities for the contractor in Clause 12.1.1:

> 11.1.1 The Subcontractor shall be bound to the Contractor by the terms of this Agreement and, to the extent that provisions of the Contract Documents between the Owner and Contractor apply to the Work of the Subcontractor as defined in this Agreement, the Subcontractor shall assume toward the Contractor all the obligations and responsibilities which the Contractor, by those Documents, assumes toward the Owner and the Architect and shall have the benefit of all rights, remedies and redress against the Contractor which the Contractor, by those Documents, has against the Owner, insofar as applicable to this Subcontract, provided that where any provision of the Contract Documents between the Owner and Contractor is inconsistent with any provision of this Agreement, this Agreement shall govern.

> 12.1.1 The Contractor shall be bound to the Subcontractor by the terms of this Agreement and, to the extent that provisions of the Contract Documents between the Owner and the Contractor apply to the Work of the Subcontractor as defined in this Agreement, the Contractor shall assume toward the Subcontractor all the obligations and responsibilities that the Owner, by those Documents, assumes toward Contractor, and shall have the benefit of all rights, remedies, and redress against the Subcontractor which the Owner, by those Documents, has against the Contractor. Where any provision of the Contract Documents between the Owner and the Contractor is inconsistent with any provisions of this Agreement, this Agreement shall govern.*

Often subcontract forms drafted by the general contractors contain a conduit clause which ties the subcontractor to the general contractor's obligations but conspicuously omits the corresponding rights of the subcontractor, such as the following:

> Contractor shall have the same rights and privileges as against the Subcontractor herein as

---

* AIA Document A401 Copyright © 1978 by The American Institute of Architects.

> the Owner in the General Contract has against Contractor. Subcontractor acknowledges that he has read the General Contract and all plans and specifications and is familiar therewith and agrees to comply with and perform all provisions thereof applicable to the Subcontractor.

It is patently unreasonable for the general contractor to attempt to bind the subcontractor to the provisions of the general contract while the general contractor does not give the corresponding rights, remedies and redress to the subcontractor.

If a conduit clause is used in the subcontract, then it is imperative that the subcontractor inspect all of the plans and specifications and contract documents, including the general and special conditions, the general contract and modifications and addenda. This is necessary because the subcontractor is agreeing to be bound by terms and conditions in the subcontract that are contained in the general contract and in plans and specifications applicable to the general contract. If the general contractor is unwilling to allow inspection of the general contract, then the general contract should be excluded from the operation of the conduit clause.

§5.09   7. Warranties   Subcontractors are well advised to limit warranty clauses to start at the time of completion of their installation rather than at the time of acceptance of the entire project. Warranty provisions in subcontracts usually require that the subcontractors warrant their work for one year from final acceptance of the entire project. On jobs where there is extensive site development which may go on for years, the subcontractors are obliged to warrant their portion of the work well beyond the time originally intended.

Subcontractors should make sure that the warranties they extend to the general contractor or owner are clearly defined and that they understand the scope of the warranties. They should be careful that they do not extend the warranties beyond the warranties given to them by manufacturers of equipment and materials installed, unless they do so knowingly and at a price at which they can afford to assume such risks.

Subcontractors not only have to contend with the written or express warranties contained in their contracts for the period of time specified, but subcontractors also must be aware of the unwritten warranties which the law implies. The law implies a warranty of merchantability or fitness for a particular use. If the subcontractor's construction or material is defective, the owner or general contractor may attempt to rely on the implied warranty for a length of time considerably longer than the express warranty. Typically, the statute of limitations periods for implied warranties are four to eight years.

Express warranties contained in the AIA Standard Subcontract Form A-401 in Article 11.7.1 do not exclude implied warranties and stipulate that:

> 11.7.1 The Subcontractor warrants to the Owner, the Architect and the Contractor that all materials and equipment furnished shall be new unless otherwise specified, and that all Work under this Subcontract shall be of good quality, free from faults and defects and in conformance with the Contract Documents. All Work not conforming to these requirements, including substitutions not properly approved and authorized, may be considered defective. The warranty provided in this Paragraph 11.9 shall be in addition to and not in limitation of any other warranty or remedy required by law or by the Contract Documents.*

---

* AIA Document A401 Copyright © 1978 by The American Institute of Architects.

This warranty in the AIA standard subcontract, which is similar to the warranty provisions that typically appear in the general or special conditions of the general contract, specially reserves the implied warranty. Even without the language which stipulates that implied warranties are reserved, the implied warranty would attach to the subcontractor's work unless the implied warranty is expressly excluded by a disclaimer. Under some circumstances, the implied warranties may be excluded by a disclaimer of all implied warranties. For such a disclaimer, the subcontract should stipulate in bold print that:

The express warranties contained herein are in lieu of all other warranties, expressed or implied, including any warranties of merchantability or fitness for a particular use and in no event shall the subcontractor be liable for consequential damages.

Unless the subcontractor excludes the implied warranties and consequential damages, unsuspected legal remedies may be available to the owner or general contractor. This may force the subcontractor to rectify defective work or materials far beyond the express warranty.

§5.10   8. Hold Harmless and Indemnity Provisions   Hold harmless and indemnity clauses in subcontracts should be limited strictly to injuries or damages arising out of the subcontractor's work, caused by the negligence of the subcontractor, or by the subcontractor's agents and employees. It is not unreasonable for the subcontractor to agree to indemnify and hold harmless the general contractor and owner for damages which are caused by the subcontractor's own negligence because the subcontractor normally is responsible for these. However, in recent years, hold harmless provisions have been broadened in scope to require the subcontractor to indemnify the owner, and general contractor and/or the architect against any and all liabilities arising out of the job, including the negligence of the owner, general contractor, and/or the architect.

Those hold harmless clauses which are limited in scope to the subcontractor's agreeing to indemnify and hold harmless the owner, general contractor and architect against the subcontractor's negligence are called limited form hold harmless clauses.

A broad form hold harmless clause, which is very objectionable, is an agreement under which the subcontractor agrees to indemnify and hold harmless the general contractor, the owner and/or the architect against all claims arising out of the work, including any claims resulting from the negligence of the general contractor, the owner, or the architect.

A third class of hold harmless clause is the intermediate form hold harmless clause, which requires the subcontractor to indemnify and hold harmless the contractor against all losses arising out of the work and resulting from the negligence of the subcontractor, even though the party indemnified may also be negligent. An example of an intermediate form hold harmless clause appears in Article 11.11 of the AIA standard form subcontract:

11.11.1 To the fullest extent permitted by law, the Subcontractor shall indemnify and hold harmless the Owner, the Architect and the Contractor and all of their agents and employees from and against all claims, damages, losses and expenses including but not limited to attorney's fees, arising out of or resulting from the performance of the Subcontractor's Work under this Subcontract, provided that any such claim, damage, loss, or expense is attributable to bodily injury, sickness, disease, or death, or to injury to or destruction of tangible property (other than the Work itself) including the loss of use resulting therefrom, to the extent caused in whole or in part by any negligent act or omission of the Subcontractor or anyone directly employed by him or anyone for whose acts he may be liable, regardless of whether it is caused in part by a party indemnified hereunder. Such obligation shall not be construed to negate, or abridge, or otherwise reduce any other right or obligation of indemnity which would otherwise exist as to any party or person described in this Paragraph 11.11.

11.11.2 In any and all claims against the Owner, the Architect, or the Contractor or any of their agents or employees by any employee of the Subcontractor, anyone directly or indirectly employed by him or anyone for whose acts he may be liable, the indemnification obligation under this Paragraph 11.11 shall not be limited in any way by an limitation on the amount or type of damages, compensation or benefits payable by or for the Subcontractor under workers' or workmen's compensation acts, disability benefit acts or other employee benefit acts.

11.11.3 The obligations of the Subcontractor under this Paragraph 11.11 shall not extend to the liability of the Architect, his agents or employees arising out of (1) the preparation or approval of maps, drawings, opinions, reports, surveys, Change Orders, designs or specifications, or (2) the giving of or the failure to give directions or instructions by the Architect, his agents or employees provided such giving or failure to give is the primary cause of the injury or damage.*

A subcontractor who signs a broad form hold harmless clause has become an insurer by agreeing to insure other parties against their negligence and fault. By signing a broad form hold harmless clause, a subcontractor undertakes the obligations of paying for damages for which the subcontractor otherwise would not be legally responsible. When a subcontractor signs a broad form hold harmless clause, a contractual liability is undertaken, as distinguished from a general liability for the subcontractor's own negligent acts. Contractual liabilities are not covered by a subcontractor's general liability insurance. Unless a subcontractor's insurance specifically includes coverage of contractual liability under hold harmless clauses, the subcontractor must pay for any losses that are incurred under these broad form hold harmless clauses arising from damages caused by the fault of someone else. It takes only one substantial uninsured loss to put most subcontracting firms out of business.

There are many recent cases in which subcontractors who were not at fault had to pay very substantial losses and legal expenses because they signed broad form hold harmless clauses and agreed to insure not only the owners, but also the architects and engineers against their own professional negligence.[3]

These recent cases caused concern for subcontractors and, through the efforts of associations representing subcontractors, laws have been passed declaring broad form hold harmless clauses invalid as against public policy. In twenty-six states[4] laws have

---

* AIA Document A401 Copyright © 1978 by The American Institute of Architects.

3 See, e.g., *Kraft Foods v Disheroon* 118 GAAp 632, 165 SE2d 189 (1968)

4 California (CA Civ Code §2782–84 (West 1974)); Delaware (DE Code Tit 6 §2704 (1975)); Florida (FL Stat Ann §725.06 (West 1969 Supp 1977)); Georgia (GA Code Ann §20–504); Hawaii (HI Rev Stat §431–453 (1968)); Idaho (ID Code §29–114 (1967 Supp 1976)); Illinois (IL Ann Stat Ch 29 §61 (Smith-Hurd 1969 Supp 1977)); Indiana (IN Stat Ann §§26–2–5–1, 26–2–5–2 (Burns 1974 Supp 1976)); Maryland (MD Cts & Jud Proc Code Ann §5–305 (1974. 1976)); Michigan (MI Code Stat Ann §26–114(1)(1974)); Mississippi (MS Code Ann §31–5–41 (1972 Supp 1972)); New Hampshire (NH Rev Stat Ann §338A; 1 (1955 Supp 1975)); New Mexico (NM Stat Ann §28–2–1 (1954 Supp 1975)); New York (NY Gen Oblig Law §5–322.1 (McKinney's 1964 Supp 1976)); North Dakota (ND Cent Code §9–08–

been passed which either prohibit, nullify or modify a subcontractor's liability under hold harmless provisions when the injury or damage arises from the sole negligence of the party indemnified under the hold harmless clause, normally the general contractor, owner and/or architect.

These laws generally invalidate broad form hold harmless clauses but usually do not invalidate intermediate hold harmless provisions where the subcontractor is jointly liable with the parties indemnified under the hold harmless provision. If a subcontractor and the party indemnified under a broad form hold harmless clause were both negligent, then even after the passage of this statute, the subcontractor may be jointly negligent with the party indemnified by the hold harmless clause. It is questionable whether the subcontractor's general liability policy covers such losses in spite of the fact that the losses arise, at least in part, from the subcontractor's own negligence. Subcontractors must check with their individual insurance agents to determine whether they are covered under specific hold harmless clauses.

Courts generally do not allow parties to limit their liability by stipulating against their own negligence. On one side are the courts which take the position that no agreement can prevent liability for one's own negligence and allow a party to avoid indirectly responsibility contrary to public policy. Other courts reason that freedom of contract requires upholding agreements, even though the agreements indirectly allow parties to avoid responsibility for the consequences of the parties' own negligence or fault, if such intent is clearly spelled out in the agreement.[5]

However, courts generally bend over backwards to avoid construing hold harmless agreements to include an agreement to indemnify the other parties for the indemnitee's own negligence. If the hold harmless clauses stipulate that the subcontractor shall indemnify the general contractor for any injury or damage arising out of the work, the courts generally have construed this language as not creating a broad form hold harmless clause, and have interpreted the language as only holding the general contractor harmless for those injuries which are caused by the fault of the subcontractor.[6]

Many general contractors will strike out broad form or intermediate form hold harmless clauses if the subcontractor asks. Alternatively, subcontractors should modify broad form hold harmless clauses to a limited form by limiting the hold harmless clauses to cover the subcontractor's negligence, to which the subcontractor already is bound under the law.

When a subcontract contains a broad form hold harmless clause, it either should be deleted, modified to a limited form hold harmless clause, or if the hold harmless clause is signed, it should be insured against loss with broad form contractual liability insurance coverage. All hold harmless clauses should be insured with blanket contractual liability coverage.

Subcontractors should read the hold harmless clauses in subcontracts very carefully,

---

02.1 (1975)); Ohio (OH Rev Code Ann §2305.31 (p 19-Supp 1976)); Oregon (OR Rev Stat §30–140 (1975)); Pennsylvania (PA Stat Ann Tit 68 §491 (Purdon 1965 Supp 1976)); Rhode Island (Bill No 76–S–2324, June 3, 1976)); South Dakota (SD Compiled Laws Ann §56–3–16 (1967 Supp 1976)); Tennessee (Tn Code Ann §62–624 (1976 Supp 1976)); Texas (TX Civ Stat §249d (Vernon 1973)); Utah (UT Code Ann §13-8–1 (1973)); Virginia (VA Code §11–4.1 (1950 Supp 1976)); Washington (WA Rev Code Ann §4.24.115 (1962 Supp 1975)); West Virginia (WV Code §55–8–14 (1966 Supp 1976))

5 See, e.g., *Kraft Foods v Disheroon* 118 GAAp 632, 165 SE2d 189 (1968)
6 *Batson-Cook Co, et al v Georgia Marble Setting Co* 112 GA Ap 226 (1965)

and should check with their attorneys and insurance agents concerning questions about their liability under the clauses. After subcontractors review several hold harmless clauses they probably will acquire working knowledge of the various types of hold harmless clauses so that they can spot problem areas of liability under such clauses in the future.

§5.11   9. FORM   **Standard Subcontract Agreement**

Developed as a guide by The Associated General Contractors of America, The National Electrical Contractors Association, The Mechanical Contractors Association of America, The Sheet Metal and Air Conditioning Contractors National Association and the National Association of Plumbing-Heating-Cooling Contractors.

Standard Subcontract Agreement, Copyright © 1966, reprinted by permission of The Associated General Contractors of America and The Associated Specialty Contractors, Inc.

THIS AGREEMENT made this _____ day of _____ in the year Nineteen Hundred and _____ by and between _____

hereinafter called the Subcontractor and _____

hereinafter called the Contractor.

WITNESSETH, That the Subcontractor and Contractor for the consideration hereinafter named agree as follows:

ARTICLE I

The Subcontractor agrees to furnish all material and perform all work as described in Article II hereof for _____
(Here name the project.)

for _____
(Here name the Contractor.)

at _____
(Here insert the location of the work and name of Owner.)

in accordance with this Agreement, the Agreement between the Owner and Contractor, and in accordance with the General Conditions of the Contract, Supplementary General Conditions, the Drawings and Specifications and addenda prepared by

hereinafter called the Architect or Owner's authorized agent, all of which documents, signed by the parties thereto or identified by the Architect or Owner's authorized agent, form a part of a Contract

between the Contractor and the Owner dated _____, 19___, and hereby become a part of this contract, and herein referred to as the Contract Documents, and shall be made available to the Subcontractor upon his request prior to and at anytime subsequent to signing this Subcontract.

ARTICLE II

The Subcontractor and the Contractor agree that the materials and equipment to be furnished and work to be done by the Subcontractor are:

(Here insert a precise description of the work, preferably by reference to the numbers of the drawings and the pages of the specifications including addenda and accepted alternates.)

The Subcontractor shall furnish the labor, materials, equipment and supervision necessary to construct the _____ work shown on drawing numbers _____ dated _____, and last revised _____, and sections _____ of the Specifications, dated _____ and Addenda numbers _____, and excluding the following:

ARTICLE III

Time is of the essence and the Subcontractor agrees to commence and to complete the work as described in Article II as follows:
(Here insert any information pertaining to the method of notification for commencement of work, starting and completion dates, or duration, and any liquidated damage requirements.)

Subcontractor shall be responsible for maintaining job progress in accordance with the owner-approved schedule of performance; provided, however, that the Subcontractor shall be afforded an opportunity to establish the activities and working time necessary to perform and complete the work under this Subcontract. In the event a schedule of progress is approved without Subcontractor's input, reasonable and sufficient time within which to complete the phases of work as they may occur. Contractor shall be responsible for providing within said schedule reasonable time in proper sequence of the performance of the Subcontractor's work.

(a) No extension of time of this contract will be recognized without the written consent of the Contractor which consent shall not be withheld unreasonably consistent with Article X-4 of this Contract, subject to the arbitration provisions herein provided.

ARTICLE IV

The Contractor agrees to pay the Subcontractor for the performance of this work the sum of _____ ($_____) in current funds, subject to additions and deductions for changes as may be agreed upon in writing, and to make monthly payments on account thereof in accordance with Article X, Sections 20–23 inclusive.

(Here insert additional details—unit prices, etc., payment procedure including date of monthly applications for payment, payment procedure if other than on a monthly basis, consideration of materials safely and suitably stored at the site or at some other location agreed upon in writing by the parties—and any provisions made for limiting or reducing the amount retained after the work reaches a certain stage of completion which should be consistent with the Contract Documents.)

Monthly progress payments shall be paid by the Contractor to the Subcontractor on or before the tenth of each month. Payments will be made for the value of work completed and on account of materials or equipment not incorporated in the Work but delivered and suitably stored at the site and, for materials or equipment suitably stored at some other location agreed upon in advance. Payments for materials or equipment stored on or off the site shall be conditioned upon submission by the Subcontractor of bills of sale or such other procedures satisfactory to the Owner to establish the Owner's title to such materials or equipment or otherwise protect the Owner's interest, including applicable insurance and transportation to the site for those materials and equipment stored off the site.

ARTICLE V

Final payment shall be due when the work described in this contract is fully completed and performed in accordance with the Contract Documents, and payment to be consistent with Article IV and Article X, Sections 18, 20–23 inclusive of this contract.

Before issuance of the final payment the Subcontractor if required shall submit evidence satisfactory to the Contractor that all payrolls, material bills, and all known indebtedness connected with the Subcontractor's work have been satisfied.

Final payment shall be due thirty (30) days after completion of the work by the Subcontractor.

ARTICLE VI   Performance and Payment Bonds

(Here insert any requirement for the furnishing of performance and payment bonds.)

If a performance bond is required by the Contractor, the premium of the bond shall be paid by the Contractor in addition to the contract price.

ARTICLE VII   Temporary Site Facilities

(Here insert any requirements and terms concerning temporary site facilities, i.e., storage, sheds, water, heat, light, power, toilets, hoists, elevators, scaffolding, cold weather protection, ventilating, pumps, watchman service, etc.)

Contractor shall, at no cost to Subcontractor, furnish utilities, services and facilities, as listed below, conveniently located at the construction site for use by Subcontractor to install its work, and of sufficient capacity to service Subcontractor's equipment and employees as well as the equipment and employees of all other subcontractors or contractors including Contractor on the Job: (a) Electricity at each floor rated for small tools, hoists, derricks, scaffolds, and welder's equipment, (b) Toilets, (c) Personnel elevators so positioned that Subcontractor's personnel are not required to walk up or down more than two floors to get to or from their place of work at the construction site, (d) Drinking water, (e) Rubbish removal from an area designated by the Contractor at each floor, (f) Accessible and adequate storage area within the building for Subcontractor's materials and equipment, (g) Adequate clear area to enable Subcontractor to perform its work without interference, (h) Should Subcontractor elect to use the Contractor's hoist, such use shall be available during regular working hours at no cost to Subcontractor and at such other times which do not cause any interference with Subcontractor's personnel working below prior trades, Contractor will be responsible for furnishing and erecting such protection and moving it as required by Subcontractor, (k) Temporary heat, (l) Perimeter protection and barricades shall be installed in compliance with OSHA regulations at no cost to Subcontractor. Such protection shall not interfere with the normal installation of the work covered under this Subcontract, it shall be removed and reinstalled by Contractor at no expense to Subcontractor.

ARTICLE VIII   Insurance

Unless otherwise provided herein, the Subcontractor shall have a direct liability for the acts of his employees and agents for which he is legally responsible, and the Subcontractor shall not be required to assume the liability for the acts of any others.

Prior to starting work the insurance required to be furnished shall be obtained from a responsible company or companies to provide proper and adequate coverage and satisfactory evidence will be furnished to the Contractor that the Subcontractor has complied with the requirements as stated in this Section.

(Here insert any insurance requirements and Subcontractor's responsibility for obtaining, maintaining and paying for necessary insurance, not less than limits as may be specified in the Contract Documents or required by laws. This to include fire insurance and extended coverage, consideration of public liability, property damage, employer's liability, and workmen's compensation insurance for the Subcontractor and his employees. The insertion should provide the agreement of the Contractor and the Subcontractor on subrogation waivers, provision for notice of cancellation, allocation of insurance proceeds, and other aspects of insurance.)

(It is recommended that the AGC Insurance and Bonds Checklist (AGC Form No. 29) be referred to as a guide for other insurance coverages.)

ARTICLE IX   Job Conditions

(Here insert any applicable arrangements and necessary cooperation concerning labor matters for the project.)

ARTICLE X

In addition to the foregoing provisions the parties also agree:

That the Subcontractor shall:

(1) Be bound to the Contractor by the terms of the Contractor Documents and this Agreement, and assume toward the Contractor all the obligations and responsibilities that the Contractor, by those documents, assumes toward the Owner, as applicable to this Subcontract. (a) Not discriminate against any employee or applicant for employment because of race, creed, color, or national origin.

(2) Submit to the Contractor applications for payment at such times as stipulated in Article IV so as to enable the Contractor to apply for payment.

If payments are made on valuations of work done, the Subcontractor shall, before the first application, submit to the Contractor a schedule of values of the various parts of the work, aggregating the total sum of the Contract, made out in such detail as the Subcontractor and Contractor may agree upon, or as required by the Owner, and, if required, supported by such evidence as to its correctness as the Contractor may direct. This schedule, when approved by the Contractor, shall be used as a basis for Certificates for Payment, unless it be found to be in error. In applying for payment, the Subcontractor shall submit a statement based upon this schedule.

If payments are made on account of materials not incorporated in the work but delivered and suitably stored at the site, or at some other location agreed upon in writing, such payments shall be in accordance with the terms and conditions of the Contract Documents.

(3) Pay for all materials and labor used in, or in connection with, the performance of this contract, through the period covered by previous payments received from the Contractor, and furnish satisfactory evidence when requested by the Contractor, to verify compliance with the above requirements.

(4) Make all claims for extras, for extensions of time and for damage for delays or otherwise, promptly to the Contractor consistent with the Contract Documents.

(5) Take necessary precaution to properly protect the finished work of other trades.

(6) Keep the building and premises clean at all times of debris arising out of the operation of this subcontract. The Subcontractor shall not be held responsible for unclean conditions caused by other contractors or subcontractors, unless otherwise provided for.

(7) Comply with all statutory and/or contractual safety requirements applying to his work and/or initiated by the Contractor, and shall report within 3 days to the Contractor any injury to the Subcontractor's employees at the site of the project.

(8) (a) Not assign this subcontract or any amounts due or to become due thereunder without the written consent of the contractor. (b) Nor subcontract the whole of this subcontract without the written consent of the contractor. (c) Nor further subcontract portions of this subcontract without written notification to the contractor when such notification is requested by the contractor.

(9) Guarantee his work against all defects of materials and/or workmanship as called for in the plans, specifications and addenda, or if no guarantee is called for, then for

a period of one year from the dates of partial or total acceptance of the Subcontractor's work by the Owner.

(10) And does hereby agree that if the Subcontractor should neglect to prosecute the work diligently and properly or fail to perform any provision of this contract, the Contractor, after three days written notice to the Subcontractor, may, without prejudice to any other remedy he may have, make good such deficiencies and may deduct the cost thereof from the payment then or thereafter due the Subcontractor, provided, however, that if such action is based upon faulty workmanship the Architect or Owner's authorized agent, shall first have determined that the workmanship and/or materials is defective.

(11) And does hereby agree that the Contractor's equipment will be available to the Subcontractor only at the Contractor's discretion and on mutually satisfactory terms.

(12) Furnish periodic progress reports of the work as mutually agreed including the progress of materials or equipment under this Agreement that may be in the course of preparation or manufacture.

(13) Make any and all changes or deviations from the original plans and specifications without nullifying the original contract when specifically ordered to do so in writing by the Contractor. The Subcontractor prior to the commencement of this revised work, shall submit promptly to the Contractor written copies of the cost or credit proposal for such revised work in a manner consistent with the Contract Documents.

(14) Cooperate with the Contractor and other Subcontractors whose work might interfere with the Subcontractor's work and to participate in the preparation of coordinated drawings in areas of congestion as required by the Contract Documents, specifically noting and advising the Contractor of any such interference.

(15) Cooperate with the Contractor in scheduling his work so as not conflict or interfere with the work of others. To promptly submit shop drawings, drawings, and samples, as required in order to carry on said work efficiently and at speed that will not cause delay in the progress of the Contractor's work or other branches of the work carried on by other Subcontractors.

(16) Comply with all Federal, State and local laws and ordinances applying to the building or structure and to comply and give adequate notices relating to the work to proper authorities and to secure and pay for all necessary licenses or permits to carry on the work as described in the Contract Documents as applicable to this Subcontract.

(17) Comply with Federal, State and local tax laws, Social Security laws and Unemployment Compensation laws and Workmen's Compensation Laws insofar as applicable to the performance of this subcontract.

(18) And does hereby agree that all work shall be done subject to the final approval of the Architect or Owner's authorized agent, and his decision in matters relating to artistic effect shall be final, if within the terms of the Contract Documents.

That the Contractor shall—

(19) Be bound to the Subcontractor by all the obligations that the Owner assumes to the Contractor under the Contract Documents and by all the provisions thereof affording remedies and redress to the Contractor from the Owner insofar as applicable to this Subcontract.

(20) Pay the Subcontractor within seven days, unless otherwise provided in the Contract Documents, upon the payment of certificates issued under the Contractor's schedule of values, or as described in Article IV herein. The amount of the payment shall be equal to the percentage of completion certified by the Owner or his authorized agent for the work of this Subcontractor applied to the amount set forth under Article IV and allowed to the Contractor on account of the Subcontractor's work to the extent of the Subcontractor's interest therein.

(21) Permit the Subcontractor to obtain direct from the Architect or Owner's authorized agent, evidence of percentages of completion certified on his account.

(22) Pay the Subcontractor on demand for his work and/or materials as far as executed and fixed in place, less the retained percentage, at the time the payment should be made to the Subcontractor if the Architect or Owner's authorized agent fails to issue the certificate for any fault of the Contractor and not the fault of the Subcontractor or as otherwise provided herein.

(23) And does hereby agree that the failure to make payments to the Subcontractor as herein provided for any cause not the fault of the Subcontractor, within 7 days from the Contractor's receipt of payment or from time payment should be made as provided in Article X, Section 22, or maturity, then the Subcontractor may upon 7 days written notice to the Contractor stop work without prejudice to any other remedy he may have.

(24) Not issue or give any instructions, order or directions directly to employees or workmen of the Subcontractor other than to the persons designated as the authorized representative(s) of the Subcontractor.

(25) Make no demand for liquidated damages in any sum in excess of such amount as may be specifically named in the subcontract, provided, however, no liquidated damages shall be assessed for delays or causes attributable to other Subcontractors or arising outside the scope of this Subcontract.

(26) And does hereby agree that no claim for services rendered or materials furnished by the Contractor to the Subcontractor shall be valid unless written notice thereof is given by the Contractor to the Subcontractor during the first ten days of the calendar month following that in which the claim originated.

(27) Give the Subcontractor an opportunity to be present and to submit evidence in any arbitration involving his rights.

(28) Name as arbitor under arbitration proceedings as provided in the General Conditions the person nominated by the Subcontractor, if the sole cause of dispute is the work, materials, rights or responsibilities of the Subcontractor; or if, of the Subcontractor and any other Subcontractor jointly, to name as such arbitrator the person upon whom they agree.

That the Contractor and the Subcontractor agree—

(29) That in the matter of arbitration, their rights and obligations and all procedure shall be analogous to those set forth in the Contract Documents provided, however, that a decision by the Architect or Owner's authorized agent, shall not be a condition precedent to arbitration.

(30) This subcontract is solely for the benefit of the signatories hereto.

ARTICLE XI

IN WITNESS WHEREOF the parties hereto have executed this Agreement under seal, the day and year first above written.

Attest: Subcontractor

_____   _____
    (Seal)   By   (Title)

Attest: Contractor

_____   _____
    (Seal)   By   (Title)

§5.12　10. FORM— **Standard Form of Agreement**
AIA DOCUMENT A401　**Between Contractor and Subcontractor**

The American Institute of Architects

1978 EDITION

This document has been reproduced with the permission of The American Institute of Architects under application number 78035. Further reproduction, in part or in whole, is not authorized.

Because AIA documents are revised from time to time, users should ascertain from AIA the current edition of the document reproduced here.

AGREEMENT

made as of the _____ day of _____ in the year Nineteen Hundred and _____

BETWEEN the Contractor:

and the Subcontractor:

The Project:

The Owner:

The Architect:

The Contractor and Subcontractor agree as set forth below.

AIA Document A401 Copyright © 1978 by The American Institute of Architects.

ARTICLE 1 The Contract Documents

1.1 The Contract Documents for this Subcontract consist of this Agreement and any Exhibits attached hereto, the Agreement between the Owner and Contractor dated as of _____, the Conditions of the Contract between the Owner and Contractor (General, Supplementary and other Conditions), the Drawings, the Specifications, all Addenda issued prior to and all Modifications issued after execution of the Agreement between the Owner and Contractor and agreed upon by the parties to this Subcontract. These form the Subcontract, and are as fully a part of the Subcontract as if attached to this Agreement or repeated herein.

1.2 Copies of the above documents which are applicable to the Work under this Subcontract shall be furnished to the Subcontractor upon his request. An enumeration of the applicable Contract Documents appears in Article 15.

ARTICLE 2 The Work

2.1 The Subcontractor shall perform all the Work required by the Contract Documents for

(Here insert a precise description of the Work covered by this Subcontract and refer to numbers of Drawings and pages of Specifications including Addenda, Modifications and accepted Alternates.)
The Subcontractor shall furnish the labor, materials, equipment and supervision necessary to construct the _____ work shown on drawing numbers _____ dated _____, and last revised _____, and sections _____ of the Specifications, dated _____ and Addenda numbers _____, and excluding the following:

ARTICLE 3 Time of Commencement and Substantial Completion

3.1 The Work to be performed under this Subcontract shall be commenced and, subject to authorized adjustments, shall be substantially completed not later than
(Here insert the specific provisions that are applicable to this Subcontract including any information pertaining to notice to proceed or other method of modification for commencement of Work, starting and completion dates, or duration, and any provisions for liquidated damages relating to failure to complete on time.)

Subcontractor shall be responsible for maintaining job progress in accordance with the owner-approved schedule of performance; provided, however, that the Subcontractor shall be afforded an opportunity to establish the activities and working time necessary to perform and complete the work under this Subcontract. In the event a schedule of progress is approved without Subcontractor's input, reasonable and sufficient time within which to complete the phases of work as they may occur. Contractor shall be responsible for providing within said schedule reasonable time in proper sequence of the performance of the Subcontractor's work.

3.2 Time is of the essence of this Subcontract.

AIA Document A401 Copyright © 1978 by The American Institute of Architects.

3.3 No extension of time will be valid without the Contractor's written consent after claim made by the Subcontractor in accordance with Paragraph 11.10.

ARTICLE 4 The Contract Sum

4.1 The Contractor shall pay the Subcontractor in current funds for the performance of the Work, subject to additions and deductions authorized pursuant to Paragraph 11.9, the Contract Sum of _____ dollars ($_____). The Contract Sum is determined as follows:

(State here the base bid or other lump sum amount, accepted alternates, and unit prices, as applicable.)

ARTICLE 5 Progress Payments

5.1 The Contractor shall pay the Subcontractor monthly progress payments in accordance with Paragraph 12.4 of this Subcontract.

5.2 Applications for monthly progress payments shall be in writing and in accordance with Paragraph 11.8, shall state the estimated percentage of the Work in this Subcontract that has been satisfactorily completed and shall be submitted to the Contractor on or before the _____ day of each month.

(Here insert details on (1) payment procedures and date of monthly applications, or other procedure if on other than a monthly basis, (2) the basis on which payment will be made on account of materials and equipment suitably stored at the site or other location agreed upon in writing, and (3) any provisions consistent with the Contract Documents for limiting or reducing the amount retained after the Work reaches a certain stage of completion.)

Monthly progress payments shall be paid by the Contractor to the Subcontractor on or before the tenth of each month. Payments will be made for the value of work completed and on account of materials or equipment not incorporated in the Work but delivered and suitably stored at the site and, for materials or equipment suitably stored at some other location agreed upon in advance. Payments for materials or equipment stored on or off the site shall be conditioned upon submission by the Subcontractor of bills of sale or such other procedures satisfactory to the Owner to establish the Owner's title to such materials or equipment or otherwise protect the Owner's interest, including applicable insurance and transportation to the site for those materials and equipment stored off the site.

5.3 When the Subcontractor's Work or a designated portion thereof is substantially complete and in accordance with the Contract Documents, the Contractor shall, upon application by the Subcontractor, make prompt application for payment of such Work. Within thirty days following issuance by the Architect of the Certificate for Payment covering such substantially completed Work, the Contractor shall, to the full extent provided in the Contract Documents, make payment to the Subcontractor of the entire unpaid balance of the

---

AIA Document A401 Copyright © 1978 by The American Institute of Architects.

Contract Sum or of that portion of the Contract Sum attributable to the substantially completed Work, less any portion of the funds for the Subcontractor's Work withheld in accordance with the Certificate to cover costs of items to be completed or corrected by the Subcontractor.

(Delete the above Paragraph if the Contract Documents do not provide for, and the Subcontractor agrees to forego, release of retainage for the Subcontractor's Work prior to completion of the entire Project.)

5.4 Progress payments or final payment due and unpaid under this Subcontract shall bear interest from the date payment is due at the rate entered below or, in the absence thereof, at the legal rate prevailing at the place of the Project.

(Here insert any rate of interest agreed upon.)

(Usury laws and requirements under the Federal Truth in Lending Act, similar state and local consumer credit laws and other regulations at the Owner's, Contractor's and Subcontractor's principal places of business, the location of the Project and elsewhere may affect the validity of this provision. Specific legal advice should be obtained with respect to deletion, modification, or other requirements such as written disclosures or waivers.)

ARTICLE 6   Final Payment

6.1 Final payment, constituting the entire unpaid balance of the Contract Sum, shall be due when the Work described in this Subcontract is fully completed and performed in accordance with the Contract Documents and is satisfactory to the Architect, and shall be payable as follows, in accordance with Article 5 and with Paragraph 12.4 of this Subcontract:

(Here insert the relevant conditions under which or time in which final payment will become payable.)
Final payment shall be due thirty (30) days after completion of the work by the Subcontractor.

6.2 Before issuance of the final payment, the Subcontractor, if required, shall submit evidence satisfactory to the Contractor that all payrolls, bills for materials and equipment, and all known indebtedness connected with the Subcontractor's Work have been satisfied.

ARTICLE 7   Performance Bond and Labor and Material Payment Bond

(Here insert any requirement for the furnishing of bonds by the Subcontractor.)
If a performance bond is required by the Contractor, the premium of the bond shall be paid by the Contractor in addition to the contract price.

ARTICLE 8   Temporary Facilities and Services

8.1 Unless otherwise provided in this Subcontract, the Contractor shall furnish and make available at no cost to the Subcontractor the following temporary facilities and services:

AIA Document A401 Copyright © 1978 by The American Institute of Architects.

Contractor shall, at no cost to Subcontractor, furnish utilities, services and facilities, as listed below, conveniently located at the construction site for use by Subcontractor to install its work, and of sufficient capacity to service Subcontractor's equipment and employees as well as the equipment and employees of all other subcontractors or contractors including the Contractor on the Job: (a) Electricity at each floor rated for small tools, hoists, derricks, scaffolds and welder's equipment, (b) Toilets, (c) Personnel elevators so positioned that Subcontractor's personnel are not required to walk up or down more than two floors to get to or from their place of work at the construction site, (d) Drinking water, (e) Rubbish removal from an area designated by the Contractor at each floor, (f) Accessible and adequate storage area within the building for Subcontractor's materials and equipment, (g) Adequate clear area to enable Subcontractor to perform its work without interference, (h) Should Subcontractor elect to use the Contractor's hoist, such use shall be available during regular working hours at no cost to Subcontractor and at such other times which do not cause any interference with Subcontractor's personnel working below prior trades, Contractor will be responsible for furnishing and erecting such protection and moving it as required by Subcontractor, (k) Temporary heat, (l) Perimeter protection and barricades shall be installed in compliance with OSHA regulations at no cost to Subcontractor. Such protection shall not interfere with the normal installation of the work covered under this Subcontract. Where protection or barricades must be removed to allow installation of the work under this Subcontract, it shall be removed and reinstalled by Contractor at no expense to Subcontractor.

ARTICLE 9   Insurance

9.1 Prior to starting work, the Subcontractor shall obtain the required insurance from a responsible insurer, and shall furnish satisfactory evidence to the Contractor that the Subcontractor has complied with the requirements of this Article 9. Similarly, the Contractor shall furnish to the Subcontractor satisfactory evidence of insurance required of the Contractor by the Contract Documents.

9.2 The Contractor and Subcontractor waive all rights against each other and against the Owner, the Architect, separate contractors and all other subcontractors for damages caused by fire or other perils to the extent covered by property insurance provided under the General Conditions, except such rights as they may have to the proceeds of such insurance.

(Here insert any insurance requirements and Subcontractor's responsibility for obtaining, maintaining and paying for necessary insurance with limits equalling or exceeding those specified in the Contract Documents and inserted below, or required by law. If applicable, this shall include fire insurance and extended coverage, public liability, property damage, employer's liability, and workers' or workmen's compensation insurance for the Subcontractor and his employees. The insertion should cover provisions for notice of cancellation, allocation of insurance proceeds, and other aspects of insurance.)

ARTICLE 10   Working Conditions

(Here insert any applicable arrangements concerning working conditions and labor matters for the Project.)

AIA Document A401 Copyright © 1978 by The American Institute of Architects.

GENERAL CONDITIONS

ARTICLE 11 Subcontractor

11.1 Rights and Responsibilities

11.1.1 The Subcontractor shall be bound to the Contractor by the terms of this Agreement and, to the extent that provisions of the Contract Documents between the Owner and Contractor apply to the Work of the Subcontractor as defined in this Agreement, the Subcontractor shall assume toward the Contractor all the obligations and responsibilities which the Contractor, by those Documents, assumes toward the Owner and the Architect, and shall have the benefit of all rights, remedies and redress against the Contractor which the Contractor, by those Documents, has against the Owner, insofar as applicable to this Subcontract, provided that where any provision of the Contract Documents between the Owner and Contractor is inconsistent with any provision of this Agreement, this Agreement shall govern.

11.1.2 The Subcontractor shall not assign this subcontract without the written consent of the Contractor, nor subcontract the whole of this Subcontract without the written consent of the Contractor, nor further subcontract portions of this Subcontract without written notification to the Contractor when such notification is requested by the Contractor. The Subcontractor shall not assign any amounts due or to become due under this Subcontract without written notice to the Contractor.

11.2 Execution and Progress of the Work

11.2.1 The Subcontractor agrees that the Contractor's equipment will be available to the Subcontractor only at the Contractor's discretion and on mutually satisfactory terms.

11.2.2 The Subcontractor shall cooperate with the Contractor in scheduling and performing his Work to avoid conflict or interference with the work of others.

11.2.3 The Subcontractor shall promptly submit shop drawings and samples required in order to perform his Work efficiently, expeditiously and in a manner that will not cause delay in the progress of the Work of the Contractor or other subcontractors.

11.2.4 The Subcontractor shall furnish periodic progress reports on the Work as mutually agreed, including information on the status of materials and equipment under this Subcontract which may be in the course of preparation or manufacture.

11.2.5 The Subcontractor agrees that all Work shall be done subject to the final approval of the Architect. The Architect's decisions in matters relating to artistic effect shall be final if consistent with the intent of the Contract Documents.

11.2.6 The Subcontractor shall pay for all materials, equipment and labor used in, or in connection with, the performance of this Subcontract through the period covered by previ-

---

AIA Document A401 Copyright © 1978 by The American Institute of Architects.

ous payments received from the Contractor, and shall furnish satisfactory evidence, when requested by the Contractor, to verify compliance with the above requirements.

11.3 Laws, Permits, Fees and Notices

11.3.1 The Subcontractor shall give all notices and comply with all laws, ordinances, rules, regulations and orders of any public authority bearing on the performance of the Work under this Subcontract. The Subcontractor shall secure and pay for all permits and governmental fees, licenses and inspections necessary for the proper execution and completion of the Subcontractor's Work, the furnishing of which is required of the Contractor by the Contract Documents.

11.3.2 The Subcontractor shall comply with Federal, State and local tax laws, social security acts, unemployment compensation acts and workers' or workmen's compensation acts insofar as applicable to the performance of this Subcontract.

11.4 Work of Others

11.4.1 In carrying out his Work, the Subcontractor shall take necessary precautions to protect properly the finished work of other trades from damage caused by his operations.

11.4.2 The Subcontractor shall cooperate with the Contractor and other subcontractors whose work might interfere with the Subcontractor's Work, and shall participate in the preparation of coordinated drawings in areas of congestion as required by the Contract Documents, specifically noting and advising the Contractor of any such interference.

11.5 Safety Precautions and Procedures

11.5.1 The Subcontractor shall take all reasonable safety precautions with respect to his Work, shall comply with all safety measures initiated by the Contractor and with all applicable laws, ordinances, rules, regulations and orders of any public authority for the safety of persons or property in accordance with the requirements of the Contract Documents. The Subcontractor shall report within three days to the Contractor any injury to any of the Subcontractor's employees at the site.

11.6 Cleaning Up

11.6.1 The Subcontractor shall at all times keep the premises free from accumulation of waste materials or rubbish arising out of the operations of this Subcontract. Unless otherwise provided, the Subcontractor shall not be held responsible for unclean conditions caused by other contractors or subcontractors.

11.7 Warranty

11.7.1 The Subcontractor warrants to the Owner, the Architect and the Contractor that all materials and equipment furnished shall be new unless otherwise specified, and that all Work under this Subcontract shall be of good quality, free from faults and defects and in conformance with the Contract Documents. All Work not conforming to these requirements, including substitutions not properly approved and authorized, may be considered defective. The warranty provided in this Paragraph 11.7 shall be in addition to and not in limitation of any other warranty or remedy required by law or by the Contract Documents.

AIA Document A401 Copyright © 1978 by The American Institute of Architects.

11.8 Applications for Payment

11.8.1 The Subcontractor shall submit to the Contractor applications for payment at such times as stipulated in Article 5 to enable the Contractor to apply for payment.

11.8.2 If payments are made on the valuation of Work done, the Subcontractor shall, before the first application, submit to the Contractor a schedule of values of the various parts of the Work aggregating the total sum of this Subcontract, made out in such detail as the Subcontractor and Contractor may agree upon or as required by the Owner, and supported by such evidence as to its correctness as the Contractor may direct. This schedule, when approved by the Contractor, shall be used only as a basis for Applications for Payment, unless it be found to be in error. In applying for payment, the Subcontractor shall submit a statement based upon this schedule.

11.8.3 If payments are made on account of materials or equipment not incorporated in the Work but delivered and suitably stored at the site or at some other location agreed upon in writing, such payments shall be in accordance with the terms and conditions of the Contract Documents.

11.9 Changes in the Work

11.9.1 The Subcontractor may be ordered in writing by the Contractor, without invalidating this Subcontract, to make changes in the Work within the general scope of this Subcontract consisting of additions, deletions or other revisions, the Contract Sum and the Contract Time being adjusted accordingly. The Subcontractor, prior to the commencement of such changed or revised Work, shall submit promptly to the Contractor written copies of any claim for adjustment to the Contract Sum and Contract Time for such revised Work in a manner consistent with the Contract Documents.

11.10 Claims of the Subcontractor

11.10.1 The Subcontractor shall make all claims promptly to the Contractor for additional cost, extensions of time, and damages for delays or other causes in accordance with the Contract Documents. Any such claim which will affect or become part of a claim which the Contractor is required to make under the Contract Documents within a specified time period or in a specified manner shall be made in sufficient time to permit the Contractor to satisfy the requirements of the Contract Documents. Such claims shall be received by the Contractor not less than two working days preceding the time by which the Contractor's claim must be made. Failure of the Subcontractor to make such a timely claim shall bind the Subcontractor to the same consequences as those to which the Contractor is bound.

11.11 Indemnification

11.11.1 To the fullest extent permitted by law, the Subcontractor shall indemnify and hold harmless the Owner the Architect and the Contractor and all of their agents and employees from and against all claims, damages, losses and expenses, including but not limited to attorney's fees, arising out of or resulting from the performance of the Subcontractor's Work under this Subcontract, provided that any such claim, damage, loss, or expense is attributable to bodily injury, sickness, disease, or death, or to injury to or destruction of tangible property (other than the Work itself) including the loss of use resulting therefrom, to the

---

AIA Document A401 Copyright © 1978 by The American Institute of Architects.

extent caused in whole or in part by any negligent act or omission of the Subcontractor or anyone directly or indirectly employed by him or anyone for whose acts he may be liable, regardless of whether it is caused in part by a party indemnified hereunder. Such obligation shall not be construed to negate, or abridge, or otherwise reduce any other right or obligation of indemnity which would otherwise exist as to any party or person described in this Paragraph 11.11.

11.11.2 In any and all claims against the Owner, the Architect, or the Contractor or any of their agents or employees by any employee of the Subcontractor, anyone directly or indirectly employed by him or anyone for whose acts he may be liable, the indemnification obligation under this Paragraph 11.11 shall not be limited in any way by any limitation on the amount or type of damages, compensation or benefits payable by or for the Subcontractor under workers' or workmen's compensation acts, disability benefit acts or other employee benefit acts.

11.11.3 The obligations of the Subcontractor under this Paragraph 11.11 shall not extend to the liability of the Architect, his agents or employees arising out of (1) the preparation or approval of maps, drawings, opinions, reports, surveys, Change Orders, designs or specifications, or (2) the giving of or the failure to give directions or instructions by the Architect, his agents or employees provided such giving or failure to give is the primary cause of the injury or damage.

11.12 Subcontractor's Remedies

11.12.1 If the Contractor does not pay the Subcontractor through no fault of the Subcontractor, within seven days from the time payment should be made as provided in Paragraph 12.4, the Subcontractor may, without prejudice to any other remedy he may have, upon seven additional days' written notice to the Contractor, stop his Work until payment of the amount owing has been received. The Contract Sum shall, by appropriate adjustment, be increased by the amount of the Subcontractor's reasonable costs of shutdown, delay and start-up.

ARTICLE 12   Contractor

12.1 Rights and Responsibilities

12.1.1 The Contractor shall be bound to the Subcontractor by the terms of this Agreement, and to the extent that provisions of the Contract Documents between the Owner and the Contractor apply to the Work of the Subcontractor as defined in this Agreement, the Contractor shall assume toward the Subcontractor all the obligations and responsibilities that the Owner, by those Documents, assumes toward the Contractor, and shall have the benefit of all rights, remedies and redress against the Subcontractor which the Owner, by those Documents, has against the Contractor. Where any provision of the Contract Documents between the Owner and the Contractor is inconsistent with any provisions of this Agreement, this Agreement shall govern.

12.2 Services Provided by the Contractor

12.2.1 The Contractor shall cooperate with the Subcontractor in scheduling and perform-

---

AIA Document A401 Copyright © 1978 by The American Institute of Architects.

ing his Work to avoid conflicts or interference in the Subcontractor's Work, and shall expedite written responses to submittals made by the Subcontractor in accordance with Paragraphs 11.2, 11.9 and 11.10. As soon as practicable after execution of this Agreement, the Contractor shall provide the Subcontractor a copy of the estimated progress schedule of the Contractor's entire Work which the Contractor has prepared and submitted for the Owner's and the Architect's information, together with such additional scheduling details as will enable the Subcontractor to plan and perform his Work properly. The Subcontractor shall be notified promptly of any subsequent changes in the progress schedule and the additional scheduling details.

12.2.2 The Contractor shall provide suitable areas for storage of the Subcontractor's materials and equipment during the course of the Work. Any additional costs to the Subcontractor resulting from the relocation of such facilities at the direction of the Contractor shall be reimbursed by the Contractor.

12.3 Communications

12.3.1 The Contractor shall promptly notify the Subcontractor of all modifications to the Contract between the Owner and the Contractor which affect this Subcontract and which were issued or entered into subsequent to the execution of this Subcontract.

12.3.2 The Contractor shall not give instructions or orders directly to employees or workmen of the Subcontractor except to persons designated as authorized representatives of the Subcontractor.

12.4 Payments to the Subcontractor

12.4.1 Unless otherwise provided in the Contract Documents, the Contractor shall pay the Subcontractor each progress payment and the final payment under this Subcontract within three working days after he receives payment from the Owner, except as provided in Subparagraph 12.4.3. The amount of each progress payment to the Subcontractor shall be the amount to which the Subcontractor is entitled, reflecting the percentage of completion allowed to the Contractor for the Work of this Subcontractor applied to the Contract Sum of this Subcontract, and the percentage actually retained, if any, from payments to the Contractor on account of such Subcontractor's Work, plus, to the extent permitted by the Contract Documents, the amount allowed for materials and equipment suitably stored by the Subcontractor, less the aggregate of previous payments to the Subcontractor.

12.4.2 The Contractor shall permit the Subcontractor to request directly from the Architect information regarding the percentages of completion or the amount certified on account of Work done by the Subcontractor.

12.4.3 If the Architect does not issue a Certificate for Payment or the Contractor does not receive payment for any cause which is not the fault of the Subcontractor, the Contractor shall pay the Subcontractor, on demand, a progress payment computed as provided in Subparagraph 12.4.1 or the final payment as provided in Article 6.

12.5 Claims by the Contractor

12.5.1 The Contractor shall make no demand for liquidated damages for delay in any sum

---

AIA Document A401 Copyright © 1978 by The American Institute of Architects.

in excess of such amount as may be specifically named in this Subcontract, and liquidated damages shall be assessed against this Subcontractor only for his negligent acts and his failure to act in accordance with the terms of this Agreement, and in no case for delays or causes arising outside the scope of this Subcontract, or for which other subcontractors are responsible.

12.5.2 Except as may be indicated in this Agreement, the Contractor agrees that no claim for payment for services rendered or materials and equipment furnished by the Contractor to the Subcontractor shall be valid without prior notice to the Subcontractor and unless written notice thereof is given by the Contractor to the Subcontractor not later than the tenth day of the calendar month following that in which the claim originated.

12.6 Contractors' Remedies

12.6.1 If the Subcontractor defaults or neglects to carry out the Work in accordance with this Agreement and fails within three working days after receipt of written notice from the Contractor to commence and continue correction of such default or neglect with diligence and promptness, the Contractor may, after three days following receipt by the Subcontractor of an additional written notice, and without prejudice to any other remedy he may have, make good such deficiencies and may deduct the cost thereof from the payments then or thereafter due the Subcontractor, provided, however, that if such action is based upon faulty workmanship or materials and equipment, the Architect shall first have determined that the workmanship or materials and equipment are not in accordance with the Contract Documents.

ARTICLE 13   Arbitration

13.1 All claims, disputes and other matters in question arising out of, or relating to, this Subcontract, or the breach thereof, shall be decided by arbitration, which shall be conducted in the same manner and under the same procedure as provided in the Contract Documents with respect to disputes between the Owner and the Contractor, except that a decision by the Architect shall not be a condition precedent to arbitration. If the Contract Documents do not provide for arbitration or fail to specify the manner and procedure for arbitration, it shall be conducted in accordance with the Construction Industry Arbitration Rules of the American Arbitration Association then obtaining unless the parties mutually agree otherwise.

13.2 Except by written consent of the person or entity sought to be joined, no arbitration arising out of or relating to the Contract Documents shall include, by consolidation, joinder or in any other manner, any person or entity not a party to the Agreement under which such arbitration arises, unless it is shown at the time the demand for arbitration is filed that (1) such person or entity is substantially involved in a common question of fact or law, (2) the presence of such person or entity is required if complete relief is to be accorded in the arbitration, (3) the interest or responsibility of such person or entity in the matter is not insubstantial, and (4) such person or entity is not the Architect, his employee or his consultant. This agreement to arbitrate and any other written agreement to arbitrate with an additional person or persons referred to herein shall be specifically enforceable under the prevailing arbitration law.

AIA Document A401 Copyright © 1978 by The American Institute of Architects.

13.3 The Contractor shall permit the Subcontractor to be present and to submit evidence in any arbitration proceeding involving his rights.

13.4 The Contractor shall permit the Subcontractor to exercise whatever rights the Contractor may have under the Contract Documents in the choice of arbitrators in any dispute, if the sole cause of the dispute is the Work, materials, equipment, rights or responsibilities of the Subcontractor; or if the dispute involves the Subcontractor and any other subcontractor or subcontractors jointly, the Contractor shall permit them to exercise such rights jointly.

13.5 The award rendered by the arbitrators shall be final, and judgment may be entered upon it in accordance with applicable law in any court having jurisdiction thereof.

13.6 This Article shall not be deemed a limitation of any rights or remedies which the Subcontractor may have under any Federal or State mechanics' lien laws or under any applicable labor and material payment bonds unless such rights or remedies are expressly waived by him.

ARTICLE 14 Termination

14.1 Termination by the Subcontractor

14.1.1 If the Work is stopped for a period of thirty days through no fault of the Subcontractor because the Contractor has not made payments thereon as provided in this Agreement, then the Subcontractor may without prejudice to any other remedy he may have, upon seven additional days' written notice to the Contractor, terminate this Subcontract and recover from the Contractor payment for all Work executed and for any proven loss resulting from the stoppage of the Work, including reasonable overhead, profit and damages.

14.2 Termination by the Contractor

14.2.1 If the Subcontractor persistently or repeatedly fails or neglects to carry out the Work in accordance with the Contract Documents or otherwise to perform in accordance with this Agreement and fails within seven days after receipt of written notice to commence and continue correction of such default or neglect with diligence and promptness, the Contractor may, after seven days following receipt by the Subcontractor of an additional written notice and without prejudice to any other remedy he may have, terminate the Subcontract and finish the Work by whatever method he may deem expedient. If the unpaid balance of the Contract Sum exceeds the expense of finishing the Work, such excess shall be paid to the Subcontractor, but if such expense exceeds such unpaid balance, the Subcontractor shall pay the difference to the Contractor.

ARTICLE 15 Miscellaneous Provisions

15.1 Terms used in this Agreement which are defined in the Conditions of the Contract shall have the meanings designated in those Conditions.

15.2 The Contract Documents, which constitute the entire Agreement between the Owner and the Contractor, are listed in Article 1, and the documents which are applicable to this

---

AIA Document A401 Copyright © 1978 by The American Institute of Architects.

Subcontract, except for Addenda and Modifications issued after execution of this Subcontract, are enumerated as follows:

(List below the Agreement, the Conditions of the Contract (General, Supplementary, and other Conditions), the Drawings, the Specifications, and any Addenda and accepted Alternates, showing page or sheet numbers in all cases and dates where applicable. Continue on succeeding pages as required.)

This Agreement entered into as of the day and year first written above.

CONTRACTOR   SUBCONTRACTOR
_____   _____
_____   _____
_____   _____

AIA Document A401 Copyright © 1978 by The American Institute of Architects.

C. AUTHORIZATION FOR EXTRA OR CHANGED WORK

§5.13   1. Introduction The typical construction contract change clause contains a requirement that the contractor or subcontractor give written notice that a particular item is considered to be a change or extra and that, unless written notice is given within a specified time, the contractor or subcontractor may be barred from claiming additional compensation under the contract. This written-notice requirement is one of the many pitfalls which await an unwary contractor.

Construction companies should give their project managers, superintendents, and supervisors detailed instructions on the notices required by the contract for the specific job on which they are working. The jobsite personnel must be instructed in the correct, contractual method of reporting any changes, extras, and delays. Contractors who establish a methodical system, which consistently recognizes circumstances requiring written notification to the owner, will not have to absorb the cost of changes because of procedural technicalities in the contract.

The notice provision which a subcontractor should follow may not be in the subcontract. Rather, it may be in the general conditions, which are a part of the specifications and which are often incorporated into and made a part of the subcontract by reference. Therefore, in preparing supervisory personnel for commencement of work on a new project, it is not enough to look at only a contract or subcontract. Every part of the subcontracts, general contract, general conditions, supplementary conditions, plans, specifications must be examined, and a list must be made of every place in those documents where notice is required.

If the general contract requires that a change order be issued in writing by the owner, then the contractor should obtain a written order from the owner or the owner's authorized representative. If a subcontract requires a change order to be issued in writing by the general contractor prior to the performance of the work as changed, the subcontractor involved should be careful to follow the contract procedures for obtaining an appropriate written order from the general contractor or the contractor's authorized representative prior to the performance of the changed work. This will avoid problems in subsequently obtaining payment for the performance of changed work.

Often, the general contractor does not follow the procedure set out in the contract for ordering changes and extra work. Instead of a written order in advance from an authorized representative, an oral order from the general contractor's field superintendent may be issued. Although the subcontractor's supervisor may be tempted to perform the extra work in expectation that the subcontractor will be paid the reasonable value of the work, the supervisor should not perform extra work ordered orally. The general contractor may dispute the fair value of the work performed or may reject the claim entirely because it was not authorized in advance in writing by the proper officer, as required by the contract. The subcontractor should abide strictly by the procedure set out in the contract for complying with change orders in order to preserve the right to compensation for extra work performed. Specifically, the subcontractor should obtain written authorization for the changed work on a form that identifies itself as being an order for changed or extra work.

Many general contractors and subcontractors supply their field supervision with a supply of extra work authorization forms, with instructions that their field personnel should not perform any extra or changed work without obtaining the signature of an authorized representative of the party ordering the extra or changed work. If the claim clearly indicates that the scope covers "authorization for extra or changed work" and it is signed by an authorized representative of the party ordering the work, the signed form is the legal basis entitling the contractor to extra compensation for the extra or changed work.

When a contractor receives oral instructions from a representative whom the contractor is not certain has the appropriate authority, it is a wise course of action to write the owner reporting the field instructions and stating that these instructions require extra work for which the contractor, if required to perform, will claim an extra. The authorized agents of the owner then may tell the contractor not to proceed with the work, in which case the contractor has no further problem; or the owner may acquiesce in these instructions either by affirmatively issuing a written change order or by silence or failure to repudiate the instructions. This notice also fairly alerts the authorized representatives of the owner to the fact that the instructions were issued by operating personnel, which provides the owner with an opportunity to clarify, define, or rescind the instructions before costs are incurred. Writing a letter confirming oral and possibly unauthorized instructions not only preserves the contractor's right to relief, but also gives the owner an opportunity to avoid any misunderstandings before work is performed. A written confirmation also avoids any disputes as to the issuance and scope of the instructions.

In addition to protecting claims for additional compensation, the general contractor or subcontractor should give notice of claims for extensions of time needed to perform changed work within the specific time limit for completion included in the contract. If the general contractor or subcontractor exceeds this limit, there may be liability for liquidated delay damages. A general contractor or subcontractor is extremely vulnerable to liquidated damages because the money can be taken out of progress payments or retention.

Most general contractors and subcontractors are required by the contract to make a claim for an extension of time, if the project is delayed for any excusable reason, in order to avoid an assessment of liquidated damages. For example, if the owner verbally orders the contractor to do extra work, which will delay completion of the project, the contractor should claim an extension of time within the time limit after receipt of the order. The contractor can obtain protection by sending one letter to the owner containing two statements:

1. The contractor has been ordered to do extra work (state here the work ordered) for which he will incur extra costs. A claim for extra costs will be forwarded later (or can be made now if known).
2. The extra work may delay completion, and the contractor claims an extension of time to cover the extra work.

Thus, when a project is delayed, two claims are required—one for an extension of time and one for extra cost. A common error of contractors who perform extra work is to claim only an adjustment of the contract price and to neglect to claim an extension of time.

§5.14   2. FORM   **Work Authorization**

WORK AUTHORIZATION #_____

SHEET NO._____ OF _____
DATE _____
CUSTOMER ORDER NO. _____
PROJECT _____ JOB NO. _____
WORK PERFORMED BY _____ FOR _____
AUTHORIZED BY _____ TITLE _____
DESCRIPTION OF WORK _____

LABOR

NAME	TRADE	ACTUAL HOURS WORKED	
		STRAIGHT TIME	PREMIUM TIME

MATERIAL

DESCRIPTION	QUANTITY

EQUIPMENT & TOOLS

DESCRIPTION	TIME	DESCRIPTION	TIME

REMARKS: _____

CONTRACTOR _____   ARCHITECT OWNER _____   SUBCONTRACTOR _____
BY _____   BY _____   BY _____
BILLING ADDRESS _____   ADDRESS _____   BILLING ADDRESS _____

JOB COMPLETED   ☐ YES   ☐ NO

WORK AUTHORIZATION NOT SIGNED BECAUSE:
☐ UNABLE TO CONTACT REPRESENTATIVE
☐ AUTHORIZED BY PHONE
☐ FORM ISSUED FOR RECORD PURPOSES ONLY
　　AUTHORIZATION IN DISPUTE

NOTE: COMPLETE A SEPARATE DAILY WORK ORDER FOR (1) EACH JOB (2) EACH DAY.
(DO NOT ATTEMPT TO COMBINE JOBS OR DAYS)

AGC - ASA 1000 ©

Work Authorization reprinted by permission of The Associated General Contractors of America and The Associated Specialty Contractors, Inc.

SIX Documents Applicable to Suppliers

Purchase Orders
§6.01 *Introduction*
§6.02 *Form—Purchase Order*

A. PURCHASE ORDERS

§6.01   1. Introduction   A purchase order should be drafted so that it protects the subcontractor's right to receive the stated quantity of materials which conform to the plans and specifications at a stipulated price on time from the supplier. The purchase order form and its general conditions on the following pages is a model of the type of provisions a contractor's purchase order should contain. A subcontractor should consult an attorney to draft a purchase order form that best suits the subcontractor's particular needs.

Subcontractors should make sure that warranties they extend to the general contractor or owner are clearly defined and that they understand the scope of the warranties. Furthermore, since the subcontractor is generally required to warrant the work to the general contractor and/or owner, the subcontractor should be certain to obtain guarantees and warranties from the suppliers as to the materials they provide. In fact, subcontractors should be careful that the warranties obtained from the supplier extend to the same duration and scope as the warranties given to the general contractor and/or owner. If the warranties given to the general contractor and/or owner extend beyond the warranties given by the supplier of the materials and equipment installed, then the subcontractor must realize that the risk has been assumed and must obtain the work at a price at which the additional warranty risk is affordable.

Accordingly, the supplier of a product should be tied into the guarantees and warranties of the subcontract and the plans and specifications. The sample purchase order in §6.02 specifically provides on its first page that the supplier: "Ship the following items and do the following work in strict accordance with plans and specifications." The warranty provision of the terms and conditions of the purchase order provides:

> All material and equipment furnished under this order shall be guaranteed by the Seller to the Purchaser and Owner to be fit and sufficient for the purpose intended, and that they are merchantable, of good material and workmanship and free from defects, and Seller agrees to replace without charge to Purchaser or Owner said material and equipment, or remedy any defects latent or patent not due to ordinary wear and tear or due to improper use or

maintenance, which may develop within one year from date of acceptance by the Owner, or within the guarantee period set forth in applicable plans and specifications, whichever is longer. The warranties herein are in addition to those implied by law.

It is, of course, necessary that the subcontractor give the supplier copies of the plans and specifications at the time the order for materials is placed in order to facilitate the supplier's compliance with the warranty that the materials be furnished "as per plans and specifications."

By requiring suppliers to guarantee that the materials and equipment they provide will meet the plans and specifications with which the subcontractor must comply, the subcontractors can protect themselves from any additional costs that might arise if damages result from the inadequacy of materials or equipment supplied. This type of protection should be sought in all supply contracts.

A wise course of action to pursue on major guarantees or warranties of the materials or equipment, as per the plans and specifications, is to make sure that the warranties are properly made by the supplier in favor of the owner, so that if problems arise after the subcontractor has completed the work, the owner can act against the supplier without necessarily involving the subcontractor in a legal problem. Should default on any of the guarantees or warranties become apparent before the subcontractor's work is completed, the subcontractor should insist on the legally implied warranties and express contractual rights and should demand that the supplier either correct the defects or provide non-defective material or equipment as replacements. If the supplier fails to do so, the available remedy is an action for breach of contract.

The law usually implies a warranty of merchantability or of fitness for use. Therefore, legal remedies may be available even if the subcontractor has neglected to write any guarantees and warranties into the purchase order, or if the supplier has not provided a warranty. But it is always wiser to provide express warranties in the supply contract terms rather than to rely upon a court later to provide implied warranty protection.

In addition, the purchase order should stipulate that it is not effective until the material or equipment is approved by the owner or the owner's agents. In the event that approval is not obtained, the subcontractor may cancel with no liability on the part of the buyer. The risk of loss during shipment often is ignored by subcontractors, but is a very important item. The risk of loss in transit should be placed on the supplier, who normally deals constantly with the shippers and controls the shipping. The risk should not be on the buyer, and the purchase order should specify that risk of loss remains with the seller.

The purchase order should state clearly that time is the essence and that the supplier is liable to the buyer for any damages caused by delay or failure of the purchases to be performed on time, including any consequential damages suffered by the buyer. The purchase order should require the seller to indemnify the buyer against any claim or loss from infringement. The purchase order also should contain a contractual requirement that the seller execute necessary lien waivers in order to obtain payments.

An oral agreement is an acceptable beginning for a contractor's or subcontractor's contractual relations with a supplier, but the contractor who does not properly follow up an oral agreement by obtaining effective, written evidence of the agreement treads on thin ice. As a practical matter, the supplier and contractor often find that they disagree as to what are the actual terms of the oral contract, and sometimes even disagree about whether the contract has been entered into at all. Then, if the misunderstandings cause problems serious enough to cause one of the parties to consider going to court to enforce that party's version of the contract, it is discovered that the law makes the oral contract unenforceable. In the words of an old maxim, "an oral contract is not worth the paper it is written on."

The statutory provisions that make many supply contracts unenforceable are found in the Uniform Commercial Code, since a supply contract, in contrast to a construction contract, is a contract for the sale of goods. UCC §2–201(1) provides that, in general, a contract for the sale of goods for the price of $500.00 or more is not enforceable unless: (1) there is some writing sufficient to indicate that a contract for sale has been made between the parties; and (2) the writing is signed by the party against whom enforcement is sought. Thus, there must be a memorandum indicating that the contract does indeed exist, and it must be authenticated in some way by the party against whom the contract is to be enforced. The memorandum may not be necessarily the contract itself, but may be merely evidence of the existence of a contract.

Whenever an oral agreement with a supplier is completed, the subcontractor should follow the special procedure provided by UCC §2–201(2) to establish the enforceability of the oral contract. This procedure requires sending a letter of confirmation and a purchase order to the supplier within a reasonable time after the making of the agreement. Upon its receipt by the supplier, an enforceable contract results unless the supplier sends written notice of rejection of the terms contained in the letter of confirmation within ten days. §2–201(2) thus provides for the self-executing memorandum to prove the existence of a contract, even though it is not signed by the other party. Obviously, it is to the subcontractor's advantage to include as completely as possible the terms of the agreement in order to facilitate proof of the terms, if necessary.

Within certain limits, additional terms, not discussed in the oral agreement, may be included in the letter of confirmation. These additional terms will become part of the contract unless they materially alter the contract or unless the supplier objects to the terms. The letter also may state that there is no contract unless such terms are accepted by the supplier, so that the signed letter of confirmation will not be used to prove the existence of a contract which does not include the additional terms desired. Of course, if the supplier sends the subcontractor a letter of confirmation, the shoe is on the other foot. The subcontractor then has the burden of objecting to the terms of the letter of confirmation, including any additional terms not discussed over the telephone, or they will become part of the contract between the subcontractor and supplier. Subcontractors should always carefully review letters from suppliers confirming telephone conversations to make sure that they have a clear understanding of the terms of the contract. If anything is unclear, written objection to the terms of the letter should be sent to the supplier within ten days of receipt.

A letter of confirmation, sought to be used as a self-executing memorandum, should confirm at least the following aspects of the purchase: (1) description of the materials or equipment, (2) quantity, price, date of delivery, and allowable substitutions, if any. For example, immediately after an agreement is reached in a telephone conversation with a supplier, the subcontractor should send the supplier a letter of confirmation such as the following:

> This letter will serve to confirm the agreement by _____ of our company and _____ of your company, during their telephone conversation of this morning.
> We have agreed to purchase and you have agreed to sell _____ (describe material and quantity) at _____ (price) for use on the _____ (name of the project) construction

project described in this morning's telephone conversation. Delivery is to take place at the jobsite according to the following schedule:
(There will be no allowable substitutions).
Enclosed are two (2) signed copies of our standard purchase order form containing the terms of our agreement which were discussed. Please sign and return one (1) copy of the purchase order.

In summary, after having negotiated an oral supply contract with the supplier, the subcontractor should send a letter of confirmation to the supplier along with a purchase order such as the model provided, specifying the quantity to be supplied, the price, and other necessary information. Should the supplier fail to respond within ten days of receipt of the letter of confirmation and purchase order, the subcontractor will have a supply contract according to the terms agreed upon in the telephone negotiation. Should the supplier sign and return the purchase order, the subcontractor will have a supply contract based upon the terms of the purchase order.

If a subcontractor has a firm contract which has been obtained from the suppliers through the use of negotiation, a letter of confirmation acting as a self-executing memorandum, and a purchase order, then the subcontractor has legal remedy against defaulting suppliers.

§6.02   2. FORM   Purchase Order

TO:

Date _____

Purchase Order No. _____

SHIP TO:

Above purchase order number MUST appear on all inquiries, invoices, packing slips and shipping documents.

Render all invoices in TRIPLICATE

Job _____

_____

Ship via:

F.O.B.

Freight Terms:

SHIP THE FOLLOWING ITEMS AND DO THE WORK IN STRICT ACCORDANCE WITH THE PLANS AND SPECIFICATIONS:
Price:

Terms:

Delivery Date(s) Required:

ALL TERMS AND CONDITIONS AS SET FORTH ON REVERSE SIDE ARE PART OF THIS PURCHASE ORDER.

ACCEPTED: _____   _____
                 Supplier   Purchaser

By: _____   _____
           Title   Title

Date: _____

General Conditions

All material and equipment furnished under this order shall be guaranteed by the Seller to the Purchaser and Owner to be fit and sufficient for the purpose intended, and that they are merchantable, of good material and workmanship and free from defects, and Seller agrees to replace without charge to Purchaser or Owner said material and equipment, or remedy any defects latent or patent not due to ordinary wear and tear or due to improper use or maintenance, which may develop within one year from date of acceptance by the Owner, or within the guarantee period set forth in applicable plans and specifications, whichever is longer. The warranties herein are in addition to those implied by law.

The Seller and all material and equipment furnished under this order shall be subject to the approval of the Owners, architect, engineer, or the Purchaser, and Seller shall furnish the required number of submittal data or samples for said approval. In the event approval is not obtained the order may be cancelled by Purchaser with no liability on the part of Purchaser.

All material and equipment furnished hereunder shall be in strict compliance with plans, specifications, and general conditions applicable to the contract of Purchaser with the Owner or another contractor, and Seller shall be bound thereby in the performance of this contract.

The materials and equipment covered by this order, whether in a deliverable state or otherwise, shall remain the property of the Seller until delivered to a designated site and actually received by the Purchaser, and any damage to the material and equipment or loss of any kind occasioned in transit shall be borne by the Seller, notwithstanding the manner in which the goods are shipped or who pays the freight or other transportation costs.

The Seller hereby agrees to indemnify and save harmless the Purchaser from and against all claims, liability, loss, damage or expense, including attorneys' fees by reason of any actual or alleged infringement of letters patent or any litigation based thereon covering any article purchased hereunder.

Time is of the essence of this contract. Should the Supplier for any reason fail to make deliveries as required hereunder to the satisfaction of the Purchaser, or if the materials are not satisfactory to the Owner, Architect, Engineer, or Purchaser, the Purchaser shall be at liberty to purchase the materials elsewhere, and any excess in cost of same over the price herein provided shall be chargeable to and paid by the Supplier on demand. Should any delay on the part of the Supplier or defects or nonconformance of the materials or equipment with the plans and specifications occasion loss, damage or expense including consequential damages to the Owner or to the Purchaser, the Supplier shall indemnify the Owner and the Purchaser against such loss, damage or expense including attorneys' fees. If for any cause, all or any portion of the materials to be furnished are not delivered at the time or times herein specified, the Purchaser may, at his option, cancel this order as to all or any portion of materials not so delivered.

Seller shall furnish all necessary lien waivers, affidavits or other documents required to keep the Owner's premises free from liens or claims for liens, arising out of the furnishing of the material or equipment herein, as payments are made from time to time under this order.

All prior representations, conversations or preliminary negotiations shall be deemed to be merged in this order, and no changes will be considered or approved unless this order is modified by an authorized representative of Purchaser in writing.

SEVEN   Joint Venture Agreements

Joint Venture Agreements
§7.01 *Introduction*
§7.02 *Parties*
§7.03 *Introductory Premises*
§7.04 *Rights and Responsibilities*
§7.05 *Name and Principal Office*
§7.06 *Interests of Parties*
§7.07 *Control of Operations*
§7.08 *Contributions and Financing*
§7.09 *Joint Venture Property*
§7.10 *Labor*
§7.11 *Employees of Joint Venture*
§7.12 *Accounting*
§7.13 *Insurance*
§7.14 *Conclusion*

§7.15 *Form—Joint Venture Agreement*

A. JOINT VENTURE AGREEMENTS

§7.01   **1. Introduction**   The joint venture has been defined as a temporary contractual association of independent companies for the purpose of entering into a single business transaction. In the construction industry, the principal purpose of the joint venture normally is to secure and perform a construction contract for a single project.

Courts have applied the law of partnerships to joint ventures to determine the rights and liabilities of the co-venturers among themselves and with respect to third parties with whom the joint venture deals. The Internal Revenue Service has followed suit by generally taxing the income generated by the joint venture to the constituent venturers, in the same fashion as each partner is taxed on that partner's distributive share of partnership income. However, the characteristic of temporariness is the principal aspect of the joint venture which distinguishes it from a partnership.

The element of temporariness has been the principal reason why the joint venture has developed as a distinct business entity form. By utilizing the joint venture form, two independent companies can join together to bid and perform work on a single construction project, and thereafter can return to their original status.

There are, of course, factors other than the limited nature and duration of joint ventures that are behind the current trend toward the use of joint ventures in the construction industry. The joint venture approach to a project allows the combination of existing skills of the co-venturers without requiring a drastic restructuring of the venturers' present organizations. The ability to attempt a large project without risking capital beyond the individual contractor's means is another advantage which is provided by the joint venture.

As noted in the definition of a joint venture, it is a contractual association; that is, a voluntary association which arises from an agreement between the venturers. As in any business undertaking where two or more independent parties are involved, it is mandatory that a written joint venture agreement be entered into which sets forth the business understanding, rights and responsibilities of the joint venture participants. The joint venture agreement will then define the legal framework of the relationship between the joint venturers.

A detailed discussion of the many legal considerations affecting joint ventures and venturers, such as liability and taxation, is beyond the scope of this work; nevertheless, these legal questions must be addressed by any prospective joint venturer. The points discussed in this book should serve as a basis for planning, discussions and negotiations by contractors who are considering entering into joint ventures. However, the following list of considerations is not exhaustive, and each joint venture agreement must be tailored to meet the circumstances of the particular project and venturers. The contractual clauses, contained in the text, for the various provisions of a joint venture agreement are provided solely for purposes of illustration. In most cases, many alternatives are possible and competent legal counsel should be consulted both in the planning and drafting of such an agreement.

§7.02   2. Parties   The first clause of the joint venture agreement should identify the parties to the joint venture, and indicate whether the parties are individuals, corporations or partnerships, and their principal place of business. It is important that the proper names of the parties be used.

§7.03   3. Introductory Premises   Following the initial statement of the parties, there may appear several paragraphs containing introductory premises, or general informational background statements regarding the joint venture. These introductory premises may state the purpose of the joint venture agreement, the location of the project, and the name of the general contractor and/or owner. Since the purpose of the joint venture is to secure and perform a construction contract, the applicable general contract or subcontract, or both, can be attached to the joint venture agreement as exhibits and incorporated into the joint venture agreement by reference.

In addition to or instead of the premises, the agreement can begin with an introductory consideration clause.

§7.04   4. Rights and Responsibilities   A rights and responsibilities provision can be used for several purposes. First, it can specifically state that the parties to the agreement constitute themselves a joint venture for the sole purpose of performing the construction contract referenced in the introductory premises or in the paragraph itself. This paragraph should specify further that the parties to the joint venture agreement do not intend to create a partnership. While this fact can be inferred from a statement limiting the joint venture to the performance of a single construction contract, it is desirable from a planning standpoint to state specifically that no partnership is intended, rather than to rely on inferences drawn from other language appearing in the agreement. It is very important to state plainly that the relationship between or among the joint venturers is a temporary association confined to the performance of a particular contract (or contracts), and that this association of the parties will not place any limitation or liability on the parties beyond the specific undertakings contained in the agreement.

This provision also should state whether or not the joint venturers are permitted to carry on their own businesses contemporaneously with joint venture operations. Language permitting other activity will diminish the possibility of a claim by a co-venturer that all of one's efforts must be devoted to performance of the joint venture work, when a party has the capacity to do work outside of the joint venture and still meet its obligations under the joint venture agreement and the underlying construction contract.

§7.05   5. Name and Principal Office   This provision of the agreement simply states the name and the location of the principal office of the joint venture. It is important that a name be selected for the joint venture to identify it as a distinct organization. Obviously, psychology plays a part in the choice of a name, as may the relative economic power of the parties, or other practical or financial considerations. One joint venturer may be locally based, while the other contractor is unknown in the area. Before deciding upon a name to be used, however, the parties must consider the effect of various state laws which will govern the joint venture, as well as the choice of a name. For example, many states prohibit the use of names other than those of the participating companies.

As a practical matter, a joint venture office should be established as a place where notices and mail can be received, and joint venture records can be kept; however, it need not be fixed inflexibly in the agreement. The initial location may be designated, with provision for change by mutual agreement. The office may be located at the construction site, at one of the offices of the co-venturers, or at any other convenient and mutually agreeable location.

§7.06   6. Interests of Parties   The joint venture agreement must provide a method for allocation of the revenue, profits or losses, and liabilities of the joint venture resulting from the performance of the construction contract. If the parties agree to divide the gross contract price, this paragraph will state the percentage, or lump sum, division of the contract price. If profits or losses are to be allocated among the co-venturers, the formula for such allocation will be set forth in this clause. In addition to specifying interests in the profits and losses of the joint venture, provision may also be made for the venturers' interests in any property and equipment held by the joint venture.

There are many methods for dividing joint venture interests among the co-venturers; however, the most common method is by a fixed percentage allocation among all parties. The percentage which each venturer will receive is, of course, part of the negotiations between the parties as they attempt to arrive at a comprehensive joint venture agreement.

The clause dealing with the interests of the parties may also contain a provision whereby the parties agree to indemnify each other against any loss or liability arising out of the joint venture work, in excess of the agreed upon percentage division.

§7.07**7. Control of Operations** Since two or more distinct business entities will be combining to form the joint venture, it is mandatory that the agreement establish some mechanism for the centralized control of joint venture operations. One option available is the designation of one venturer as the joint venture sponsor, having control over the joint venture and performance of the construction contract. More often, the joint venture agreement provides for the establishment of a management committee, consisting of one or more representatives of each joint venturer.

The management committee can have full responsibility and authority concerning the performance of the construction contract. This responsibility includes the assignment of work among the parties, preparation of the work schedule, settlement of disputes with the owner or general contractor, and the selection of key personnel.

This portion of the agreement either should designate the representatives of the respective venturers who will serve on the management committee or provide a procedure for their selection. Also, provision should be made for the appointment of alternate representatives to serve when the principal representatives are absent, incapacitated or otherwise unable to serve.

One issue which must be resolved and expressly stated in the agreement is whether a unanimous or majority vote of the representatives will be necessary for approval of certain actions by the management committee. In either event, for ease of administration, the agreement should clearly spell out that the decisions and actions of the management committee are final, binding and conclusive upon the parties to the joint venture. In the alternative, a method for final review of management committee decisions must be specified.

§7.08**8. Contributions and Financing** Arrangements for the initial and continued financing of the joint venture must be specified in the joint venture agreement. A decision must be made as to the amount of any initial capital contributions by the co-venturers. Initial contributions are normally specified in the agreement, and are usually in proportion to the percentage interests of the parties.

The financing clause should provide for the establishment of a bank account or accounts in the name of the joint venture. The choice of the particular bank or banks in which joint venture accounts are to be established is a decision which can be left to the discretion of the management committee. In connection with expenditures from joint venture accounts, each party should choose an individual who will have the authority to sign checks on behalf of that party. A prudent practice to follow is that of requiring the signature of a representative of each venturer on any check drawn on a joint venture account.

It is possible that the initial capital contributions of the parties, coupled with the revenues generated by the joint venture throughout the project, at times will be insufficient to finance the joint venture operations. This potential problem can be dealt with effectively by including in the agreement a clause which requires the parties to remit additional capital contributions to the joint venture in proportion to their respective interests in the joint venture, when and if the management committee feels that additional funds are necessary. Occasions can arise where one venturer is unable to contribute the capital required by the joint venture and specified in the agreement. If any venturer is unable to make a required capital contribution, provision should be made for the remaining venturers to contribute the difference. Where any of the parties contribute funds to make up such a deficiency, the agreement can provide for repayment from the first joint venture revenues available for distribution, with interest from the date the deficiency was advanced. The interest, paid to the contributing party or parties advancing funds to cure the deficiency, then should be charged against the percentage share of the delinquent venturer. Another method of dealing with advances by one party is to provide for a readjustment of the interests of the parties to coincide with the new ratio of invested capital. In such cases, the agreement can provide for a readjustment of the profit percentage only, or of the interest in both profits and losses.

In the opposite case, the joint venture may find that it has excess funds on hand. In anticipation of that event, a joint venture agreement usually will provide for a periodic distribution of excess funds in the discretion of the Management Committee. However, when a distribution of excess funds is provided for, it is important to state that such a distribution will not affect the parties' liability for future losses and expenses of the joint venture.

§7.09   9. Joint Venture Property Many aspects of the law of partnerships and, in the vast majority of states, the Uniform Partnership Act are applied to joint ventures. An important aspect of partnership law generally applied to joint ventures is that governing the rights of the venturers in specific joint venture property. Under applicable legal principles, a joint venturer possesses an equal right to possess property owned by the joint venture for joint venture purposes; however, the venturer has no right to possess such property for any other reason without the consent of his co-venturers. Further, a joint venturer's rights in specific joint venture property are not assignable except in connection with the assignment of rights by all of the co-venturers in the particular property. On the legal death of a joint venturer (that is, the actual death of an individual, or liquidation and dissolution in the case of a business entity), the joint venturer's interest in specific joint venture property goes to the surviving venturer or venturers. The surviving co-venturers then have exclusive right to the possession of the joint venture property.

As can be seen from the preceding discussion, applicable law places significant restrictions upon a joint venturer's interest in the specific property of the joint venture. Thus, it is important to determine what property used by the joint venture will be considered joint venture property, and what property will remain within the sole ownership of the respective parties to the joint venture. The laws of the majority of states provide that the initial capital contribution of the co-venturers, whether in cash or other property, becomes property of the joint venture immediately upon contribution. In addition, all property subsequently acquired on behalf of the joint venture becomes part of the joint venture's assets. On the other hand, when a venturer contributes only the use of particular property to the joint venture, then the joint venture will not become the owner of the property.

Accordingly, the joint venture agreement can provide that property contributed to, or acquired by the joint venture is joint venture property. The difficulty arises in determining whether property has been so contributed or acquired. The intention of the co-venturers is the controlling factor in determining what is joint venture property and what remains the property of the individual venturers. In determining the intention of the parties, the joint venture records, the conduct of the co-venturers, and most importantly, the joint venture agreement will control. Thus, it is imperative that the joint venture agreement deal directly with the question of property ownership, specifying the property to be owned by the joint venture, as well as the property which is provided only for use by the joint venture.

§7.10 **10. Labor** A joint venture agreement for the performance of a construction contract must contain a provision dealing with the obligations of the respective parties to supply the work force necessary to perform the contract. A common method of specifying this obligation is to allocate the responsibility to supply labor on a percentage basis, or merely to agree on the amount of labor to be supplied by each venturer; that is, the agreement states that each venturer "shall furnish the labor required to perform the work on the project from time to time, in approximately equal proportions." Of course, the parties also can commit specific persons (subject to their continued employment), or agree to staff specified positions.

Whatever method of allocating responsibility for providing labor is utilized, the co-venturers must be aware, and the joint venture agreement should reflect, that the agreement by the parties to supply labor is subject to the terms of any applicable collective bargaining agreements to which any of the co-venturers is a party. It is possible that the business agent of a local union will interpret an applicable collective bargaining agreement so as to permit only one of the co-venturers to supply labor on a job and thus, refuse to provide union labor to the remaining co-venturers. The joint venture agreement should provide for such a contingency, allowing one of the venturers to be the conduit through which all labor is supplied.

§7.11 **11. Employees of the Joint Venture** Many construction contractors have established their own pension and profit-sharing plans, while many others contribute to jointly administered multi-employer pension and profit-sharing plans created pursuant to the terms of collective bargaining agreements negotiated by the employer or by an employer association and a union. Where a co-venturer has established its own pension or profit-sharing plan, problems may arise if the employees participating in such plans terminate their employment with the co-venturer to become employees of the joint venture.

The principal, applicable law in the area of pension and profit-sharing plans is the Employee Retirement Income Security Act of 1974 (ERISA). Within the requirements of ERISA, pension and profit-sharing plans may be drafted to meet the needs of the particular business establishing the plan. Thus, as a preface to the following discussion, it should be noted that the terms of any particular pension or profit-sharing plan must be examined to determine whether they are more or less restrictive than the general provisions of law discussed below. In order to determine precisely the effect of employment with the joint venture upon a participant in such a plan, the actual plan documents and the facts of each situation must be reviewed.

The most important issue affecting the status of an employee of a joint venturer, who terminates employment with the company to become employed by the joint venture, is whether the employee thereby will incur a one-year break in service. This is defined generally as a period of 12 consecutive months during which the employee has not completed more than 500 hours of service with the employer (IRC §411(1)(6)(A)).

The consequences of a one-year break in service are very unfavorable for the employee. The most immediate consequence is that the employee forfeits accrued but non-vested benefits. This can cause a serious monetary loss to the employee whose interest in the plan is not 100% vested.

In addition, joint venture employees who return to their respective companies after incurring a one-year break in service may find that the resumption of participation in the pension or profit-sharing plan of their employer is delayed. The terms of the pension or profit-sharing plan may provide that the employee must complete a full year of service after return, as a condition for eligibility for the particular plan (IRC §410(a)(5)(C)).

Even after returning to the employ of a venturer, the one-year break in service may continue to have detrimental effects when the number of years of service with the employer are computed for vesting purposes. The plan may require a one year waiting period before the employee's pre-break and post-break service must be aggregated under the plan; in certain cases, the plan may disregard the employee's pre-break service if the period of absence equals or exceeds the years of service prior to the break.

Thus, a termination of employment with one of the co-venturers to work directly for the joint venture itself, which may result in a one-year break in service, can prejudice severely the employee's participation in and benefits under a company's pension or profit-sharing plan. Even where there is no break in service, the terms of a particular plan may affect an employee who terminates employment to work for the joint venture.

The problems created by terminating the employee's employment with a company to service the joint venture directly throughout its duration can be alleviated by proper planning. While pension and profit-sharing plans typically include only those persons who are directly in the employ of the legal entity sponsoring the plan, it is possible to provide in the pension or profit-sharing plan involved that persons who are indirectly employed by the company sponsoring the plan, and in particular, those employed by the joint venture, be included in the plan.

Another method of avoiding the problems resulting from termination of employment is through the joint venture agreement. Many joint ventures provide that the personnel actually involved in the construction of the project are not the employees of the joint venture, but rather retain their status as employees of the respective joint venturers. Such a provision may eliminate completely the termination of employment problem.

§7.12   12. Accounting The joint venture agreement should provide for maintenance of separate records and books of account for the joint venture. The management committee usually will designate the accounting method or methods to be used by the joint venture and also will select a location where the joint venture records and books of account will be kept and made available for inspection by all of the co-venturers. In many instances, the management committee also will be authorized to select one individual to act as the treasurer or chief fiscal officer of the joint venture.

The agreement may provide for periodic independent audits of the joint venture books at the request of any co-venturer; of course, a final independent audit upon completion of the construction contract is advisable. Language in the agreement, stating that the certified figures of the independent accountant selected to perform the audit are to be conclusive, final and binding on the parties, is very useful in avoiding potential disputes.

§7.13   13. Insurance A construction contracting joint venture needs the same types of insurance coverage as any other contractor, and policies should be secured which protect the joint venture. Each contractor participating in the joint venture should maintain the individual insurance coverage carried prior to entering the joint venture. Before entering into the joint venture, the advice of an experienced insurance adviser should be sought to establish the joint venture insurance program. The insurance adviser can play a crucial role in recommending adequate insurance protection for the joint venture, as well as in reviewing the sufficiency of the coverage maintained by the individual venturers. Insurance coverage for joint venture participants may often be excluded by individual insurance policies. Endorsements or separate policies to cover joint venture activities must be obtained.

As a matter of practice, the obligations of the joint venture to acquire insurance in its own behalf, and of the individual venturers to maintain adequate insurance coverage, should be reflected in the joint venture agreement.

§7.14   14. Conclusion It can readily be seen that there are many aspects of entering into a joint venture and performing a construction contract as a member of a joint venture which must be considered. Advising the contractor of the essential elements of an agreement will enable the contractor to negotiate with the co-venturers for the performance of a contract as a joint venture. After the manner and means of securing and performing a contract have been discussed, the terms and conditions of the agreement specifically defining the rights and responsibilities of all of the co-venturers should be set down in writing.

The provisions discussed above are those most frequently encountered in a construction industry joint venture agreement, but are by no means exhaustive. Each individual joint venture requires a carefully considered written agreement tailored to the specific circumstances. In the planning of a joint venture and drafting of the joint venture agreement, it is highly advisable for the contractor to seek the advice of competent legal and accounting counsel.

§7.15   B. FORM   **Joint Venture Agreement**

This JOINT VENTURE AGREEMENT made and entered into this 1st day of May, 19XX, (hereinafter referred to as the "Agreement") between ABC, INC. (hereinafter referred to as "ABC"), a Georgia Corporation having its principal place of business at 100 Magnolia Avenue, Atlanta, Georgia, and XYZ COMPANY (hereinafter referred to as "XYZ"), a Georgia corporation having its principal place of business at 250 Poplar Drive, Atlanta, Georgia.

WITNESSETH:

WHEREAS, the parties hereto desire to associate themselves in a Joint Venture for the purpose of securing a contract and performing mechanical construction on an Office Building to serve as a Corporate Headquarters for the Cavalier Company, located on Peachtree Street, Atlanta, Georgia (the contract hereinafter referred to as the "Construction Contract" and the building hereinafter referred to as the "Project"); said Construction Contract being attached hereto as Exhibit A and made a part of this Agreement by reference; and,

WHEREAS, the parties hereto have agreed as to the method and means of performing said Construction Contract; and,

WHEREAS, the parties hereto desire that their interest in the services to be rendered in the work to be performed under the Construction Contract (including any supplements, changes, and additions thereto, or work in connection therewith) and all rights, liabilities, profits and losses arising out of the performance or non-performance thereof be defined by an agreement in writing;

NOW, THEREFORE, in consideration of the mutual promises and covenants contained herein, it is mutually agreed as follows:

[Instead of the premises, the agreement can begin with a clause such as the following:
For and in consideration of the mutual covenants contained herein, and other good and valuable consideration, the receipt and sufficiency of which is hereby acknowledged, the parties agree as follows:]

1. Rights and Responsibilities

The parties hereto constitute themselves a Joint Venture for the purpose of performing and completing the Project hereinabove described, and for the purpose of furnishing or performing the necessary work, labor, materials and services in connection therewith, and for no other purpose, it being expressly understood that nothing contained in this Agreement shall be construed as creating any partnership between the parties hereto, or one party the general agent of the other, or in any way preventing or hindering either party hereto from carrying on its respective business or businesses for its own benefit.

2. Joint and Several Liability

The Construction Contract shall be made in the name of the Joint Venture for the mutual benefit of the parties hereto, and the obligations under the Construction Contract shall be joint and several.

3. Name and Principal Office

The name of this Joint Venture shall be "ABC, INC.-XYZ COMPANY JOINT VENTURE". The principal office of the Joint Venture shall be located at the Project, or at such other location as may be mutually agreed upon by the parties.

4. Interests of the Parties

a. The interest of the parties in and to the Construction Contract, and in and to any and all property and equipment acquired in connection with the performance thereof and in and to any and all monies which may be derived from the performance thereof, and the obligations and liabilities of each of the parties hereto as among themselves in connection with the Construction Contract and with respect to any and all liabilities and losses in connection therewith shall be:

ABC:	X PERCENT (X%)
XYZ:	Y PERCENT (Y%)

b. Each party agrees to indemnify the other against any loss or liability exceeding the proportions hereinabove stated by reason of any liability incurred or loss sustained in and about the Construction Contract, or by reason of the execution of any surety company bonds or indemnity agreements in connection therewith.

5. Representatives and Management Committee

a. Each party shall designate a Principal Representative to serve on a Management Committee (hereinafter referred to as the "Management Committee") who shall have complete responsibility to act on behalf of that party in any matter involving, in connection with, or arising out of the performance of the Construction Contract by the Joint Venture.

b. Each party shall also designate an Alternate Representative to the Management Committee who shall serve only when the Principal Representative of that party is absent or incapacitated or unable to serve. The Principal and Alternate Representatives shall serve as such without compensation, or for such compensation from the funds of the Joint Venture as may be agreed upon by the Management Committee.

c. Subject to the terms of this Agreement, the Management Committee shall have full responsibility and authority for the performance of the Construction Contract, including, but not limited to, assignment of work between the parties, preparation of schedules of work, settlement of disputes with the (General Contractor) (Owner), and any other matters affecting the performance of the Construction Contract. Actions and decisions of the Management Committee shall be by (unanimous) (majority) vote and shall be final, conclusive, and binding upon the parties.

 d. Should any of the representatives of the respective parties die, become disabled, resign, or for any reason cease to be connected with the party which nominated him, such party shall promptly, by written notice served upon the other party, name his successor.

 e. Each of the parties hereto may at any time replace either the Principal or Alternate Representative designated by it, or all such representatives, by a notice in writing served upon the other party.

 f. Meetings of the Management Committee for the transaction of the business of the Joint Venture may be called at such time and such place, subject to reasonable notice, by either party or their representatives as they may consider necessary or desirable.

6. Contributions and Financing

 a. The initial capital contribution of each party to the Joint Venture shall be as follows:

ABC:	X DOLLARS
XYZ:	Y DOLLARS

 b. A joint bank account or joint bank accounts (hereinafter collectively referred to as the "Joint Venture Account") shall be opened in such banks or trust companies as may be determined by the Management Committee.

 c. Within five (5) days after the execution of this Agreement, the parties shall each advance and pay into the Joint Venture Account, the initial capital contributions specified in Subparagraph 6a above, or execute such other documents or perform such other services as is necessary to make the initial capital contribution available to the Joint Venture.

 d. All monies contributed by the parties and all monies received as payment under the Construction Contract or otherwise received by the Joint Venture are hereby declared to be trust funds for the performance of the Construction Contract and for no other purpose, until the Construction Contract shall have been fully completed and accepted by the Owner, and all obligations of the Joint Venture have been paid or otherwise discharged, or adequate reserves have been established to cover any such obligations; and such reserves likewise are declared to be trust funds which shall be disbursed only for the purpose for which such reserves were created, or returned to the parties when that purpose has been served. Proper fidelity bond coverage shall be maintained on all persons who are directly connected with the performance of the Construction Contract, and the cost of such fidelity bond premiums shall be part of the Construction Costs, as defined herein (see "Construction Costs," below).

 e. All payments received by the Joint Venture under the Construction Contract or from others in connection with the Project shall be promptly deposited in the Joint Venture Account and all invoices received by the Joint Venture shall be paid by check drawn on the Joint Venture Account.

f. Checks drawn against the Joint Venture Account shall require the signature of two (2) persons, each representing a different party. Each party shall designate an individual or individuals authorized on its behalf to endorse checks deposited and to sign checks drawn on the Joint Venture Account.

g. When and if the Management Committee of the Joint Venture determines that additional funds are required or desirable for carrying out the Construction Contract, or to pay any losses arising therefrom, or to make good any deficits by reason of prior overpayments to the parties, then, and in such event, the parties shall within ten (10) days after such determination contribute such additional funds in accordance with the respective percentage interests of the parties. Should any party be unable, or fail or neglect to contribute and deposit such additional funds in the Joint Venture Account, then the other party advancing such deficiency shall receive interest on the funds advanced at a rate computed at X percent (X%) per annum from the time of their advancement to the time of their repayment. Such excess funds shall be repaid in full with interest (from the time of their advancement to the time of their repayment) from the first monies thereafter received in connection with the Project distributable to the parties and before any other payments are made to the parties. The interest paid for funds thus advanced shall be charged against the party on account of whose failure the said funds were advanced.

h. When and if the Management Committee of the Joint Venture determines that the funds in the Joint Venture Account are in excess of the needs of the Project, such excess funds shall be first applied to the return of the parties' capital contributions until such capital contributions have been entirely repaid, and the balance of such excess shall be distributed to the parties in their respective percentage interests set forth above.

i. In no event will advance distribution of any funds pursuant to Subparagraph 6h, above, reduce the obligation of the parties for future expenses of the Joint Venture.

j. Neither party nor its agents shall have the power to borrow money on, or otherwise pledge, the credit of the other party to the Joint Venture.

7. Preliminary Expenses

Subject to the approval of the Management Committee, all preliminary, traveling, out-of-pocket and other expenses related to the Project incurred by any party up to and including the date on which the Construction Contract was awarded shall be borne proportionally by the parties as set forth in Subparagraph 4a, above.

8. Joint Venture Property

a. The capital contributions described in Paragraph 6 above, shall become Joint Venture property.

b. Other property obtained with funds of the Joint Venture shall likewise become Joint Venture property.

c. Joint Venture property shall be so recorded in the Joint Venture books of account.

d. Property made available for Joint Venture use shall remain the property of the contributing party. A schedule of the property made available for Joint Venture use by each party is attached hereto as Exhibit "B" and made a part hereof by reference. Upon termination of this Agreement, or at such other time as the parties may agree upon, this property may be returned to the contributing party. Nothing contained herein shall limit the parties hereto from making additional property available for use by the Joint Venture. Property made available for use by the Joint Venture, in addition to that which is specified in Exhibit "B", shall be subject to the provisions of Subparagraph 6e and f, below.

e. Property made available for Joint Venture use, once contributed, shall not be withdrawn from Joint Venture use prior to the termination of this Agreement, without the consent of the Management Committee of the Joint Venture.

f. Subject to the approval of the Management Committee, any party to this agreement which makes property available for use by the Joint Venture shall be entitled to payment from Joint Venture funds of the fair rental value for the use of such property. The receipt of any such rental payments from the Joint Venture by a party hereto shall in no way limit or affect that party's interest in the Joint Venture as specified in Subparagraph 4a.

9. Labor

a. The parties hereto shall furnish the labor required to perform the work on the Project in the following proportions:

ABC:	X PERCENT
XYZ:	Y PERCENT

Provided, however, that notwithstanding the foregoing, the provision of labor for the Project by the parties hereto shall be in compliance with the terms of any applicable collective bargaining agreements to which either ABC, XYZ, or both, may be a party.

b. Each party shall be reimbursed for all expenses incurred in providing said labor, including but not limited to salaries, insurance, employee benefits, workmen's compensation insurance, public liability insurance, Federal old age taxes, State unemployment taxes, and any other taxes levied by Federal, State or local authorities; provided, however, that such reimbursement shall not exceed the reimbursement received by the Joint Venture from the Owner for such items pursuant to the Construction Contract. The receipt of such payments shall in no way affect or limit the parties' interest in the Joint Venture as specified in Subparagraph 4a. Each party shall invoice the Joint Venture monthly for its costs of providing such labor.

10. Employees

Unless otherwise mutually agreed, the Joint Venture shall have no employees, and all personnel rendering services to the Joint Venture shall remain the employees of the respective parties hereto. All necessary personnel shall be provided from the staffs of the parties. New personnel employed specifically for work on the Project will become employees of one of the parties by mutual agreement at the time of employment with distribution of new persons as agreed upon between the parties.

11. Cost of Construction

The Cost of Construction of the Project shall include: The cost of all subcontracts, labor, material, plant, tools and equipment purchased or leased (including any of the foregoing items purchased or leased from either of the parties hereto); bonds, insurance, taxes of all types (excepting income); miscellaneous charges; legal fees; consultants' fees; administrative and accounting expenses; liabilities not covered by insurance; and all other expenses and obligations incurred or suffered in and about the performance of the Construction Contract of a nature properly charged as a cost of performance of the Construction Contract under generally accepted accounting principles.

12. Project Profits

Upon completion of the Construction Contract and after paying or adequately providing for the payment of all Costs of Construction (as specified in Paragraph 11) incurred for its performance and completion, including all costs and charges properly allocable to the Construction Contract, payment of any and all claims not secured by insurance, or the establishment of adequate reserves therefor, whether such claims actually have been brought or may be reasonably anticipated, and after providing any other reserves for contingency that may be determined by the Management Committee to be necessary, and after repaying to the parties all advances for capital contributions, any profits thereafter remaining shall be divided between and distributed to the parties hereto in the proportions specified in Subparagraph 4a. Any reserves when no longer required, or so much thereof as shall remain, shall be similarly divided and distributed.

13. Project Manager and Assistant Project Manager

The representatives of the respective parties to the Management Committee shall appoint a Project Manager and an Assistant Project Manager for the Project who shall (1) be responsible for the direction and management of the work in accordance with policies and procedures established by the Management Committee, (2) coordinate the work, and (3) be responsible for contact with the General Contractor and other necessary parties in order to perform the work.

The Project Manager shall be appointed by the representative of ABC, and the Assistant Project Manager shall be appointed by the representative of XYZ.

The Project Manager and Assistant Project Manager shall be subject to removal and reappointment by the representative of the party empowered to appoint same; provided, however, that any such removal and reappointment shall be subject to the approval of the Management Committee.

14. Policy Disputes

a. All disputes between the parties on matters of policy with respect to the performance of the Construction Contract shall be submitted to an independent arbiter mutually agreed upon by the parties. Unless otherwise mutually agreed by the parties hereto, or unless he is unwilling or unable to serve, the parties hereto do hereby appoint Mr. T of U Company, to act as the abovesaid independent arbiter with respect to all disputes between the parties on matters of policy in connection with the performance of the Construction Contract.

b. The decision rendered by the independent arbiter, provided for in Subparagraph a, above, shall be final, conclusive and binding upon the parties.

c. Notice of submission of the policy dispute to the independent arbiter shall be filed with the other party to this Agreement by the party submitting same. The policy dispute shall be submitted to the independent arbiter within a reasonable time after the dispute has arisen.

d. In rendering a decision with respect to a policy dispute, the independent arbiter shall proceed in accordance with either the Construction Industry Arbitration Rules of the American Arbitration Association as its guide, or such rules as may otherwise be mutually agreed upon by the parties hereto and the arbiter.

15. Accounting

a. One person designated by the Management Committee shall be appointed Treasurer of the Joint Venture. The Treasurer shall keep for the Joint Venture a separate set of full and current books of account, upon such basis as the Management Committee may determine. Such books of account shall be kept and maintained at the principal office of the Joint Venture, and, along with all other records of the Joint Venture, shall be open for inspection by the parties to the Joint Venture at mutually convenient times.

b. A periodic audit of such books of account shall be made by an independent firm of certified public accountants as may be mutually agreed upon by the parties, and a like audit shall be made upon completion of the Construction Contract. With respect to the periodic audits, there shall be included, if requested by the parties, a periodic comparison between the items of cost and the items set up in the estimate of cost. The cost of these audits shall be a part of the Construction Costs of the Project as defined in Paragraph 11. For purposes of this Agreement, the certified figures of the firm of accountants retained to perform the periodic and/or final audits shall be final, conclusive and binding upon the parties.

c. Records of the Joint Venture which are required to be kept subsequent to the completion of the Construction Contract pursuant to the provisions of law shall be kept at such place or places as determined by the Management Committee, and the costs thereof shall be borne by the parties in accordance with their respective interests as described in Subparagraph 4a.

16. Insurance

a. Each party to this Agreement shall effect and maintain insurance to protect itself from: claims under the Workmen's Compensation Act; claims for damages because of bodily injury including personal injury, sickness or disease, or death of any of its employees or of any person other than its employees; and, from claims for damages because of injury to or destruction of tangible property including loss of use resulting therefrom.

b. The Joint Venture will effect and maintain insurance to protect all parties from claims arising out of the performance under this Agreement for which the Joint Venture is legally liable. The Joint Venture shall acquire all necessary bonds, completed operations insurance, personal liability insurance, workmen's compensation insurance, automobile liability insurance, and in such amounts as the Management Committee believes necessary to protect the Joint Venture. To the extent that any party hereto provides these coverages for the Joint Venture, the party shall be reimbursed for its cost of obtaining same, which payment shall not affect or limit the party's interest in the Joint Venture as specified in Subparagraph 4a.

17. Bankruptcy, Insolvency or Liquidation

a. Notwithstanding any other provision contained herein, in the event of the insolvency, bankruptcy or liquidation of either party, this Joint Venture Agreement shall terminate, and the insolvent, bankrupt or liquidated party shall share only in the profits earned or loss or liability incurred to the date of such insolvency, bankruptcy or liquidation. The profits earned or loss or liability incurred to the date of such insolvency, bankruptcy or liquidation shall be deemed to bear the same proportion to the total profits earned or loss or liability incurred upon the final completion of the Construction Contract as the amount of the work completed on the date of such insolvency, bankruptcy or liquidation bears to the total work required at the completion of the Construction Contract. Such share in any profits shall in no event be payable to the insolvent, bankrupt or liquidated party before the completion of the Construction Contract and the collection of all receipts and the payment of all liabilities.

b. In the event of the insolvency, bankruptcy, or liquidation of either party, the remaining party, being the one not insolvent, bankrupt, or liquidated, shall be privileged to complete the Construction Contract without incurring liability of any kind to the other party to this Agreement for the profit earned after such date of insolvency, bankruptcy, or liquidation, and such earnings or accruals after such happening shall belong to the surviving party.

18. Assignment of Interest

Neither party may assign, pledge, transfer or hypothecate its interest in this Agreement or in any monies belonging to or which may accrue to the Joint Venture in connection with the Construction Contract or any interest in the Joint Venture Account, or in any property, real or personal, loaned to or belonging to, or employed by the Joint Venture, except with the prior written consent of the other party.

19. Legal Counsel

The Joint Venture may retain, as and when necessary, legal counsel to be mutually agreed upon for use in connection with any matters of concern to the Joint Venture which may require legal counsel or assistance.

20. Commencement and Termination

a. This Joint Venture will commence on_____.

b. Except as otherwise provided herein, this Agreement shall remain in full force and effect until terminated by written agreement duly signed by all of the parties hereto, or until all of the purposes for which this Joint Venture has been undertaken have been accomplished and completed.

21. Technical Assistance of Each Party

Except as otherwise provided herein, each party shall make available for the Project such of its personnel, facilities, experience, and records as may be reasonably necessary or desirable to the end that the Project may be promptly and successfully carried out.

22. Fiscal Year

The books of account of the Joint Venture shall be maintained on a fiscal year basis. The fiscal year shall begin on_____and end on_____.

23. Notices

Any and all notices required or permitted to be given under this Agreement will be sufficient if furnished in writing, sent by United States Mail, postage prepaid to his last known residence in the case of an individual, or its principal office in the metropolitan area of Atlanta, Georgia in the case of a corporation or other business entity.

24. Applicable Law

All questions relative to the execution, validity, interpretation and performance of this Agreement shall be governed by the laws of the State of Georgia.

25. Binding Agreement

This Agreement shall be binding upon and inure to the benefit of the parties hereto, their heirs, successors, and assigns as the case may be.

26. Merger

This Agreement, and the exhibits attached hereto and referenced herein, contain and embody the entire Agreement of the parties hereto, and no representations, inducements, or agreements, oral or otherwise, between the parties not contained and embodied herein shall be of any force or effect; and this Agreement may not be modified or changed, in whole or in part, orally or in any other manner than by an agreement in writing duly signed by all of the parties hereto.

IN WITNESS WHEREOF, the parties hereto have caused this Agreement to be executed, and their seals affixed hereto, by their duly authorized officers on the day and year first above written.

"ABC"

(CORPORATE SEAL)   ABC, INC.

By: _____
          President

ATTEST:

_____
Secretary

                                    "XYZ"

(CORPORATE SEAL)   XYZ COMPANY

                                    By: _____
                                                           President

ATTEST:

_____
Secretary

EIGHT   Privity Agreements

§8.01   Introduction
§8.02   Form—Privity Agreement

§8.01   A.   INTRODUCTION

The general contract usually states that the disputes procedure under the contract is applicable to disputes between the owner and the general contractor. In most situations, there is no privity of contract between a subcontractor and the owner. A subcontractor whose dispute is ultimately with the owner may obtain the general contractor's agreement to provide cooperation and contract privity in order to give the subcontractor access to the disputes procedure. Although a direct appeal in the name of the subcontractor generally is not available in the case of a direct appeal of a dispute with the owner under the disputes clause, a subcontractor's claim can be prosecuted either by the general contractor on behalf of the subcontractor or by the subcontractor using the general contractor's name and privity.

The procedure for indirect appeals in the name of the general contractor is a matter of form because the general contractor need not be involved in prosecuting the subcontractor's claim. The general contractor typically is motivated to extend to the subcontractor indirect appeal rights because it results in all the parties' rights being adjudicated in one forum at the same time between the owner and the subcontractor, who are the real parties in interest. If the general contractor does not grant to the subcontractor the right to an indirect appeal through the general contractor's disputes clause, the result may be that the general contractor and the contractor's surety may be sued in court by the subcontractor while the general contractor is required to pursue the administrative disputes remedy against the owner.

In many instances the subcontract will incorporate by reference all the boilerplate of the general contract, and it may be argued that the subcontract also includes the disputes clause. This often creates an issue as to when the subcontractor is bound to proceed under the disputes article, and when the subcontractor is bound by an administrative decision which the general contractor may institute under the article on behalf of the subcontractor. However, because all disputes are between the owner and the general contractor, arguably the conduit clause in a subcontract is not meant to apply to any disputes arising under a subcontract.

Since an indirect appeal technically is made in the name of the general contractor, the general contractor obviously would be bound by the decision; it does not necessarily follow that the subcontractor is also bound. The legal relationship between the general contractor and the owner may be substantially different from that between the subcontractor and the general contractor. The owner may have certain defenses against the general contractor which the general contractor may not have against the subcontractor. Moreover, a dispute may be solely between the general contractor and the subcontractor but may not involve any substantial issues concerning or any liability of the owner. Therefore, the dispute would be beyond the coverage of the disputes clause between the owner and the general contractor. There also may be disputes between the general contractor and the subcontractor which solely relate to matters of law, in which case the administrative remedies under the disputes clause may be inapplicable because the scope of a disputes clause typically is limited to adjudications of questions of fact or mixed questions of law and fact.

Since the subcontractor's indirect appeal must proceed through the offices of the general contractor, it is vital that the general contractor preserve the subcontractor's right of indirect appeal and not take any action that would destroy the possibility of appeal, such as the general contractor's executing a release to the owner or not giving timely notice of a subcontractor's indirect appeal. The agreement should stipulate that the general contractor will cooperate with the subcontractor in presenting any appeal, and that the general contractor will make witnesses available and give the subcontractor access to information in the files of the general contractor that may be necessary for a complete and accurate presentation of the claim.

The agreement sometimes stipulates that the parties settle all matters, and apportion any funds received from claims, between themselves. This type of agreement is a liquidation agreement, in which the parties liquidate all claims that they may have against each other, arising out of the subject matter of the dispute, and agree on a common course of action against the owner. The agreement should never stipulate that the subcontractor gives the general contractor a full release without at least placing on the general contractor liability to the subcontractor for any amounts recovered on claims.

A subcontractor's right to indirectly appeal to the owner may be lost inadvertently. If the subcontractor agrees to exculpatory language which releases or eliminates any liability that the general contractor may have to be the subcontractor, the owner may argue that the owner cannot be liable to the general contractor, who has been released from any liability to the subcontractor under the doctrine of *Severin v United States* 99 CCl 435 (1943), cert den 332 US 733 (1944). The *Severin* doctrine is that an exculpatory clause which relieves the general contractor of liability to the subcontractor precludes the general contractor from suing the government on the subcontractor's behalf. Fortunately, the Armed Services Board of Contract Appeals and even the Court of Claims have subsequently limited the application of the *Severin* doctrine in indirect appeals to the Board, and there are specific situations where the *Severin* doctrine does not apply.

The way to ensure that the *Severin* doctrine does not apply to an indirect appeal is to provide that the general contractor remains liable to the subcontractor for any amounts recovered pursuant to the indirect appeal of the subcontractor. Subcontractors and general contractors should be careful to see that any exculpatory clauses in subcontracts or in supplemental agreements are drawn so that they do not completely release the general contractor, causing the subcontractor to fall into the *Severin* trap. A conditional release can be achieved by having the general contractor agree to remain liable to the subcontractor for any monies received by the general contractor on the subcontractor's appeal.

§8.02   B. FORM   Privity Agreement

This Agreement entered into this _____ day of _____, 19___, by and between _____, hereinafter referred to as "General Contractor", and _____, hereinafter referred to as "Subcontractor", whereby the parties enter into this Agreement for the purpose of allowing the Subcontractor to pursue a claim, administrative appeal or litigation against _____, hereinafter referred to as the "Owner", arising out of a dispute in connection with the construction of the _____, hereinafter referred to as the "Project", that arises under the subcontract with the general contractor being more particularly described as follows:

The parties agree as follows:

1. General Contractor agrees to allow the Subcontractor to proceed directly against the Owner in all claims, appeals and litigation pertaining to the above described dispute in the name of the General Contractor.

2. The Subcontractor agrees to bear the cost and expense to conduct research, compile evidence, produce witnesses and engage counsel for and in connection with the preparation, substantiation, presentation, trial and appeal of aforesaid claim; and the General Contractor shall have no obligation in regard to paying any expenses pursuant to said appeal by the subcontractor.

3. The General Contractor agrees to cooperate with the Subcontractor in preserving its right to present said claim and appeals, and the General Contractor shall not take any action which would jeopardize the Subcontractor's right to appeal said dispute. The General Contractor shall make available access to its files, documentation and will fully and completely, without reservation, share all information and records so that an accurate and complete claim presentation to the Owner may be made.

4. The General Contractor shall be liable to the Subcontractor for any amounts paid by the Owner to the General Contractor with respect to the aforesaid claim; and said funds paid to the General Contractor shall be held as trust funds to be paid to the Subcontractor.

IN WITNESS WHEREOF the parties hereto, on the date set forth above, cause this Agreement to be executed by their respective fully authorized officers.

_____
General Contractor

_____
Subcontractor

PART THREE

Documents to Secure and Obtain Payment

Robert F. Cushman, Esq.

The forms set forth in this Part are those most commonly used in the construction industry in the United States to insure payment and to collect money for labor and/or material supplied. For this reason, documentation pertaining to letters of credit arrangements (often used in foreign construction projects and foreign supply arrangements), as well as to commercial and political risk insurance and guarantee program documentation, are not included. (The Foreign Credit Insurance Association and the Export-Import Bank of the United States maintain a number of programs to facilitate the export of American goods and services.) Letters of credit arrangements and credit insurance, although available, are seldom used in domestic construction projects.

This Part is tailored to present commonly used collection forms and is not intended to cover in depth the many devices and procedures available to secure and obtain payment. Stopping work for nonpayment and other breaches of contract rights, the right of contract rescission, the rights granted under the Uniform Commercial Code which are applicable to construction situations, the rights granted suppliers of labor and material under state trust-doctrine statutes, the practical and legal effect of notifying third parties with or without interests, the use of credit insurance, etc., must be left to other commentary.[1]

Local law should at all times be examined before making use of the forms presented herein.

---

1 For an overview of collective procedures, see M. Koenig, "Collection Procedures in the Construction Industry" in *McGraw-Hill Construction Business Handbook* (1978)

NINE   Assignments, Joint Checks, Guarantees

Assignment of Monies Due or to Become Due
§9.01 *Introduction*
§9.02 *Form—Assignment*
§9.03 *Form—Notice of Assignment*

Third Party Joint-Check Arrangement
§9.04 *Introduction*
§9.05 *Form—Agreement by General Contractor to Issue Check to Joint Order of Subcontractor and Supplier or Labor and/or Material to that Subcontractor*
§9.06 *Form—Agreement by Owner to Issue Check to the Joint Order of General Contractor and Supplier of Labor and/or Material to that General Contractor*

Guarantees
§9.07 *Introduction*
§9.08 *Form—Guarantee of Payment to Building Material Supplier*
§9.09 *Bank Guarantees—Generally*
§9.10 *Form—Agreement by Bank to Set Aside, Earmark, and Pay Contractor*
§9.11 *Form—Bank Guarantee to Prime Contractor (Construction Manager-Shell Owner Situation) with Additional Guarantee to Pay Change Orders*

A. ASSIGNMENT OF MONIES DUE OR TO BECOME DUE

§9.01   1. Introduction   Unless forbidden by statute, common law, or contract, a right created by contract may be assigned. Thus, the right to receive money due or to become due under a contract may be effectively assigned, even though the contract itself is not assignable, unless an intent to forbid an assignment of contract proceeds is manifest.

§9.02 2. FORM Assignment Form

For and in consideration of the sum of $1.00 and other
value received,
    Problem Construction Company
    124 Wicker Way
    New York, New York
        Assignor

hereby assigns to:
    Careful Construction Company
    4000 Brandywine Street
    Los Angeles, California
        Assignee

the sum of $10,050.00
part of the funds now or hereafter to become due Assignor from:
    Owner Development Corporation
    1 Seaside Drive
    Newport Beach, California
        Owner

under a certain Agreement dated October 1, 1977 (the Agreement) between Assignor and Owner for work performed on the project known as:
    Crickelwood Hill Apts.
    1 Seaside Drive
    Newport Beach, California

Assignor agrees that it will hold any funds in trust for Assignee and promptly turn same over to Assignee in the form received (check, drafts, cash), supplying any and all necessary endorsements, in the event that all or any part of the assigned sum is paid directly to Assignor.

Assignor agrees to perform and execute at the request of Assignee any act as shall be reasonably required to effectuate the purpose of this assignment.

All Assignor's right, title and interest hereunder may be re-assigned by Assignee.

Assignor constitutes Assignee, its successors and assigns, Assignor's attorney, irrevocably, with full power in the name of Assignor otherwise to demand, receive and give releases for any and all monies and claims for money due or to become due or arising out of the Agreement, to endorse any checks or other instruments or orders in connection therewith, to give all or any of the notices, consents, instructions or other communications reserved to Assignor under the Agreement, to file any claims or take any action or institute any proceedings which Assignee deems necessary. This Power of Attorney is irrevocable and coupled with an interest.

Assignor shall remain liable under the Agreement to perform all of its obligations under the Agreement. Assignor agrees to perform its obligations under the Agreement, to exercise promptly and diligently any right it may have under the Agreement, to promptly notify Assignee or any subsequent assignee of which it has notice of any default or alleged default by any party to the Agreement or any termination or alleged termination thereof.

Assignor does hereby warrant and represent that the Agreement is in full force and effect, that it has the power to make this assignment hereunder, that said assignment has been duly authorized, and that it has not assigned or pledged and hereby covenants that it will not assign or pledge, the whole or any part of the rights hereby assigned to anyone other than Assignee, it successors or assigns.

WITNESS (ATTEST)   PROBLEM CONSTRUCTION COMPANY
ASSIGNOR:

_____   _____

_____   _____

Acknowledged and Agreed to By:

_____

_____

Owner

§9.03 3. FORM Notice of Assignment

Date

Owner Development Corporation
1 Seaside Drive
Newport Beach, California

Gentlemen:

We are enclosing herewith a copy of an assignment of the sum of $10,050.00, part of the monies now owed to us (or to become due hereafter) under a certain agreement dated October 1, 1977 between you and the undersigned for work performed by the undersigned on the project known as Crickelwood Hill Apts., 1 Seaside Drive, Newport Beach, California to Careful Construction Company, 4000 Brandywine Street, Los Angeles, California, who is now the owner thereof.

We request that you make all payments sufficient to satisfy this assignment to Careful Construction Company prior to making any other payments under our agreement and declare that payment of said sum to Careful Construction Company shall discharge your obligation to the undersigned under our agreement to the extent of said payment.

PROBLEM CONSTRUCTION COMPANY

_____

_____

B. THIRD PARTY JOINT-CHECK ARRANGEMENT

§9.04   1. Introduction   A joint-check arrangement is an agreement by the owner to issue a check, payable to the joint order of the contractor and the contractor's supplier of labor or material (or an agreement by the contractor to issue a check to the subcontractor and the subcontractor's supplier). There is some question whether the agreement is legally enforceable. Practically, it is a most useful way of effecting payment. The promisor's (payor's) obligation is fulfilled when the check is issued. The check, however, is not negotiable without the endorsement of both payees. If the other payee (for example, the general contractor) is in bankruptcy, that payee's trustee may want to do some negotiating (claiming the check belongs to the bankruptcy estate of the general contractor) before signing the check. Consequently, it is recommended that suppliers attempt to procure a guarantee of full payment from the owner or general contractor.

The forms which follow are, admittedly, most favorable to suppliers seeking security. Most contractors will sign forms of this type because they are simple and to the point. More cautious contractors will insist upon clauses such as:

> Such joint check payments shall be made monthly as progress payments . . . only for materials and/or labor supplied to the project . . . which were ordered by the subcontractor pursuant to the above subcontract . . . and which comply with the specifications . . . and which are incorporated into the project . . . and for which the contractor has been provided a complete invoice, lien, waivers and certifications of compliance with the specifications by the architect.

They will further insist that:

> All joint check monies shall be applied to labor and material pertaining to this project . . . in no way create liability on the contractor's part for sums owed the supplier by the contractor's subcontractor . . . joint payments shall not be construed as a waiver of the contractor's rights against the subcontractor or others . . . that payment may be terminated if the subcontractor does not perform . . . that there is no obligation to make payments in excess of the amounts due the subcontractor.

§9.05   2. FORM   Agreement by General Contractor to Issue Check to Joint Order of Subcontractor and Supplier of Labor and/or Material to that Subcontractor

Date

Cautious Air Conditioning Corporation
1492 Torresdale Avenue
Philadelphia, Pennsylvania

In consideration of you, Cautious Air Conditioning Corp., 1492 Torresdale Avenue, Philadelphia, Pennsylvania, furnishing labor, material and equipment on open account to our subcontractor

        Weak Subcontracting Company
        999 Jones Street
        Philadelphia, Pennsylvania

and assisting us and our above subcontractor in completing our contract with

        Clover Department Store
        Ocean City, New Jersey

Contract dated October 1, 1977 for revamping of air conditioning and heating system, we hereby agree to pay a total of
        $50,000.00
by check made jointly to our subcontractor and you, Cautious Air Conditioning Corp., no later than forty-five (45) days from date of invoice of such labor, material and equipment.

It is expressly understood that Cautious Air Conditioning Corp. does not waive any right accorded it by law as a labor, material or equipment supplier on this project.

        PRIME CONSTRUCTION COMPANY
        123 Lancaster Avenue
        Villanova, Pennsylvania

        By: _____

CONFIRMED AND ACCEPTED:

WEAK SUBCONTRACTING COMPANY
999 Jones Street
Philadelphia, Pennsylvania

        By: _____

§9.06   3. FORM   **Agreement by Owner to Issue Check to Joint Order of General Contractor and Supplier of Labor and/or Material to that General Contractor**

Date

Cautious Air Conditioning Corp.
1492 Torresdale Avenue
Philadelphia, Pennsylvania

In consideration of you, Cautious Air Conditioning Corp., 1492 Torresdale Avenue, Philadelphia, Pennsylvania, furnishing labor, material and equipment on open account to our contractor,

Prime Contracting Company
123 South Jones Street
Philadelphia, Pennsylvania

and assisting the above company in the completion of its contract with the undersigned

said contract being dated October 1, 1977—
contract for the revamping of the air
conditioning and heating system at:

Owner Pharmaceutical Company
345 Smith Street
Philadelphia, Pennsylvania

we hereby agree to pay a total of
    $20,000.00
by check made jointly to the above contractor and you, Cautious Air Conditioning Corp., no later than forty-five (45) days from date of invoice price of such labor, material and equipment.

It is expressly understood that Cautious Air Conditioning Corp. does not waive any right accorded it by law as a labor, material or equipment supplier on this project.

OWNER PHARMACEUTICAL COMPANY
345 Smith Street
Philadelphia, Pennsylvania

By: _____

CONFIRMED AND ACCEPTED:

PRIME CONTRACTING COMPANY
123 South Jones Street
Philadelphia, Pennsylvania

By: _____

C. GUARANTEES

§9.07   1. Introduction   In many situations a guarantee is a most effective tool. It is a must when dealing with a dummy corporation or a limited partnership with a weak general partner.

A contract of guarantee must be in writing to be enforceable under the Statute of Frauds.

§9.08   2. FORM   Guarantee of Payment to Building Material Supplier

Date

Baker Construction Supply Company
400 Broad Street
Lancaster, Pennsylvania

      Re: Johnson Retail Outlet
            1018 Spruce Street
            Lancaster, Pa.

In order to induce you to supply materials to the above referred to construction project, the undersigned as owners do hereby jointly and severally guarantee full payment of the account of

      Slippery Construction Company
      1000 Maiden Lane
      New York, New York

(hereinafter "Slippery") for all material delivered by you to the construction project in accordance with the terms and conditions of Slippery's purchase order No. 40296 attached to this letter.

Upon any failure by Slippery to make payment when required, all amounts owed by Slippery in respect to such material shall become due and payable by the undersigned, immediately following your demand therefore. It is understood that you have no obligation to proceed first against Slippery or any collateral security before proceeding against the undersigned. This guarantee is the irrevocable, absolute and unconditional obligation of the undersigned and shall not be affected by any waiver or forebearance which you may extend for Slippery's benefit.

      _____
      Alvin Bright

      _____
      Betty Bright

3. Bank Guarantees

§9.09 **a. Introduction** From a practical point of view, guarantees of financial institutions can be most effective documents to secure payment. A guarantee of a bank, however, must be fashioned with extreme care to meet local banking codes. In many states, a guarantee issued by a bank is in violation of banking statutes.

§9.10 b. FORM Agreement by Bank to Set Aside, Earmark and Pay Contractor

AGREEMENT made this _____ day of _____, 1977, by and between PRUDENT CONSTRUCTORS CORPORATION and MERCANTILE BANKING & TRUST COMPANY

WITNESSETH:

(a) WHEREAS, PRUDENT CONSTRUCTORS CORPORATION (hereinafter called "Contractor") is about to enter into a construction agreement with FORT WASHINGTON PROPERTIES, INC. (hereinafter called "Owner") for the furnishing and installation of the caissons, grade beams, etc. at the four story office building on Franklyn Avenue, Fort Washington, Springfield Township, Montgomery County, Pennsylvania, to be erected by Owner (a copy of said construction agreement being annexed hereto and marked Exhibit 1); and

(b) WHEREAS, MERCANTILE BANKING & TRUST COMPANY has committed the sum of $110,000.00 to Owner for the purpose of the payment by Owner to Contractor under Exhibit 1; and

(c) WHEREAS, Owner and Contractor are mutually desirous of providing for the segregation and application of said construction funds as hereinafter is more particularly set forth,

NOW, THEREFORE, for and in consideration of the sum of One Dollar ($1.00) and other good and valuable consideration the MERCANTILE BANKING & TRUST COMPANY for itself and its successors does irrevocably agree to set aside and earmark the entire construction sum of $110,000.00 otherwise payable to Owner referred to in subdivision (b) hereof to the payment of monies due and payable to contractor under the agreement set forth in subdivision (a) hereof and hereby further agrees to apply and pay all sums due and payable under the contract referred to in subdivision (a) to contractor as and when the same become due and payable at such times and in such amounts as may have been approved by the architect under the construction agreement referred to in subdivision (a) hereof without other or further writings from Owner.

In the event that a dispute arises between Owner and Contractor, then MERCANTILE BANKING & TRUST COMPANY agrees to hold such funds until such time as the dispute is resolved in accordance with the general conditions of the contract agreement or otherwise.

MERCANTILE BANKING & TRUST
COMPANY

By: _____

APPROVED AND AGREED TO:
FORT WASHINGTON PROPERTIES, INC.

By: _____
              President

Attest:

_____
              Secretary

§9.11   c. FORM   Bank Guarantee to Prime Contractor (Construction Manager—Shell Owner Situation) with Additional Guarantee to Pay Change Orders

CASH GUARANTEE

THIS GUARANTEE given this 12th day of June, 1977 by THE MERCANTILE BANK, a _____ corporation, with offices at _____ ("Bank") to HARRISON CONCRETE CORP., a _____ corporation having its principal office at _____ ("Prime Contractor").

WITNESSETH:

A. Bank and SHELL CORP., INC. ("Owner") have entered into a construction loan agreement of even date herewith, by which Bank has agreed to lend to Owner Thirty-Two Million Five Hundred Thousand Dollars ($32,500,000.00) for the construction of a forty-seven (47) story building containing condominium apartments, commercial space, together with two (2) levels of underground parking (the "Improvements") on the property located in _____, _____ at _____ (the "Property"). The loan is evidenced by a note made by Owner in favor of Bank and the note is secured, inter alia, by a mortgage on the Property.

B. Owner and CONSTRUCTION MANAGEMENT COMPANY, INC. ("Construction Manager") have entered into a Construction Management Contract dated March 20, 1977 ("Construction Management Contract") by which Construction Manager has agreed to cause the erection and completion of the Improvements pursuant to the terms of the Construction Management Contract. The Construction Management Contract provides that Owner will contract directly with certain prime contractors (which prime contractors are referred to in the Construction Management Contract as "bonded subcontractors") to supply certain labor and materials for the erection and completion of the Improvements.

C. Owner and Prime Contractor have entered into a contract (the "Contract") dated June 11, 1977, by which Prime Contractor has agreed to furnish certain labor and materials for the erection and completion of the Improvements as more fully described in the Contract, a copy of which Contract is attached hereto and made a part hereof as Exhibit "A". The amount of the Contract is Five Million Four Hundred Thousand Dollars ($5,400,000.00).

D. Prime Contractor has requested that Bank guarantee payment of (i) the $5,400,000.00 Contract price to become due Prime Contractor under the Contract, and (ii) the agreed amount payable to Prime Contractor upon proper performance of permitted change orders which shall have been approved in writing by Bank and funded by Owner.

NOW, THEREFORE, for good and valuable consideration and intending to be legally bound hereby, Bank agrees as follows:

1. Subject to the terms and conditions hereinafter set forth, Bank hereby guarantees to Prime Contractor payment of all sums as and when they become due Prime Contractor for labor and materials furnished pursuant to the Contract; provided, however, that nothing in this Paragraph shall be construed as a guarantee of payment of any sums in excess of the aggregate amount of $5,400,000.00 except as otherwise specified in Paragraph 2 of this Guarantee.

2. Notwithstanding the limitation contained in Paragraph 1 of this Guarantee setting $5,400,000.00 as the maximum amount of this Guarantee, this Guarantee shall apply to, and Bank shall guarantee payment of, any amounts as and when they become due Prime Contractor upon proper performance by Prime Contractor of change orders ("Change Orders") provided that the following conditions precedent have been fulfilled with respect to each Change Order:

   (i) Each Change Order shall be in writing, signed by Owner or Owner's authorized representative, and shall meet all the requirements of the Contract as to form and substance; and

   (ii) Owner shall have deposited with Bank a fully executed copy of the complete Change Order; and

   (iii) Owner shall have deposited with Bank in cash or in such other form as Bank may require, the funds required to pay Prime Contractor for the cost of the Change Order; and

   (iv) Bank shall have given to Owner its written approval of the Change Order and the deposit of funds; and

   (v) Bank shall have given Prime Contractor written notice that the conditions set forth in clauses (i), (ii), (iii), and (iv) of this Paragraph 2 have been satisfied; and

   (vi) Bank shall have received from Prime Contractor the fee applicable to the Change Order (as hereinafter specified); and

   (vii) Bank shall have issued a written endorsement to this Guarantee to include the specific amount to become due Prime Contractor pursuant to the Change Order, identifying it.

3.

   (a) This guarantee shall not be effective until Bank shall have received from Owner the basic initial fee charged by Bank for this Guarantee.

   (b) Bank shall be entitled to receive from Prime Contractor a fee equal to one-quarter of one percent (1/4%) of the amount to be guaranteed under each Change Order; and no guarantee shall be effective as to any change until Bank shall have received the applicable fee and given its written receipt therefor.

4. Payment by Bank under this Cash Guarantee is subject to the following terms and conditions:

   (a) Satisfactory performance of labor and physical incorporation of materials into the structure or delivery and proper storage of materials at the site in a manner satisfactory to Bank, in accordance with the terms of the Contract, free of any chattel mortgage, conditional sale, security interest or any other lien or encumbrance; and

   (b) Only upon and pursuant to vouchers payable to the order of Prime Contractor, properly signed by Prime Contractor, together with a requisition for payment and architect's certification signed by

    (i) a representative of the Construction manager; and

    (ii) a representative of Robert F. Wright and Associates (architects); and

    (iii) a representative of Owner, which vouchers shall constitute evidence of performance of the labor and incorporation of the materials or delivery and proper storage of the materials at the site and acceptance thereof in accordance with the terms and conditions of the Contract; and

(c) Inspection and approval by a representative of Bank of performance of the labor and incorporation of the materials or delivery and proper storage of the materials at the site, the inspection of Bank to be performed within three (3) days after receipt of the fully executed and fully documented voucher, it being understood that the inspection and approval when made and given shall be solely on behalf of Bank and not as agent for any other person or entity.

5. In the event of any dispute between Prime Contractor and any of the parties whose signatures are required under Paragraph 4(b) to document vouchers, involving Prime Contractor's right to receive payment, Bank will hold funds (within the limits of this Agreement) sufficient to pay the disputed item, for disbursement to the party entitled thereto as finally determined, beyond appeal, in accordance with the Contract or as otherwise provided by law.

6.

(a) Notwithstanding anything contained herein to the contrary, and subject to the provisions of subparagraph (b) of this Paragraph 6, Bank shall be liable to Prime Contractor under this Guarantee only for work done or materials supplied and incorporated into the structure or properly stored at the site by Prime Contractor on behalf of Owner until such time as the Bank shall have given written notice to Prime Contractor that Owner is in default under the construction loan agreement, note and mortgage and any amendments and modifications thereof.

(b) However, if, upon Owner's failure to perform its obligations under the construction loan agreement, note and mortgage and any amendments and modifications thereof, Bank requests Prime Contractor, pursuant to the terms of the letter of even date herewith from Prime Contractor to Bank (a copy of which is attached hereto as Exhibit "B") to perform on behalf of Bank Prime Contractor's obligations under the Contract, this Guarantee will continue in full force and effect, subject to the terms and conditions hereof, for (i) all work theretofore performed or materials theretofore supplied and incorporated into the structure or properly stored at the site by Prime Contractor on behalf of Owner pursuant to the Contract and Change Orders approved by Bank and (ii) all work to be performed or materials to be supplied and incorporated into the structure or properly stored at the site by Prime Contractor on behalf of Bank.

IN WITNESS WHEREOF, Bank has caused these presents to be signed by its duly authorized officers under its corporate seal the day and year first above written.

                    THE MERCANTILE BANK

                    By: _____
                              President

                Attest: _____
                              Secretary
               (CORPORATE SEAL)

Accepted and Agreed to:

HARRISON CONCRETE CORP.

By: _____
      President

Attest: _____
         Secretary

(CORPORATE SEAL)

    SHELL CORP., INC., named as owner in the Contract between the undersigned and Harrison Concrete Corp. referred to above, hereby accepts notice of the execution of the foregoing Guarantee; hereby approves the Guarantee; authorizes THE MERCANTILE BANK (the "Bank") to charge against the construction loan account at any time all or any part of the sums guaranteed pursuant to this Contract or any approved Change Orders; and agrees to indemnify Bank, as guarantor therein, against any loss, liability, cost or expense incurred by Bank thereunder by reason of any default under the Contract on the part of the undersigned as Owner.

                    SHELL CORP., INC.

                  By: _____
                            President

              Attest: _____
                          Secretary
             (CORPORATE SEAL)
             (ATTACH EXHIBIT "A" AND EXHIBIT "B")

TEN   Mechanics' Liens

Mechanics' Lien of Private Projects
§10.01 *Introduction*
§10.02 *Form—Contents of Claim*

Waivers
§10.03 *Waiver of Lien Clauses in Construction Agreements*
§10.04 *Interim Waiver Affidavits—Author's Comments*
§10.05 *Standard Form Interim Waiver*
§10.06 *Suggested Form Interim Waiver*
§10.07 *Final Waiver Affidavit (Release of Liens)—Author's Comments*
§10.08 *Form—Suggested Final Waiver Affidavit*
§10.09 *Trust Receipt for Waiver—Author's Comments*
§10.10 *Form—Trust Receipt for Waiver*

Mechanics' Lien on Public Projects
§10.11 *Introduction*
§10.12 *Form—Notice of Municipal Mechanics' Lien*
§10.13 *Author's Comments*

A. MECHANICS' LIEN OF PRIVATE PROJECTS

§10.01   1. Introduction   If a contractor, subcontractor or material supplier has a perfected mechanics's lien, that party has perhaps the most effective tool to secure payment. In most states a perfected mechanic's lien can be used to force a foreclosure and sale of the owner's land. Further, an owner would find it most difficult to sell or borrow against the property without first discharging the lien. In some states, the lien is limited to the amount due the general contractor; in others, the owner may limit liability in the contract price; in still others, the lien liability is unlimited.

All state legislatures have created this special statutory remedy for the benefit of contractors, and certain subcontractors and material suppliers. The remedy is based on the belief that those who enhance the value of real estate by means of their labor are entitled to charges against the owners' equity in the property to secure their payment. The mechanic's lien thus prevents unjust enrichment.

The statutes that create these lien rights are technical and overly complex. No two lien statutes are exactly alike, and most of the statutes are undergoing revision at the urging of subcontractors and material suppliers, who are discovering their bargaining power with owners and with financial institutions which own the mortgages. It is impossible to summarize the fifty lien statutes. Contractors and suppliers should have local, professional advice to make sure that they do not waive lien rights and to help them to perfect liens.[1]

In order for a lienor to gain priority over other creditors, strict compliance with the provisions of the statute covering form and content of the claim is necessary. The requirements are different in each state, as are the requirements for notice and filing of the lien. Statutes differ as to the duration and priority of the claim, and also as to foreclosure procedures. Mechanic's lien procedures are very technical; failure to follow strictly the intricate legal requirements usually will defeat the right to perfect a lien.

§10.02   2. Contents of Claim   It is suggested that in every state the mechanic's lien claim should contain and state, at a minimum, the following:

(a)
  (1) The name and address of the party claimant and whether he is filing as a contractor, subcontractor or material supplier;
  (2) the name and address of the owner or reputed owner;
  (3) the date of completion of the claimant's work.
(b) If filed by a subcontractor or material supplier, the name of the person with whom he contracted and the date on which any required preliminary notice was given and the date on which formal notice of intention to file the claim was given (if notice is necessary).
(c) If filed by a contractor under a contract or contracts for an agreed sum, an identification of the contract and a general statement of the kind and character of the labor and materials furnished.
(d) In all other cases other than set forth in clause (c) immediately above, a detailed statement of the kind and character of the labor and materials furnished or both, and the prices charged for each thereof, and if required by state law, the time when each such term of labor or material was furnished.
(e) The amount of sum claimed to be due.
(f) A description reasonably necessary to identify the improvement and the property claimed to be subject to the lien.

B. WAIVERS

§10.03   1. Waivers of Lien Clauses in Construction Agreements   Contractors and subcontractors should weigh carefully the wisdom of executing printed form construction agreements which contain provisions waiving lien rights, or provisions requiring removal, at their own expense, of liens placed against the property by lower-

---

1   See, R. Ager, "Mechanics Liens on Private Projects" in *McGraw-Hill Construction Business Handbook*

tier suppliers of labor or material.[2] Moreover, the state statutes should be consulted to ascertain whether the General Contractor has the power to waive lien rights on behalf of those subordinate.[3]

2. Interim Waiver Affidavits

§10.04   **a. Author's Comments**   Contractors, subcontractors and material suppliers should neither waive their lien rights until they have been paid; nor should they waive rights to file liens for work to be performed or material to be supplied in the future. If requested to execute an interim waiver or release of lien in order to receive partial payment, the waiver or release should be modified by contingent language. The Associated General Contractors of America, as well as the American Subcontractors Association, suggest the following as a fair standard interim waiver:

---

2   Massachusetts (MA Ann Laws, Ch 254 §32 (Supp 1975) and New York (NY Consol Laws Ann, Book 32 §34 (McKinney's Supp 1975); NY Acts 1975 (Bill No 5947-A)) invalidated waivers of lien as being against public policy

3   For example, in Pennsylvania the contractor can enter into an agreement with the owner waiving the right of the contractor and of all persons under the contractor to file or to maintain a mechanic's lien claim. Such an agreement is binding upon a subcontractor, provided the subcontractor has had actual notice of this waiver before furnishing any labor or material, or a signed copy of the waiver has been filed in the office of the prothonotary of the Court of Common Pleas of the county where the structure is situated prior to the commencement of the work upon the ground, or within ten days after the execution of the principal contract, or in less than ten days, prior to the contract with the claimant. This waiver of lien is indexed by the prothonotary. (The owner may, under certain circumstances, and by an appropriate agreement, restore this right to lien by waiving the waiver either entirely or in part)

b. Forms

---
§10.05   i. FORM   Standard Interim Waiver

In consideration of the payments received and upon receipt of the amount of this request, the undersigned does hereby waive, release and relinquish all claim or right of lien which the undersigned may now have upon the premises above described except for claims or right of lien for contract and/or change order work performed to extent that payment if being retained or will subsequently become due.

The following form, likely to be acceptable to general contractors, owners and architects, is suggested to suppliers of labor and material:

---
§10.06   ii. FORM   Suggested Interim Waiver

NOW, THEREFORE, for and in consideration of the payment by General Construction Company to the undersigned of the sum of $ _____, (_____ Dollars) the receipt of which is hereby acknowledged, the undersigned does hereby waive and release, only however to the extent of said payment, any and all liens, claims or rights of lien on or against said construction or improvement, for and on account of labor or material or both furnished by the undersigned to the General Construction Company only and used or intended for use in said construction or improvement.

WITNESS the due execution hereof this _____ day of _____, 19 _____.

AMERICAN STEEL SUPPLY COMPANY

By: _____

(The above document should be signed only after monies have been paid.)

3. Final Waiver Affidavit (Release of Liens)

§10.07**a. Author's Comments**   Signing a release of liens or final waiver before final payment has been made may bar the lien rights of a contractor, subcontractor or material supplier. The affidavit should be a contingent affidavit so that it is not effective until final payment actually is received. To do this, the words "upon receipt of the sum of X dollars" should be inserted in the tendered document. Should the monies not be received, the waiver acknowledgment of receipt will not be effective.

§10.08   b. FORM   Suggested Final Waiver Affidavit

WHEREAS General Construction Company is now indebted to the undersigned in the amount of $ _____ for and on account of labor and/or material furnished by the undersigned for use in the above referred to construction project; and

WHEREAS General Construction Company has requested the undersigned to furnish to it this Release prior to payment by General Construction Company to the undersigned of said sum of $ _____.

NOW, THEREFORE, for and in consideration of the payment by General Construction Company to the undersigned of the sum of $1.00, the receipt of which is hereby acknowledged, the undersigned does hereby waive and release any and all liens, claims or rights of lien on or against said construction or improvement for and on account of labor or material or both furnished up to this date by the undersigned to the General Construction Company and used or intended for use in said construction or improvement.

Anything herein contained to the contrary notwithstanding, it is understood that this Release shall take effect and shall be enforceable only upon and after receipt by the undersigned of payment to it of said outstanding indebtedness of General Construction Company to the undersigned in the amount of $ _____, and this Release is given by the undersigned and is accepted by General Construction Company subject to such understanding.

WITNESS the due execution hereof this _____ day of _____, 19_____.

AMERICAN STEEL SUPPLY COMPANY

BY _____

Dated:

4. Trust Receipt for Waiver

§10.09   **a. Introduction**   The trust receipt is an effective tool to assure payment from contractors or subcontractors tendering lien waivers, when they are unable to pay until they receive their own payments for the project. A trust receipt is a document in which the contractor or subcontractor agrees to hold in trust monies received until disbursement to the beneficiary of the trust receipt. A violation of this trust normally will subject the violator to state criminal prosecution.

§10.10 B. FORM Trust Receipt for Waiver

SOLARAIR SHEET METAL, INC.
411 Jones Street
Chicago, Illinois 60185

Receipt for Waiver

Received in trust from Supplier, Inc.

This 20th of June, 1977 the following waiver of lien,

        Amount $3,100.00

        For temperature controls

        Job address Fox Hunt, Madison, Ill.

Which waivers of lien are acknowledged by the undersigned to be the sole property of Supplier, Inc. The undersigned agrees to hold said above described waivers for the sole benefit and subject to the order of said Supplier, Inc.

The undersigned agrees that it has received these waivers for the sole purpose of presenting waivers for collection and to immediately pay to Suppliers, Inc. the sum of $ Three thousand, one hundred dollars and no cents and the undersigned acknowledges that it is the bailee of said waivers and the property or sums of money for which said waivers may be exchanged for said described purposes and for the sole benefit and account of said Supplier, Inc., the said owner of said waiver of lien.

        SOLARAIR SHEET METAL, INC.

        By - Donald E. Smith
        President

Subscribed and sworn to before me this 20th day of June, 1977.

        Notary Public

C. MECHANIC'S LIEN ON PUBLIC PROJECTS

§10.11   1. Introduction   This statutory remedy, sometimes referred to as the municipal mechanics' lien, is available in nineteen states.[4] It is usually intended to create lien rights in the labor or material supplier against funds due or to become due the contractor from the public agency. Municipal mechanics' lien rights are rights given in addition to state statutory surety bond rights. The technical notice, time and form requirements differ under each state statute.[5] A form follows.

---

[4] California, Colorado, Illinois, Indiana, Iowa, Kentucky, Louisiana, Maine (but only to public buildings), Massachusetts, New Hampshire, New Jersey, New York, Ohio, South Dakota, Texas (on certain contracts) Washington (state), Wisconsin. An early Kansas decision indicates that there is some such right (*Fidelity & Deposit Co v Stafford* 165 P 837). Similarly, Utah (*Mellon v Vondor-Horst Bros* 140 P 130)

[5] See, L. Auerbacher Jr., "Mechanics Liens on Public Projects" in *McGraw-Hill Construction Business Handbook*

§10.12 2. FORM **Notice of Municipal Mechanics' Lien**

To: Board of Education
Seaview Township
Ocean County, NJ

Notice is hereby given by American Sheet Metal Co., Inc., a municipal mechanic's lien claimant of 410 East Fredericksburg Avenue, in the City of Ventnor, County of Atlantic, New Jersey, that it has performed labor and has furnished materials which have actually been performed and used in the execution and completion of a certain contract for the erection of a public school house made by and between the Board of Education of Seaview County, New Jersey and Inferior Contractors, Inc., a building contractor, on the 20th day of August, 1977, and duly filed with the Clerk of the County of Ocean.

1. The aforesaid public school is located at Ocean Avenue and Bay Street, Oceanville, New Jersey.

2. The aforesaid labor and materials have been performed for and furnished to Inferior Contractors, Inc. by the claimant in pursuance of a Subcontract made by and between the claimant and Inferior Contractors, Inc. and dated September 20, 1977.

3. The labor and material furnished by American Sheet Metal Co., Inc. to Inferior Contractors, Inc. is described in the aforementioned Subcontract, a copy of which is attached hereto as Exhibit A.

4. The amount of the claimant's demand after the deduction of all just credits and offsets, is the sum of $7,500.00, which is the amount claimed as justly due and owing to the claimant by Inferior Contractors, Inc.

5. A lien is hereby claimed for the sum of $7,500.00, being the full value of the labor and materials furnished by the claimant, on the monies in the control and possession of the Board of Education of Ocean County, New Jersey, which are due or to become due on the aforesaid contract between the Board of Education of Ocean County and Inferior Contractors, Inc.

Dated: December 24, 1977

AMERICAN SHEET METAL CO., INC.

Affidavit
Exhibit

By _____

§10.13   3. Author's Comments   The municipal mechanics' lien remedy is particularly valuable in a state like New Jersey where suit cannot be commenced under the statutory surety bond until eighty days after the project has been accepted.

ELEVEN   Bonds

Requirement
§11.01 *Payment Bonds*
§11.02 *Obtaining Copies of Bonds and Contracts*
§11.03 *Form—Affidavit to Comptroller General to Obtain a Copy of the Bonded Federal Contract and a Copy of the Payment Bond*

Notice
§11.04 *Introduction*
§11.05 *Timeliness of Notice*
§11.06 *Contents of Notice*
§11.07 *Form—Notice and Demand for Payment to Contractor and Surety*

Time to Institute Suit
§11.08 *Miller Act Suit—Author's Comments*
§11.09 *Form—Miller Act Suit*
§11.10 *Freeze Agreement—Author's Comments*
§11.11 *Form—Freeze Agreement*

§11.01   A. PAYMENT BONDS

Recognizing an equitable obligation to secure payment to labor and material suppliers on public projects, the federal government and every state require payment bonds.[1] Each state differs as to what is included as labor and material covered by the bond, to whom payment coverage is extended, and the notice and time for suit requirements.[2] Many private owners also require that prime contractors furnish payment bonds to insure payment of subcontractors and material suppliers.[3]

---

1 See, K. Lewis and R. Cushman, "Surety Bonds" and P. Wolf, "Claims against Bonding Companies" in *McGraw-Hill Construction Business Handbook*
2 For a summary of both federal and state requirements, see, "Credit Manual of Commercial Laws" in *Bonds on Public Works,* published yearly by the National Association of Credit Management
3 The most commonly used bond form on private projects is AIA Form 311. This form of bond requires

§11.02   B. OBTAINING COPIES OF BONDS

Every condition of the bond must be complied with by the supplier who has not been paid, for, contrary to belief, bonds are not insurance policies. They are contracts which state that if the supplier complies with the strict letter of the bond, the Surety will stand by its obligations. The best time to become aware of the conditions of the bond is before the project is commenced. In practice, it is easier to obtain copies of the bond from the owner or the contractor at that time. Sometimes, when the notice or time for filing suit limitations period is expiring rapidly, bonds can't be located. Contacting the architect, who usually has the most complete set of contract documents, is often the easiest way to obtain a copy of the bond. The architect usually is persuaded by the argument that the bond is a matter of public record, and consequently will make a copy available.

If a federal contract is involved, a bond is required by the Miller Act.[4] The Comptroller General of the United States is required to furnish a certified copy of the bond and the contract upon receipt of an affidavit from an unpaid supplier of labor or material, such as the following:

---

notice within 90 days by labor and material suppliers who did not have a direct contract with the principal contractor. This notice must be served upon any two of the following: the general contractors, the owner, the surety

4   The Miller Act (40 USC §§270a–270f)

§11.03 C. FORM   Affidavit to the Comptroller General to Obtain a Copy of the Bonded Federal Contract and a Copy of the Payment Bond

STATE OF
COUNTY OF

John Lawyer, being duly sworn according to law, deposes and says that he is an attorney for Atlas Steel Corporation, a corporation (hereinafter called "claimant"), and that he is authorized to make this application and affidavit on its behalf:

1. Heretofore, the United States of America, acting by and through the General Services Administration, Public Building Services, entered into an agreement dated Oct. 15, 1974, being Contract No. GS-02B, with Heavy Construction Corporation, a corporation (hereinafter called "contractor"), of Jersey City, New Jersey for the construction of (insert here contract designation and location of project), in accordance with drawings and contract documents prepared by S. Walter Jones & Associates of Newark, New Jersey, architects.

2. Pursuant to the provisions of said contract and the Act of Congress in such case made and provided, said Heavy Construction Corporation, as principal, and United Surety Co. of Philadelphia, Pennsylvania, as surety (hereinafter called "surety"), furnished to The United States of America their certain joint and several payment bond dated Oct. 15, 1974 in the penal sum of $5,460,000.00, conditioned for the payment to all persons supplying labor and material in the prosecution of the public work described herein.

3. On Dec. 15, 1974 claimant entered into a written agreement with contractor to furnish and to provide steel beams required in the construction and completion of the said project.

4. Thereafter, claimant furnished all of the material required of it by the aforesaid agreement, and was paid from time to time by contractor the aggregate sum of $27,000.00, leaving due, owing and payable a balance of $18,400.22, with interest; which balance contractor, without legal justification or excuse, has failed and neglected to pay to claimant.

5. The material upon which the aforesaid indebtedness is based was furnished by claimants and supplied upon the faith and credit of the payment bond referred to in Paragraph 2 hereof.

6. Wherefore, claimant applies to the Comptroller General of the United States for a certified copy of the contract and the payment bond referred to in Paragraphs 1 and 2 hereof, for the purpose of maintaining legal proceedings for the recovery of the aforesaid indebtedness against contractor and/or surety on the said payment bond.

7. Claimant hereby offers to pay for such certified copy such fee as the Comptroller General has fixed or may fix to cover the cost of supplying a copy thereof.

Sworn and Subscribed
before me this_____
day of_____, 197___.

Atlas Steel Corporation

By _____
   John Lawyer, Esq.
   Attorney

_____
   Notary Public
My Commission Expires

(This form should be mailed to the Comptroller General in Washington, D.C.)

D. NOTICE

§11.04 **1. Introduction** One of the most important tasks the unpaid supplier of labor or material has in protecting rights under the payment bond is giving notice in accordance with the law. Under the Miller Act (and the vast number of state laws which are, in effect, "little Miller Act" statutes), where the claimant has a direct contractual relationship with the prime contractor, the claimant is not required by law to give any notice. If the claimant has not been paid within 90 days of the date on which labor or delivered materials last were supplied, the claimant may institute suit on the bond. It makes sense to give notice of the delinquency to the prime contractor's surety as well as to the contractor. Where the claimant has a direct contractual relationship with a subcontractor, but no contractual relationship with the contractor, the statute requires written notice to the prime contractor of the delinquency and demand for payment. While not technically required, it is recommended that a carbon copy of this notice be sent to the payment bond surety.

§11.05 **2. Timeliness of Notice** When notice is required by law, it must be sent to the prime contractor within 90 days of the date on which the claimant last furnished materials or labor for which payment is claimed. This date is most obvious in a single delivery case. For example, assume that on March 1, 1977 the claimant delivered carpet to a subcontractor under a single purchase order. If the claimant does not give notice to the prime contractor by May 30, 1977, the payment bond cannot be recovered. If deliveries of carpet had been made on March 1, 1977 and April 1, 1977, under a single purchase order, notice would have to be given to the prime contractor by July 1, 1977, 90 days from the date of the last delivery.

Assume, however, that the April 1, 1977 delivery had been made pursuant to a separate purchase order. Must notice be given on May 30, 1977 for the delivery of March 1 and again on July 1, 1977? This will depend upon whether the purchase orders are of such independent significance as to be considered two separate contracts. Counsel should be consulted, before May 30, 1977, to decide this question.

Now assume that after a March 1, 1977 initial delivery, the claimant returns to the site on April 1, 1977 to deliver two yards of carpet that has been mistakenly omitted from the March 1 delivery. Does notice have to be given by May 30, 1977 or July 1, 1977? Where only corrective work is performed at the subsequent date, the deadline runs from the time of initial delivery. If notice was not given by May 30, 1977 the claimant would lose the rights under the payment bond.

Finally, assume that deliveries are made on March 1, 1977 and April 1, 1977 but no payment is received. As a result, the next delivery, on May 1, 1977 is made C.O.D. In order to recover for the March and April deliveries, when must the claimant give notice? Notice must be given by July 1, 1977, 90 days from the April 1 delivery. Since the May 1 delivery was C.O.D., the last date on which the claimant furnished materials for which payment is claimed is April 1, 1977.

In each of these cases, care should be taken to structure files so that the appropriate notice is mailed not 90 but 75 days after the deadline began to run, so that notice reaches the prime contractor by the 90-day deadline.

§11.06 **3. Contents of Notice** The written notice required by the law must state, with substantial accuracy, the amount claimed and the subcontractor to whom the labor or materials were furnished. It either should be sent to the prime contractor with a carbon copy to the surety or jointly (see forms following) to the contractor's and surety's regularly maintained offices, via certified mail, return receipt requested.

§11.07 4. FORM **Notice and Demand for Payment to Contractor and Surety**

Date

Imperial Construction Company
401 W. 47th Street
Dallas, Texas

American Fidelity and Surety Company
1010 St. Paul Street
Baltimore, Maryland

Gentlemen:

By writing dated January 10, 1976, The United States of America, acting by and through the General Services Administration entered into an agreement (Contract No. 107-D 462) with Imperial Construction Company for the construction of *(description of project and location)*. Imperial Construction Company, as principal, and American Fidelity and Surety Company, as surety, furnished to The United States of America a joint and several payment bond dated January 10, 1976, in the penal sum of $410,777.26, conditioned upon the payment to all persons supplying labor and material in the prosecution of the project described herein.

On Feb. 20, 1976 Unpaid Material Supply Company entered into a written agreement with Imperial Construction Company to furnish and to provide *(description of material, equipment, etc. furnished)* required in the construction and completion of the project described above. A true and correct copy of this agreement is attached hereto.

Thereafter, Unpaid Material Supply Company supplied all of the material required by its agreement, whereupon there became due, owing and payable to Unpaid Material Supply Company, the sum of $14,110.00, made up as is more particularly set forth in the summary attached. Imperial Construction Company has paid Unpaid Material Supply Company the aggregate sum of $10,000.00 leaving due, owing and payable a balance of $4,110.00, with lawful interest.

Imperial Construction Company, without legal justification or excuse, has failed, neglected and refused to make payment to Unpaid Material Supply Company of this indebtedness in the sum of $4,110.00, with interest, or any part thereof.

Unpaid Material Supply Company states that the materials were supplied to, for, toward, in and about the construction of the project referred to herein upon the faith and credit of the bond furnished by American Fidelity and Supply Company inuring to the use of laborers and materialmen, including Unpaid Material Supply Company.

Demand is hereby made upon you and each of you, the contractor and surety for the payment of this indebtedness in the amount of $4,110.00, with lawful interest. You and each of you are hereby further notified that, unless the amount due and owing is forthwith paid, suit will be instituted upon the bond.

Unpaid Material Supply Company

By: _____
Title

E. TIME TO INSTITUTE SUIT

1. Miller Act Suit

§11.08**a. Author's Comments** If the unpaid supplier of labor or material has given timely notice of the delinquency in payment, suit on the Miller Act bond may be commenced after the 90-day deadline expires. Suit must be instituted within one year of the date on which labor or material was last furnished, or bond rights will be lost.

§11.09   b. FORM   **Miller Act Suit**

IN THE UNITED STATES DISTRICT COURT
FOR THE EASTERN DISTRICT OF PENNSYLVANIA

UNITED STATES OF AMERICA
For the Use and Benefit of
American Insulation Company, Inc.
15th & Wyoming Avenue
Philadelphia, Pennsylvania
    Plaintiff

VS.

GENERAL CONSTRUCTION COMPANY, INC.　　　　CIVIL ACTION
1520 Mt. Carmel Avenue　　　　　　　　　　　　No. 75–635
South Hills, Pennsylvania

AND

ARIZONA CASUALTY COMPANY
2020 Philadelphia Savings Fund Building
Philadelphia, Pennsylvania
    Defendants

COMPLAINT

1. The Use Plaintiff, American Insulation, is a Pennsylvania corporation with its principal place of business at 15th and Wyoming Avenue, Philadelphia, Pennsylvania at all times relevant hereto, American Insulation Company, Inc. was engaged in the business of supplying and/or installing insulation.

2. Defendant, General Construction Company Inc., (hereinafter called "General") is a corporation with its principal place of business at 1520 Mt. Carmel Avenue, South Hills, Pennsylvania at all times relevant hereto, General was engaged in the business of general construction contracting.

3. Defendant, Arizona Casualty Company, (hereinafter called "Arizona") is an Arizona corporation, with business offices at 2020 Philadelphia Savings Fund Building, Philadelphia, Pennsylvania. At all times relevant hereto, Arizona was engaged in the business of corporate paid suretyship.

4. Jurisdiction of this case is conferred by Sections 270 a and b of Title 40 of the United States Code Annotated, commonly known as "The Miller Act."

5. On or about May 30, 1976, the United States of America, acting by the Contracting Officer, Robert Morris, General, U.S. Army, Corps of Engineers, District Engineer, and Defendant, General, entered into a written contract, No. DA 2143–76, whereby the said Defendant, General, agreed to furnish all the labor and materials and perform all the work required for the construction of the U.S. Army Reserve Center, Frankford Arsenal, Philadelphia, Pennsylvania, for the consideration of the sum of $1,902,500.00. A true and correct copy of said Contract is attached hereto, made a part hereof and marked Exhibit "A".

6. Pursuant to the provisions of The Miller Act, Defendant, General, as principal and Defendant, Arizona, as surety, bound themselves jointly and severally in the sum of $951,-250.00 to assure the payment by said principal of the claims of all persons supplying labor and materials in the prosecution of the work provided in said Contract, and any and all modifications thereof. A true and correct copy of said Payment Bond (No. 5642096) is attached hereto, made a part hereof and marked Exhibit "B".

7. The said Bond, Exhibit "B" hereof, was duly accepted by the United States of America, and upon such acceptance, the contract for the construction of said U.S. Army Reserve Center referred to in paragraph 5 hereof was awarded to Defendant, General.

8. Thereafter, Defendant, General, entered into a direct contractual relationship with Perry, Inc., (hereinafter called "Perry") whereby Perry was to perform certain mechanical contracting work in and about the prosecution of the work required of Defendant, General, under its aforesaid Contract with the United States, Exhibit "A" hereof. A true and correct copy of said contract between Defendant, General and Perry is not attached hereto, since it is in the exclusive custody and control of adverse parties.

9. On or about July 15, 1976, said Perry issued to Use Plaintiff its work order in the amount of $57,500.00, which was accepted by Use Plaintiff in July 20, 1976, whereby Use Plaintiff agreed to furnish Perry with the labor and materials to perform certain insulation work required of Perry under its subcontract with Defendant, General, and required of Defendant, General, under its Contract with the United States, Exhibit "A" hereof. A true a correct copy of such work order is attached hereto, made a part hereof and marked Exhibit "C".

10. The Use Plaintiff has furnished all of the labor and materials required of it under its subcontract with Perry for the project, whereupon Use Plaintiff became entitled to the payment from Perry of the sum of $57,500.00, as aforesaid.

11. After giving credit for payments on account thereof aggregating $27,500.00, there is a balance of $30,000.00 presently due and owing to Use Plaintiff in connection with the above project.

12. Said Perry has failed and neglected to pay to Use Plaintiff said sum of $30,000.00 due and owing to Use Plaintiff under said subcontract, whereupon Use Plaintiff, on October 20, 1976, within ninety (90) days from the last day upon which Use Plaintiff furnished labor and materials on the above project under said subcontract, duly notified Defendant, General, and Defendant, Arizona, that the said Perry had failed to pay said sum to Use Plaintiff, as aforesaid and demanded payment of the aforesaid sum. A true and correct copy of said notice and demand for payment is attached hereto, made a part hereof and marked Exhibit "D".

13. The Use Plaintiff has made timely demand upon Defendant, General and Defendant, Arizona, for the payment of the aforesaid sum of $30,000.00, but the Defendants have refused and continue to refuse to pay same or any part thereof.

14. By reason of the failure of Perry, Defendant General and/or Defendant Arizona, to pay Use Plaintiff said sum of $30,000.00 justly due and owing to it as aforesaid, and in accordance with the provisions of the Payment Bond heretofore identified as Exhibit "B" hereof and The Miller Act, Defendant, General as principal, and Defendant, Arizona, as surety, have become indebted, jointly and severally, to the Use Plaintiff in the sum of $30,000.00.

15. More than ninety (90) days, but less than one year, has expired from the last date upon which the Use Plaintiff furnished labor and materials on the above project, as aforesaid.

16. The Use Plaintiff has conformed and complied with all of the conditions required of it under the aforesaid Payment Bond, Exhibit "B" hereof, and The Miller Act.

17. All of the foregoing labor and materials furnished by Use Plaintiff for the above project were furnished within the Eastern District of the Commonwealth of Pennsylvania.

WHEREFORE, The United States of America, for the use and benefit of American Insulation Company, Inc. demands judgment against Defendant, General Construction Company, Inc., and Defendant, Arizona Casualty Company, in the sum of $30,000.00 with interest and costs of suit.

KETCHUM AND SKINNER, ESQS.

By: _____

Exhibits as above

2. Freeze Agreement

§11.10   **a. Author's Comments**   Legal action is expensive. If authorized representatives of the surety are willing to bind their company to extend the time for suit while they investigate the merits of the unpaid supplier's claim, it is advantageous to all parties to enter into a freeze agreement.

§11.11 b. FORM   **Freeze Agreement**

Dated: Jan. 10, 1978

The parties to this Agreement are Keystone Wire Corporation (hereinafter referred to as "Keystone"), Slow Pay Construction Co. (hereinafter referred to as "Slow Pay") and Surety Company of Wisconsin (hereinafter referred to as "Surety").

It is hereby agreed by and between the above parties as follows:

1. In the event that a suit is commenced or claim is asserted by any of the parties hereto which claim or suit relates to or arises out of General State Authority Project No. GSA 428–1977 (Penn State Veterinary School, Spring City, Pennsylvania), each party hereto agrees that it will not allege or assert that said suit or claim is untimely filed or that said suit or claim is barred by any contractual or statutory limitation of action or statute of limitations, which assertain could not have been raised as of Jan. 10, 1978.

2. Except for the foregoing paragraph 1 hereabove, Keystone, Slow Pay and Surety specifically reserve and do not waive by this Agreement each and every right which each has or may have against either of the other two parties of this Agreement.

SURETY COMPANY OF WISCONSIN

By: _____

SLOW PAY CONSTRUCTION CO.

By: _____

KEYSTONE WIRE CORPORATION

By: _____

TWELVE Arbitration

Advantages
§12.01 *Advantage of Arbitration*

Considerations Prior to Commencement of Arbitration Proceedings
§12.02 *Existence of Arbitration Agreement Between Parties*
§12.03 *Enforcement of Arbitration Agreement by Courts*

Initiation of Proceedings Under Contract Arbitration Agreement
§12.04 *Standard American Arbitration Association (AAA) Construction Industry Arbitration Demand Form—Author's Comments*
§12.05 *Form—AAA Standard Arbitration Demand*
§12.06 *Combining Claim for Unpaid Contract Balance with Claim for Interference and Delay in Undetermined Amount—Author's Comments*
§12.07 *Form—Demand for Arbitration*

Initiation of Proceedings Under Submission
§12.08 *Author's Comments*
§12.09 *Form—AAA Submission*

Compelling Arbitration
§12.10 *Author's Comments*
§12.11 *Form—Petition to Compel Arbitration*

Judgment
§12.12 *Turning Award into Judgment—Form—Motion to Confirm Award of Arbitrators*

Waiver
§12.13 *Inadvertent Waiver of Arbitration Rights*

§12.01 A. ADVANTAGE OF ARBITRATION

Arbitration may be the last hope for the unpaid claimant, short of instituting litigation. Much has been written on the advantages and disadvantages of arbitration.[1] Generally, it is believed that arbitration is faster and less expensive than litigation, and that the procedures are more practical and flexible. A benefit sometimes overlooked is that the attorney who drew and/or approved the construction contract, and who is familiar with the client's business, usually can appear on the client's behalf in an arbitration proceeding, wherever held. (If the attorney is not a member of the bar of the state where the litigation is required to take place, the attorney could not appear for the client where the case litigated rather than arbitrated.)

Since approximately 25% of the business failures in the United States are construction companies, it is often more advantageous for a claimant to arbitrate rather than litigate, because the award in arbitration often comes more quickly than the judgment in litigation. The claimant is better off obtaining an award while the debtor is still solvent.

B. CONSIDERATIONS PRIOR TO COMMENCEMENT OF ARBITRATION PROCEEDINGS

§12.02 1. Existence of Arbitration Agreement Between Parties

There are two chief areas of concern for the construction claimant seeking to settle the dispute and obtain payment through arbitration procedures. The first is whether the other party to the dispute has agreed to arbitrate; the second is whether a court will enforce the arbitration agreement.

A party to a contract cannot be required to arbitrate unless the party has agreed by contract to submit to arbitration. Consequently, an examination of the agreement between the parties is crucial. The 1976 edition of AIA Form 201 is the owner-general contract used most frequently in the United States today; it calls for the resolution of disputes by means of arbitration, pursuant to the Construction Industry Rules of the American Arbitration Association. Clearly, if a dispute arises between the owner and the contractor, arbitration may be invoked.

The now-outdated 1970 edition of AIA Form 201 (Owner-General) contained the following language:

> All claims, disputes and other matters in question arising out of, or relating to, this Contract, or the breach thereof. . .

Courts have held that, although agreements between contractors and subcontractors do not specifically contain arbitration provisions, incorporation by reference clauses in the contractor-subcontractor agreement pick up the broad arbitration wording of the 1970 edition of AIA Form 201. Therefore, arbitration is required between the contrac-

---

1 See, G. Aksen, "Arbitration of Construction Disputes"; G Visconti, "Arbitration May Help You Collect Faster"; M Greenberg, "The Disadvantages of Arbitration" in *McGraw-Hill Construction Business Handbook* (1978)

tor and the subcontractor where there is an incorporation by reference clause in the subcontract and a broad arbitration clause in the agreement between the owner and the general.[2]

The arbitration language of the 1976 edition of AIA Form 201 is not as broad:

> All claims, disputes and other matters in question *between the Contractor and Owner* arising out of or relating to the Contract Documents or the breach thereof. . . .*

As a result, it is likely to be given a more limited interpretation by courts, and one who seeks to arbitrate will be less able to rely upon the incorporation by reference cases that were decided under the 1970 edition of AIA Form 201.

§12.03   2. Enforcement of Arbitration Agreement by Courts

Generally, the cases decided under early common law held that, by providing for arbitration in construction contracts, the parties ousted the courts of their jurisdiction, and that this was against public policy. Even today, some courts allow arbitration agreements to be revoked unilaterally at any time before an award, or they hold that only agreements to arbitrate existing controversies are valid.[3]

Over the years, contractors and subcontractors, material suppliers, architects and engineers (as well as busy judges) have taken a major role in suggesting to their legislators the advantages of arbitration to resolve disputes. Consequently, statutory law has gradually revised the early, common-law concepts. Today thirty-six states, the District of Columbia, and the U. S. government (the Federal Arbitration Act)[4] have enacted modern arbitration statutes to enforce provisions to arbitrate. These statutes provide a method by which a claimant can bring a recalcitrant party to the arbitration table. Under these statutes, agreements to arbitrate are liberally considered in favor of arbitration.[5]

C. INITIATION OF PROCEEDINGS UNDER CONTRACT ARBITRATION AGREEMENT

1. Demand for Arbitration

a. Standard American Arbitration Association (AAA) Construction Industry Arbitration Demand Form

§12.04   i. AUTHOR'S COMMENTS

Arbitration is commenced by one party's making a demand for arbitration under the

---

*AIA Document A201 Copyright © 1976 by The American Institute of Architects.

2   *J S H Constr Co v Richmond County Hosp Auth* 473 F2d 212 (1973); *W V Pangborne & Co Inc v Wark & Co* 64 PA D & C 109 (1974)
3   Askin, "Resolving Construction Contract Disputes Through Arbitration" 23 Arb J 141 (1968)
4   9 USC §2 (1970)
5   *Lundgren v Freeman* 307 F2d 104 (9th Cir 1962); *Metro Indus Painting Corp v Terminal Constr Co* 287 F2d 382, 384 (2d Cir 1961), cert den 368 US 817 (1961)

agreement. If the Construction Industry Arbitration Rules of the American Arbitration Association are applicable, the party upon whom a demand for arbitration is served has seven days to file an answer. If an answer is not filed within the stated time, the claim will be denied.

This demand under AAA rules should contain a statement setting forth the nature of the dispute, the amount involved, and the remedy sought.

Set forth below is the standard AAA Construction Industry Arbitration Demand Form, recommended for use in the simplest type of an arbitration situation (for example, an unpaid contract balance claim).

§12.05   ii. FORM   **AAA Standard Arbitration Demand**

Reprinted by permission of The American Arbitration Association

CONSTRUCTION INDUSTRY ARBITRATION RULES

DEMAND FOR ARBITRATION

Date:

TO: (Name) _____
                  (of party upon whom the Demand is made)

        (Address) _____

        (City and State) _____

Named claimant, a party to an arbitration agreement contained in a written contract, _____ dated _____, providing for arbitration, under the Construction Industry Arbitration Rules, hereby demands arbitration thereunder.

NATURE OF DISPUTE:

CLAIM OR RELIEF SOUGHT: (amount, if any)

HEARING LOCALE REQUESTED: _____
                                   (City and State)

You are hereby notified that copies of our Arbitration Agreement and of this Demand are being filed with the American Arbitration Association at its _____ Regional Office, with the request that it commence the administration of the arbitration. Under Section 7 of the Arbitration Rules, you may file an answering statement within seven days after notice from the Administrator.

Signed _____
(May be Signed by Attorney)

Name of Claimant _____

Address (to be used
in connection with
this case) _____

City and State _____

Telephone _____

Name of Attorney _____

Address _____

City & State _____

Telephone _____

To institute proceedings, please send three copies of this Demand and the arbitration agreement, with the filing fee, as provided in Section 47 of the Rules.

Note that a copy of the arbitration clause should be attached to this demand, so that the other party and the AAA know the basis for arbitration.

b. Combining Claim for Unpaid Contract Balance with Claim for Interference and Delay in Undetermined Amount

§12.06   i. AUTHOR'S COMMENTS

A well-prepared demand for arbitration can be a valuable tool in convincing the arbitrators of the merit of the claimant's position. Preparing a claim in a fashion similar to a legal complaint, with exhibits and/or schedules attached, is helpful in the organization and marshaling of the facts, as well as in the presentation of the evidence before the arbitrators. Such preparation will impress on them the genuineness and sincerity of the claimant's position better than simply filling in the blanks of the AAA standard form.

The following demand for arbitration contains two counts. The first count is the demand of a subcontractor against a general for an unpaid contract balance. The second count is the demand of the subcontractor against the general for denying proper access to the job site by failing to coordinate properly, for requiring extra work not contemplated by the agreement, and by delaying and otherwise interfering with the performance of the subcontractor.

§12.07   ii. FORM   **Demand for Arbitration**

January 2, 1975

TO: Eastern State Construction Company
      10 South 20th Street
      Philadelphia, PA

DEMAND FOR ARBITRATION

Claimant, Federal Steel Co., Inc., 123 S. Broad Street, Philadelphia, Pennsylvania, 19109, a party to the Arbitration Agreements contained in the written contracts described herein, which agreements provide for arbitration pursuant to the Construction Industry Rules of the American Arbitration Association, hereby demands arbitration as follows:

Count I

1. By writing attached hereto as Exhibit A and dated July 4, 1970 ("Subcontract"), claimant Federal Steel Co., Inc. ("Federal") and Respondent Eastern State Construction Company ("Eastern") entered into an agreement whereby Federal would perform the work itemized in Schedule A to said Subcontract plus all agreed-upon extras, that Eastern would pay to Federal the agreed-upon contract amounts in exchange for that performance. All terms of said Subcontract are incorporated herein by reference.

2. Federal performed and furnished in a good and workmanlike manner all of the labor and materials which it was required to furnish pursuant to the terms and conditions of said Subcontract and performed certain extra work incidental thereto, completing all such work on August 10, 1973.

3. Whereupon there became due, owing and payable to Federal by Eastern the sum of $25,000.00 together with lawful interest accruing from September 10, 1973.

4. From time to time, Federal has demanded payment of the aforesaid amount from Eastern, but Eastern, without legal justification nor excuse, has failed and refused to pay said amount or any part thereof.

5. Paragraph 23 of the foregoing Subcontract provides as follows:

Any controversy or claim arising out of or relating to this contract, or the breach thereof, shall be submitted to arbitration, upon the written notice by either party to the other. The arbitration shall be as follows: The rules of the American Arbitration Association shall control and any award rendered in the arbitration shall be binding and conclusive upon the parties and shall not be subject to appeals or retrying by any court. The arbitrators shall, among all their own rights, have the right to decree specific performance. Three arbitrators shall be appointed; Contractor shall designate an arbitrator, Subcontractor shall designate an arbitrator, and the two arbitrators so chosen shall designate a third. In the event that the arbitrators so designated cannot agree upon the selection of a third arbitrator within 10 days from their appointment and acceptance of their appointment, or if a party shall fail to designate an arbitrator, the arbitrator shall be appointed by the then current administrator of the American Arbitration Association and a decision shall be rendered within 3 weeks of the appointment of the three arbitrators. Judgment upon the award rendered by the arbitrators may be entered in any court having jurisdiction thereof. The costs of said arbitration shall be borne equally by the parties hereto.

WHEREFORE, Federal demands arbitration of its foregoing claim for unpaid contract balances in the amount of $25,000.00 plus lawful interest thereupon accruing from September 10, 1973, until date of payment, plus all reasonable costs and attorneys' fees incurred in connection with said arbitration.

Count II

6. Federal incorporates by reference herein the allegations contained in the foregoing Count I.

7. In the course of performing its work pursuant to the Subcontract of July 4, 1970, referred to in the foregoing Count I, Federal was impeded, hindered and delayed by the acts and omissions of Eastern and/or Eastern's agents in that Eastern failed to properly coordinate and supervise the work, failed to compel other subcontractors to perform their work in a timely and proper manner, delayed the commencement of Federal's work, required Federal to perform work out of sequence, required Federal to perform work in a time period not contemplated by the Subcontract, required Federal to perform work beyond the requirements of the Subcontract, failed to allow Federal to use normal and standard construction methods or technique in a timely access to the project site, failed to make timely payments to Federal as required by the Subcontract, interfered with Federal's performance of its work, deprived Federal of its method of performance, delayed Federal's performance, disrupted the normal procedure and sequence of performance as contemplated by the Subcontract and forced Federal to perform in a manner and at times which greatly increased the costs of said performance, all of which foregoing acts and omissions were in breach of Eastern's contractual obligations to Federal.

8. As a result of the foregoing breaches, Federal incurred additional expenses in connection with its work and was otherwise damaged and continues to be damaged in an amount yet to be determined. Federal has from time to time notified Eastern of said damages and expenses, but Eastern, without legal justification nor excuse has failed and refused to pay same.

WHEREFORE, pursuant to Paragraph 23 of the Subcontract referred to in the foregoing Count I, Federal demands arbitration of its foregoing claim for delay damages in an amount to be determined finally at the arbitration of said claim, plus all reasonable costs and attorneys' fees incurred in connection with said arbitration.

9. Federal reserves until itself the right to amend this Demand for Arbitration to set forth the precise amount of damages suffered as a result of the matters set forth herein.

Appointment of Arbitrator

Federal hereby appoints as its party-selected arbitrator the following person and demands that Eastern appoint its party-selected arbitrator in accordance with the arbitration agreement of the parties prior to the expiration of ten days from the date of receipt of this Demand and notify Federal of said appointment. Federal appoints as its arbitrator:

        James Pious
        Professional Engineer
        300 Main Street
        Lancaster, PA

        Robert Righteous
        President
        Federal Steel Co., Inc.

Exhibit A
  with Schedules

D. INITIATION OF PROCEEDINGS UNDER SUBMISSION

§12.08   1. Author's Comments   Parties to a dispute, who are not required to arbitrate under an existing agreement, may still agree to arbitrate under the Construction Industry Arbitration Rules by filing a voluntary submission to arbitration, signed by the parties, with the American Arbitration Association. Like the demand for arbitration, it should contain a statement of the matter in dispute, the amount of money involved, and the remedy sought.

§12.09   2. FORM   **AAA Submission**

Reprinted by permission of The American Arbitration Association

SUBMISSION TO ARBITRATION

Date:

The named Parties hereby submit the following dispute to arbitration under the CONSTRUCTION INDUSTRY ARBITRATION RULES of the American Arbitration Association:

Amount of money involved:

Number of Arbitrators desired: one   three

Place of Hearing:

We agree that we will abide by and perform any Award rendered hereunder and that a judgment may be entered upon the Award.

Name of Party _____

Address _____

Signed by _____

Name of Party _____

Address _____

Signed by _____

PLEASE FILE TWO COPIES
Consult counsel about valid execution

E. COMPELLING ARBITRATION

§12.10   1. Author's Comments   The procedural method used to compel a resisting party to arbitrate is a motion or petition to compel arbitration. The following example is a petition that is filed pursuant to both the Federal Arbitration Act and the Pennsylvania Arbitration Act. It is also an example of a petition filed in a situation where the arbitration provisions of the owner-general contract were incorporated by reference into the subcontractor's agreement with the general contractor.

§12.11 2. FORM Petition to Compel Arbitration

COMMONWEALTH OF PENNSYLVANIA
COUNTY OF PHILADELPHIA

Peerless Electrical Construction
Company, Inc.

      Plaintiff

v.

Hospital Construction Co., Inc.

      Defendant

PETITION TO COMPEL ARBITRATION

Petitioner, Peerless Electrical Construction Company, Inc. ("Peerless"), by its attorneys, hereby petitions the Court to compel Hospital Construction Co., Inc., ("Contractor") to proceed with the arbitration of all of the disputes set forth in Peerless' Demand for Arbitration filed on January 2, 1977 before the American Arbitration Association as Case No. 17-10-4275-77D upon the following facts:

1. Peerless Electrical Construction Company, Inc., is a New York corporation with an office located at 123 S. Broad Street, Philadelphia, Pennsylvania 19109.

2. Hospital Construction Co., Inc. is a Pennsylvania corporation with an office located at 20 South 10th Street, Philadelphia, Pennsylvania.

3. On or about July 5, 1970, Peerless entered into a written agreement with Contractor whereby Peerless agreed to complete the electrical work required in the construction of the Moore Building for the General Hospital at 15th and Market Streets in Philadelphia. A copy of the written agreement is attached hereto and labelled Exhibit A.

4. Article 1 of the January 5, 1970 Agreement provides *inter alia* that: "Drawings, specifications and general conditions are hereby made a part hereof [of the Agreement.]"

5. The General Conditions include *inter alia* Article 7.10 Arbitration, a copy of which is attached hereto and labelled Exhibit B.

6. Section 7.10.1 of the General Conditions provides for the resolution of all claims, disputes and other matters in question arising out of, or relating to the contract, with certain exceptions not pertinent here, by arbitration in accordance with the Construction Industry Arbitration Rules of the American Arbitration Association. Section 7.10.1 further provides that the agreement so to arbitrate shall be specifically enforceable under the prevailing arbitration law.

7. The written agreement between Peerless and Contractor is a contract evidencing a transaction involving interstate commerce within the scope of the Federal Arbitration Act, 9 U.S.C. §§2 and 4 in that substantial amounts of materials and supplies furnished to the Moore Building project for use by Peerless in the completion of the electrical work were manufactured outside of the Commonwealth of Pennsylvania. This petition is therefore being filed pursuant to, and Peerless' right to proceed to arbitration is governed by, federal law under section 2 of the United States Arbitration Act of 1925, 9 U.S.C. §2.

8. This petition is also being filed pursuant to section 3 of the Pennsylvania Arbitration Act, 5 P.S. §163.

9. By a writing dated August 9, 1975, a copy of which is attached hereto and labelled Exhibit C, Contractor was advised of Peerless' claims for damages.

10. By a writing dated June 10, 1976, a copy of which is attached hereto and labelled Exhibit D, Peerless formally advised Contractor of its intention to arbitrate damage claims against Contractor.

11. On January 2, 1977, Peerless filed with the American Arbitration Association the Demand for Arbitration, a copy of which is attached hereto and labelled Exhibit E. The Demand, has been designated as Case No. 17-10-4275-77D.

12. By filing the demand for arbitration, Peerless was acting pursuant to its contract rights with Contractor and in accordance with the Construction Industry Arbitration Rules of the American Arbitration Association.

WHEREFORE, Peerless Electrical Construction Company, Inc., prays this Court to Grant its Petition and ORDER that Hospital Construction Co., Inc. proceed with the arbitration of all of the disputes set forth in Peerless' Demand for Arbitration filed on January 2, 1977 before the American Arbitration Association as Case No. 17-10-4275-77D.

§12.12   F. FORM   **Turning Award Into Judgment—
Motion to Confirm Award
of Arbitrators**

In order for an arbitration award to have the same effect as any other judgment, the prevailing party must move the appropriate court to confirm the award as a judgment. The following is a suggested form of a motion to confirm the arbitrator's award.

Roadway Construction Company, Inc.
1000 Broad Street
Pittsburgh, PA 18014

v.

City of Springtown
1 Main Street
Springtown, PA 19018

MOTION TO CONFIRM AWARD
OF ARBITRATORS

1. This is a motion to confirm an award of arbitrators brought pursuant to the provisions of the Act of April 25, 1977, D.C. 381, Pa. Stat. Ann. tit. 5 §169.

2. Movant herein, Roadway Construction Company, Inc. (hereinafter "Roadway") is and was at all times relevant hereto, a corporation organized and existing under the laws of the Commonwealth of Pennsylvania, with its main office and principle place of business located at 1000 Broad Street, Pittsburgh, Pennsylvania.

3. Respondent, City of Springtown, (hereinafter "Springtown") is the owner of the Springtown Water Treatment Plan Project (hereinafter "Project") in Springtown, Pennsylvania, with offices located at 1 Main Street, Springtown, Pennsylvania.

4. By writing dated September 15, 1976, Roadway and Springtown entered into a contract (hereinafter "Contract") for the general construction by Roadway of the Project. A true and correct copy of said contract is attached hereto, marked as Exhibit "A", and made a part hereof. Said contract incorporated by reference certain "Contract Documents", which are bulky and contain numerous pages. Roadway has not attached said Contract Documents to this motion, but refers to same as if fully set forth herein, and respectfully requests leave to produce same at any hearing in this cause with the same force and effect as if said documents had been pleaded at length herein.

5. A provision was contained in said Contract Documents to settle by arbitration controversies between the parties arising out of the contract.

6. Thereafter, a controversy arose out of the Contract, between the parties, as to their respective rights and liabilities, all as is more fully set forth in the transcript of testimony of the proceedings hereinafter described.

7. On January 20, 1977, Roadway demanded arbitration against Springtown. A copy of the Demand for Arbitration is incorporated herein and attached as Exhibit "B".

8. The controversy was submitted for administration to the American Arbitration Association under the caption, CASE NUMBER: 19 40 0162 77 R.

9. The parties selected Joe Doe, Richard Roe and William Stone as Arbitrators to hear and decide said controversy.

10. Three hearings were held before said Arbitrators, under the Construction Industry Rules of the American Arbitration Association, in Philadelphia County, Pennsylvania between April 15, 1977 and July 16, 1977 during which the parties presented evidence and their respective positions pertaining to the controversy. A transcript of testimony of approximately 1500 pages in length was compiled at said hearings.

11. On September 1, 1977 a written award (hereinafter "Award") was issued by the Arbitrators in Philadelphia, in favor of Roadway. A copy of said Award is attached as Exhibit "C" and a part hereof.

12. Signed copies of the Award were delivered to each of the parties on or about September 2, 1977.

13. Said Award of Arbitrators provide as follows:
I, (WE), THE UNDERSIGNED ARBITRATOR(S), having been designated in accordance with the Arbitration Agreement entered into by the above-named Parties, and dated September 15, 1976 and having duly heard the proofs and allegations of the Parties, AWARD, as follows:

1. In favor of Roadway Construction Company, Inc. in accordance with Stipulation A-1 which was agreed to at the hearings, and Change Order #8 which incorporates Stipulation A-1, copies of Stipulation A-1 and Change Order #8 are attached. The City of Springtown shall pay to Roadway Construction Company, Inc. the sum of $227,250.00.

2. The administrative fees and expenses of the American Arbitration Association shall be borne equally by the parties and paid as directed by the Association.

3. The compensation of the Arbitrators shall be borne equally by the parties and paid as directed by the Association.

WHEREFORE, Roadway Construction Company, Inc. prays for an Order confirming said Award and directing the entry of judgment thereon in its favor and against the City of Springtown, together with the costs of this Motion, and such other and further relief as this Court may deem just and proper.

COMMONWEALTH OF PENNSYLVANIA:
                                      ss

COUNTY OF PHILADELPHIA   :

AFFIDAVIT

JOHN LAWYER, being duly sworn, deposes and says that he is the attorney for Roadway Construction Company, Inc., Movant herein, that he is familiar with the facts set forth in the foregoing Motion to Confirm Award of Arbitrators, and that the averments of fact set forth therein are true and correct to the best of his knowledge, information and belief.

_____

JOHN LAWYER

SWORN TO AND SUBSCRIBED

before me this   day
of   , 1977.

_____

Notary Public

§12.13 G. INADVERTENT WAIVER OF ARBITRATION RIGHTS

The law is clear that if a party to an arbitration agreement submits the claim to a court, that party waives any right to enforce the arbitration agreement.[6]

---

6 *Galion Iron Works & Mfg Co v J D Adams Mfg Co* 128 F2d 411 (7th Cir 1942); *Gutor Intl A G v Raymond Packer Co Inc* 493 F2d 938 (1st Cir 1974); *Devin Products Co v B Bornstein & Sons Inc* 359 A2d 923 (1976).
But, see also, *McElwee-Courbis Constr Co v Rife* 133 FSupp 790 (ED PA 1955)

Index

A

ACCEPTANCE OF WORK
   design-build contract §1.19
   management contract §1.12
ACCESS TO JOB SITE, arbitration
   demand for failure to allow §12.07
ACCOUNTING, joint venture agreement
   §§4.01, 7.12, 7.15
ACTIONS
   arbitration rights, inadvertent waiver of §12.13
   payment bond as basis for §§11.08, 11.09
   subcontractor, privity contract §§8.01, 8.02
ADDITIONAL COSTS
   design-build contract §1.19
   management contract §1.12
ADDITIONAL SERVICES
   design-build contract §1.17
   extra work. See EXTRA WORK
ADDRESS, mechanic's lien claim §10.02
ADVANCES, joint venture by subcontractors §7.08
AFFIDAVITS, subcontractor's application for payment §2.08
AGENTS, subcontract agreement §2.04
AGREEMENTS
   generally this index
ALLOWANCES
   contract for construction §1.05
   design-build contract §1.19
   management contract §1.12
AMBIGUITY
   See CONSTRUCTION OF CONTRACTS
AMENDMENTS
   changes in work. See CHANGES IN WORK
   guaranteed maximum price management contract §§1.09, 1.10

APPEALS, subcontractor, privity contract §§8.01, 8.02
APPLICATIONS FOR PAYMENT
   construction contract §1.05
   management contract §1.12
   subcontractors §§2.08, 2.09, 5.11, 5.12
ARBITRATION
   advantages of §12.01
   agreement to arbitrate, existence of §12.02
   compelling §§12.10, 12.11
   confirmation of award §12.12
   contract for construction §1.05
   demand for §§12.04—12.07
   design-build contract §§1.17, 1.19
   incorporation of arbitration agreement by reference §12.02
   joint venture agreement §§4.01, 7.15
   management contract §§1.08, 1.12
   privity contract §§8.01, 8.02
   subcontract agreement §§5.11, 5.12
   voluntary submission §§12.08, 12.09
   waiver, inadvertent §12.13
ARCHITECTS
   generally this index
ASSETS, joint ventures §§4.01, 7.09
ASSIGNMENTS
   contract for construction §1.05
   design-build contract §§1.17, 1.19
   joint venture agreements §7.15
   management contract §1.08
   money due under contract §§9.01—9.03
   subcontract agreement §§2.04, 5.11
ATTORNEYS AT LAW
   arbitration proceeding, appearance at §12.01
   joint venture agreement §§4.01, 7.15
AUDITS, joint venture §7.12
AUTHORIZATION OF EXTRA WORK, subcontract agreement §§5.13, 5.14
AWARDS, arbitration, confirmation §12.12

B

BACKCHARGES, subcontract agreement §5.07
BANK ACCOUNTS
  checks. See CHECKS
  joint ventures §§4.01, 7.08, 7.15
BANKRUPTCY, joint venture agreement §7.15
BANKS, guarantee of payment by §§9.09—9.11
BIDS AND BIDDING
  joint venture §4.01
  subcontractors. See SUBCONTRACTORS
BOARD OF DIRECTORS, joint venture agreement §4.01
BONDS
  payment bonds. See PAYMENT BONDS
  performance bonds. See PERFORMANCE BONDS
  surety bonds. See SURETY BONDS
BOOKS AND RECORDS
  accounting, joint venture agreement, §§4.01, 7.12, 7.15
  daily report of contractor §§3.01, 3.02
BREACH OF CONTRACT, purchase orders by subcontractors §6.01
BUILDING CODES, subcontract agreement requiring compliance with §2.04
BUILDING MATERIALS
  See MATERIALS
BUSINESS RECORDS, daily report of contractor as hearsay exception §§3.01, 3.02

C

CANCELLATION OF CONTRACT
  See TERMINATION OF CONTRACT
CAPITAL, joint ventures §§4.01, 7.08
CERTIFICATES, payment under construction contract §1.05
CERTIFIED MAIL, notice given under payment bond §11.06
CHANGES IN WORK
  conditions generally §1.05
  design-build contract §§1.17, 1.19
  management contract §§1.08, 1.12
  payment of change order guaranteed by bank §9.11
  subcontract agreement §§2.03, 2.04, 5.11—5.14
CHECKS
  joint-check arrangements §§9.04—9.06
  joint venture agreement §7.15

CLAIMS
  mechanic's lien §10.02
  subcontract agreement §§2.03, 2.04, 5.12, 8.01, 8.02
CLEANING UP
  contract for construction §1.05
  design-build contract §1.19
  management contract §1.12
  subcontract agreement §§2.04, 5.11, 5.12
COLLECTIVE BARGAINING, joint venture agreement §§7.10, 7.11, 7.15
COMMUNICATIONS
  contract for construction §1.05
  design-build contract §1.19
  management contract §1.12
  subcontract agreement §5.12
COMPENSATION
  fees. See FEES
  joint venture agreement §4.01
COMPETITION, joint venture agreement §4.01
COMPLAINTS, Miller Act suit on payment bond §11.09
COMPLETION OF CONSTRUCTION
  conditions generally §1.05
  design-build contract §§1.17, 1.19
  management contract §1.08
  subcontract agreement §5.11
  substantial completion. See SUBSTANTIAL COMPLETION
CONDITIONS OF CONSTRUCTION
  general conditions §§1.04, 1.05
  index to construction contract §1.05
CONDUIT CLAUSES
  See INCORPORATION OF CONTRACTS
CONFIRMATION, oral purchase order by subcontractor §6.01
CONFLICT OF INTERESTS, management contract §1.07
CONFLICT OF LAWS
  contract for construction, general conditions §1.05
  design-build contract §§1.17, 1.19
  joint venture agreement §§7.05, 7.15
  management contract §1.08
  subcontract agreement §2.04
CONSEQUENTIAL DAMAGES
  purchase order by subcontractor §§6.01, 6.02
  subcontractor's proposal §§5.01, 5.02
CONSTRUCTION OF CONTRACTS
  arbitration agreements §12.03
  indemnity and hold harmless provisions §5.10
  management contract §1.12
  purchase order, long form §2.07
  subcontract agreement §2.03

CONTINGENT PAYMENT, subcontract
   agreement §5.04
CONTRACTORS
   generally this index
CONTRACTS
   generally this index
CONTRIBUTIONS, joint venture
   agreement §§7.08, 7.15
COPIES
   arbitration clause, demand for
      arbitration §12.05
   notice given under payment bond
      §§11.04, 11.06
   payment bonds, obtaining copies of
      §§11.02, 11.03
CORPORATIONS
   dummy, payment guarantees §9.07
   joint venture agreement §§4.01, 4.02
CORRECTIONS OF WORK
   conditions generally §1.05
   design-build contract §1.19
   management contract §1.12
COST OF PROJECT
   additional costs. See ADDITIONAL
      COSTS
   design-build contract §1.17
   extra work, claim by subcontractor
      §5.13
   joint venture agreement §7.15
   management contract §§1.07, 1.08
COST PLUS CONTRACTS
   design-build agreement, preliminary
      work §1.14
   plans and specifications §1.01
   subcontractor, payment §2.08
COUNSEL
   See ATTORNEYS AT LAW
COURTS
   indemnity and hold harmless provisions,
      construction of §5.10
   joint ventures, view of §7.01
   jurisdiction of courts. See
      JURISDICTION OF COURTS
CRIMINAL LAW, trust receipt violation
   §10.09
CUTTING AND PATCHING
   contract for construction §1.05
   design-build contract §1.19
   management contract §1.12

D

DAILY REPORT OF CONTRACTOR
   §§3.01, 3.02
DAMAGES
   consequential damages. See
      CONSEQUENTIAL DAMAGES

DAMAGES—Cont.
   contract for construction §1.05
   design-build contract §1.19
   indemnity. See INDEMNITY
   management contract §1.12
   subcontractors. See
      SUBCONTRACTORS
DEATH, joint venturer, property
   disposition §7.09
DEFAULT
   joint venture agreement §4.01
   subcontract agreement §5.12
DELAYS
   arbitration demand for causing §12.07
   contract for construction §1.05
   design-build contract §§1.17, 1.19
   management contract, general conditions
      §1.12
   subcontractors §§5.01, 5.02, 5.11, 5.13
DEMAND
   arbitration §§12.04—12.07
   payment, notice of demand under
      payment bond §11.07
DESCRIPTIONS
   mechanic's lien §10.02
   subcontractor's work, scope of §§5.01,
      5.05
DESIGN
   contractor, liability of §1.13
   management contract §1.08
DESIGN-BUILD CONTRACTS
   conditions generally §§1.18, 1.19
   joint ventures §4.01
   preliminary work
   –agreement §1.15
   –fees, cost plus arrangement §1.14
   standard form §§1.16, 1.17
DIRECTORS, joint venture agreement
   §4.01
DISCHARGE, payment made to
   subcontractor/supplier §§2.10, 2.11
DISCLAIMERS, subcontract agreement
   §5.09
DISCOUNTS, design-build contract §1.17
DISSOLUTION, joint venture agreement
   §§4.01, 7.09
DISTRICT OF COLUMBIA, arbitration
   statutes §12.03
DOCUMENTS
   conditions of construction §1.05
   design-build contract §1.19
   management contract §1.12
   stipulated sum agreement §1.03
   subcontract agreement §§2.04, 5.12
DRAGNET CLAUSE, subcontract
   agreement §5.05
DRAWINGS
   contract for construction §1.05
   design-build contract §1.19

DRAWINGS—Cont.
  management contract §1.12
  subcontract agreement §5.11

E

EMERGENCIES
  design-build contract §§1.17, 1.19
  management contract §§1.08, 1.12
EMPLOYEES, joint venture agreement §§7.11, 7.15
ENGINEERS
  generally this index
EQUIPMENT AND MACHINERY
  contract for construction §1.05
  design-build contract §1.19
  management contract §1.12
  subcontract agreement §5.11
  tools. See TOOLS
ERRORS
  See CORRECTIONS OF WORK
ETHICS
  conflict of interests, management contract §1.07
  joint venture entities checking canons of ethics §4.01
EVIDENCE, daily report of contractor §§3.01, 3.02
EXHIBITS, attachment to arbitration demand §12.06
EXPENSES, joint venture agreement §§4.01, 7.15
EXPRESS WARRANTIES, subcontract agreement §5.09
EXTENSIONS OF TIME
  contract for construction §1.05
  design-build contract, general conditions §1.19
  management contract §§1.08, 1.12
  subcontract agreement §§5.11, 5.13
EXTRA WORK
  arbitration demand §12.07
  notice, subcontract agreement §§5.13, 5.14

F

FEDERAL GOVERNMENT
  See UNITED STATES GOVERNMENT
FEES
  contract for construction §1.05
  design-build contract §§1.17, 1.19
  management contract §§1.07, 1.08, 1.12
  subcontract agreement §§2.04, 5.12
FINAL PAYMENT
  conditions generally §1.05
  design-build contract §1.19

FINAL PAYMENT—Cont.
  management contract §§1.08, 1.12
  stipulated sum contract §1.03
  subcontract agreement §§2.04, 5.04, 5.11, 5.12
  waiver, release and discharge of subcontractor/supplier §§2.10, 2.11
FINAL WAIVERS, mechanics' liens §§10.07, 10.08
FINANCING
  See FUNDS
FINES AND PENALTIES, design-build agreements violating licensing statutes §1.13
FISCAL YEAR, joint venture agreement §7.15
FORECLOSURE, action based on mechanic's lien §10.01
FREEZE AGREEMENTS, payment bonds §§11.10, 11.11
FUNDS
  design-build contract §1.17
  joint venture agreement §§4.01, 7.08, 7.15

G

GENERAL CONTRACTORS
  generally this index
GOVERNING LAW
  See CONFLICT OF LAWS
GUARANTEED MAXIMUM PRICE
  design-build contracts §§1.16, 1.17
  management contracts. See MANAGEMENT CONTRACTS
GUARANTY
  joint-check arrangement §9.04
  payment §§9.07—9.11

H

HEARINGS, locale of arbitration hearing §12.05
HEARSAY, daily report of contractor §§3.01, 3.02
HIGHWAYS, unit price contract §1.01
HOISTING, subcontractor's proposal §§5.01, 5.02
HOLD HARMLESS
  See INDEMNITY

I

IMPLIED WARRANTIES, subcontract agreement §5.09

INCORPORATION OF CONTRACTS
  arbitration agreement §12.02
  joint venture agreement §7.15
  subcontract agreement §§2.03, 5.01, 5.02, 5.08, 5.13, 5.14
INDEMNITY
  contract for construction §1.05
  design-build contract §§1.13, 1.17, 1.19
  management contract §§1.08, 1.12
  purchase order by subcontractor §§6.01, 6.02
  subcontract agreement §§2.04, 5.10, 5.12
INDEXES, conditions of construction, AIA Document A201 §1.05
INSOLVENCY
  arbitration award made before §12.01
  joint venture agreement §7.15
INSPECTIONS
  general contract, inspection by subcontractor §5.08
  subcontract agreement §2.04
INSURANCE
  conditions of construction §1.05
  joint venture agreement §§7.13, 7.15
  liability insurance. See LIABILITY INSURANCE
  management contract §§1.08, 1.12
  property insurance. See PROPERTY INSURANCE
  subcontract agreement §§2.04, 5.11, 5.12
  subrogation. See SUBROGATION
INTENT
  design-build contract §1.19
  management contract §1.12
INTEREST (ON MONEY)
  contract for construction §1.05
  management contract §1.12
  subcontractor's proposal §§5.01, 5.02
INTERIM WAIVERS, mechanics' liens §§10.04—10.06
INTERPRETATION OF CONTRACTS
  See CONSTRUCTION OF CONTRACTS

J

JOB SITE
  arbitration demand for failure to allow access to §12.07
  temporary facilities, subcontract proposal and agreement §§5.01, 5.02, 5.07, 5.11, 5.12
JOINT-CHECK ARRANGEMENTS §§9.04—9.06
JOINT VENTURE CONTRACTS
  prime contractors §§4.01, 4.02
  subcontractors §§7.01—7.15

JUDGMENT, confirmation of arbitration award §12.12
JURISDICTION OF COURTS
  arbitration agreements §§12.03, 12.12
  subcontract agreement §2.04

L

LABOR AND LABOR UNIONS
  contract for construction §1.05
  design-build contract §1.19
  joint venture agreement §§7.10, 7.11, 7.15
  management contract §1.12
  payment bonds. See PAYMENT BONDS
  subcontract agreement §§2.04, 5.11, 5.12
LAWSUITS
  See ACTIONS
LAWYERS
  See ATTORNEYS AT LAW
LETTER OF CONFIRMATION, purchase order by subcontractor, oral §6.01
LIABILITY INSURANCE
  conditions of construction §1.05
  design-build contract §§1.17, 1.19
  management contract §§1.08, 1.12
  subcontract agreement §2.04
LICENSES AND PERMITS
  contract for construction §1.05
  design-build contract §§1.13, 1.19
  joint venture entities §4.01
  management contract §1.12
  subcontract agreement §5.12
LIENS
  See MECHANICS' AND MATERIALMEN'S LIENS
LIMITATION OF ACTIONS
  payment bond §11.08
  warranties, implied §5.09
LIMITED PARTNERSHIPS, payment guarantees §9.07
LIQUIDATED DAMAGES, subcontractors §§5.01, 5.02, 5.06, 5.11, 5.13
LIQUIDATION, joint venture agreement §§7.09, 7.15
LOSSES, joint venture agreement §§7.06, 7.15
LOSS OF USE INSURANCE, conditions of construction §1.05

M

MACHINERY
  See EQUIPMENT AND MACHINERY
MAIL, notice given under payment bond §11.06

MANAGEMENT
contract for construction §1.05
design-build contract §1.19
joint venture agreement §§7.07, 7.15

MANAGEMENT CONTRACTS
generally §§1.06, 1.11, 1.12
guaranteed maximum price contract
–amendment §§1.09, 1.10
–option §1.08
standard form §§1.07, 1.08

MARK-UP CONTRACTS, plans and specifications §1.01

MATERIALS
contract for construction §1.05
design-build contract §1.19
liens. See MECHANICS' AND MATERIALMEN'S LIENS
management contract §1.12
payment
–guarantee §9.08
–joint check arrangement §§9.05—9.06
–waiver, release and discharge §§2.10, 2.11
payment bonds. See PAYMENT BONDS
purchase orders. See PURCHASE ORDERS
subcontractors §§2.04, 5.02, 5.11

MAXIMUM PRICE
See GUARANTEED MAXIMUM PRICE

MECHANICS' AND MATERIALMEN'S LIENS
private projects §§10.01, 10.02
public projects §§10.11, 10.13
subcontract agreement §2.04
waiver
–generally §§10.03—10.10
–subcontractor, purchase order by §2.04

MERGER OF CONTRACTS
See INCORPORATION OF CONTRACTS

MILLER ACT, payment bonds on federal projects §§11.02—11.09

MINORITIES, joint ventures §4.01

MISCELLANEOUS CONTRACT PROVISIONS
conditions of construction §1.05
design-build contract §§1.17, 1.19
management contract §§1.07, 1.08, 1.12
stipulated sum contract §1.03
subcontract agreement §5.12

MISTAKES
See CORRECTIONS OF WORK

MOTIONS, arbitration §§12.10, 12.12

MUNICIPAL MECHANICS' LIENS §§10.11—10.13

MUTUALITY OF OBLIGATION, subcontract agreement §§2.03, 5.08

N

NAMES
joint venture agreement §§4.01, 7.02, 7.05, 7.15
mechanic's lien claim §10.02

NEGLIGENCE
design-build contracts §§1.16, 1.17
indemnity. See INDEMNITY
liability insurance. See LIABILITY INSURANCE
subcontract agreement §§5.10, 5.12

NEGOTIATIONS, subcontract agreement §5.03

NOTICE
assignment of money due under contract §9.03
changes or extra work, subcontract agreement §§5.13, 5.14
contract for construction §1.05
design-build contract §1.19
joint venture agreement §7.15
management contract §1.12
municipal mechanics' lien §10.12
payment bonds §§11.04—11.07
subcontract agreement §§5.11, 5.12

O

OFFICES, joint venture §§7.05, 7.15

ORAL CONTRACTS
purchase order by subcontractor §6.01
statute of frauds. See STATUTE OF FRAUDS

ORDERS
See PURCHASE ORDERS

ORDINANCES, subcontract agreement requiring compliance with §2.04

OWNERS
generally this index

OWNERSHIP, joint venture agreement §4.01

P

PARTNERSHIPS
joint ventures. See JOINT VENTURES
payment guarantees §9.07

PATCHING
See CUTTING AND PATCHING

PATENTS
contract for construction, general conditions §1.05
design-build contract §§1.17, 1.19
management contract, general conditions §1.12

PAYMENT
   applications. See APPLICATIONS FOR PAYMENT
   arbitration. See ARBITRATION
   assignment of money due §§9.01—9.03
   bonds. See PAYMENT BONDS
   conditions generally §1.05
   design-build contract §1.17
   final payment. See FINAL PAYMENT
   guarantees §§9.07—9.11
   joint-check arrangements §§9.04—9.06
   management contract §§1.08, 1.12
   materials. See MATERIALS
   mechanics' and materialmen's liens. See MECHANICS' AND MATERIALMEN'S LIENS
   progress payments. See PROGRESS PAYMENTS
   stipulated sum contract §1.03
   subcontractors. See SUBCONTRACTORS
PAYMENT BONDS
   actions, institution of §§11.08, 11.09
   copies, obtaining §§11.02, 11.03
   design-build contract §1.19
   explained §11.03
   federal projects §§11.01—11.09
   freeze agreements §§11.10, 11.11
   necessity of obtaining §11.01
   notice §§11.04—11.07
   subcontractors §§2.04, 2.08, 5.11, 5.12
PENALTIES, design-build agreement violating licensing statutes §1.13
PENSIONS, joint venture employees §7.11
PERCENTAGES, joint venture interests §§4.01, 7.06, 7.15
PERFORMANCE BONDS
   contract for construction §1.05
   design-build contract §1.19
   subcontract agreement §§2.04, 5.11, 5.12
PERFORMANCE OF CONTRACT, see specific headings
PERMITS
   See LICENSES AND PERMITS
PETITIONS, compelling arbitration §§12.10, 12.11
PLANS AND SPECIFICATIONS
   design-build contracts §§1.13, 1.19
   drawings. See DRAWINGS
   management contract §1.12
   purchase order of subcontractor §§6.01, 6.02
   stipulated sum agreement §§1.01—1.03
   subcontract agreement, scope of work §5.05

PRELIMINARY WORK
   See DESIGN-BUILD CONTRACTS
PRICE
   guaranteed maximum price. See GUARANTEED MAXIMUM PRICE
   plans and specifications, stipulated price §§1.01—1.03
   unit prices, subbid proposal §2.02
PRIME CONTRACTORS
   generally this index
PRIVITY CONTRACTS, subcontractors §§8.01, 8.02
PROFITS,
   joint venture agreement §§4.01, 7.06, 7.15
PROFIT-SHARING PLANS, joint venture employees §7.11
PROGRESS PAYMENTS
   conditions generally §1.05
   design-build contract §1.19
   management contract §1.12
   stipulated sum contract §1.03
   subcontractors §§2.04, 5.01, 5.02, 5.11, 5.12
PROPERTY, joint venture §§7.09, 7.15
PROPERTY INSURANCE
   conditions of construction §1.05
   design-build contract §1.19
   management contract §1.12
   subcontractor's proposal §§5.01, 5.02
PROPOSALS, subcontractors §§5.01, 5.02
PUBLIC CONTRACTS
   payment bonds §§11.01—11.09
   unit price contract §1.01
PURCHASE ORDERS
   importance of §2.05
   long form §§2.05, 2.07
   short form §§2.05, 2.06
   subcontractors §§6.01, 6.02

R

RECORDS
   See BOOKS AND RECORDS
REGULATIONS
   joint venture entities checking §4.01
   subcontract agreement requiring compliance with §2.04
REIMBURSEMENT
   See INDEMNITY
RELATED WORK, subcontract agreement §2.04
RELEASES
   mechanics' liens, final waiver of §§10.07, 10.08
   subcontractor/supplier, payment made to §§2.10, 2.11

REPORTS
    daily report of contractor §§3.01, 3.02
    subcontract agreement, progress reports §5.11

REPRESENTATIVES
    joint venture agreement §§4.01, 7.15
    subcontract agreement §2.04

REQUESTS FOR PAYMENT
    See APPLICATIONS FOR PAYMENT

RETENTION OF PAYMENT, subcontract agreement §5.04

RETIREMENT, joint venture employees §7.11

ROYALTIES
    contract for construction §1.05
    design-build contract §§1.17, 1.19
    management contract, general conditions §1.12

S

SAFETY
    conditions of construction §1.05
    design-build contract §1.19
    management contract §1.12
    subcontract agreement §§5.07, 5.12

SAMPLES
    contract for construction §1.05
    design-build contract §1.19
    management contract §1.12
    subcontract agreement §5.11

SCHEDULES
    arbitration demand, attachment to §12.06
    contract for construction §1.05
    design-build contract §§1.17, 1.19
    management contract §1.12
    subcontract agreement §§5.06, 5.11

SCOPE OF WORK, subcontractors §§2.04, 5.01, 5.05

SEPARATE SUBCONTRACTS, design-build contract §1.19

SEPARATE TRADE CONTRACTS, management contract §1.12

SEWER FACILITIES, joint ventures §4.01

SOLID WASTE TREATMENT FACILITIES, joint venture project §4.01

SPECIFICATIONS
    See PLANS AND SPECIFICATIONS

STATUTE OF FRAUDS
    payment guarantees §9.07
    purchase order by subcontractor §6.01

STATUTE OF LIMITATIONS
    See LIMITATION OF ACTIONS

STATUTES
    arbitration §12.03

STATUTES—Cont.
    bank guarantee of payment as violation of §9.09
    mechanics' liens, variations in §§10.01, 10.11
    payment bonds §§11.01—11.09
    subcontract agreement requiring compliance with §2.04
    waivers of mechanics' liens §10.03

STIPULATED SUM AGREEMENTS, plans and specifications §§1.01—1.03

STIPULATIONS, subcontract agreement form stipulated in bid §5.03

STORAGE, subcontractors §§2.04, 5.01, 5.02

STRIKES, subcontract agreement §2.04

SUBBID PROPOSAL §§2.01, 2.02

SUBCONTRACTORS
    agreement with contractor
    —neutral forms §§5.03—5.14
    —prime contractor favored §§2.03, 2.04
    arbitration agreement §12.02
    bids and bidding
    —safety requirements §5.07
    —stipulation as to subcontract form §5.03
    —subbid proposal §§2.01, 2.02
    —temporary site facilities §5.07
    conditions of construction generally §1.05
    damages
    —generally §§2.03, 2.04, 5.12
    —consequential §§5.01, 5.02
    —liquidated §§5.01, 5.02, 5.06, 5.11, 5.13
    —purchase orders §§6.01, 6.02
    design-build contract §§1.17, 1.19
    payment
    —generally §§2.03, 2.04, 5.04
    —application for §§2.08, 2.09, 5.11, 5.12
    —joint-check arrangement §9.05
    —waiver, release and discharge §§2.10, 2.11
    privity contracts §§8.01, 8.02
    proposals §§5.01, 5.02
    purchase orders §§6.01, 6.02
    subbid proposal §§2.01, 2.02
    sub-subcontractors. See SUB-SUBCONTRACTORS
    trade subcontractors, management contract §1.12
    warranties
    —agreement with prime contractor §§2.04, 5.09, 5.11, 5.12
    —proposal by subcontractor §§5.01, 5.02
    —suppliers, obtaining warranties from §§6.01, 6.02

SUBLEASES, subcontract agreement §2.04

SUBROGATION
   design-build contract, insurance clause §1.17
   management contract, insurance clause §§1.08, 1.12
   waiver, generally this heading

SUBSTANTIAL COMPLETION
   conditions generally §1.05
   design-build contract §1.19
   management contract §1.12
   subcontract agreement §5.12

SUB-SUBCONTRACTORS
   design-build contract §1.19
   subcontract agreement §2.04

SUCCESSORS
   contract for construction §1.05
   design-build contract §1.19

SUITS
   See ACTIONS

SUPERVISION
   See MANAGEMENT

SUPPLIES
   See MATERIALS

SURETY BONDS
   management contract §1.12
   municipal mechanics' lien statutes, effect of §§10.11, 10.13

T

TAXES
   contract for construction §1.05
   design-build contract §1.19
   joint ventures §§4.01, 7.01
   management contract §1.12
   subcontract agreement §2.04

TEMPORARY SITE FACILITIES, subcontract proposal and agreement §§5.01, 5.02, 5.07, 5.11, 5.12

TERMINATION OF CONTRACT
   conditions generally §1.05
   design-build contracts §§1.16, 1.17, 1.19
   joint venture agreement §§4.01, 7.15
   management contract §§1.08, 1.12
   subcontract agreement §§2.03, 2.04, 5.12

TESTS AND TESTING
   contract for construction §1.05
   design-build contract §1.19
   management contract §1.12

THIRD PARTIES, joint-check arrangements §§9.04—9.06

TIME OF PERFORMANCE
   conditions generally §1.05
   delays. See DELAYS
   design-build contract §1.17
   extensions of time. See EXTENSIONS OF TIME

TIME OF PERFORMANCE—Cont.
   guaranteed maximum price contract §1.10
   management contract §§1.08, 1.12
   purchase order by subcontractor §§6.01, 6.02
   schedules. See SCHEDULES
   stipulated sum contract §1.03
   subcontract agreement §§2.04, 5.11, 5.12

TOOLS
   contract for construction §1.05
   design-build contract §1.19
   management contract §1.12

TRADE CONTRACTS, management contract §§1.07, 1.08, 1.12

TRANSPORTATION
   contract for construction §1.05
   design-build contract §1.19
   management contract §1.12

TRUST RECEIPTS, mechanics' lien waiver §§10.09, 10.10

TURNKEY CONTRACTS
   See DESIGN-BUILD CONTRACTS

U

UNCONSCIONABLE CONTRACTS, enforceability of subcontract agreement §2.03

UNCOVERING OF WORK
   contract for construction §1.05
   design-build contract §1.19
   management contract §1.12

UNIFORM COMMERCIAL CODE, oral purchase order by subcontractor §6.01

UNIONS
   See LABOR AND LABOR UNIONS

UNITED STATES GOVERNMENT
   arbitration statutes §§12.03, 12.11
   payment bonds §§11.01—11.09

UNIT PRICE CONTRACTS
   plans and specifications §1.01
   subcontractor, payment of §2.08

UNIT PRICES, subbid proposal §2.02

UTILITIES, contract for construction §1.05

W

WAIVER
   arbitration rights, inadvertent waiver of §12.13
   mechanics' and materialmen's liens. See MECHANICS' AND MATERIALMEN'S LIENS
   payment made to subcontractor/supplier §§2.10, 2.11
   subrogation. See SUBROGATION

WARRANTIES
  contract for construction §1.05
  design-build contract §§1.17, 1.19
  management contract, general conditions §1.12
  plans and specifications, §1.01
  subcontractors. See
    SUBCONTRACTORS

Y

YEAR, fiscal year, joint venture agreement §7.15